THE STUDENT-RUN AGENCY

Transitioning from Student to Professional

Analysis ← Research

STRATEGY

CREATIVE

- brainstorm

DO!

PROCESS

Time

& Focus on Quality

JUST MAKE THE BEST THINGS!

ABILITY

BENEFIT

Kendall Hunt
publishing company

LEE BUSH • JEFF RANTA • HAL VINCENT
Elon University   **Coastal Carolina University**   **Elon University**

D0078044

Cover © Shutterstock.com

www.kendallhunt.com
Send all inquiries to:
4050 Westmark Drive
Dubuque, IA 52004-1840

Copyright © 2018 by Kendall Hunt Publishing Company

ISBN: 978-1-5249-1967-2

All rights reserved. No part of this publication may be reproduced,
stored in a retrieval system, or transmitted, in any form or by any means,
electronic, mechanical, photocopying, recording, or otherwise,
without the prior written permission of the copyright owner.

Published in the United States of America

Dedicated to the many students who have come through the doors of our student agencies and gone on to become accomplished professionals. You inspire us!

About the Authors

Lee Bush is an associate professor in the School of Communications at Elon University. Prior to teaching, she spent 18 years in both advertising and PR agencies, most recently as a senior vice president of Ketchum Communications in Chicago, and as senior vice president of Ogilvy Public Relations in both Chicago and London. She specialized in brand marketing and worked for clients including Quaker Oats, Jim Beam Brands, Kimberly-Clark, Horizon Organic, Eurotunnel, Wendy's, and Unilever. In 2007, she founded Elon's student agency, Live Oak Communications, and served as the faculty director for its first 7 years. She has conducted extensive research on the structures and learning benefits of student agencies, their impact on graduates' careers, and employer awareness and perceptions of student agencies. Her research has been published in *Journal of Advertising Education*, *Public Relations Review*, *Journalism and Mass Communications Educator*, and *PRSA's The Strategist and Tactics Online*. At Elon, she teaches undergraduate Strategic Communications courses, as well as the Organizational Communications course in Elon's M.S. in management program. She has a B.A. from Missouri Western State University and an M.S. in communications from Northwestern University.

Jeff Ranta is an assistant professor of communications, media, & culture at Coastal Carolina University. Prior to his teaching debut 16 years ago, he was a Naval officer and marketing communications executive. His career highlights include vice president for RBB/Weber Shandwick Miami; executive positions in Atlanta and Columbia, SC boutique agencies; service as a division officer/public affairs officer for a U.S. Navy destroyer, Yokosuka Japan; public affairs officer for the aircraft carrier USS Constellation; assistant public affairs officer for Naval Base Philadelphia; acting director for the Navy Office of Information in Atlanta; and founder/principal for two, full service, marketing communications agencies. Some of his clients include Coca-Cola, BellSouth, Chick-fil-A, NewellRubbermaid, Shoney's, Golden Corral, and various automobile dealerships. He established The Carolina Agency at the University of South Carolina in 2005 and turned it into a PRSSA nationally affiliated agency with more than 20 award-winning campaigns and four Bateman national championships. He recently established Coastal Carolina's student agency, Teal Nation Communications. Ranta has a Ph.D. from the University of South Carolina, where his dissertation examined the interface between student-run agencies and the current shift from public relations to strategic communications.

Hal Vincent is a lecturer in communications at Elon University and the current faculty director of Live Oak Communications. A graduate of VCU's Brandcenter, he spent nearly 15 years in advertising and integrated communications agencies in New York, Philadelphia, and Tampa working for clients such as Nabisco, Tropicana, Independence Blue Cross, AmeriHealth New Jersey, The Pennsylvania Lottery, The Florida Aquarium, and the Orlando Convention and Visitors Bureau. He has supervised numerous industry internship programs and is the former interim director of the Zimmerman Advertising Program at the University of South Florida. He took over the faculty director position of Live Oak in 2013. Since then he has guided the agency in winning several academic and professional awards, and established Project ECHO, an insight and innovation partnership with global content marketing firm PACE. He was previously an advisor to numerous student advertising clubs and an AAF National Student Advertising Competition (NSAC) coach and is a current board member of the Triangle Ad Fed and the AEJMC Advertising Division.

Table of Contents

History of advertising and PR agencies; agency ownership and holding companies; types of agencies; agency structures; the agency of the future; industry trade associations, media, and awards.

Agency needs, resources, and mission; agency structures, titles/ roles, organizational charts, and funding sources; office space and equipment; agency branding and culture; mining, prospecting, and cultivating student staff.

Categories of client organizations; types of client/agency relationships; developing a new business plan including prospecting, preparing materials, and conducting outreach; the agency search process (RFIs and RFPs); making a new business pitch.

Recruiting and hiring processes; developing client contracts, staffing the account and holding your first meeting; moving work through the agency using workflow processes, briefs, status reports, and shared agency drives; internal agency communications; measuring agency success.

Reasons to promote your agency; ways to engage in agency promotion including doing a brand audit, documenting case studies, establishing and communicating thought leadership, and displaying your professionalism and culture; planning and executing agency promotion through content marketing, media, and messaging.

Using your student agency experience to get in front of employers and land your perfect job; building your personal brand, developing materials and an online portfolio; gathering intelligence and prospect targeting; techniques to prepare for and conduct interviews; using your experience in your first position.

Introduction

If you are reading this book, you are about to embark on the experience of working at a student-run agency. You are in good company. There are more than 150 student agencies at colleges and universities in the United States (Swanson, 2017). And the number is growing. While some have been in operation for decades, more than half of student agencies have been established in the past 10 years (Busch, 2013; Bush & Miller, 2011; Maben, 2010). This growth is attributed to the rise in experiential learning and the need to prepare strategic communications graduates for the real world of the profession.

Due to their proliferation and an increase in student-focused research, we know more about the learning benefits of student agencies today than we ever have before. There are many benefits to working at a student agency. These include

- Gaining real-world, hands-on experience working for real clients
- Learning business processes and protocols inherent in professional agencies and organizations
- Building a professional identity, including valuable organizational skills and working with a diversity of people
- Learning to work well within a team and build team dynamics
- Developing self-efficacy and confidence
- Experiencing corporate culture and becoming a valued member of that culture
- Gaining leadership and decision-making skills
- Achieving personal growth and positive change
  (Aldoory & Wrigley, 2000; Bush, 2009; Bush & Miller, 2011; Kearns, Puglisi, & Shelton, 2014; Ranta & Davis, 2017; Swanson, 2011)

These learning benefits are both immediate and sustainable. Not only do students report doing better in their academic classes and internships, but also graduates report their student agency experience differentiated them in the job market and had a direct or indirect impact on getting hired for their positions. And, graduates are still utilizing this learning many years into their careers (Bush, Haygood, & Vincent, 2016).

As our understanding of the structure and benefits of student agencies grows, so too does the need for materials to guide students through the process. And that brings us to this book.

WHY WE DEVELOPED THIS TEXT

As founders, advisors, and faculty directors of student-run agencies, the authors saw a need for a textbook that could help students navigate the student agency environment. Many agencies have a wide range of student participants, from first year to seniors. Some students have progressed through several communications courses already, while others are just starting out. And, all are embarking on an experience that is very different from traditional classroom learning.

Student agency members are unique in that they are still learning some of the basics, but are working with clients who expect students to conduct themselves professionally and understand how the business world operates. This text serves as a comprehensive resource to help you navigate those waters and begin making the transition from student to professional. And, because the situations are similar, this text can also be valuable for students in Strategic Campaigns courses and those who are embarking on professional internships.

The authors developed the content of this text based on three perspectives:

- *Years of experience founding and managing student-run agencies.* This experience has taught us what students already know, what they don't know, and what they need to know to make their time in the student agency meaningful. We understand the transient nature of student agency staff, the short-term timeline of the student agency semester, and what students require to ramp up quickly and dive into the work. We recognize when students need guidance, and when we should get out of the way and let them shine. We know what clients expect of students and the types of programs students can execute most effectively. We've worked with administrators to get agencies up and running, and managed agencies through years of progression. Most importantly, we know where student agencies can fail (we've experienced it personally), and what it takes for them to be successful. And, we're still learning.

- *Extensive research on student agencies.* Each of the authors has conducted academic research on the structures, learning benefits, and professional value of student-run agencies. We've interviewed students, advisors, agency graduates, and employers. We've published papers, spoken at conferences, and networked with other student agencies. The learning and insights from this research and networking are manifested throughout this book. In addition, some of our research has told us what student agencies are NOT teaching students that they should be, or what they need to do better. Thus, we've included content in this text to help fill those gaps.

- *Years of professional agency experience.* Each of the authors has worked in the corporate and professional agency world before joining academics—from small and mid-sized agencies, to large conglomerates, to starting our own agencies. We know the stresses and frustrations of the agency world, as well as the overwhelming joys of winning a pitch or watching a client campaign take off. We've been account executives and senior vice presidents. We've filled out time sheets, dealt with difficult clients, and managed millions of dollars in client programming. We understand that, first and foremost, an agency is a business, and are familiar with agency best practices.

Our professional experience was instrumental in designing content that helps student agencies mimic as closely as possible the structure and dynamics of the professional world so they can prepare students to be valuable contributors in the industry.

HOW TO USE THIS TEXT

This book was designed to work in two ways: (1) to serve as a comprehensive resource for your complete student agency experience, and (2) to serve as a reference guide as specific situations arise. By reading the text from cover to cover, you will have a full understanding of the agency business, how agencies are structured, and the type of work you will do in your student agency tenure. Then, as situations arise, the book will serve as a reference. For example, when you are asked to write a strategic communications plan, Chapter 8 will walk you through the steps. When a client asks for help with social media, the Professional Practice article, Social Media Marketing, will get you started.

The text is divided into four sections:

Part I—Shaping the Student Agency—Agency Structure and Processes

This section provides a comprehensive overview of the advertising and PR industry, and digs into the key components that keep the agency engine running. If you are just starting your agency, this section will be invaluable in thinking through how and why to set up your structure. If you are joining a well-established agency, this section will help you understand agency processes and how to work within those processes. The section helps you recognize that agencies are businesses that rely on client revenues and well-managed budgets to keep the agency fires burning. You'll learn how to build business, develop and manage the processes to maintain that business, and the ways in which you can become a valued and diverse contributor to your student agency culture. In essence, this section covers what you need to know to be an agency employee, and sets the stage for the work you will be conducting in your student agency tenure.

Part II—Program Planning and Management

This section will be most helpful as you begin working with clients on the programs that will make their businesses successful. This section gives you the tools to develop and manage client programming, establish a professional identity, and build healthy client relationships. You'll learn how to develop and "sell" your ideas to clients, the legal and ethical ramifications of your work, and how to effectively manage your time and become a resilient problem solver. In essence, this section helps you navigate the day-to-day of your agency work.

Part III—Professional Practices

Ten agency professionals contributed to this section. These are executives who are experts in their fields, with many years' experience working on various aspects of client campaigns. To develop this section, we first determined the types of programming student agencies most often execute, and then recruited professionals within those categories to share their best practices. From conducting research, to producing a video, to writing copy, and more, these professional articles give you insights into how programs are executed in professional agencies. In essence, this section provides a "how-to" when you need a quick primer on a specific communications technique or discipline.

Part IV—Leaving a Legacy

The culmination of your client work is that it builds credibility for both you and your agency. In this section, we outline how you can package and promote agency successes to build a positive reputation for your agency and to get in front of potential employers. As your agency becomes more visible and respected, the value of listing that agency on a resume or talking about it in an interview increases. In essence, this section is about branding: developing your agency's brand, and developing your personal brand. You'll also read testimonials from graduates who have used their agency experiences to shape their own personal brand and launch successful careers.

A FINAL THOUGHT ABOUT "BECOMING" A PROFESSIONAL

You don't suddenly "arrive" at being a professional one day. It's a lifelong transition that goes on long after you graduate.

One of the concepts we discuss in our textbook is that of the learning organization (Senge, 2006). Learning organizations are those that are continually learning, growing, and transforming their organizations and the people who work for them. That's what the student agency experience is all about. As each new group of students comes into the organization, they transform the agency down new paths and in new directions. Rather than simply "being," the student agency is always "becoming."

YOU are a big part of that transformation.

Each of you brings a unique background and perspective to the student agency and how others experience it. Not only are you transforming the agency, you're transforming each other. We hope you'll add your own experiences and knowledge to the content of this text and discuss that learning with your colleagues. Use the review and discussion questions at the end of each chapter as conversation starters. Share your thoughts with your team, other agency members, or even agency professionals in your area. Teach each other, learn from each other, and add to the content as you go. By doing so, you'll transform this textbook from something static into something dynamic.

And, let us hear from you. Like you, we are also continually "becoming." We want to learn from you, too. We're eager to hear about your experiences and the knowledge you've gained from your time at a student or professional agency, and to add that knowledge to future editions of the book.

Now, let's get started. Go!—Start becoming.

Lee Bush
Associate Professor, Communications
Elon University
Founder of Live Oak Communications
lbush3@elon.edu

Jeff Ranta
Assistant Professor, Communications, Media & Culture
Coastal Carolina University
Founder of The Carolina Agency at USC, and Coastal Carolina's Teal Nation Student Agency
jranta@coastal.edu

Hal Vincent
Lecturer, Communications
Elon University
Faculty Director of Live Oak Communications
hvincent@elon.edu

REFERENCES AND ADDITIONAL READINGS

Aldoory, L., & Wrigley, B. (2000). Exploring the use of real clients in the PR Campaigns course. *Journalism & Mass Communication Educator, 54,* 47–58.

Busch, A. M. (2013). A professional project surveying student-run advertising and public relations agencies at institutions with AEJMC accredited programs. *Thesis and Professional Projects from the College of Journalism and Mass Communications, Paper 35,* 1–75. Retrieved from http://digitalcommons.unl.edu/cgi/viewcontent.cgi?article=1040&context=journalismdiss

Bush, L. (2009). Student public relations agencies: A qualitative study of the pedagogical benefits, risks and a framework for success. *Journalism & Mass Communication Educator, 64*(1), 27–38.

Bush, L., Haygood, D., & Vincent, H. (2017). Student-run communications agencies: Providing students with real-world experiences that impact their careers. *Journalism & Mass Communication Educator, 72,* 410–424.

Bush, L., & Miller, M. (2011). U.S. student-run agencies: Organization, attributes and advisor perceptions of student learning outcomes. *Public Relations Review, 37*(5), 485–491.

Kearns, E., Puglisi, G., & Shelton, A. (2014, October 11). Service learning: Strategic partnerships between universities and businesses. Presentation to the PRSA Educators Academy Super Saturday Session, Washington, DC.

Maben, S. K. (2010). *A mixed method analysis of undergraduate student-run public relations firms on U.S. college campuses.* Doctoral dissertation, University of North Texas, Denton, TX. Retrieved from http://digital.library.unt.edu/ark:/67531/metadc30486/m2/1/high_res_d/dissertation.pdf

Ranta, J., & Davis, D. (2017, March). *Student self-efficacy and student agencies.* Presentation to the International Public Relations Research Conference, Orlando, FL.

Senge, P. (2006). *The fifth discipline: The art & practice of the learning organization.* New York, NY: Doubleday.

Swanson, D. J. (2011). The student-run public relations firm in an undergraduate program: Reaching learning and professional development goals through real-world experience. *Public Relations Review, 37*(5), 499–505.

Swanson, D. J. (2017). *Real world career preparation: A guide to creating a university student-run communications agency*. New York, NY: Peter Lang Publishing.

Part I

Shaping the Student Agency

Overview of the Agency Industry

The goal for any student agency should be to create an environment that mimics as closely as possible the professional world of advertising and public relations (PR) agencies. By creating a real-world agency environment, students learn how to work within a professional agency structure and are better prepared to enter the industry—whether working on the agency side or the client side of the business.

To create such an environment, it's important to understand the ins and outs of the agency industry. From its early days more than 150 years ago, the industry has grown and evolved significantly. This evolution has been marked by economic ups and downs, dramatic media technology transformations, consolidation and conglomeration, cultural and social evolution, and changes in the needs and demands of both clients and audiences.

According to Brian Regienczuk, founder of the agency search firm Agency Spotter, today there are approximately 120,000 agencies in the United States and more than 500,000 agencies worldwide (Regienczuk, 2014). And while each agency may be unique in its focus and offerings, and although agencies are continually evolving based on the trends and media technologies of the day, agencies often share a similar structure and work environment.

In this chapter, we cover the basics of the history, development, and structure of professional agencies, and a bit about where the business might be headed in the future. In this chapter, you learn about

- History of advertising and PR agencies
- Ownership of professional agencies
- Types of communications agencies in the 21st century
- Common departments found in professional agencies
- Evolution in agency structures
- Industry associations and awards

HISTORY OF THE AGENCY BUSINESS

If you look at the evolution of media and communications—from oral societies, moving through print, photographic, moving images, and today's digital society—you can easily track the development and evolution of professional advertising and PR agencies. From an economic standpoint, wherever there were goods or services to sell, and a means of communicating information about those goods, advertising and PR agencies developed.

In addition, we can observe the progression of the industry through the lens of our country's geographic evolution (moving from East Coast to West Coast to global), and cultural evolution (from the Civil Rights movement, to the women's movement, and waves of immigration from Europe, Asia, and Latin American countries). All of these factors played a role in where, when, and why agencies developed.

U.S. Advertising Agency History

While shop owners, shipping merchants, and land developers used town criers and handbills to advertise their goods, it was the proliferation of newspapers and magazines during the early days of the Industrial Revolution that initiated the establishment of the first advertising agencies. In the United States, the first known agency was Volney Palmer in Boston in 1841. However, this agency was very different than the agencies we see today. In selling ads to local merchants, newspapers found themselves in a tough

© Everett Collection/Shutterstock.com

economic spot when clients placed ads but then didn't pay. Volney Palmer stepped in and became a broker of sorts, paying newspapers up front for advertising space, and then selling that space at a commission to advertisers. In essence, Volney Palmer worked for newspapers rather than advertisers.

A few decades later, we see the first, full-service agency—one that created ads for clients, as well as placing them in print outlets. N. W. Ayer & Son opened its doors in 1869 in Philadelphia, bought out Volney Palmer in 1877, and by the late 1800s was hiring artists and writers to develop ads, becoming the prelude to modern-day advertising agencies. In addition to newspaper ads, the agency developed slogans, logos, and taglines for clients such as Morton Salt (When it rains, it pours®), De Beers diamonds (A diamond is forever®), and AT&T (Reach out and touch someone®). You can see images of the Morton Salt Girl through the years here: http://www.huffingtonpost.com/2014/01/29/morton-salt-girl-_n_4690728.html.

Ayer revolutionized the advertising agency business in many ways. It was one of the first agencies to establish a creative department and hire commercial artists and copywriters; the first to develop "open contracts" with clients (where advertisers pay commission based on advertising placement volume); and Ayer was a founding member of the Advertising Council in 1945. Ayer was in business for more than a hundred years, closing its doors in 2002 after a series of mergers.

During the 1960s, the advertising business went through a creative revolution. Spearheaded by innovators such as Bill Bernbach, Leo Burnett, and David Ogilvy, agencies moved from selling product "features and benefits" to focusing on brand personalities, colorful imagery, humorous situations, and real-life scenarios. Bernbach paired copywriters and art directors for the first time at his agency, Doyle Dane Bernbach (DDB), and the creative department became the mainstay of the industry (see History of Advertising, n.d.). Memorable ads during this time include DDB's Volkswagon "Lemon" ad and Hertz "We try harder" campaign; Alka Seltzer's "I can't believe I ate the whole thing" commercial by Wells Rich Greene; and many advertising characters such as Tony the Tiger, Charlie the Tuna, and the iconic Marlboro Man created by Leo Burnett.

© Sheila Fitzgerald/Shutterstock.com

Despite the *MadMen* stereotype of the advertising industry, women have been involved in the business since its inception. In fact, according to *Advertising Age* (Russell, 2012), women (mostly white) likely had more opportunities in the early days of advertising than they did in the 1960s era depicted by the show *MadMen*. For example, a prominent advertising journal in 1895 was owned and edited by Kate Griswold. Mathilde Weil opened the first woman-owned shop in New York in 1880. In 1885, J. Walter Thompson hired Alice Stoddard as a media buyer, and added its first female copywriter in 1911. That copywriter, Helen Lansdowne Resor, became the industry's first female creative director. Resor pioneered the use of "sex appeal," celebrity endorsements, and editorial advertising copy for clients such as Woodbury soap and Pond's cold cream. She and her husband later owned and ran the agency, and by 1918, the "Women's Editorial Department" led by Resor accounted for more than half of J. Walter Thompson's revenues (Lavelle, 2015). You can see one of her early ads in *Ladies Home Journal* here: https://contentequalsmoney.com/3-copywriting-tips-from-helen-lansdowne-resor/.

Though women weren't allowed to vote, women's perspectives were valuable during the early days of the Industrial Revolution because many products were marketed to women. However, this also stereotyped women into only having a "female perspective" and by the 1960s, women were segregated into more clerical roles. Many women broke through, however. Mary Wells, an executive at DDB during the creative revolution of the 1960s, launched Wells Rich Greene in

© Monkey Business Images/Shutterstock.com

1966. Wells embarked on her own agency venture after an executive role in an Interpublic agency, where she was told she could have the salary of the president but not the title because "the world is not ready for women presidents" (Wells Lawrence, 2002, p. 44). By 1969, Wells was reportedly the highest paid executive in the industry. Other women who broke barriers in the 1960s include Carol Williams, who became Leo Burnett's first female and first African American VP-creative director; and Caroline Jones, J. Walter Thompson's first African American copywriter in the early 1960s (Davis, 2017). Both women went on to open their own agencies.

For the first century of the U.S. agency business, ads were targeted to a mass and mostly white market. By the 1960s, however, clients began to target more niche audiences and acknowledge ethnic markets as viable areas for growth.

With his wife, Marian, and partner Emmitt McBane, Vincent Cullers opened the first African American owned, full-service agency in Chicago in 1956. At the time, there were few black employees in the industry and few clients who saw African Americans as a viable market segment. Vince Cullers Agency changed that by convincing large clients such as Kent cigarettes and Bristol-Myers (Bufferin) that the market existed and by mentoring and encouraging young black professionals to enter the business (Gordon, 2013). Later, in 1970, Barbara Gardner Proctor opened Proctor and Gardner Advertising, the first African American woman to own and operate an agency.

At the time, agencies had to convince white marketers that "black people were not simply dark-skinned white people," as Thomas Burrell, who opened Burrell Communications in 1971, described it in an interview with National Public Radio (Glinton, 2015). Burrell recalled when one of his first clients, Marlboro cigarettes, wanted to create a black version of the celebrated Marlboro Man cowboy, which would not have resonated with black audiences. Instead, Burrell took the cowboy out of the country and gave him a more cool, urban feel with the slogan "Where the flavor is." Burrell went on to work for clients including Coca-Cola, McDonald's, and Procter & Gamble, bringing more culturally relevant depictions of African Americans to the mainstream.

In the early 1960s, led by a wave of immigrants from Cuba, the first Hispanic advertising agencies began to appear in Miami and New York. Spanish Advertising and Marketing Services, the first full-service Hispanic advertising agency established in 1962, marketed products to the Latin American market mostly through Spanish language ads and creative.

In the 1980s and 1990s, a second wave of Latin American immigrants entered the United States and media outlets such as Telemundo and Univision were growing exponentially. During this time, agencies like Sosa, Bromley, Aguilar & Associates in San Antonio, and Orci Advertising in Los Angeles (founded by Hector and Norma Orci) created campaigns not only to sell products, but also to address issues important to Latin American communities (Anderson, 2016). Hispanic agencies subsequently evolved to develop bilingual and cultural campaigns, and many were (and still are) women-owned or family-owned agencies.

In 2015, the Association of Hispanic Advertising Agencies (founded in 1996) collaborated with the Smithsonian to curate a Hispanic advertising collection as part of the National Museum of American History's advertising archives. Among the collection is the first Clio award presented to a Hispanic agency, awarded to Sara Sunshine in 1987 (Smithsonian, 2015).

After several waves of immigration from Asian countries following the Korean and Vietnam Wars, marketers began looking at Asian Americans as a growth market beginning in the 1980s. The first Asian American advertising agency, L3 (founded by Joe Lam, Lawrence Lee, and Wing Lee), opened its doors in New York in 1984, and launched a Los Angeles office in 1990 (see http://www.l3advertising.com/about/history/). The agency has developed advertising for Fortune 500 companies including Metropolitan Life and JP Morgan Chase. L3 was also one of the founding agencies in the Asian American Advertising Federation (3AF) in 1999. Today, 3AF lists more than 30 agencies and media companies as part of its membership.

PR Agency History

To understand the history of PR agencies, it is helpful to start with a history of PR. In the United States, a widely cited model to track the evolution of PR is the Hunt-Grunig model (1984). This model outlines four stages of PR development: press agentry (agents involved in securing positive publicity for clients), public information (disseminating accurate and objective information), two-way asymmetrical (researching audiences and persuading them to a particular point of view), and two-way symmetrical (communications as a means of achieving mutual understanding). It is worth noting, however, that this model does not necessarily apply to countries outside of the United States, where governments and capitalistic structures may be different.

Press agentry was used in the early days of the Industrial Revolution by entities such as P. T. Barnum (circus) and Williams F. Cody (Buffalo Bill's Wild West show), who often staged extravagant events to gain coverage in local newspapers. At this point, the term "public relations" did not yet exist. It is in the second stage—the public information model—that we see the dawn of PR agencies.

Ivy Ledbetter Lee established the first PR firm with partner George Park in 1904. Some of his clients included the Pennsylvania Railroad and oil giant John D. Rockefeller, both of which asked for his help during fatal incidents at their facilities. Evolving from the press agentry days of PR, Lee advised clients to be honest and open with the press and the public, instead of hiding or covering up information, and established a "Declaration of Principles" to outline this public information model. Lee was also the first to develop the "press release," disseminating information to the press before they heard other versions of a story.

While Lee was influential in early PR, he did not necessarily see it as a profession. It wasn't until Edward Bernays opened a PR agency in 1919 (Edward L. Bernays Council on Public Relations), subsequently teaching the first PR class at New York University and writing the first PR text in 1923, that PR became a true profession. Bernays moved the industry to the third and fourth Hunt-Grunig models—two-way asymmetrical and two-way symmetrical. A nephew of Sigmund Freud, Bernays used principles of psychology and sociology to research audiences and develop campaigns to influence public opinion (not always for the better), and advocated that PR should be a two-way street—communicating the public's opinions back to the client. Some of his clients included the American Tobacco Company, the United Fruit Company, General Electric, and Procter & Gamble.

While Bernays gets much of the credit for being the "father" of PR, his wife, Doris Fleischman, was an equal business partner in the firm. She was a prominent writer and book author, developed and wrote the firm's newsletter (Contact), and worked on many of Bernays' campaigns, including managing media coverage for the first NAACP convention held in the South (Henry, 1997). She was especially active in the women's movement advocating for Women's Suffrage and pay equity. Throughout her life, Fleischman worked with organizations like the Association for Women in Communications to open doors for other young women to enter the PR field.

By the mid-20th century, most large corporations and associations were hiring in-house PR professionals as part of their senior management. Some professionals who advanced the field during this time include Arthur Page (AT&T); Paul Garrett (GM); Betsy Plank (Illinois Bell/SBC); and Denny Griswold, who founded the first PR trade publication, *Public Relations News* (see The Museum of Public Relations, n.d.). The mid-20th century saw the proliferation of PR agencies. These include Hill + Knowlton, established in 1927; Edelman, established in 1952; Burson-Marsteller, established in 1953; and Golin Harris, established in 1956, all of which are global agencies today.

It's also worth noting that many advertising agencies housed PR or publicity departments at this time. For example, in 1947, when Frances Gerety at N. W. Ayer created the legendary De Beers' slogan "A Diamond is Forever®," Dorothy Dignam in Ayer's "publicity" department became known as "Diamond Dot Dignam." She made sure the press knew about diamond-clad Hollywood celebrities by sending monthly letters to newspapers, penning guest columns, and providing celebrities with diamonds to wear at red carpet events (Sullivan, 2013).

As with the advertising industry, the mid-20th century also saw the dawn of multicultural PR firms. Inez Kaiser founded Inez Kaiser & Associates in 1957, the first African American, women-owned firm in the country. The National Black Public Relations Society (NBPRS) was established in 1957, and the Hispanic Public Relations Association (HPRA) was established in 1984.

MERGER MANIA—AGENCY OWNERSHIP

Advertising and PR agencies, much like law firms, often carry the name/s of the founder or founders on the door. When two people partner to open an agency, both names go on the door. Then, as agencies merge with and acquire other firms, new names are added.

For example, in 1906, William D'Arcy opened a small advertising firm in St. Louis called simply D'Arcy Advertising. After expansion into Atlanta and New York in the following decades, the agency merged with a Detroit firm in 1970 and became D'Arcy-MacManus;

with a British firm in 1972 to become D'Arcy-MacManus & Masius; and with New York firm Benton & Bowles in 1986 to become D'Arcy Masius Benton & Bowles. In the late 1990s, the company acquired N. W. Ayer and merged with The Leo Group (owner of Leo Burnett Advertising) and became a holding company called the MacManus Group.

Beginning in the 1960s and accelerating significantly in the 1980s, the agency industry has experienced hundreds (if not thousands) of **mergers and acquisitions (M&As)** through the decades—so many, in fact, that there are whole companies whose sole purpose is to manage M&As for the marketing communications industry. In the late 1980s, one of the authors of this text worked with Don Tennant, former worldwide creative director of Leo Burnett and legendary creator of Tony the Tiger. Tennant often joked that one day all the agencies would merge and all the clients would merge and then the client would go in-house (have its own internal agency), at which point we'd all work for the same company. He wasn't that far off.

M&As have led to significant agency consolidation under a handful of global **holding companies**. And today, it's not just agencies purchasing other agencies. Global technology and consulting companies like IBM, Deloitte, and Accenture are purchasing digital agencies to improve their marketing offerings to clients, rivaling the world's largest agency holding companies (Gianatasio, 2017).

Mergers and acquisitions (M&As): The process of joining (merging) with another company or purchasing (acquiring) another company.

© maxsattana/Shutterstock.com

Holding company: A company whose purpose is to own other companies or the majority stock in other companies or business entities. Often referred to as a "parent" company.

To understand the agency industry and working environment, it's important to understand the shifts and changes in agency ownership. These shifts often result in a "changing of the deck chairs" where employees are laid off from one agency and hired by another. Thus, the resumes of those who work in the industry are often long, and include work for several agencies over a short period of time.

Factors That Influence M&As

There are many factors that have influenced the need for M&As throughout the decades. Briefly, some of these include

1. *The move from "Mom & Pop" to mass retail:* Beginning in the 1960s, grocery stores became "supermarkets," hardware stores became "big box stores," and local restaurants gave way to fast-food franchises. As retail moved from "mom & pop"

ownership to consolidated ownership through regional and national chains, agencies had to respond to client needs with added services and locations. M&As in the agency business often mirror M&As happening on the client side.

2. *Changes in media technology:* The advent of radio in the 1940s and television in the 1950s and 1960s changed the industry landscape significantly. Creative departments that once hired print illustrators added experts in filming and editing technology, jingle writers, media-buying experts who understood the expanding media landscape, and researchers who could track listening and watching habits. Because the backbone of advertising and PR is disseminating messages through the media, with each new wave of media technology comes the need for agencies to adapt and change.

   Rather than hiring waves of new talent, it is often more economically beneficial for agencies to merge with or buy out firms that already have those capabilities. For example, as social media took off in the mid-2000s, larger agencies often merged with or bought out niche agencies with expertise in social media. And, with each new technology comes the need to measure that technology with media analytics. So, the continuum usually begins with startup agencies that see an emerging technology need, growth of those startups as the new technology becomes mainstream, and then a wave of M&As where larger agencies buy out the startups. For example, in the past couple of years, M&As of digital and analytics firms have surged, with 204 M&A deals in the first half of 2016 alone (Slefo, 2016).

3. *Globalization:* As clients expanded from national to multinational companies, advertising and PR agencies expanded as well to service the needs of those clients. Let's say, for example, you are an agency of record for a client in St. Louis who decides to expand its business to China. By merging with or buying out agencies in key centers in China, you would be able to maintain and expand your business with that client. Today, most of the large advertising and PR agencies have offices all over the world. Instead of starting these agencies from scratch, many large firms will buy out agencies in other countries to expand their geographic reach.

4. *Agency integration:* In the 1980s, we called it the "whole egg" approach. In the 1990s, the term "seamless communications" appeared. Today, we call it **integrated marketing communications** (IMCs). Rather than a siloed approach to communications with separate advertising, PR, promotional and digital strategies, these functions are being integrated into one communications strategy. Larger clients often demand that their agencies be able to handle all communications functions under one roof. In addition, as digital communications becomes the prominent technology for disseminating messages, the walls are coming down between what is considered social media versus PR versus advertising versus word-of-mouth marketing, and so on. Thus, agencies will merge with other agencies to offer clients full-service communications.

> **Integrated marketing communications:** A planning process that ensures all communications functions (such as advertising, PR, sales promotion) are unified and communicating consistent messages to target audiences.

In addition, as demographics shift in the United States, the general market is becoming more multicultural. Rather than having separate strategies for the general market and the multicultural market, general market agencies are realizing the need to merge with or acquire agencies with expertise in multicultural marketing to offer clients a Total Market approach to communications (see Chapter 6).

5. *Conflicts of interest:* Let's say you are an agency specializing in branded food products, and the agency of record for a large food conglomerate client. The client markets more than 50 different food brands, and you've signed a contract saying you won't take on any clients that compete with the conglomerate's brands. A portfolio that large is going to limit the new business you can go after in the category.

   Agencies will often spin-off another business unit, merge with or acquire another agency to avoid client conflicts of interest. In this case, for example, the agency might pitch the business of a juice brand, and then spin-off or acquire another agency to handle the business to avoid any conflicts of interest with its large conglomerate client.

6. *Financial growth:* It all comes down to money. As the agency industry became more competitive in the 1960s and 1970s, M&As became a way to significantly grow market share. Rather than trying to start and win business for a new function from scratch, which takes time, M&As allow agencies to increase market share all at once. The agency business is a volatile one, where revenues are often fixed and business is vulnerable to client impulses. One major account loss can devastate a small or mid-sized agency. M&As allow agencies to grow in sluggish economies, expand their global capabilities, buffer their businesses against sudden client losses, and achieve **economies of scale**.

   > **Economies of scale:** As agencies increase in size, they can share resources and spread those costs over a larger scale, thus achieving increased productivity at lower costs.

There are upsides and downsides to agency consolidation. For large clients, consolidation gives clients access to a variety of functions and geographies under one entity. For employees, working in a conglomerate can make it easier to move from one location to another, or one agency to another, once you've gotten your foot in the door. However, many feel that consolidation has everything to do with increasing profits for agency shareholders, and little to do with producing excellent work for clients. When a smaller agency is bought out by a larger one, it often loses its autonomy and must do business the way its new owner dictates. This can often stifle creativity and innovation. Regardless, M&As are a fact of life in the agency business and show no signs of abating.

The Big Four + One

As a result of M&As through the decades, four giant conglomerates, called holding companies, control more than 50% of all marketing communications revenues and media spending in the world, and have for many years. The big four include WPP (London), Omnicom

(New York), Publicis (Paris), and Interpublic Group (IPG) (New York). Coming in a close fifth in revenues is Dentsu out of Tokyo, which controls a large slice of the Asian market and has been expanding into the other countries in recent years.

What's more, there are agency networks within the larger holding companies. For example, the Ogilvy companies are **wholly owned subsidiaries** of WPP Group and include Ogilvy & Mather (advertising), Ogilvy Public Relations, and Ogilvy One (direct marketing). Ogilvy has more than 450

Wholly owned subsidiary: A company or entity that is owned by another company, such as a holding company.

offices in 169 cities around the globe (see http://www.ogilvy.com/our-history/). And, there are mergers within conglomerates. For example, Omnicom's U.S.-based Ketchum and U.K.-based Pleon merged in 2009 to give both entities a larger global footprint in the PR industry.

In essence, conglomeration has created a complex matrix of agencies, networks, marketing disciplines, and geographic locations, which are continually changing and evolving. Below is a brief outline of each of the largest holding companies, based on 2016 revenues (AdAge Agency Report, 2017).

Table 1.1   World's Largest Agency Holding Companies

Company	Revenues (2016)
WPP Group, London	19.4 billion
Omnicom, New York	15.4 billion
Publicis, Paris	10.7 billion
Interpublic Group, New York	7.8 billion
Dentsu, Tokyo	7.2 billion

Source: AdAge Data Center, 2017 Agency Report.

WPP Group, London: In 1985, Sir Martin Sorrell took a financial interest in Wire & Plastics Products, PLC to set up a holding company through which he could buy marketing services agencies. In 1987, WPP purchased J. Walter Thompson, which included Hill & Knowlton PR agency. In 1989, the Ogilvy Group became part of WPP, which included Ogilvy & Mather Worldwide, Ogilvy Direct, and Ogilvy Public Relations Worldwide. In 1997, the company launched the media planning and buying entity MindShare. Over the decades, WPP has purchased entities in advertising, PR, media buying, healthcare, sports and entertainment, research, e-commerce, branding, and digital media. The company currently owns more than 400 agency brands and employs more than 200,000 people worldwide (see https://www.wpp.com/wpp/).

Omnicom, New York: Omnicom boasts 30 marketing disciplines across 1,500 agencies worldwide (see http://www.omnicomgroup.com/about/). Some of its most well-known agency groups include BBDO, DDB, TWBA, Ketchum, Fleishman, and DAS. Omnicom was created in 1986 as a merger between BBDO Worldwide, DDB, and Needham Harper. In 2013, Omnicom was slated to merge with Publicis, but the deal didn't go forward.

Publicis Groupe, Paris: Marcel Bleustein-Blanchet founded Publicis in 1926, and named it after the French word for advertising and the number "6," his favorite number. In an effort to integrate its more than 130 agencies, the company recently announced a new organizational structure around four "Solution Hubs": Publicis Communications, Publicis Sapient, Publicis Media, and Publicis Health (see http://www.publicisgroupe.com/en/services/the-power-of-one). Some of its agencies include Leo Burnett; Saatchi & Saatchi; Burrell Communications; Digitas; Fallon; Manning, Selvage and Lee; and Starcom MediaVest.

IPG, New York: Some of the main brands for IPG include Foote, Cone & Belding (FCB); Golin; McCann; MullenLowe Group; Weber Shandwick; and Campbell Ewald. IPG began as McCann-Erickson in 1930 and became IPG in 1961. It currently has nearly 100 agency brands in as many countries (see https://www.interpublic.com/about).

Dentsu, Tokyo: Dentsu was established in 1901 as both a news agency and a broker selling advertisements for newspapers. After successes organizing the Tokyo Olympic Games in 1964 and Osaka Expo in 1970, the company diversified its offerings and in 1974 was the world's largest advertising agency in revenues. After several acquisitions in Europe, the United Kingdom and the America's in the mid-2000s, Dentsu acquired the Aegis Group in 2013 and formed a new global operating unit. It has accelerated its rate of acquisitions in the past few years and now serves clients in nearly 150 countries (see http://www.dentsu.com/history/).

Middle Market Players

In between the big four conglomerates and the smaller independent agencies (discussed below), are mid-sized holding companies. As silos between marketing communications functions come down and clients demand a variety of services, these networks give clients more to choose from while still maintaining the customer service and feel of a smaller shop. Some of the middle-market holding companies include CHR Group, Engine Group, and Project Worldwide.

Independent Agencies

Independent agencies comprise the rest of the agency world. These agencies are not under the purview of any holding company and are usually independently owned by one or a handful of private owners. While this group encompasses the majority of small- to medium-sized local or regional agencies, independent agencies can also be very large. For example, Edelman Public Relations, founded by Daniel J. Edelman in 1952, is the world's largest independent PR firm with 65 offices around the world. The agency grew by opening its own offices in most countries in which it expanded, and in some cases acquiring other agencies.

The advantage of being independent is that the owner (or owners) can call the shots, rather than being tied to the edicts of a corporate bureaucracy. This allows the agency to be more flexible, more responsive to client needs, and more entrepreneurial in its culture. For employees, independent agencies can often have tight-knit cultures where working relationships are like family. In addition, in smaller shops, titles are less important and employees frequently wear many hats. For entry-level employees, working at an independent agency can help you learn a broader set of skills than being pigeonholed into, say, only doing media pitching.

On the advertising side, independent agencies can also be the most creative. For example, independent agency Wieden+Kennedy out of Portland is widely known for its breakthrough campaigns like the Old Spice Guy and the Nike Equality campaign.

The downside of independent agencies is financial risk. As stated previously, the agency business is volatile. An independent agency with one large client and a handful of small clients is at risk if that one large client moves to another agency. For example, one of the authors worked in the Chicago office of Toronto-based Saffer Advertising in the 1990s. The agency had about 80 employees and served one large client—Montgomery Ward. When the client took its business to another agency, the Chicago office of Saffer was closed and those 80 employees were out of a job. While this isn't as big of a problem in cities like Chicago, where dozens of other agencies exist, it is a bigger issue in a smaller city like, say, Indianapolis where there are only a handful of agencies.

TYPES OF AGENCIES

There are as many different types of agencies as there are marketing communications disciplines. In general, agencies are broken into two overarching categories: Full-service agencies and specialty/niche agencies.

Full-service agencies are those that offer a full range of services and capabilities for their clients. In the advertising industry, this means an agency can conduct research, set brand or campaign strategy, develop and produce creative, plan and buy media, and monitor/track a campaign's results. Full-service PR firms perform similar functions, though instead of purchasing

> **Full-service agencies:** Agencies that offer a full range of services and capabilities for their clients— from research and planning to execution and measurement.

advertising they will design other means of message dissemination and campaign execution. In addition to marketing to consumers, customers, donors, and other end-users of a product or service, full-service agencies may also develop communications aimed toward the sales force and trade industry (like producing end-aisle displays for grocery stores).

Besides full-service advertising and PR agencies, there are also full-service IMC agencies, where advertising, PR, and other disciplines are combined under one roof. While the larger industry players maintain separate advertising and PR agencies, many smaller local or regional agencies will handle both functions for clients.

Some agencies are experts in certain industries or marketing categories and will work for clients within those industries—like the food and beverage industry, the pharmaceutical industry, or the real estate market. Honing in on an expertise can be a competitive advantage for agencies if there are only a handful of players in that category. For example, some agencies, like The Food Group, specialize in food and beverage marketing. They are still a full-service agency able to handle a client's campaign from research through execution, but have added benefits for food clients like research and development facilities, test kitchens or culinary and nutrition experts on staff.

Being a full-service agency does not mean the agency will handle absolutely everything a campaign entails. For example, when developing a commercial, an ad agency will likely concept, design and write the script for the commercial, but will then hire outside directors and casting agents to help with filming. Likewise, a PR agency wanting to research attitudes toward a particular client might hire a research company to carry out focus groups in several geographic markets. For example, 20/20 out of Charlotte (with offices also in Nashville and Miami) has focus group facilities with one-way mirrors, client viewing rooms, mock trial courtroom setups and staff who handle participant recruiting. These are not facilities that would normally be housed in a PR agency.

Specialty/niche agencies are those that focus on a specific expertise in a certain niche. For example, a client may already have a full-service marketing agency but need help with sales promotion strategy. Many agencies specialize in sales promotion, where they help clients with building customer databases, direct marketing, couponing, sweepstakes, encouraging product trial, and

> **Specialty/niche agencies:** Agencies that focus on a specific marketing or communications expertise for a client, such as crisis communications, direct marketing, or search engine optimization.

other sales-driven activities. Likewise, APCO Worldwide is an independent consultancy specializing in public affairs communication. The agency works with clients around the world on issues related to public opinion, issues management, and government relations.

While full-service agencies go wide, handling a diverse range of services for clients, specialty agencies go deep becoming experts in one marketing or communications discipline. You will find specialty agencies in the areas of word-of-mouth marketing, search engine optimization, media planning and buying, product placement, sports marketing, employee workplace performance, crisis communications, mobile marketing, brand identity, direct marketing, environmental communications, and many others.

AGENCY STRUCTURES

While every agency has its "signature" way of doing business, you will notice similar structures at most advertising and PR agencies. These structures evolve and change as new technologies, disciplines, and cultural insights are adopted. However, these changes have traditionally transformed the thinking and capabilities within agencies, but not necessarily the structure.

You can think of agency structures in terms of who is being served by agencies, the work they do and how they do it. In essence, agencies are in the business of serving clients. These are the folks who pay the bills and hire and fire agencies, so successfully meeting clients' needs is at the center of any agency structure.

Clients come to agencies because they need to communicate and engage with stakeholders and target audiences—consumers, publics, voters, donors, members, and the like. To do so, you have to understand those audiences and their needs. Thus, most agencies will have researchers on staff to gather information and insights, people to interpret those insights for others in the agency, and people or departments that will in turn transform those insights into strategies.

Then, those insights and strategies are converted into messages and content, often through visual and written storytelling. To engage with targeted audiences and disseminate that content, agencies will use many tactics, including media relations, advertising placement, social media, sponsorships, experiential marketing, customer relationship management, digital marketing, corporate social responsibility, and so on. Thus, you need people in the agency who can execute these tactics and others who will measure whether those programs were effective.

But who else is served by agencies? Employees are. To keep the agency engine running smoothly, agencies have people and departments (often called human resources) that hire and support those who are serving clients' needs. Lastly, agencies support the owner/s and shareholders in the business. At the end of the day, agencies are profit centers in business to earn money, pay employees and put money back into the business. The finance department handles all the billing and financial services needed to keep the agency financially viable and profitable.

Advertising Agency Structure

Below are the standard departments and functions found in most advertising agencies.

Client/account services: Client service, often called account service, is responsible for working directly with clients to determine their needs, bring in other departments to serve those needs, and to communicate with clients throughout the process. This is where you will find titles such as account executives, account supervisors, or account managers. Clients depend on account services to be responsive to changing client or market needs, to represent them with other departments in the agency and to keep programs running effectively on deadline. The client service team is essentially the liaison between the client and the agency. Client service is organized into client account teams—such as the Dove client team or the Quaker client team. Account executives will coordinate and execute a diverse range of program tactics for their particular clients.

Research: Research takes place at many stages in the communications process. At the beginning of the process, researchers gather audience insights through both qualitative and quantitative research to determine audience attitudes, preferences, and behaviors. Once create strategies and tactics are developed, researchers will pretest ads and other creative strategies through focus groups and other methods, and may also conduct campaign tracking to determine how the campaign is doing as it is being executed. Finally, the research group will develop and execute a measurement plan to determine if a program or campaign met stated goals outlined at the beginning of the strategic process. As digital media has proliferated, researchers rely a great deal on **digital analytics** to measure the performance of online ads, mobile applications, websites, and social media.

Digital analytics: Measuring and tracking performance on websites, social media sites, blogs, and other digital platforms through the use of data gathering tools such as Google Analytics.

Research departments also utilize syndicated data such as GfK MRI or Simmons data to supplement primary research.

Account planning: Working closely with the research department, account planners will determine the research that needs to be conducted and then interpret those audience insights for the client and others in the agency. Account planners often set the strategy for the program or campaign. Account planning emerged in the 1990s, when agencies realized that the consumer and other end-users were not being properly represented in the agency process. Account planners essentially represent the audience in the agency process, keeping the client and agency members on track with audience insights throughout the planning and execution process.

Creative services: In the creative services department, you will find copywriters, illustrators, graphic designers, digital design experts, videographers, art directors, and producers. These are the people who develop the creative content for advertising programs under the direction of a creative director. With the insights of the account planning team, creative members are given a **creative brief** (see Chapter 4) often developed by the account executive, which outlines all the necessary information and audience insights needed to develop ads and other creative materials. In essence, the creative group brings the program strategy to life, grabbing the audience's attention, and driving them to action.

> **Creative brief:** A document that provides insights into the brand, target audience, and project goals and logistics to guide the work of the creative team in producing a campaign.

Production: The production department often reports to the creative department. This department manages the tangible process of producing and placing advertisements. For example, if a campaign includes billboard ads, the production team will determine the specs needed for producing that billboard. They will work with printers to ensure the size, color, and printing quality are up to standards; liaise with the art and create directors to sign off on those processes; and work with the owner of the billboard to coordinate the physical application of the ad. Similarly, when producing a commercial, the production team will work with directors, casting agents, and videographers to coordinate the production of the commercial. Within the department are different types of production, for example, print production, television production, digital production, and so on.

Media department: The media department develops plans for disseminating content through a variety of media platforms and channels, including billboards, mobile, digital ads, print, television, film, radio, and point of purchase. **Media planners** develop the strategy for disseminating creative content, including determining where ads should be placed, when they should be placed, how frequently and for how long. Media planning is a complex process that involves a great deal of statistical research on what the target audience is reading, watching, hearing, and consuming, as well as which

> **Media planners:** People who develop the strategy for disseminating creative content, including where ads should be placed, when they should be placed, how frequently and for how long.

platforms and channels will be most effective in reaching audiences with specific messages. **Media buyers** then negotiate and purchase the advertising time and space in those platforms and channels. The greater the volume of advertising purchased, the less per unit the advertising costs. Thus, media buyers will work with publishers and brokers to purchase the optimum media package for reaching the target audience. For more information, see the professional article on Media Planning and Placement in Part III.

Media buyers: Those who negotiate media prices and purchase advertising time and space across platforms such as television, print, outdoor, and digital media.

Finance: The finance department develops financial plans for the agency, seeks out investments, determines billing rates, calculates overhead, sets budgets and profit margins, and prepares client financial contracts, among other things. Within the department, there are usually those who work on accounts receivable (money coming into the agency) and accounts payable (money going out of the agency in the form of staff salaries, facility management, and vendor payments). In Chapter 5, we outline in more detail the processes involved in the Business Side of Communications.

Human resources and agency support services: The HR department is responsible for hiring employees and maintaining programs and systems to support those employees. This includes managing employee recruitment, interviewing and hiring processes; developing and maintaining employee benefits programs; communicating with employees; and managing legal and ethical issues involved in employee interactions. Often, other support services will be bundled under the HR department, including the IT department, office managers, administrative staff, and other support services.

New business/agency branding: Sometimes, agencies have people or departments to manage the new business process and promote the agency to potential clients (see Chapter 3 on Building Business). People in this department would develop new business databases, handle outreach to potential clients, manage proposals and pitch processes, and execute PR programs to generate awareness and credibility for the agency.

PR Agency Structure

PR agency structures are similar in many ways to advertising agencies, but there are also several differences. These differences center around the type of work PR agencies do for their clients and how they disseminate their content.

First, **PR** agencies are not usually producing paid media content in the form of commercials and advertisements (though this is changing). Instead, their content comes in the form of news releases, annual reports, social media content, brochures, and the like. Because of this, traditionally **PR** agencies did not have large, separate creative departments. Instead of copywriters, account executives in **PR** agencies write most of the informational and creative content, whether it is writing a news release or a script for a public service announcement (PSA). When the need arose for creative such as web design, graphic design, or video production, **PR** agencies traditionally hired out to specialty agencies or freelancers to create these materials.

Today, this is changing quite a bit. We have become a much more visual society. Rather than reading long-form articles and 10-page brochures, we want our content in snackable form with lots of visuals. In addition, as mentioned earlier in this chapter, digital media has blurred the lines between what is considered advertising and what is considered PR. For these reasons, many **PR** agencies have formed separate creative and production departments, especially in larger agencies.

The second area where **PR** agencies differ is in the ways they disseminate content. While media departments in ad agencies focus on paid advertising placements, **PR** agencies focus more on earned media placement (see **PESO** discussion in Chapter 14). **PR** professionals pitch stories to journalists, bloggers, and television news directors. And again, this type of function often is carried out by each of the account teams for their particular clients. However, many agencies do have a separate media relations department. In advertising agencies, media planners and buyers work with the sales staff of media companies, but in **PR** agencies members of a media relations department are experts in working with the editorial side of the media, and have developed relationships with journalists, editors, and news directors.

In a typical **PR** agency, client account teams (account executives, account supervisors, etc.) manage and conduct much of the work for agency clients. In addition, these account teams are often supported by other departments including research, media relations, creative, and digital/social media.

PR Agency Practice Groups

Many of the larger, multinational **PR** agencies are also organized by what are called **practice groups**. Each of these practice groups focuses on an industry category or functional expertise within the industry. Why distinguish by practice group? Because certain industry

Practice groups: PR agencies will often organize people and resources across multiple offices into groups that specialize in areas such as brand marketing, corporate communications, or health and medical PR.

categories have unique business needs, stakeholder relationships, media outlets, legal issues, and ways of doing business. Thus, it is helpful to work with professionals who understand that industry or specialty.

Typical practice groups found at larger PR agencies include

Brand marketing: This is essentially the consumer side of marketing. Brand marketing experts understand brand identity/image, consumer behavior, and buying habits, and have unique experience marketing products and services to consumers. Members in this practice group stay up-to-date on trends in popular culture and integrate these cultural insights into client programs.

Corporate communication: Corporate communication professionals understand the unique issues facing those occupying the C-Suite within organizations—chief executive officers, chief financial officers, chief operating officers, chief communications officer, and so on. These specialists have experience communicating with company shareholders, employees, strategic partners, and business media like the *Wall Street Journal*. They help companies build and maintain corporate reputation, work on corporate social responsibility and sustainability programs, and often help with company mergers and change management initiatives.

Health and medical: The healthcare industry must adhere to strict governmental laws and guidelines. For example, to make a claim about a certain drug or health benefit, companies must back up that claim with extensive medical research. Audiences to which this practice group communicates would include doctors and other healthcare professionals, nutritionists and dietitians, hospital administrators, and medical associations. PR experts in this area understand the unique rules and guidelines of these industries.

Sport and entertainment marketing: Programs that involve sports or entertainment sponsorships, events, or partnerships (like NASCAR, the Olympics, the Chicago Marathon, and red carpet events at the Oscar's), would fall under the purview of this practice group. Some agencies combine sport and entertainment into one practice group, while others separate them into two.

Technology: This practice group would work with consumer electronics companies, digital businesses, or software companies. Clients like IBM, Apple, Microsoft, or GoPro might be clients you'd find in this practice group. Tech companies have unique go-to-market strategies, as well as specific industry analysts and trade media that experts in this area would be familiar with. The language of technology differs from other industries and thus companies benefit from working with communications experts who understand the technology field.

Public affairs: Issues relating to government and public policy are managed under the Public Affairs practice group. Experts in this area would communicate with government officials, policy decision-makers, nongovernmental organizations (NGOs), constituency groups, and the public on a regional, national, or global level. Public Affairs practice groups are often housed within an agency's Washington DC office.

Practice group employees may be spread across geographic offices and clients. For example, the head of the global brand marketing practice might be housed in a New York corporate headquarters, but would work with brand marketing people and accounts in Chicago, Atlanta, Los Angeles, London, Beijing, San Paolo, and so on. Sometimes, several geographic offices are involved in serving one brand marketing client. For example, a Chicago-based client would work primarily with the Chicago account team, but teams in Los Angeles or New York might be pulled in to help with national media pitching, special events, or other activities. Likewise, a brand marketing client may have a special need, such as experiencing a crisis, when the corporate practice group would be brought in to help. Thus, account team members will not only have a direct line of reporting in their own office, but also report horizontally to account supervisors or practice heads in other geographic locations. This is referred to as a **matrix organization** structure.

> **Matrix organization:** An organizational structure that has both direct lines of reporting (vertical) and horizontal lines of reporting. This structure breaks down departmental barriers, where employees can work horizontally with teams across functions and departments.

AGENCIES OF THE FUTURE—WHAT WILL THEY LOOK LIKE?

Ask 10 people what the future of the agency business will look like and you may get 10 different answers. However, if we look at the current trends in the industry we can gather a few clues.

Beginning in 2013, many companies began moving their marketing in-house, disrupting the traditional agency model. Why? According to Harvard Business Review (Schaefer, 2015), clients want to connect with target audiences in new ways, faster, continuously, and on a personalized basis. The behemoths created by decades of megamergers and consolidation in the agency business make it difficult for larger agencies to change from a "campaign-based" model to one that is more flexible and dynamic.

In response to this, agencies are turning to what is called an **omnichannel** approach. For example, in 2016 Omnicom launched an agency called "We Are Unlimited" specifically dedicated to one client—McDonald's. The agency is made up of staffers from a variety of Omnicom agencies across disciplines such as digital, social, word-of-mouth marketing, creative, behavioral marketing, multicultural

> **Omnichannel agency:** An agency formed by combining the expertise from several agencies across a holding company. An omnichannel agency provides one or more clients with access to a variety of marketing communications disciplines under one roof.

marketing, and many others, as well as embedded team members from companies like Facebook, Twitter, Adobe, and The Marketing Store—some 200 staffers in all (Stein & Wohl, 2016). This omnichannel model gives the client the best of all Omnicom agencies under one roof. Most importantly, at the center of the model is a data center called "Cortex" where real-time media, behavioral, and purchasing data drive agency decisions and programs.

When we look at this model, we can glimpse the future of the agency business. Within this omnichannel model are five clues: the agency is integrated, collaborative, flexible, results-based, and focused on digital data.

Today's digital world generates data—big data, tons of data, and every imaginable type of data. Your online footprint generates a digital profile that maps your needs, desires, attitudes, and behaviors. When you search for a pair of skinny jeans, make a comment on the service at Starbucks, donate to an environmental group, or Tweet about a contestant on Dancing With the Stars, the Internet is keeping track. Marketers who want your business need to reach you in real time, giving you personalized information as you are making those decisions and forming those attitudes. We saw an example of this in the 2016 election where campaigns used data to send specific information to voters based on their attitudes and political views.

© Rawpixel.com/Shutterstock.com

This data-rich world is disrupting the conventional agency business model. Traditionally, advertising agencies made most of their money through commissions on large television and print media buys. But today's digital media and **programmatic media buying** are changing that. Media purchases are becoming more personalized and based on individual behavior rather than large target markets.

Programmatic media buying: A digital process that automates media buying, allowing media planners and buyers to reach and track audiences, and optimize advertising across multiple platforms and channels in real time.

This also allows advertisers to test ideas and then change them over a short period of time, instead of launching one, big yearlong campaign and then waiting for the results.

This model is changing the PR landscape, too. Traditionally, PR practitioners dealt with gatekeepers—editors, journalists, news directors, and the like. But digital technology has broken down barriers between brands and consumers. Today, PR practitioners communicate directly to the consumer, customer, or potential donor, truly creating the two-way symmetrical relationship of the Hunt-Grunig model. This also means organizations need to be less corporate and more human, communicating more authentically, as Lellis and Eggleston discuss in their book, *The Zombie Business Cure* (2017).

So how will these trends affect the agency of the future? First, rather than force-fitting their businesses into current agency models, clients expect agencies to create signature models that will best fit their needs. This might be an omnichannel model or a model where the client works independently with a series of specialty firms and freelancers. Second, digital media has allowed us to be much more collaborative in our thinking. Rather than one creative team coming up with the "big idea," agencies are collaborating with clients, other agencies, digital media suppliers, and even consumers to develop ideas. Additionally, rather than brands tightly controlling their image, today's consumers are cocreators of brands through branded selfies, social media sharing, live video, and online reviews. Remember Chewbacca Mom? She played a significant role in cocreating and personalizing the Star Wars brand.

Alexei Orlov, CEO of Rapp, says this type of collaboration means fewer creatives and account executives, and more creative "communities" within agencies. "These communities include graphic designers, copywriters, analysts, strategists, and big thinkers," Orlov said. "It is an integrative team brought together to combine left and right brain thinking into superior strategy and creative" (Whitler, 2016).

There are also new players coming into the agency market. Accenture, IBM, Deloitte, and other consulting firms are purchasing digital agencies at a significant rate. Tech companies like Google and Snapchat are also dipping their toe into the advertising and publishing mix, as well as traditional publishers like the *Financial Times* and *New York Times*, both of which purchased agencies in 2016. Everyone is trying to capitalize on the content-rich digital space. And, as PR agencies add more creative and production capabilities, and advertising agencies add more relationship-building capabilities, they'll become more competitive with each other, too.

Lastly, the digital landscape requires new ways of measuring our results, in real time and down to personalized statistics. This is why we see data and media analytics being added as majors in university business and communications departments.

All of these changes will transform the agency landscape in the coming decade. And, they provide a great deal for student agencies to contemplate. How will you organize your agency to take advantage of these new trends? What capabilities do you have in place to stay on top of emerging media and data analytics? And, how can you make your agency process more collaborative and focused on client results?

TRADE ASSOCIATIONS, MEDIA, AND AWARDS

Throughout this text, we will often reference organizations such as the American Association of Advertising Agencies, Public Relations Society of America, or AHAA: The Voice of Hispanic Marketing. Industry associations play an important role in the business by supporting the growth and development of agencies, establishing ethical guidelines for the industry, organizing national and regional professional events, and recognizing agencies for successful work. Like any trade industry, associations bring professionals and agencies together to share best practices and discuss issues affecting the industry. In Table 1.2, you will find a list of the larger trade associations in the advertising and PR business. Many of these associations have regional chapters and also student chapters.

In addition to these associations, there are also organizations focusing on specialty practices. These include the Word of Mouth Marketing Association (WOMMA), the Social Media Association (SMA), the Data and Marketing Association (DMA), the Promotion Marketing Association (PMA), Sport Marketing Association (SMA), and many others.

Another important player in the industry is advertising and PR trade media. These publications report on trends in the industry, client account changes, influential leaders, and agency campaigns. Some trade publications include *PR News*, *PR Week*, *Advertising Age* (AdAge), *Advertising Week* (AdWeek), and *Media Post* publications to name a few. There are also publications that report on specialty agencies or disciplines in the industry, like the *Social Media Examiner*.

Table 1.2   Key Industry Associations

Association	Purpose
AHAA: The Voice of Hispanic Marketing	Represents Hispanic marketing communications professionals and advocates for increased investment in multicultural marketing.
American Advertising Federation	Helps professionals build their careers; works to protect and promote the industry. Has 200 local AAF clubs and 200 student clubs.
American Association of Advertising Agencies (4As)	Works to elevate and educate member agencies and promote the industry in general. Represents 740 member agencies across 1,400 offices.
American Marketing Association	Connects academics and marketers to promote marketing excellence.
Arthur Page Society	Advances the role of senior-level PR and corporate communications professionals.
Asian American Advertising Federation (3AF)	Works to grow the Asian American advertising industry and promote the importance of the Asian American market.
Association for Women in Communications	Promotes the advancement of women across all communications disciplines including journalism, broadcast, PR, and marketing.
Association of National Advertisers	Represents the client side of the ad business working to advance the interests of marketers.
Hispanic Public Relations Association	Network of Latinx marketing communications professionals. Helps advance careers and promote best practices in Hispanic marketing.
Institute for Public Relations	Dedicated to research in, on, and for the PR industry.
International Association of Business Communicators	Global network of corporate and strategic communications professionals; committed to improving organizational effectiveness.
National Black Public Relations Society	Strives to nurture, enlighten, and inform its membership about new technologies and techniques. Serves communications professionals, administrators, and media specialists.
PR Council	Represents PR agencies; advocates and advances the business of communications firms in the market.
Public Relations Society of America	Nation's largest organization representing communications professionals. Works to make professionals smarter and better prepared in the field. Also encompasses the Public Relations Student Society of America.

Lastly, agency awards play a significant role in recognizing and applauding breakthrough campaigns, agencies, and industry leaders. There are two ways to know you have succeeded in the business. First, your clients are pleased. And second, you receive recognition through an industry award. Awards give you bragging rights. These are important not only to individuals but to agencies as well. The more awards an agency wins, the more recognition they will receive in the industry. The more recognition they receive, the more business they will win and the more qualified employees they will attract.

And, there is another advantage to awards programs, especially for student agencies: They give you access to some of the best campaigns in the business. As you likely know, creative ideas don't come from a blank sheet of paper. They come from putting as many great ideas into your head as possible, and then synthesizing, evolving, and reapplying those ideas to your own campaigns. Most awards programs have websites where you can review case studies on the winning campaigns. This is a great way to review trends in the industry and gather ideas for your own creative brainstorming. In Table 1.3, you'll find a list of some of the most renowned awards programs in the industry.

Table 1.3   Top Industry Awards Programs

Program	Sponsor and Purpose
American Advertising Awards (ADDYs)	Includes local, district, national, and student competitions for creative excellence.
¡BRAVO! Awards	Awarded for outstanding innovation, creativity, and cultural competence for Hispanic PR campaigns.
Bronze & Silver Anvil Awards	Sponsor: Public Relations Society of America. Silver Anvils recognize the best PR campaigns/programs of the year, while Bronze Anvils recognize individual elements such as media kits, videos, social media, annual reports, etc.
Bulldog Stars of PR Awards	Sponsor: Bulldog Reporter. Recognizes top agencies of the year in several categories (e.g., small, medium, large, boutique, public affairs, etc.) and top professionals of the year.
Cannes Lions International Awards	Separate entity. Recognizes creativity for all types of communications campaigns in a variety of categories. Held in Cannes, France each summer.
Clio Awards	Separate entity. Recognizes high achievement in advertising including work, agencies, and people.
Design and Art Direction Awards (D&AD)	Separate entity. Recognizes outstanding work in design and advertising. Includes Impact Awards, Professional Awards, Next Awards, and New Blood Awards.
Effie Awards	Separate entity. Honors effectiveness in marketing communications with emphasis on results.

(Continued)

(*Continued*)

Program	Sponsor and Purpose
OBIE Awards	Separate entity. Awards creative excellence in advertising in a variety of categories and media.
OMMA Awards	Recognizes excellence in digital advertising. Media Post has several other awards programs including awards for out-of-home, mobile apps, automotive advertising, and exceptional agencies and talent.
PR News Awards	Awards excellent in PR across a variety of categories and media.
PR Week Awards	Sponsor: PR Week. Awards excellence in PR across a variety of categories and media.
SABRE Awards	Sponsor: The Holmes Report. Awards the best work produced by PR agencies and departments in a variety of categories.
The One Club	Awarding creative excellence in advertising and design. The One Club is the nonprofit umbrella for the One Show Awards and ADC Awards given during its annual Creative Week.
Webby Awards	Presented by the International Academy of Digital Arts & Sciences (IADAS). Awards for work on the Web/Internet in six major media types: websites, film/video, advertising, media & PR, mobile sites and apps, and podcasts and digital audio.

If you plan to work for an agency after graduation, joining professional or student communications associations and reading industry publications on a regular basis will be invaluable in keeping abreast of industry happenings. They can also help you make contact and network with professionals in the industry, creating a path for future employment. And, winning a student agency award is a nice bonus to add to your resume.

CONCLUSION

The agency business has had a long and illustrious history with many twists and turns along the way. No doubt by the time you read this text, the business will have evolved and adapted again as new technologies, cultures, and approaches disrupt the traditional way of communicating with target audiences. This chapter should help you understand the foundations of the industry so you can track those changes as they occur.

In addition, this knowledge will help clarify your role within the student agency and how it fits within the larger framework of the agency and the industry. If you choose to work for an agency after graduation, or in-house in a client organization, having a working knowledge of the industry will make you that much more prepared to provide counsel to clients and work more seamlessly with your colleagues. Employers often complain that entry-level applicants don't understand how the industry works. Now you do. In subsequent chapters, you will learn even more about working within an agency structure and becoming a stalwart communications professional. Who knows; someday YOU might win a Clio or Silver Anvil, or develop a unique approach that will revolutionize the industry once again.

REVIEW AND DISCUSSION QUESTIONS

1. What was the name of the first advertising agency that developed and produced ads for clients, becoming the precursor to modern advertising agencies?
2. Name the four phases in the Hunt-Grunig model of PR.
3. Helen Lansdowne was the first woman to become a creative director in the advertising industry. What was the name of the agency she worked for and later ran with her husband?
4. Who is known as the "father" of PR and what were his main contributions to the industry?
5. What were some of the key reasons that multicultural agencies developed in the United States?
6. During the 1960s, the advertising business went through a "creative revolution." What were some of the characteristics that marked this time in advertising history?
7. Name and discuss two reasons that agencies merge or acquire other agencies.
8. Who are the four largest advertising and PR agency holding companies? Take a few minutes to review the websites of each and the list of agencies each conglomerate owns.
9. If you were planning to work for an agency after graduation, which position would you most like to hold and what would your responsibilities be?
10. Review the current issue of one advertising, PR, or specialty trade publication such as *Ad Age,* or *PR Week* (you may need to use your university's library database to gain full access). With your teammates, discuss two articles from the issue and why you find them of interest.

REFERENCES AND ADDITIONAL READINGS

Agency Report 2017 (2017). *Advertising Age, 88*(9), 020. Complete report in *AdAge Data Center*.

Anderson, M. (2016). American history curators seek Don Drapers of Hispanic ad world. *Smithsonian Insider*. Retrieved from http://insider.si.edu/2016/09/curator-seeks-don-drapers-hispanic-ad-world/

Davis, J. F. (2017). *Pioneering African American women in the advertising business: Biographies of MAD Black women*. Abingdom, UK: Routledge.

Gianatasio, D. (2017, March 12). Global consultancies are buying up agencies and reshaping the brand marketing world. *Advertising Week*. Retrieved from http://www.adweek.com/brand-marketing/global-consultancies-are-buying-up-agencies-and-reshaping-the-brand-marketing-world/

Glinton, S. (2015, June 15). How an African-American ad man changed the face of advertising. *National Public Radio*. Retrieved from http://www.npr.org/2015/06/15/414561593/how-an-african-american-ad-man-changed-the-face-of-advertising

Gordon, R. (2003, October 13). Founder of the first African-American agency. *Advertising Age*. Retrieved from http://adage.com/article/news/founder-african-american-agency/96394/

Grunig, J., & Hunt, T. (1984). *Managing public relations*. Independence, KY: Cengage Learning.

Henry, S. (1997). Anonymous in her own name: Public relations pioneer Doris Fleischman. *Journalism History*, 23(2), 51-62.

History of Advertising. (n.d.). *The creative revolution*. Retrieved from http://historyofads.old.the-voice.com/the-creative-revolution

Lavelle, C. (2015, April 16). The forgotten history of the women who shaped modern advertising. *Bitch Media*. Retrieved from https://www.bitchmedia.org/post/the-forgotten-history-of-the-women-who-shaped-modern-advertising

Lellis, J., & Eggleston, M. (2017). *The zombie business cure*. Wayne, NJ: Career Press.

Regienczuk, B. (2014, April 22). How many agencies are in the U.S.? *Quora*. Retrieved from https://www.quora.com/How-many-ad-agencies-are-in-the-US

Russell, M. (2012, September 4). Forget Peggy Olson: Mad women made their mark long before the 60s. *Advertising Age*. Retrieved from http://adage.com/article/special-report-100-most-influential-women-in-advertising/mad-women-made-history-long-time-peggy-olson/237372/

Schaefer, M. (2015, July 30). 6 reasons marketing is moving in-house. *Harvard Business Review*. Retrieved from https://hbr.org/2015/07/6-reasons-marketing-is-moving-in-house

Slefo, G. (2016, August 10). Acquisition of digital agencies, ad tech firms. *Advertising Age*. Retrieved from http://adage.com/article/agency-news/digital-properties-dominated-mergers-acquisitions/305397/

Smithsonian. (2015, October 27). Smithsonian collects Hispanic advertising history. *National Museum of American History, Smithsonian*. Retrieved from http://americanhistory.si.edu/press/releases/hispanic-ad-history

Stein, L., & Wohl. J. (2016, November 17). Omnicom launches dedicated McDonald's agency We Are Unlimited. *Advertising Age*. Retrieved from http://adage.com/article/agency-news/omnicom-launches-mcdonald-s-agency-unlimited/306783/

Sullivan, J. C. (2013, May 3). How diamonds became forever. *New York Times*. Retrieved from http://www.nytimes.com/2013/05/05/fashion/weddings/how-americans-learned-to-love-diamonds.html

The Museum of Public Relations. (n.d.). *Public relations through the ages: A timeline of social movements, technology milestones and the rise of the profession*. Retrieved from http://www.prmuseum.org/pr-timeline/

Wells Lawrence, M. (2002). *A big life in advertising*. New York, NY: Touchstone.

Whitler, K. (2016, April 3). The new era of advertising: What agencies and clients must do differently to succeed. *Forbes*. Retrieved from https://www.forbes.com/sites/kimberlywhitler/2016/04/03/the-new-era-of-advertising-agencies-what-agencies-and-clients-must-do-differently-to-succeed/#262f258748b6

Organizing the Student Agency

Of the many ways to build your portfolio and experience real work for real clients, the student-run agency is an exciting option. Whether you plan to work in a professional agency after you graduate or have broader goals within the business or communications industries, participating in a student agency can help you make the transition from student to professional.

Student-run agencies come in all shapes and sizes (Bush & Miller, 2011). Some are student organizations with a handful of students working with one or two clients. Others are organized as a class with more than 50 students working for several clients. In some agencies, faculty advisors are hired to work full-time on the student agency. In others, graduate students serve as advisors with limited guidance from faculty. Some agencies develop traditional campaigns for regional or national clients while others specialize in social media for local nonprofits (Gibson & Rowden, 1994–1995; Hazdovac, 2012).

So, how do you decide which organization is right for your agency?

The answer to that question depends on many factors. Starting a student agency is much like establishing an actual business—you are essentially proposing to provide a service to real clients in exchange for money and/or experience. To provide that service, you'll need to think through the goals of your organization, the strengths you bring to the table, the resources and funding available to you, and the market environment in which your business will operate.

The breadth of what you learn in a student agency also depends largely on how the agency is structured. While most of the student agencies help build portfolios, agencies that include more layers of structure can also help students develop their professional identities, build business and management skills, experience client relationships, and gain first-hand knowledge of how a real agency works. For these reasons, it's important to think through the purpose of your agency and build something you can not only be proud of, but also fulfill your student learning goals. In this chapter, you will discover

- How do you organize your student-run agency?
- What type of agency should you be?
- What are some strategies for assigning jobs?
- What titles are used in agency life?
- What kind of resources do you need to locate/invest in?
- What will your brand identity be?

© Kzenon/Shutterstock.com

DISCOVERY AND DECISION MAKING

While it's tempting to jump in with both feet and just start doing the work, smart entre-preneurs know to take a step back, assess the environment, and make educated decisions about how to approach organizational development. This section outlines the questions to ask and decisions to be made when starting the process of developing a student agency.

First Step—Determine the Need(s) for a Student Agency

Entrepreneurs start a business because they see an unfulfilled need or opportunity their business can fill. What need or needs will your student agency fulfill? Start the process by asking one seemingly simple question—Why? Why do we need or want to start a student agency? The answer to this question will set the stage for everything that follows.

You may want to start a student agency because everyone else is doing it. This is a legit-imate reason. After all, you don't want your university to lag behind others. But dig a little deeper to determine what a student agency can accomplish for students, your university, and the community at large (Sallot, 1996).

Just like a small business, a student agency is created to fulfill a need, or many needs. For example, a dean at one university noted that portfolios of his journalism and broad-cast students were much more extensive than those of his strategic communications stu-dents. Why? Because the campus newspaper and television station provided portfolio work for journalism and broadcast students, but no such outlet existed for strategic communica-tions students. Thus, a need emerged for a student-run agency.

In addition, as faculty began to investigate agencies at other universities, they observed agencies that went beyond just building portfolios. Agencies also gave students the oppor-tunity to work with a diversity of people, think quickly on their feet, engage in leadership opportunities, and solve problems in a team environment (Todd, 2014).

Student learning goals are important factors to consider when structuring your student agency. If the purpose of your agency is simply to give students experience applying classroom learning to real client situations, you'll structure your agency accordingly. However, if there is a need for students to understand the business side of communications, you'll want to include budgeting and billing practices that achieve this goal. In particular, if you are charging fees, you will need to know how to calculate **billable hours**. Or, you may find that students need more opportunities to experience how a real agency works. Thus, you'll want your agency to mimic a professional agency as closely as possible.

Billable hours: Billable hours refers to the number of worked hours that can be billed to the client as compensation.

At another university, faculty members noted continuous requests from nonprofit and small businesses looking for students to help with various projects. These included conducting market research, producing videos, developing logos, and launching social media pages. Together, these requests revealed not only a need for communications assistance in the community, but also shined a light on the type of work local businesses required. Understanding these needs can help you determine the capabilities you'll want to include in your agency.

There may also be institutional needs that a student agency could fulfill. For example, many universities strive to become accredited by one or more academic associations. A student-run agency may fulfill certain requirements of those accrediting bodies. Or, your institution may want to rank as one of the top universities in advertising or public relations (PR) education. Thus, starting a cutting-edge student agency would serve as a proof point toward that goal (Swanson, 2011).

Lastly, student agencies can fulfill needs in the industry. For example, as social media becomes a standard form of communication, there is an industry demand for graduates who are well versed in social media analytics. Your agency could become the training ground for supplying these graduates to the industry.

Think through all the reasons you need or want to start a student agency. Consider the needs of students, the department or university, the industry, and the community at large. List them in order of priority. Then you can work toward organizing an agency that fulfills the most critical needs. And, just like a business must make a case for funding, knowing the needs your agency fulfills will help you build a case with administrators for funding your student agency.

Assess Your Organic Resources

While you may want to become the hottest creative shop in student agency history, this goal will be hard to fulfill if your university doesn't teach communications design. Take an inventory of the available organic resources that you can realistically tap into. Unlike physical resources, organic resources relate to the people, programs, skills, and even relationships that can help shape your agency.

One way of assessing organic resources is to think in terms of assisters and resisters. What are the organic resources that can assist you in establishing an agency? And, what might be the barriers, or resisters, to starting an agency? For example, lack of funding is often a resister. Or, as mentioned above, not having a program to teach specific skills might be a resister to providing that capability in your agency. Once you've listed your assisters and resisters, you can then determine ways to utilize your assisters to the fullest and overcome the resisters.

In Box 2.1, you'll find a list of questions to help assess your organic resources and other structural issues in terms of faculty, students, and stakeholders.

Box 2.1   Assessing Your Organic Resources

Faculty

- What are your relative faculty strengths?
  - What are the specific areas where your faculty have research or work experience?
    - Can any of it be leveraged or associated with a student-run agency?
    - Can agency students or faculty be used to help find/grow clients?
  - Do you have the organic capabilities/commensurate experience necessary to fulfill the requirements of the desired organization?
    - Are there appropriate majors available to serve in leadership positions?
    - Is there a level of training sufficient to create a critical mass for student agency work?
    - Do you have experienced specialists in the areas of videography, graphics, social media, SEO, copywriting, consulting, and so on?
  - What is the climate at the institution you serve?
    - Is there a strong interest in a for-credit course?
    - If not, is there a strong interest in keeping this agency as a club?
    - Are there financial resources available to
      - Up fit or acquire a dedicated space?
      - Pay students in leadership?
      - Invest in equipment as needed to outfit the agency for the desired capacity?

- ○ What other organic resources do you have to commit to this agency?
  - Computers
  - Software
  - Video editing
  - Video production
  - Others

Stakeholder relationships

- Are there existing relationships with organizations or corporations who are interested in having you perform specific services for them? Will you have the opportunity to work with professionals as advisors in PR, graphic design, social media, internal communications, and advertising.

Student relationships

- What is your relative student strength?
  - ○ Do you have a depth of talent and experience that can take on your desired agency structure?
  - ○ How strong are your internship programs?
    - Do you have experienced graduates of internship programs who can assist in managing the agency?
  - ○ Is there a graduate program at your institution?
    - Can graduate students assist in the management of the agency?
  - ○ What will be your relationship with student clubs/interest groups? Is there a strong relationship between _____ and the agency?
    - PRSSA chapter
    - American Advertising Federation (AAF) chapter
    - International Association of Business Communicators (IABC)
    - Others
  - ○ What kind of culture do you want to present to the world?
    - What do the students get out of participating?
    - Will this be a course?
    - What will be the benefits to your clients for associating with you?
    - How will the students profit?
  - ○ How will you ensure client work gets done in a timely fashion?
    - What safeguards will be in place if it is not done?
    - How will you ensure clients hold up their end of the engagement/relationship?
  - ○ What are your expectations in terms of deliverables?
    - What client services will you provide/NOT provide?
    - How will you manage workflow?
    - Billing?
    - Accountability?
    - Evaluation/Assessment?

Determine Your Agency Mission

What kind of agency do you want to be? There are ad agencies, PR agencies, marketing communications agencies, internal communications agencies, media relations firms, strategic consultants, and so on. Is your agency especially adept at one, some or all of these functions?

In Chapter 1, we discussed the different types of agencies in today's communications business. You'll want to decide if your agency will focus on niche capabilities or be a full-service firm. This decision will largely depend on the organic resources you've identified and the client market for your services. Following are some capabilities to consider:

- Are you specialists in internal promotions for university-based clients or nonprofits?
- Will your agency be small, with a high degree of specialization (e.g., a social media solution lab)?
- Do you want to form an alliance with entrepreneurs and promote start-ups/new ventures?
- How about working specifically for university sports and entertainment initiatives? Would it make sense to work closely with those teams and organizations?
- Perhaps you have a large international community and you want to work on a more global or specialized audience in a specific culture or language?
- Maybe you see yourself in a broader context? Helping national clients penetrate regional markets or the obverse, local clients seeking a national presence with their brand.
- Another popular option is to become an integrated marketing communications agency with strategic communications plans that incorporate PR, branding, advertising and social media prowess, with client type taking a back seat to the level of service and favoring an integrated approach.

STRUCTURING THE AGENCY

Once you have a solid understanding of the needs, organic resources and the type of agency you want to become, it is now important to design the organizational structure of the agency.

Which Entity Will Oversee the Agency?

One of the first things to consider is how your agency will be structured in terms of university reporting. Just like departments in businesses report to certain divisions, you'll want to determine which university body will take responsibility for your agency. Your agency could be managed as its own distinct student club, housed within an existing student organization such as PRSSA or SAF, or placed within an academic department.

Some agencies are organized and maintained as separate clubs or chapters. An offshoot of student organizations, or perhaps its own student organization, student agency clubs can take on clients as group work. The student agency club is typically more casual in its reporting requirements than the structured agency. Commonly the student agency club offers no grade incentive for participation; however, it can be a strong resume builder and allow students to focus mainly on the work. As it is defined as a club, meeting times may be less formal than the structured agency. A club may or may not be eligible for student activities' status and funds.

On the downside, as a club there may be competition for students' time from other extracurricular activities and classwork. This competition could hinder your ability to meet client deadlines. It may also be difficult for the students to be taken seriously so client participation could suffer. And finally, it will be difficult to raise your organization's profile as a club with voluntary participation.

Similar to the above, some student agencies are housed within an existing student organization, such as SAF or PRSSA. These organizations may take on a student agency as part of a larger mission. The existing advisor of the student organization may also serve as the advisor of the student agency, or the agency could enlist the assistance of an additional advisor. This type of organization has similar benefits and drawbacks to a separate student club. In addition, some universities report difficulties in juggling the student agency with the organization's other activities, which could harm the organization's larger mission. In this case, you'll want to consider appointing separate student directors so that all activities receive ample attention.

Another popular structure is the agency placed within an academic department for minimal-course credit, usually one- or two-hours of elective credit. A hybrid between a club and a formal class, this structure allows students to take the course multiple times and expand their portfolio. Unlike the student agency club, the minimal-credit class meets the criteria of scheduled meeting times, attendance requirements, and so on. Under the academic department's jurisdiction, a faculty advisor is assigned to the agency and will take more than a casual interest in the agency's success. This can be beneficial when it is necessary to plow through bureaucratic red tape or gain access to funds and department resources.

The fourth option is the full-credit course, where the agency is taught as a regular class for required or elective credit. Typically, a semester or a year-long engagement, the structured, student-run class has regular meeting times taught by a faculty advisor. Class performance is linked to a grade and the class has a formalized curriculum structure. The structured course also offers additional lesson content as well as client service. (Box 2.2).

Box 2.2   Four Entities for Student Agency Management

1. As a student club
2. Within existing student organization
3. Within department; minimal-credit course
4. Within department; full-credit course

Formal Versus Casual Structure

Whether your agency is structured under an academic department or as a student organization, studies in best practices indicate that a more formal agency structure can increase the sustainability of the program. (Bush, 2009; Ranta, 2014). In essence, a solid structure will sustain your agency through the high turnover of students between semesters, preventing your agency from going in and out of business. More specifically, an established agency structure can increase performance, enhance quality, and assist in accomplishing the following goals:

- *Efficiency:* A structured agency is more efficient in the use of client time and student workflow as students have the opportunity to focus on needs and work quickly and effectively.
- *High-quality work:* Increased scrutiny and higher levels of quality control are more likely in a structured agency. The organization offers enhanced project management, thereby allowing scrutiny of work. The more sets of eyes on a project, the higher the chances of identifying and rectifying errors.
- *Exceptional portfolio results:* A structured agency will provide opportunities for creative collaboration and group input which often creates a better product than solo work.
- *Increased opportunities for leadership:* A structured agency can allow for increased leadership opportunities for students. By ensuring leadership roles are assigned, the structure of the agency retains focus on productivity.
- *Specialization:* A structured agency can allow for some specialization. By clearly defining roles in the agency structure, students who wish to specialize and hone their specific brand or skill can do so while ensuring overall workflow is not compromised.
- *Greater accountability:* When formally organized, assignments can be clearly given and evaluated according to the organizational chart.
- *Standardized training:* By having one or more persons assigned to ensure training is conducted, it is more likely to be completed.
- *Better client service:* With defined client points of contact and students whose primary mission is client service, that very important task is accomplished properly.

Agency Titles and Roles

To determine which titles you will have in your agency, you'll first want to think through all the different functions necessary to maintain a successful agency and serve your clients' needs. Breaking down agency management into functions, there are several important tasks that have to be accomplished:

- *Administrative management:* This agency function ensures things such as billing sheets, invoices, travel requisitions, and other management functions are completed. Agency management is one of the most important functions of the professional agency in terms of making money and keeping the doors open.

- *Brand communication:* This function helps maintain the integrity of your communication across platforms with a central theme. Brand communication is often useful for maintaining "mind share" of a particular product or category of service. Brand communication is different than direct selling as it does not usually translate into a direct appeal for sales but rather pushes for association with positive concepts, emotions, and traits.
- *Client acquisition:* Also called client development, or new business, this function in the agency contributes to the solicitation and securing of business. The process often involves identifying potential clients, performing competitive analyses, identifying insights, and "pitching" clients for the opportunity to do their work.
- *Client management:* This function involves interfacing with the client to ensure tasks are understood, the communication approach is specified, deadlines are met, and expectations are fulfilled. Client management is one of the most critical aspects of long-range planning and the viability of the student-run agency.
- *Creative development:* Working with the creative content providers, this function is commonly one of the most sought after features of agencies everywhere. Good creative development helps govern the themes and execution of creative ideas needed to communicate with target audiences in memorable, meaningful ways. In the case of student agencies, the creative development of college students' ideas is a highly sought commodity.
- *Creative production management:* In the student agency, this function ensures creative ideas become usable products such as flyers, brochures, social media postings, television and radio commercials, and so on. Those involved in creative production management alternate between being order takers and being trusted consultants on a project.

Once you outline the functions needed in your agency, you can begin determining the titles and roles. Following are some suggested titles commonly used in student agencies. This list is by no means comprehensive. Depending on your agency's structure, you may utilize all of these titles or only a few of them. However, the titles are fairly standard and a good jumping off point for the next step, the organizational chart.

- *Faculty advisor:* In a student-run agency, the faculty advisor provides informed, experienced advisement to the agency. Typically, the faculty advisor has duties teaching other classes in addition to the student agency. Advisors are usually hired because of their past experience in the industry. Depending upon the size of the agency, experience of the advisor and needs of the clients, there may be more than one faculty advisor. Typically, the faculty advisor is the last word on work that is done within the agency.
- *Graduate student:* In a student agency, graduate students are commonly tapped to assist the team with their tasks. Graduate students can fill the role of assisting the faculty member in advising the agency. They can also serve as a liaison between student leadership and the faculty advisor, and on some occasions, they can serve as a VP or account supervisor. Like the faculty advisor, the graduate student will

typically have additional responsibilities at the university, not the least of which is completing his/her course of study. Graduate students may be paid as part of a graduate assistantship or fellowship.

- *Agency president:* The agency president is usually a rising senior or junior whose job is to maintain workflow, documentation, and client service for the agency. Depending upon the size of the agency, the president may report directly to the faculty advisor or via a graduate student/graduate assistant. Presidents are commonly elected or appointed to the position by the faculty advisor or an advisory board. At some student agencies, the president is a paid position.

- *Agency vice president:* The agency vice president position(s) serve(s) to assist the president with specific tasks. In some student agencies, the vice president may have additional duties to liaise with the student PRSA, IABC, AAF, and/or other para-professional student communications chapters. Depending upon the size and organization of the agency, vice presidents may have established responsibilities within the agency including internal communications, supervising account teams, or providing professional training. At some student agencies, the vice president is a paid position.

- *Account supervisor:* The account supervisor is responsible for the success of the account executives under her/him. An account supervisor's primary responsibility is to ensure their account executive(s) have all the resources necessary to succeed and service their clients. Other duties are to act as an experienced resource for issues the account executives face and to advocate for time and resources needed by specific account teams under their tutelage.

- *Account executive:* The account executive is one of the key positions in the agency. He/she works for the agency and the client, ensuring a plan is formulated, goals are set, results are monitored, and the agency team stays on task. They are the frontline for managing client expectations and ensuring things are delivered on time and to the client's satisfaction.

- *Traffic manager:* The traffic manager ensures the creative process synchs up with deadlines and coordinates the delivery of creative product to its final destination. Traffic managers are very much like a traffic cop on the street, making sure resources and flow is maintained in the creative and implementation processes. In the real world, traffic managers would typically be the first step in production and the last step in implementation.

- *Social media chairperson/coordinator:* One of several specialty positions in a typical student agency is the social media chairperson. This individual coordinates the social media aspects of client campaigns. A subject-matter expert, the social media chairperson fills a critical role on a wide variety of platforms.

- *Media relations:* Another specialty function of PR and integrated communications is that of media relations. The media relations person(s) is charged with garnering earned media coverage on behalf of clients. Tactics used by media relations teams include press events, press releases, frequently asked questions, and so on. The goal is for that individual to secure "earned media" (as opposed to paid media) for clients.

- *Creative services director:* For larger student agencies, there may be a creative services department. For smaller ones, there is the creative services director. The lead for graphics, photography, logos, creative strategies, and other requirements, creative services fills a very important role in designing and implementing the creative approach for various client campaigns. In agencies where there is a creative services director, commonly the graphics person(s) and the copywriter(s) report to the creative services director.

- *Production manager:* The production manager is responsible for ensuring production gets done. This ranges from supervising people to ensuring the final product is of the best quality. Typically, production managers are platform-specific resources, for example, print production manager or video production manager or animation production manager. In the brave new world of convergence, these distinctions are falling away and there is increasing demand for production managers to become multi-platform literate.

- *Creative content provider:* As the title suggests, the creative content provider provides creative content for whatever application is required. Some creative content providers work in print, others in photography and still others in videography. Content providers can also be responsible for enhancing a written message for event planning or other activities.

- *Graphics:* Another specialty position at the student agency, the graphics person (or team), fulfills the role of visual communications specialist(s). While there may be subspecialties within the graphics position, the goal is to have a central point of contact for all graphics including infographics, layouts, logos, photography, videography, wordmarks, and so on. Depending upon the size of the agency and client load, graphics may report to creative services or directly to the agency president.

- *Copywriter:* Copywriters assist the creative services director in generating written content that supports the creative mission. Copywriters often work alongside graphics personnel in writing copy for various communications such as print ads, videos, broadcast commercials, or mobile copy.

- *Web/Internet-based media:* Digital communications for use on the Internet or other digital media may require special skills not possessed by every student. The web/Internet specialist is familiar with the nuances of Internet publishing and content creation. They also know the importance of search engine optimization to be sure their content is seen. This position often works closely or is combined with the social media chairperson.

- *Videography/photography:* Image capture can be difficult and requires special skills. The expectation is that videographers/photographers will take the lead in setting the stage and capturing video images. Like other specialists, those fulfilling this slot should also be able to assist others in setting up images and managing equipment.

- *Internal promotion and brand communications teams:* Often the student agencies ignore their own needs for self-promotion. The best solution for this problem is an internal communications team. This team will help solve the need to promote the student agency using blogs, social media sites, websites, award entries, and press releases.

To Pay or Not to Pay—Valuing Student Positions in the Student Agency

In some agencies, senior leadership and/or specialty positions are paid positions. The justification for paying some, but not all, has to do with available funding and the amount of time required in fulfilling the responsibilities of the position. Compensation can also provide additional motivation for students to excel or choose your agency over another activity. Student wages/grants are typically paid from departmental budgets, student-activity funds, gifts from patrons, and/or client revenue proceeds. For agencies not financially compensating their students, participants are still "paid" in terms of portfolio additions, contacts, internships, and real-world experience.

Overall, in terms of best practices, all non-club student agencies should provide some form of academic credit for the class. Those that do not compensate their students financially may also offer more hours of class credit than one that compensates with a stipend. For example, one major state-owned university rewards top performers by allowing them to enroll in an additional three hours the next semester with the goal of building recognized leadership opportunities.

Developing an Organizational Chart

As mentioned earlier in this chapter, organizing an agency can be an important step toward success. One of the best ways to map out an organization's titles and relationships is through an **organizational chart**. These tools are used by businesses and other organizations to explain

Organizational chart: Organizational charts are used by businesses and other organizations to explain relationships and reporting responsibilities between titles.

relationships and reporting responsibilities between titles. This information can be valuable to agency representatives when determining answers to questions like "Who do I need to ask about this?" "Who is in charge of this account?"

Following are some suggested organizational charts for various forms of student agencies. These organizational charts can be adjusted as needed to fit the designs of any student agency.

You will note some of these organizational charts are very vertical, meaning there is a substantial chain of reporting and organization within the framework. Vertical organization mimics large- to middle-sized corporate organizations and can also be found at large agencies, particularly those with multinational offices or large clients. The advantages of a vertical organization include the ability to ensure all procedures are followed, all considerations are made in terms of legal, ethical and social responsibilities, and a synergy is developed in terms of branding and image.

In contrast, horizontal organizations do not have such a restrictive hierarchy and can allow for nimble responses to changing priorities. Horizontal organizations are often seen in smaller agencies where a more hierarchical infrastructure would discourage engagement with smaller clients. Horizontal organizations more closely resemble an entrepreneurial organization where responsibilities are shared among its members and a high degree of multitasking takes place. The advantages of a horizontal organization include quick implementation, empowerment of the individual, and encouragement across all members for creativity, autonomy, and ownership of an account.

Below are suggested organizational charts based on several different types of organizations outlined in Chapter 1.

The specialty agency: Specialty agencies are designed for specializing in specific functions, categories, or audiences. Commonly, specialty agencies provide expertise in specific functions like social media, video production, animations, and so on. Following is a suggested organization structure for a digital specialty agency:

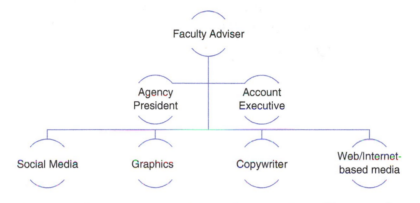

Commonly, the specialty agency would work for a few clients and would be ideally suited for small agencies (5–12 students). The specialty agency model can also be incorporated as part of a larger agency's organization if necessary.

The traditional agency: The traditional agency is organized along the lines of a traditional medium-sized organization. This structure works for medium-sized agencies to handle 6–8 clients with very specific needs. This organizational chart works for 12–18 students. Following is a traditional student-run agency organizational chart:

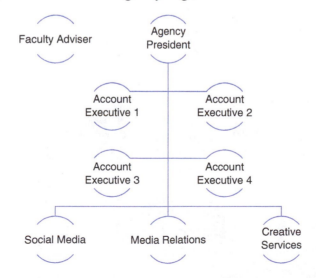

Large full-service agencies: For very large programs the organizational chart gets more robust. This structure is best used for managing 20 or more students. The advantage of having a large agency is there are many clients that can be serviced. Many students can be rotated into different positions and people can divide their time between leadership and client service. A large student agency is also the logical home for the full-service functions found in most commercial agencies today. Following are two large agency organizational charts. The first recognizes creativity as its own autonomous department. The second makes account services central and creative services subordinate.

In the first large full-service agency example, the creative department operates with some autonomy, serving all of the accounts on an as-needed basis. This arrangement fosters a parallel growth plan, ensuring that students grow in both their creative skills as well as their client service and team leadership skills. The branding communications organization ensures creative continuity.

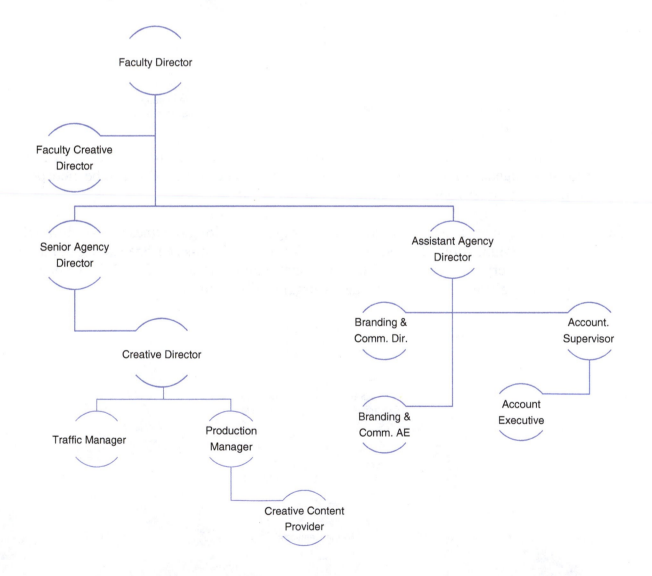

In the second large agency example, creative and other services report directly to account teams. Each account team has its own independent structure under a vice president as well as a support team servicing each account team. This arrangement can be extremely useful for integrated communication accounts as well as fostering collaborative efforts within each team.

One more note on account team organizations. These are four examples of possible organizational charts. Each can be flexed, slid, or rearranged depending upon the needs of the agency and the needs of the client.

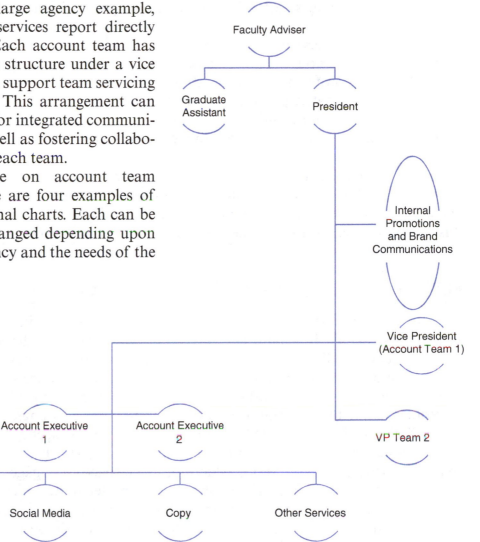

Organizational Philosophy

It can be frustrating trying to figure out structure and departments. As student-run agencies are made up of individual students with lives and responsibilities, interests, and strengths, a lot of time can be spent inventing and reinventing organizational charts and responsibility lists.

The first best priority to consider when assembling/organizing a student agency is "Will this organization help us to do a better job?" If the answer is "yes" then it is good for the agency. Consider if the organization helps students do good work—they will enjoy doing the work more. If they enjoy doing the work, they will do a better job. Similarly, if the clients receive good work, they will be more inclined to help the agency succeed. Nothing breeds success like success.

A helpful set of suggested rules for designing/organizing a student agency include

- Does it help service the client better?
- Does it access our particular expertise?
- Does it allow for more accountability?
- Does it ultimately provide a higher quality product?
- Does it allow for positive collaboration?
- Does it give every student seeking leadership experience an opportunity?

Above all, the final goal should be is the client delighted to receive your work? Sometimes situations develop requiring a different set of skills to ensure quality service. Leadership and management require occasional evaluation and adjustments. So, as the year progresses, it is certainly acceptable to change the organization or mix and match responsibilities.

EQUIPPING THE AGENCY: NEEDS VERSUS WANTS

Once you have decided to go forward with the student agency, in addition to the organizational discussions, it is important to start a parallel effort to determine where/how the agency will do the client work. For this, you need to do an inventory. You may have all you need to stand up a student agency or, in contrast, you may require some substantial investment in space, equipment (hardware), and/or software to establish the agency.

Studies show that student agencies need, among other things, a dedicated space for their efforts. Having a dedicated office space legitimizes the agency, helps build an agency culture, and increases the organization's sustainability (Bush & Miller, 2011). Meeting space for clients, workspace for production, social space for engagement, and office space for administration are all things that should be considered. Remember, the student agency is an area where students will spend many hours thinking, working, writing, revising, and producing end products that ultimately benefit the client, the student, and the institution itself. To increase the likelihood of the agency's success, an administration should make concessions for this type of effort.

When considering a space, some questions you can ask include

- How accessible is this space?
  - How hard will it be for students to gain access after-hours for client work?
    - How close is it to other buildings on campus?
    - How secure is it for equipment?
    - How secure is it for protecting the in-progress work?
  - How easy will it be for clients to access this space?
    - Is there sufficient parking?
    - Is there adequate signage?
    - How close to an entrance to the building is this space?
- How private is this space? Will there be competition from other classes for use of this space?

- How prestigious is this space? Does its location inspire confidence or question the organization's credibility?
- Is there sufficient space to accomplish the goals of the agency?
- How accommodating is this space for growth?
  - Is there sufficient space for equipment?
  - Is there sufficient space for presentations?
  - Can we accommodate increased demand for students?

More than likely not all of the answers to the above questions will be in the affirmative. Some of the answers will require compromise or further development. However, once you have space identified, the next question is what to put in that space?

Items can include anything from office chairs to a computer with software applications. Often, but not always, hard assets can drive the type of client a student agency takes on. For example, if a client needs a wide format plotter to print suggested billboard ideas or posters and you do not have such a machine, then perhaps this is not a client you can help. Or, more positively, if your client needs to host monthly stakeholder meetings and your university can offer easy access to a large event venue with sufficient parking, then perhaps you are the ideal agency this client needs. So, as you are considering which clients you would like to represent, it is important to consider hard assets.

elenabsl/Shutterstock.com

The following section lists suggested equipment a student agency should consider:

Computers and software: Obviously, computers are a critical necessity for any student-run agency. Software applications for these computers may include a creative suite of photo, text and graphic manipulation; media relations data mining software; social media publishing software; research/survey software; video editing software; digital publishing/website software; file-swapping software, digital analytics software, presentation software; and so on.

In terms of sharing documents, it is also important to ensure your agency has software applications that are compatible with those used by agency clients. Nothing is more frustrating than discovering a client cannot see your firm's work because they do not have the correct viewer or software application. Similarly, if a client desires to share files with your firm, it is imperative that your agency has the necessary plug-ins and applications to permit this to happen.

Social media capabilities: Solid social media capability is a necessity for a student-run agency. In addition to the basics of Twitter, Instagram, Snapchat, and Facebook, student agencies may also want to consider software used for developing blogs, apps, and other device-specific social media. The natural outflow of these efforts also includes software for media analytics and analysis.

Photography and Video equipment: Whether it is product shots, interviews, events, or any combination of those activities, a student agency must have access to solid photography/videography equipment. In addition to the proper camera, lighting is also a key component of solid photography or videography. The student agency should have access to functional, portable lighting to support good photography.

When deciding what videography and photography equipment to acquire, attempts should be made to ensure compatibility with any existing equipment ordered for other sequences/majors offered at the university. Key components for solid video storytelling include camera, tripod, light kits, lenses, multichannel sound recording, memory storage, and editing software.

Very often student agency work requires a high level of production value with elements of art and creative capability. Macro photography tables and tents can be a nice addition for product shots. Sophisticated video editing software with creative graphics and/or 3D and 4D capabilities would also be strong assets to have when equipping your agency. Other nice-to-have capabilities might include a soundproof space for recording voiceovers, a green screen, a shooting studio, and a highly capable character generator.

Printing equipment: While the rise of online document sharing software and the proliferation of text and e-mail have reduced the need for the printed product, the printed page has not been totally replaced. It is important to ensure printing capabilities of your agency are of high quality and compatible with existing print capabilities organic to the college or school sponsoring the agency. Wide format printing is often necessary to display finished work. In addition, oversized document printing capability can also be used for flyers, advertisements, and other applications.

Telephony/voicemail/conference call capabilities: It is imperative that student-run agencies find ways to support multiperson conversations using some sort of universally accessible devices. Online chats, texts, and e-mails are all effective at some level, but short of face-to-face meetings, the conference call or the video conference call often makes for a better client communication solution. The ability to hear another person expressing thoughts or even see and hear their enthusiasm or hesitancy can enhance understanding and reduce confusion. Many universities have conference call services managed through their IT departments or administrative departments. It is important to be included in that list of authorized users.

Focus group recording equipment: One of the most important qualitative research tools available to communicators is the focus group. The ability to measure reactions and beliefs, approvals or disapprovals, and garner information that can inform quantitative research is extremely valuable to a student-run agency. To conduct focus group research, certain equipment is necessary including ways to record responses, facilitate conversation and present samples of work. As you plan your student agency, review the access/availability of equipment to conduct this research. It is preferable to record both audio and video during a focus group session. There are also automated transcription software solutions that make the tedious job of transcribing more convenient and efficient.

Quantitative survey software: With the rise of big data and quantitative survey methodology, student agencies are sometimes called upon to perform statistical research for predictive and diagnostic studies. For many research institutions, this ability is seen as a highly desirable capability among faculty and clients who understand the process. As possible, your student agency should consider the need for this asset to deliver a high degree of client service.

FINANCING THE AGENCY

So, now that you have determined what you need to start your agency, there comes the question of how to pay for it. Just as there are several ways to organize an agency, there are several ways to pay for it. Following are some options for raising funds. Typically, student-run agencies will adopt a variety of these methods. Just like a business, an agency should take on some responsibilities toward funding its existence, if for no other reason than to increase the reality of the agency model. It is also important to consider the mechanism of how you will get paid. Typically, student-run agencies will have an account at a local bank, or through the university's accounting department, to manage deposits and purchases (Box 2.3).

Box 2.3   Agency Financing Sources/Models

- Department funded
- The benefactor
- Gifts in kind
- Student fees
- Contest prizes, grants, and scholarship programs
- Client billings

Department funded: If your student agency is managed under a university department such as journalism or communications, you may be able to secure funding as part of the department's annual budget. Typically, this would entail developing a line-item estimate of the agency's anticipated funding needs for the coming year and submitting the budget to the dean or department chair. They will then determine which part of the department's budget to allocate for agency funding. For example, equipment needs might come out of the department's technology budget, while payment for student managers might come out of a university fund for student workers.

The benefactor: Many student agencies profit from associating with some type of benefactor. Commonly structured as charitable contributions, benefactors profit from deductions to their income taxes by donating cash, or services to the agency. In addition to tax deductions, benefactors may also receive professional communication service, naming rights or perhaps an honorary award or other appreciative gesture for supporting the agency.

Gifts in kind: Similar to the benefactor relationship, the gift in kind is another potential source of equipment/services for your agency. Gifts in kind represent products or services provided to an organization in lieu of cash. For example, a copier company may provide some printing/copying equipment to your agency instead of a monetary donation. The gift will be given a value from the agency, which can then count as a charitable donation. Gifts in kind can be useful for generating brand loyalty toward future purchases or serve to develop relationships for additional for-profit business.

Student fees: Most universities charge a variety of fees to students to offset the costs of programs to benefit students. Descriptions of these fees include student activity fees, technology fees, or student development fees. This revenue can be accessed as a way to offset operating or equipment acquisition costs.

Contest prizes, grants, and scholarship programs: Revenue generated as a result of research-related work or some other type of educational services can also be a valuable source of funding.

Client billings: Seemingly one of the most obvious sources of revenue for your agency, clients can be billed for your work done on their behalf. Just as professional agencies bill for their services, student-run agencies can bill for theirs. See Chapter 5 for more information about billing practices.

AGENCY BRANDING AND CULTURE

Naming and Branding Your Agency

Once you have started to organize your agency, it is time to start thinking about a name and logo/wordmark for it. The goal is to select a name that has some brand value or "legs." You want a name that is memorable, differentiating and one that can easily be developed into a logo.

Some existing student agencies have a tie to their university mascots like Temple University's PROwl agency or Ball State's Cardinal Communications (Ranta, 2014).

Other opportunities for naming your agency can range from physical locations or nearby landmarks like the University of Oklahoma's Lindsey + Asp (named after the physical intersection closest to the agency's building) or the Texas Tower Agency at the University of Texas in Austin. Finally, there are those names that tie directly to the name of the host university like the Carolina Agency at the University of South Carolina or the more esoteric Live Oak Communications at Elon University (Elon is Hebrew for oak tree).

Once you've selected your agency name, there are myriad opportunities to promote your brand through letterhead, business cards, e-mail mastheads, PowerPoint™ templates, or premium items such as pens, t-shirts, polo shirts, or book bags. Depending upon your budget, you may want to spend some time and money investing in branded items to give your clients as a way to promote professionalism and showcase your firm's talent.

However, before you get too far into creating branded materials, make sure to do a trademark search on the name you have selected. See Chapter 12 for more information on legal considerations.

Creating the Student Agency Guidebook

As a way to train students for the student agency environment and to standardize the efforts put forth by student agencies, PRSSA publishes a student agency guidebook, which provides step-by-step instructions for student PR agencies to receive national affiliate designation.

This checklist addresses successful completion of the requirements, along with a self-study of compliance issues, and includes various management functions, client contracts, a formalized structure, adherence to the PRSA code of ethics, and accountability for hours used and clients served. Once completed, a student PR agency's affiliation package is sent to PRSSA for evaluation.

While PRSA's recommendations are specifically for PR agencies, any type of agency can benefit from following the guidelines. Specifically, as you hire agency personnel, you'll want to communicate with them important branding and protocol information about your agency. A suggested means of accomplishing this is through an agency handbook or employee manual. Below is a list of key elements that should be included in a student agency guidebook:

- *Agency mission statement:* reminds students what the agency mission is and what they should aspire to.
- *Agency vision statement:* Describes the ultimate, long-term vision for the organization
- *Agency goals statement:* Describes day-to-day goals for the handling of agency business. (see Box 2.2).
- *Time sheet/weekly activity report:* Provides accountability for the client and the students, helps justify fees charged. Also, provides a valuable planning tool for students who will soon be required to track their project/client hours.
- *Agency job sheet:* An internal document that establishes a chain of custody and a status for every major job. Allows for solid records keeping and established redundancy for tracking the completed work.
- *Client contract:* A contract between the client and the agency to ensure everyone is working together for a specified outcome at an agreed upon fee.

- *Staff expectations and ethics:* Addresses the ethical expectations in terms of behavior by agency members and cements behavioral expectations as part of the student-run agency.
- *Client evaluation form:* Provides a common theme for an evaluation between clients and student teams. Allows side-by-side comparison of performance by students in servicing diverse selections of clients.

These elements can take the form of PDF documents, writable PDFs, or other downloadable applications (Box 2.4).

Box 2.4   Agency Goals

1. We will aspire to provide every member with the opportunity to serve as an account executive for at least one project and be a contributing team member for three or four other projects.
2. Agency members will receive ongoing instruction in best practices of PR, advertising and marketing communications.
3. Agency members will support the stated goals of the university's chapter of PRSSA.
4. Agency members consistently practice a "client first" degree of professionalism.
5. Agency members will maintain PRSA and the university's codes of ethics.

Agency Culture—Setting the Mood

To complete the student agency planning, you must also consider the very soft but very important question of agency culture— the lifestyle/vibe/feel of the agency. A good leader creates a workplace that attracts, equips, informs, and motivates employees to do great work. Sometimes this may be something simple like free snacks on every Wednesdays or sometimes it is a cadre of guest speakers talking about trends in the industry.

The real challenge is to arrive at a compromise that combines the traditions of the university with the type of work to be done in the space and the hopes and dreams of those participating. Make sure to inject a strong amount of brand identity into the agency and a personality that is similar to those who participate.

Very often clients will base their business decisions on hiring people they trust, people they can get along with and people who share their values. To this end, it is important that your agency exudes a level of shared professionalism that shows you are trustworthy, and actively concerned about the outcome of your clients' efforts.

MINING, PROSPECTING, AND CULTIVATING STUDENT STAFF

Who's Got Talent?

Once you've completed your agency planning and branding, you're ready to recruit your student staff. The acquisition and steady supply of student talent are critical to maintaining a strong agency. Agencies are a storehouse of opportunity for students of multiple disciplines to thrive. Visual communications, mass communications, media arts, digital communications, advertising, and PR students can all gain meaningful experience from a student agency. The challenge is finding those students and presenting them with the opportunity.

The most obvious place to start the talent search for your agency is in your own backyard. Mine the database of majors within your school and identify potential candidates. Faculty and student services can help with this endeavor. Your faculty advisor can also be a big help here.

Another way to find talent is to prospect outside your college or department. Look to other schools and colleges at your university for specialized talent. For example, you may want to talk to the business school about marketing students, or the media arts department for some of their key video and graphic artists. Cast a wide net and see if you can find what you need.

Finally, you can also cultivate talent from your student body by offering workshops and other training opportunities to prepare solid recruits for eventual incorporation into your organization. Tactics for presenting students with the opportunity might include e-mail blasts, in-class presentations, digital and printed flyers, direct mail, student-activity fairs, table events, sponsored events, sponsored awards for student work, and conversations with faculty about what type of students you want in your agency. Again, enlist the help of your faculty advisor to make some of these requests. Remember, your goal is to get the best quality students for your agency.

CONCLUSION

Establishing a student agency requires a great deal of planning and decision-making, and a fair amount of trial and error. When something works well, you can expand on it. When something doesn't work well, you can change course. While it's important to think through all of the decisions outlined in this chapter, you don't have to achieve your ideal agency on the first day. You can start small, launch a trial student agency for a semester or two, and then build on it from there. Just remember to keep in mind your student learning goals and purpose for starting the agency.

Lastly, make sure to bring in the right decision makers when planning your student agency. Often, agencies are started by a handful of motivated students who see the potential a student agency can have. That's great! But remember, those students will soon graduate. You need to enlist the help of faculty or administrators who will champion the student agency for the long haul.

In all, congratulations on taking a major first step in becoming a student agency. It is an exciting opportunity that benefits students, the university, and the community at large, and will better prepare students to fulfill the needs of the industry.

# # #

REVIEW AND DISCUSSION QUESTIONS

1. When considering establishing a student agency, there are several resources that may be consulted to help define what type of agency you can become. Name three resources and some of the benefits they can bring to your student agency mission. For example, faculty and existing research.
2. The chapter discusses four student agency models in terms of university reporting: the club, the existing student organization, the one-credit hour, and the three-credit hour models. Discuss all four of the pros and cons associated with each other.
3. What is the first best priority when considering assembling/organizing a student agency?
4. Instead of money, in what other ways can students be "paid" for their participation in the student agency?
5. Describe the role of a faculty advisor in a student agency.
6. Describe the role of an account executive in a student agency.
7. Describe the role of a traffic manager in a student agency.
8. When equipping the agency, list five factors that should be addressed when considering physical office space.
9. When buying technology for your student-run agency, compatibility is seen as a very important factor in ultimately deciding what to purchase. Give two examples where technological compatibility is important.
10. In discussing client acquisition, why is trust seen as a critical element?

REFERENCES AND ADDITIONAL READINGS

Bush, L. (2009). Student public relations agencies: A qualitative study of the pedagogical benefits, risks and a framework for success. *Journalism & Mass Communication Educator, 64*(1), 27–38.

Bush, L., & Miller, B. M. (2011). US student-run agencies: Organization, attributes, and advisor perceptions of student learning outcomes. *Public Relations Review, 37*, 485–491.

Gibson, D. C., & Rowden, V. C. (1994–1995). Profile of an undergraduate public relations firm. *Public Relations Quarterly, 39*(4), 26–30.

Hazdovac, H. (2012). *The creation of student-run public relations firms: A historical look at student-run firms* (p. 15). Thesis for CA Polytechnic State University, San Luis Obispo, CA.

Ranta, J. A. (2014). Best practices for student-run agencies, Presentation to the PRSA International Conference, Educator's Super Saturday Conference, Washington, D.C. Aug. 2014.

Sallot, L. M. (1996). Using a public relations course to build university relationships. *Journalism and Mass Communications Educator, 51*, 51–60.

Swanson, D. J. (2011). The student-run public relations firm in an undergraduate program: Reaching learning and professional development goals through "real world" experience. *Public Relations Review, 37*, 499–505.

Todd, V. (2014). Public relations supervisors and millennial entry-level practitioners rate entry-level job skills and professional characteristics. *Public Relations Review, 40*, 789–797.

Where do clients come from? How do we find them? What kind of clients are a good fit for our agency? How do we win their business? These are some of the questions you'll likely ask as you set about building business for your agency.

As professional agencies can attest, building client business is not a one-time effort. While some clients may come to you with immediate needs, for others you'll need to reach out to key stakeholders, let them know your capabilities, and make consistent, ongoing contact to ensure your agency is top of mind when these clients have a need for your skills. This process can take months, or even years. Building new business is a continual endeavor to bring in clients now, for this semester, while keeping potential clients in the new business pipeline for subsequent semesters.

For some student-run agencies, the advisor is responsible for setting up clients each semester. In other agencies, one or more students are assigned to work on the agency's new business team. But regardless of who takes on the primary responsibility of building business, every student in the agency plays a role in finding and engaging potential clients.

For example, did you conduct an internship this past summer where you developed a relationship with your supervisor? This person might have potential projects for the agency or know people at other organizations who need your agency's services. Do you volunteer at a nonprofit organization (NPO) that could use communications assistance? Maybe you participated in a service project with your fraternity or sorority, or know a family friend who works in the communications profession. Everywhere you make contact in the professional world you'll find avenues to potential new business.

Keeping your agency top of mind with potential clients is essential to building a new business pipeline. That's why new business efforts go hand in hand with consistent agency promotion. Chapter 14 outlines in detail how to craft your brand identity and promote your agency to critical stakeholders. Developing a sound agency promotion plan can make your new business efforts that much more successful.

But keeping your agency top of mind is only part of the new business equation. Once you've gained their interest, you need to showcase your abilities and persuade clients to take the next step to hire your agency for their project or communications program. This means presenting your agency credentials and capabilities or showing the client how your agency will specifically address a given situation or problem. The agency "pitch," like pitching a baseball, needs to land in the strike zone.

In this chapter, you will learn

- The different types of client organizations and their fit with student agencies
- How client–agency relationships are categorized
- How to develop a new business plan and begin reaching out to potential clients
- The agency search process
- The process for developing an effective pitch to win the client's business

CATEGORIES OF CLIENT ORGANIZATIONS

In Chapter 2, you identified the type of communications work your agency will do based on your organic and tangible resources. To build new business, you'll want to identify the categories of clients that best fit those capabilities. To fully understand these categories, it's also important to understand how these organizations are structured and the terminology used to describe their stakeholders. Below we discuss three broad categories of clients and their potential fit with student-run agencies.

It's beneficial to work for a mix of client organizations to avoid being pigeonholed as one type of agency. If you always work for on-campus clients, you will be seen as the university's internal agency. This can lead to problems when, say, the dean of a department expects you to take on a project when you are already fully booked. It's tough to say no to a dean, especially when he or she knows you are working for several other departments. Likewise, if you take on all pro-bono clients, you'll gain a reputation as the agency that does client work for free. When establishing your agency, determine the types of clients you want to work for, how many you can serve each semester, and then recruit clients based on those parameters.

Nonprofit Organizations

NPOs are organizations that advocate for a social cause, provide services to a specific community, or promote the welfare of the common good. While there are many different types of NPOs, in general an NPO's mission is something other than making a profit.

NPOs are sustained through private donations, grants, fundraisers, membership fees, dues, or other means such as selling Girl Scout Cookies. Some examples of NPOs include national organizations like the Red Cross and United Way; foundations like the Susan G. Komen Foundation for curing breast cancer; membership organizations like the Public Relations Society of America and the National Restaurant Association; or local

© Rawpixel.com/Shutterstock.com

entities like community food banks, museums, animal shelters, and churches. Chances are the college or university you attend operates as a nonprofit.

Typically, a voluntary board of directors oversees the planning, funding, and management of an NPO. In addition, NPOs are staffed with a combination of full-time, paid employees, and unpaid volunteers. These staff members may have expertise in managing and marketing a nonprofit, or their expertise may relate to the NPOs mission. For example, the staff director of an environmental organization might have a degree in environmental science. It's important to understand how familiar clients are with marketing communications terms and tactics when pitching their business.

There are a variety of stakeholders an NPO might need to communicate with. For example, the organization may need to reach donors for fundraising purposes; increase its number of members if it is a dues-based organization; bring in strategic partners or cosponsors for events or programs; or communicate with government representatives to garner support for its cause.

Student agency fit: Local NPOs in your region make excellent clients for student-run agencies. They often need marketing communications assistance but don't have the larger budgets required to hire professional agencies. Thus, they are very open to working with student agencies to create mutually beneficial relationships. Because local NPOs often have small staffs, they are also open to your suggestions about the communications programs they should be executing. Doing work for NPOs shows goodwill on the part of your university to provide service to the local community, and gives the agency and its members the opportunity to bring about real change in the community or even the world.

Some student agencies charge NPOs fees for their services while others work on a pro-bono basis. **Pro-bono** clients are not charged an agency fee beyond paying for out-of-pocket expenses such as printing, advertising placement, or event costs. When working on a pro-bono basis, it's important to manage client expectations and set a clear scope of work (see Chapter 4). When a client is getting services

Pro-bono: Work conducted for a client voluntarily without receiving payment.

for free, it's easy to take advantage of this goodwill and make requests of the agency beyond what was outlined in the semester plan. Likewise, students may think they can slack off or not complete the work in a timely manner because they are working for free. You'll need to be cautious that both sides take the work seriously.

For-Profit Clients

Simply put, the purpose of a for-profit company is to make a profit. For-profit companies may be privately owned by a single owner, privately owned by two or more owners, or publicly owned by shareholders.

For-profit companies are categorized as either **B2C companies** (business to consumer),

B2C company (business to consumer): A company such as a consumer products manufacturer, online marketer, or retailer that markets its products directly to consumers.

or **B2B companies** (business to business). B2C companies both manufacture and sell goods and services marketed to consumers. These companies could include consumer goods manufacturers like Nike or Coca-Cola, online sellers like Amazon, or retailers like grocery stores, restaurants, and clothing stores.

> **B2B company (business to business):** A company that markets its products to other businesses rather than to consumers.

B2B companies are businesses that manufacture and sell products or services to other businesses. For example, think of the technology needs of a company with 20 or more employees. The company will need Internet servers, computers, monitors, copying machines, telephones, projectors and other electronic equipment. Rather than purchasing these products at a retailer, the company can save money by purchasing them at a bulk price directly from manufacturers. Nearly every business purchases products from other businesses. Automobile manufacturers, for example, may purchase parts like engines, air bags or Global Positioning Systems (GPS) from other manufacturing companies.

The terminology used to describe target audiences will differ depending on the type of for-profit business you are working on. Consumer goods companies market their products to consumers, whereas businesses such as retailers, restaurants, or B2B companies refer to their target audiences as customers.

© Uber Images/Shutterstock.com

Student agency fit: It is beneficial for your agency to have at least a few for-profit clients. Research shows students learn more about the "business-side" of communications when working on for-profit versus nonprofit accounts (see, e.g., Bush, 2009; Bush, Haygood, & Vincent, 2016). Commercial businesses have larger budgets for communications work and are focused on **return on investment (ROI)**. This means the company expects agency work to contribute to the company's bottom line equitable to the company's investment in agency fees and out-of-pocket expenses. Working for for-profit companies also looks good on students' resumes when they are ready to seek a job in the corporate world.

Many local businesses in your area—such as restaurants, local retailers, or area manufacturers—need communications assistance and will be open to working with student agencies. This is especially true if business owners

> **Return on investment:** A financial term that describes the potential profit gained relative to the amount invested. In the agency business, "profit" can be measured in terms of how much an advertising or PR program generated in sales, awareness, donations, and so on based on the client's goals.

have a connection to the university, such as alumni or business executives who are on the university's board of trustees. In addition, some large, for-profit businesses like Chevrolet have programs or contests where student agencies are paid to develop or execute campaigns.

On-Campus Clients

Many student agencies work for on-campus clients—various departments, majors, or schools within the university. In this case, target audiences would include students, faculty, staff, or audiences outside of the university such as parents or the larger community. On-campus clients are a particularly good starting point for newly established student agencies. Although most universities are nonprofit entities, on-campus clients often have budgets with which they can pay student agencies for their work.

University administrators usually lead departments within a university. These individuals may have advanced degrees in business or higher education, or they may have taught within an academic major before becoming an administrator. Faculty members may also have leadership positions within academic departments and university programs, such as leadership programs, Honors or Fellows programs, or other curricular and cocurricular programs.

Student agency fit: Many university departments are focused on the mission of the department or program, and are thus open to students who can provide the communications expertise that department staff may lack. Because the university's overarching mission is to educate students, employees of the university are often willing to provide work for students as part of that mission. In addition, working for on-campus clients can raise the visibility of your student agency with key stakeholders in the university.

Similar to nonprofit clients, you'll want to be cautious of managing client and student expectations and setting a clear scope of work. In addition, on-campus clients may treat agency employees as students rather than professionals. In turn, you'll want to draw boundaries between the student agency and the department or program. For example, let's say you are launching a new program for the Spanish department and secure a media placement in the on-campus newspaper. Who should be interviewed for that article—an agency member or a member of the department? The answer, of course, is the member of the department. Just as you wouldn't serve as a spokesperson for an outside client, the same is true for on-campus clients. This is often a difficult boundary for both the university department and agency students to grasp.

CATEGORIES OF CLIENT–AGENCY RELATIONSHIPS

In addition to the categories of clients you solicit, you'll also want to think about the type of relationships the agency will have with those clients. As outlined in a white paper developed jointly by the Association of National Advertisers and the American Association of Advertising Agencies (2011), there are several different types of client–agency relationships that can be categorized by the type of work, the amount of work, and whether an organization works with one or multiple agencies.

One of the most common client–agency relationships is called an **agency of record**. In this relationship, the client works with one agency on a continuing basis for all its marketing communications needs. An agency of record often sets the overall strategic communications direction for a brand or company.

> **Agency of record:** Serves as the primary agency for a client and usually sets overall communications strategy and direction.

Agencies of record may work on several different programs for a client in a variety of areas. For example, let's say your agency was the AOR for a local arts institution. You may develop an overall brand strategy for the agency in the first semester. Then, in subsequent semesters, the client may ask you to organize and promote their annual arts festival, redesign their website, or develop a fundraising campaign. All of these projects would then fit within the larger brand strategy. With AORs, the client might pay your agency a set retainer each semester or give you a semester budget and ask you to develop programs within that budget.

Clients may also have a roster of agencies that work for various divisions or departments in the company. For example, a company may have one agency working on its B2B division, while another agency develops programs for its B2C division. A client may hold a **roster agency** search in which it approves an agency to work on its brands without yet assigning a specific project. When a need arises, the client then turns to one of the agencies on its approved roster to work on that program.

> **Roster agency:** An agency that has been approved among a roster of agencies to work on a client brand, division, or department. Roster agencies are one of many that work for a particular client.

As either part of or separate from its roster agencies, clients may conduct a **specialty agency** search. Specialty agencies are agencies that have expertise in one specific area. These types of agencies may be tapped because of their knowledge with a specific target audience (such as Hispanic marketing) or for their expertise in a distinctive strategic or tactical area (such as social media strategy, videography, or crisis communications).

> **Specialty agency:** An agency hired for a specific expertise, such as digital strategy, brand identity, or crisis communications.

Often a larger client will combine its agency of record with roster or specialty agencies. For example, an organization could use its AOR for developing its national brand strategy while using a promotional agency for its retail division, a corporate communications agency to handle shareholder relations, and a digital media agency to manage its social media accounts. For student agencies, it may also be beneficial to do subcontract work with an AOR agency in a specific area, such as Millennial research or social media strategy. This helps align your agency with professional work while building your visibility with potential clients down the road.

Most often, student-run agencies are hired to do **project-based work**, where clients seek your assistance for a limited time to carry out a specific task. This might include developing

> **Project-based work:** When a client hires an agency for a specific project, such as creating a website or shooting a video.

a promotional video or PSA, helping the client organize or promote an event, redesigning a website or creating a new logo for a local NGO. In this case, you'll want to focus on very specific capabilities when pitching your work to the client rather than overwhelming them with all of your credentials.

When approaching a potential client, it's important to understand the type of agency relationship both you and the client are looking for to determine what you will present to the client, as well as how to structure your program budgets or agency fees (see Chapter 5).

DEVELOPING A NEW BUSINESS PLAN

The overarching goal of any new business effort is, of course, to bring new clients into the agency. As mentioned in the introduction to this chapter, building business for your student agency is not a one-shot effort. It is a continual endeavor to bring in clients now—for this semester—while identifying **prospects** whom could become clients in subsequent semesters. In the professional agency business, we often use the term **new business pipeline** to describe the process of developing a steady stream of client prospects and continually connecting with them until they become actual clients. In other words, you identify a prospect and put them into one end of the your pipeline; after steady, continual contact and persuasion they come out the other end as a client.

Prospects: Potential clients for whom you have the probability of working.

New business pipeline: A sales term used to describe the process of moving a prospect from initial contact through several stages of contact until they become an actual client.

Building a pipeline is only one aspect of an agency's new business efforts. In addition to identifying potential clients, new business efforts involve developing materials that can be used in communicating with a prospect, mapping out consistent points of contact with prospects, and preparing presentations or "pitches" to win a client's business.

In general, there are two ways in which student agencies potentially win business: either a client comes to you asking for assistance or you reach out to a prospect to solicit their business. In either case, you want to be prepared with materials and content to make your case.

© ADE2013/Shutterstock.com

In this section, we discuss the components of new business outreach. In subsequent sections, we outline the process of agency searches and the issues to consider when making a persuasive pitch to a potential client—whether you approach them or they approach you.

Identifying New Business Objectives

One of the first steps in creating a new business plan is to develop a list of measurable objectives—what you want to accomplish with your new business plan. Do you want to diversify your portfolio of work? Expand your geographic reach? Increase the number of opportunities to present to a prospect in person? Bring in more for-profit clients? Your new business objectives will outline the issues that should be addressed in your new business activities.

Your new business plan should directly relate to your overarching goals for the agency, as well as address any situational needs that arise each year. This is where you want to revisit the goals you set for your agency in Chapter 2. For example, a goal for your agency might be to become an expert in social media strategy. Subsequently, a new business objective would be to identify and connect with 20 organizations in the next semester that need this service. Perhaps you have accomplished your goal of becoming social media experts but your reach is limited to local companies. In this case, one of your new business objectives might include connecting with organizations in specific, targeted regions.

Look at what the agency is doing well to bring in new business and where it is falling short. Then ask how a new business plan can address any shortcomings. In addition, your new business plan should align with your agency promotion plan outlined in Chapter 14. If there are two different teams working on these plans, you'll want to work together to make sure the plans align.

Identifying Prospective Clients

One of the first steps in developing a new business pipeline is to develop a list of **prospects** that could become clients. To develop a prospect list you can

1. Identify organizations or people with which the agency or one of its members already has a connection. Everyone in the agency has, at one time or another, connected with people or organizations that could become clients. Think about your internships, service-learning projects, organizations where you volunteer, or connections with family or friends.

2. Identify organizations or people with which you do not currently have connections but with which you have the potential to become a viable partner. Start by looking at a list of businesses and NPOs in the immediate area. You can also look at your university's board of trustees, alumni from your school or major, or members of university advisory boards who have jobs outside of the university.

3. Develop a list of referrals from current clients. Clients who are happy with the agency's work will also be happy providing you with referrals to other clients, and perhaps even making an introduction.

4. Identify a list of "dream clients"—potential clients or organizations you would love to have, but that could be a long shot. These clients will be in the pipeline longer and will need steady contact to move them down the pipeline.

Once you have developed an extensive list, you'll want to compile full contact information for each—name, title, organization, address, phone number, email address —as well as a short profile on the prospect. For those with which you or an agency member already has a connection, it should be fairly easy to obtain this information. For organizations or people with which you do not have a connection, you'll need to do some research. Look at organization websites to identify appropriate communications decision makers with an organization. LinkedIn is also an excellent resource for finding people and connecting with them to obtain information. You'll need to keep these lists updated should a prospect be promoted or move to a position with another organization.

Then, categorize your list based on your new business objectives. For example, you might categorize prospects by the type of organization—NPO, for-profit, or campus client—to ensure you are looking at a diverse range of clients for your agency. Another way to categorize prospects is by their potential for becoming actual clients. For example, you might have three or four categories of viability—dream prospects (we might have them someday), stretch prospects (those with which you have potential but it will be a stretch), viable prospects (those with which you have a real opportunity but need to work on them), and low-hanging fruit (prospects that are ripe for becoming a client and ready to be picked soon). Each will require different types and frequencies of outreach.

Categorizing your list will help you determine how and when to make contact with the prospect as you attempt to move them through the pipeline. Also, keep an eye out for prospects to add to your list. For example, your local newspaper will announce new retail establishments coming into the area. Reading city business journals will also keep you up to date on the happenings at area businesses, including people and promotions. In addition, investigate the potential of being added to a professional vendor list in your area. Some municipalities, such as local chambers of commerce, generate lists of service providers for new and growing companies to reference when they need specific types of services.

Prepare New Business Materials

Rather than reinventing the wheel every time you have an opportunity to connect with or present to a potential client, there are materials you can prepare ahead of time to make communication quicker and easier. Below is a list of materials every agency should have in their new business "ice box."

Creative archives

It's not enough to simply tell a prospect about the awesome banner you developed for an on-campus event, or how you took a client's website from bland and boring to bold and engaging. Prospects want to see visual proof. To do so, you need to create an archive of creative materials. Creative teams should have a central location to keep copies of any design work including videos, posters, print ads, brochures, direct mail materials, newsletters, and so on. If you're redesigning a website, take screenshots of the site both before and after to show how it evolved.

You can also develop creative archives for programs that *don't* involve visual design by having an agency photographer or videographer document the work on every program. For example, is a client team conducting a grand opening event for a local restaurant? Photograph it. Take pictures of the client cutting the ribbon or of the crowd gathered for the opening. Take a screenshot of any social media posts or media articles that were placed as a result of your efforts.

Each time a client team begins a client program, determine how the program could be visually depicted in a new business presentation. If you wait until it's over, it will be too late. As your archive builds, you'll have a bank of materials to draw from for your new business efforts.

Credential/capabilities presentation

Every student agency should have a presentation that outlines your agency **capabilities** (the type of work you are capable of doing as an agency) and **credentials** (your qualifications and the work that you have done for various clients). Capabilities include tactical areas such as social media, media relations, digital advertising, search engine optimization, and so on; and strategic capabilities such as brand positioning, crisis communications or working with international audiences.

Capabilities: The type of work your agency is capable of doing for a client, such as social media, digital advertising, or media relations.

Credentials: Your agency's qualifications and experiences, such as awards won and work done for previous clients.

These might include strategies and tactics that the agency has actually done for a client or those that members of the agency are experienced in doing.

Credentials would include facts and information on your agency that help a potential client better understand your qualifications. For example, you might outline the year the agency was founded, the number of clients you've worked with, how many students are in the agency, the industries you've worked with, the names of client organizations, awards you've won, or even testimonials from previous clients. You can also summarize important agency processes, as well as the culture of your agency.

A capabilities/credentials presentation should be in presentation form (e.g., PowerPoint, KeyNote, etc.) and have a visual template that matches your brand identity and agency culture. Rather than bulleted lists of your credentials or capabilities, find graphically interesting ways to present your information. For example, include screenshots of client logos, websites you've created, or other materials from your archives.

A credentials/capabilities presentation can be used in a variety of situations. For example, you can use it to introduce your agency to a prospect or cut and paste different elements for a specific client proposal. Prepare as much information as possible on your agency and then you can choose different elements to customize presentations for different clients.

Case studies

Case studies are summaries of the work you've done for clients—including program goals, strategies, tactics, and results—that help tell the story of your agency's success. Case studies can be used on your agency's website, in capabilities presentations or in direct mail pieces to prospects. It is helpful to have case studies prepared on every project or program your agency has executed for clients. Then, when you need to make a presentation to a prospect, you can pull the case studies that best fit the prospect's situation and drop them into your presentation.

Your case studies should be succinct, include graphics and shots of creative work, and focus on how your agency successfully solved a problem or capitalized on an opportunity for a client. Take a look at professional agency websites to see how they showcase their case studies. You can also look at other student agency websites. Here's an example of how Brigham Young University's AdLab features its case studies on its website: http://byuadlab.com/work/

Agency reel

Your agency reel is an edited video that showcases any film work that has been done by the agency. This might include clips of television spots, public service announcements, YouTube videos, or cuts from longer videos posted on client websites. Rather than just editing together footage, use graphics and typeface to make sure the video tells your story. For example, if a viral video you filmed garnered 10,000

© Marta Design/Shutterstock.com

views, find a way to highlight that figure along with clips from the video. Use music where appropriate and make sure to include your agency logo at the beginning and/or end of the video. You can find an example of a professional agency reel from RKCR/Y&R here: https://vimeo.com/153240895

If your agency is a public relations (PR) agency, you may not have as much film work as an advertising agency would. Your work is likely in the form of special events, contests, media clips, social media campaigns, or other **PR** tactics. To compensate for this, many professional PR agencies develop what is called a **sizzle reel**. A sizzle reel highlights the agency's successes through photos, video clips taken of events, screenshots of media placements or social media pages, photos of awards, or other visual documentation of your work.

> **Sizzle reel:** A video that makes your agency's work "sizzle" by highlighting client work, campaign results, awards, and other agency successes.

Agencies and organizations often use sizzle reels to showcase the success of one specific PR campaign, but agencies also use them for new business purposes. The purpose of the reel is to bring your agency and its work to life and make it "sizzle" for a prospect. Again, having an archive of creative work will assist greatly in developing a sizzle reel. You can find an example of a PR agency sizzle reel from Coyne PR here: https://www.youtube.com/watch?v=xzwMTQWpvMo. A production company called Sizzle It! specifically develops sizzle reels for PR agencies and clients. You can take a look at their work and how they put their sizzle reels together at sizzleit.com.

© Visual Generation/Shutterstock.com

New Business Outreach

The key to new business outreach can be summed up in one phrase: frequency of contact. Just like you wouldn't develop an advertising campaign that only reaches a consumer once, you also don't want to reach out to a prospect once and then give up.

Some of the goals of continuous outreach include the following:

- Make a prospect aware that your agency exists
- Determine the prospects communications needs and identify how your agency's capabilities can fulfill those needs
- Promote your agency capabilities and successes to a prospect
- Build a relationship between the prospect and your agency
- Show your agency's interest in a prospect's business
- Ultimately, make a "final" pitch or presentation to the prospect.

Developing continuous new business outreach to a prospect is more difficult for student agencies than for professional agencies for two reasons. First, unlike a professional agency, a student agency doesn't have a dedicated, full-time professional working on new business outreach. Thus, you'll have limited time to carry out this outreach. The second difficulty comes with agency turnover. In a professional agency, the same people will reach out to the same prospects on an ongoing basis. In a student agency, a member that made initial contact with a prospect may graduate or not work in the agency the following semester. Thus, several different people will be making contact with the prospect over time.

To help overcome these barriers, it is critical for the agency to develop an efficient spreadsheet that keeps track of each point of contact, who made the contact, how the contact was made (phone call, email, face-to-face, direct mail), and notes on any outcome from the contact. For example, agency member Katie has a phone conversation with a local environmental organization. She learns they will be partnering with a Costa Rican university on water conservation in the next 6 months and may need help promoting it. This would be an important piece of information for Katie to include in the spreadsheet. Or, perhaps agency member Jason finds that a local restaurant wants to update its website, and asked the agency to contact them again in the fall. Without making a note of this in the spreadsheet, this information wouldn't be available to the next student working on this prospect.

In addition to organizational plans, include other personal or professional information on the spreadsheet. Perhaps you learn that a prospect will be taking maternity leave in the spring. Maybe a prospect mentions that his son plays basketball or that his daughter has applied to your university. Any information that helps the agency better understand the professional needs or personal values of prospects will help you, and future agency members, build a better relationship with them.

Continuous contact can take on many forms. Below are a few ways to connect with your list of prospects.

Cold calling

One of the ways agencies make initial contact with a prospect is through what is called cold calling. Cold calling is when you call a prospect with whom you have never made contact. The purpose of the call is twofold; to introduce your agency to prospects and to find out more about their communications needs. Prepare a list of points you want to make in the call as well as a list of questions you want to ask the prospect. According to *Entrepreneur* magazine (Porter, 2012), you should "Get Information Before You Give It" in a cold call. In other words, ask the prospect about their business before you sell them on yours. Doing so can help you pinpoint the agency capabilities that will best fit their needs.

You also want the call to lead to another point of contact in the future. Before you make the call, determine what this might be. For example, if the prospect doesn't have an immediate need for your agency, ask them when would be a good time to call them again. Or, ask them for a face-to-face contact as discussed below.

Face-to-face contact

In-person contact is the preferred method of connecting with a prospect because of its more personal nature. When connecting with a prospect early on, ask them out for coffee or lunch to find out more about their business. Or, you could invite them to an agency open house.

There are also more informal ways of intentionally or unintentionally "running into" a prospect. For example, if you know a prospect plays in a charity golf tournament, attend the reception afterward and introduce yourself to the prospect. Professional association meetings are also excellent ways to cross paths with potential clients. Pay attention to who is speaking at your regional PRSA, AAF, or AMA luncheons. Listen to their presentation and then approach them afterward to introduce yourself, discuss their presentation, and then ask if you can make contact with them later.

Once you get past your initial contact with a prospect, you can move on to more formal contact. This could include making a capabilities presentation at the client's offices or, eventually, pitching your agency to work on their business.

Electronic or mail contact

In between making phone calls and soliciting face-to-face contact, you can connect with prospects through emails, social media, direct mail, or other means included in your agency's promotional plan. The key to making contact with a client is to focus on their business first. A prospect wants to know what you can do for them, rather than what they can do for you.

There is a big difference between simply "contacting" a prospect and "connecting" with them. Sending an email is making contact, but it's the *content* of the email that will make the connection. For example, perhaps you come across an article that discusses trends in social media marketing. You're aware that a prospect wants to increase its organization's engagement with customers through social media. Send the link to the article with a quick note: "Hi Jennifer, I ran across this article today on social media marketing that I thought might interest you. We've been experimenting with some of these tactics for our other clients and have had great success. I'd be happy to talk with you about them in more detail."

Connecting with a client goes back to doing your homework on a prospects needs, staying abreast of what is happening in their industry, and then reaching out to them to connect their needs with your capabilities. Doing so will show the potential client that you have a genuine interest in helping them solve problems and succeed.

You should use a variety of methods discussed above in reaching out to potential clients. Each point of contact—and connection—moves a prospect further down the new business pipeline until you eventually have the opportunity to pitch their business.

AGENCY SEARCH PROCESS

While student-run agencies will rarely (if ever) be involved in a competitive agency search, it's important to understand the search process for several reasons. First, on the rare occasion that you are asked to participate in a competitive search, you'll want to be prepared.

Second, working in a student agency means learning everything you can about professional agency practices; competitive agency searches are an integral part those practices. If you work on either the agency or client side after graduation, you'll likely come across this process in your work. Lastly, a client may utilize many of the components of a competitive agency search even if they are solely looking at your agency for a project or campaign. Thus, it is important to familiarize yourself with the process to effectively respond to a client's request.

Below we outline the typical process for a typical agency search.

Internal Client Preparation

Clients decide to conduct an agency search for numerous reasons. Some of these reasons include changes in the client's business or personnel, adding new products or services, or changing trends in the industry. What most often occurs, however, is a breakdown in the relationship with a current agency partner. The decision to embark on an agency search is not something a client takes lightly. The process can be extensive and time-consuming. It can also be costly; pulling people off of the work they normally do costs the company money and human resources.

Once the client makes the decision to conduct an agency search, they will put together an internal agency search team to lead the effort. This may include members of the marketing and communications teams, members of any department or company division that will be working with the agency, and financial or procurement executives who will be involved in financial decisions. The search team will determine what they are looking for in an agency partner, the **scope of work** required of the agency and budgets for the corresponding scope of work. They may also develop selection criteria for picking the winning agency.

Once the client's needs are clearly outlined, they will develop a process and timeline for the search. Some searches include several rounds of contact with the agencies capped off with a final presentation. Others are more streamlined into one or two rounds.

Scope of work: Outlines the parameters of a client assignment, such as the type of work to be done, required deliverables and deadlines.

© Raxpixel.com/Shutterstock.com

Request for Information

A typical first-round review in an agency search process will include a **request for information** (RFI). The client search team will develop a list of agencies from which it would like to review additional information than what can be found on the agencies' websites or what is known about the agencies from previous contact. According to guidelines jointly developed by the Association of National Advertisers and the American Association of Advertising Agencies:

> **Request for information:** A client request for detailed information from an agency with the goal of determining the agency's credentials/capabilities and fit with the potential client. An RFI is one of the first stages of the agency search process.

> The purpose of the RFI is to request detailed information regarding the agency's profile, management team, organization chart, business approach, financial, credentials, client list and capabilities, and to motivate the best and most relevant agency candidates to apply. It typically also includes case studies and creative work samples that might further help the client understand the agency's capabilities. (AAAA/ANA, 2011, p. 5)

An RFI will be sent to 10 to 15 agencies, depending on the size of the client organization and the scope of the project. Agencies are given a deadline for returning the RFI. Some agencies may choose not to participate in the RFI process (usually for financial reasons). In this case, it's important for the agency to make contact with the client search committee to thank them for being included and provide a reason for not participating. Some client organizations permit agency phone calls to clarify information in the RFI or ask additional questions, while others reserve that type of contact for later rounds of the process.

Once search team members have reviewed all RFI's against the selection criteria, they will determine which agencies to ask to the next round. This process usually culls the list by half. While the client is looking for the best agency fit, not answering all of the questions in the RFI or returning an RFI with typos, grammatical errors or inconsistent formatting can result in an agency not being considered for the next round.

Request for Proposal

Traditionally, the next round in an agency search process will include a **request for proposal** (RFP). RFPs go deeper than RFIs by inviting agencies to develop proposals that specifically address the client's challenge or opportunity. Beyond simply determining the agency's capabilities, this part of the process gives clients a sense of an agency's strategic thinking, problem-solving abilities, and the overall approach to the client's business.

> **Request for proposal:** A document that outlines a client's specific needs and asks for a detailed proposal on how an agency could meet those needs. An RFP is often the second stage in an agency search process.

Typically, RFPs also ask the agency to provide background on the account team that would work on the business. The client will also provide agencies with more information on their brand and business at this point, and commonly ask RFP agencies to sign a **nondisclosure agreement** before giving them the RFP. This means an agency agrees to keep the client's information confidential. Clients will likely provide the agency with proposed budget ranges so they can determine if the business will be financially viable for the agency.

The RFP process may also include a visit to the agency by the client search team. An important component of determining client-agency fit is assessing whether the organizations share similar cultures. By visiting the agency, the client can meet the team in person, tour the offices, and get a sense of the agency's culture. For example, are employees quietly working by themselves in their offices, or are they actively engaged with each other in shared workspaces? Are the agency's physical offices "trendy" and modern, or more conservative? Are employees dressed in suits or are they more casual? Client-agency fit goes both ways. Agency visits also give the agency a chance to determine if the client is a good fit for the agency.

Nondisclosure agreement: A binding agreement in which the agency and its members agree to keep nonpublic client information confidential. Also called a confidentiality agreement.

© Constantin Stanciu/Shutterstock.com

Final Pitch Presentations

Once the client search team reviews agency RFPs, they will determine the two or three agencies to invite to a final pitch. Agencies will be given a specific assignment for the pitch and may be asked to develop strategies, tactics, and creative work to present at the pitch. At this point in the process, agencies have much more leeway to ask questions and request additional information.

The client may hold an agency briefing at the client's offices where all agencies are invited to hear client presentations on the assignment and ask questions. Asking questions in a joint briefing is tricky. You want to get valuable information from the client and impress them with intelligent questions, but you don't want to give away your potential strategies to competing agencies. Often clients will give agencies an opportunity to ask questions separately or to conduct follow-up phone calls where more tactical questions can be asked and answered.

At this point in the process, clients will often ask agencies to develop **spec** (speculative) creative to address the client

Spec creative: Developing creative work to demonstrate an agency's capabilities without being paid for it under the "speculation" that the client will be impressed enough to hire you for the job.

challenge. **Spec** work means that an agency develops creative—such as advertising layouts, commercial storyboards, or other graphic designs—to demonstrate the agency's creative skills. Professional agencies frown upon doing spec work because it is essentially giving away the work for free. However, it is often the sacrifice you make to win the business.

PUTTING YOUR BEST PITCH FORWARD

What does it mean to "pitch" a potential client? The term **new business pitch** is used in the industry to describe the act of selling a client on your ideas and your agency. Often agencies spend most of their time developing and selling clients on their proposals. Of course, that is the heart of any new business pitch—creating a proposal that will successfully address the client's situation and get results. But new business pitches are much more than that. You are not only selling your plan, you are also selling your agency, its people, its processes, and your passion for working on the client's business.

© aslysun/Shutterstock.com

New business pitch: An agency presentation made to a potential client with the goal of winning the client's business.

Put yourself in the client's shoes for a moment. What types of things would you want to be persuaded of to hire an agency? In Box 3.1, you'll find a list of potential questions a client may want answered before hiring an agency.

Box 3.1 Questions Clients Ask to Evaluate an Agency

Before embarking on a new business pitch, ask yourself what the client will want to know about your agency. Then, make sure you are addressing each of these issues in your pitch. Below are potential questions to which a client may want answers:

- How did the agency approach the proposal, what was the process? Will they use the same process for my business? What is the process for executing the proposal?
- What do they know about my business? Did they take the time to educate themselves?
- Are they experienced in this type of work? If not, what have they shown me that gives me confidence they can learn and get up to speed quickly?
- Are they creative? Have I seen their ideas a hundreds times before, or did they bring something different to the table?
- Are they passionate about my business and industry? What shows me that?
- Who would work on my business? Can I trust them? Do I like them? Will I like working with them?
- How do they present themselves? Are they professional and enthusiastic? Or are they monotone and ill prepared?

In Chapter 11, we discuss in detail ways to effectively present your ideas, whether in a new business pitch or to an existing client. In this section, we provide an overview of what you should consider when embarking on a new business pitch.

Before the Pitch

Perhaps the most important work in a new business pitch happens before the client presentation. Create opportunities to meet with the client before the pitch to get to know them and ask questions. Invite them for lunch or coffee, or ask for a time you can call them. Not only does this better prepare you for developing a proposal, but it also helps build a relationship (see discussion on chemistry later in the chapter).

Prepare intelligent questions that will both impress the client and give you insightful information about the client's business. Remember that every opportunity you have in front of the potential client is a chance to sell yourself and your agency. Pay attention to what the client is saying, both in preliminary conversations and in any RFI or RFP. One of the authors participated as a client in an agency search where the client visited all the agencies before the pitch and briefed them extensively on the situation. When one of the agencies made their pitch, their creative and strategic thinking were excellent, perhaps the best of the four agencies presenting. But they didn't win the business. Why? Because they designed their creative for the wrong target audience. They didn't listen well when the client discussed their needs.

Do your research on the client's industry and situation. Familiarize yourself with their organization, brands, and terminology. In addition, find out what you can about the people who will be in the room. What are their titles and responsibilities? What is important to them? What do they do outside of work? For example, through social media, you may find that one of the clients serves on the board of a local children's museum, or another likes to go cycling on the weekend. This tells you something about the client's values and can help you make a more personal connection with them.

Putting Together the Team

Just as the client has an agency search team, your agency will put together a new business team. Who should be on the team? What will their role be? Much of the decision will depend on the communication needs of the client. Below are some examples of members to include on your new business team:

- *Members who represent the leadership of the agency*—the advisor, director, and/or other manager. Leadership participation demonstrates that the agency takes the client's business seriously. Leaders can also answer questions other members may not know about the agency.
- *A "lead" facilitator*—the person who will have primary client contact during the new business pitch process, will serve as coordinator of the new business team, and will facilitate the presentation. This could be the agency's new business coordinator or the team leader who would work on the account.

- *Client account team members*—the potential team leader and account executives who would work on the client's account team. Clients often accuse agencies of "bate and switch"—showcasing the agency's best people at the pitch and then replacing them with lower level members once the business has been won. You want to make sure the people who will actually work on the business play a central role in the pitch.
- *Creative team members*—the creative director and/or web designers, video producers or graphics coordinators likely to produce work for the client. In addition, you'll want to assign a creative coordinator to produce the presentation itself—boards, multimedia, and PowerPoint templates—to creatively showcase your proposal and agency brand.
- *Specialty team members*—those with special skills who would contribute to the account. This would include members such as brand specialists, media relations specialists, or others in the agency whose job entails a strategic or tactical expertise.
- *Financial manager*—the "money" person. If your agency has a member whose job it is to manage client budgets and agency finances, it's a good idea to include them in the new business process. They may or may not be present at the pitch, but they can help the team assess the financial viability of an account and the feasibility of proposed fees or budgets.

The new business team should meet early in the new business process to review the RFP or other client brief, clarify roles, assign tasks and develop a timeline for each stage of the process—from research and brainstorming to proposal preparation and final printing deadlines. It is also helpful if the lead facilitator (or a research director if your agency has one) develops a **research brief** to hand out to team members. A research brief summarizes key information found on the client, category, and/or media placements through online and secondary research. This saves the team time and makes sure everyone is working from the same information.

> **Research brief:** In the initial stages of a client pitch process, online and secondary research is conducted on a potential client and summarized in a document that is distributed to the new business team. A research brief ensures that the team has as much information as possible to develop new business proposals.

Developing the Pitch

Bob Sanders of Sanders Consulting Group, a firm specializing in agency consulting, asserts that there are four elements to any agency pitch: Content, Format, Style, and Chemistry (Sanders Consulting website). According to Sanders, content refers to the content of the presentation itself—what goes on the slides or boards. Format refers to whether the content is structured in a logical and compelling way and tells an engaging story. Style is *how* you present the props or boards you use, whether you use PowerPoint, if you serve refreshments, any items you would give to the client to bring the presentation to life, and so on; in essence, style refers to how you put on the "show." Chemistry, the most important of the four, is whether the client likes the agency and its people. You can put in hours and hours of work on the other elements, but it doesn't matter if the client doesn't warm up to you.

Sanders asserts that clients and agencies view new business pitches very differently (see the pie chart below). While agencies view proposal content as the main attraction in a client pitch, clients give style and format much more weight. And, chemistry is the determining factor in winning the business, regardless of how well you do on the other three. Thus, agencies would do well to complete their content as early as possible in the process, and spend time focusing on format and style.

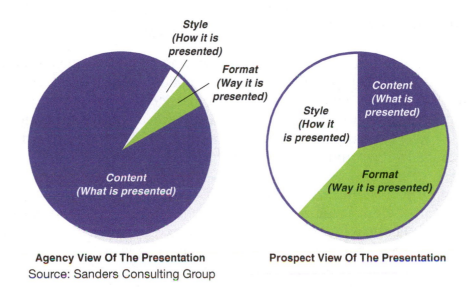

Agency View Of The Presentation
Source: Sanders Consulting Group

Prospect View Of The Presentation

Format can be improved by finding memorable ways to highlight the key points of your content, and then making sure each section of your presentation flows together to back up those memorable points. For example, Steve Jobs introduced the iPod with a simple, memorable line—"your entire music library fits in your pocket" (Shedden, 2014). In one sentence, he encapsulated a rather complex device. Agencies often err on the side of providing too much information for the client, rather than highlighting key points and trusting the client to be intelligent enough to fill in the blanks. As discussed in detail in Chapter 11, your presentation is a narrative, with an engaging beginning that draws the listeners in; a middle that carries them along the narrative path without losing their interest; and a big finish that leaves them wanting more.

When clients have to sit through several agency presentations in a row, it can be hard to remember which agency presented what. This is where style can make a big difference. Agencies often call this the "dog and pony show." How much style you bring to your pitch should depend on the client to whom you are presenting. Is it a rigid, no-nonsense client or one who is expecting to be entertained and "wowed" by your presentation? If you've done your research, you will know. The key is to provide enough style to make your presentation memorable without sacrificing substance for style.

You can add style to your presentation by bringing key threads of your pitch to life. For example, one of the authors worked for an agency that pitched a fall campaign to a state tourism bureau. At the pitch, the agency served hot apple cider and played a looped video of a fireplace in the background. When the same agency pitched a food brand targeted to men, the room was designed as a "man cave" to set the mood for their concepts. In another example, the agency created a lounge atmosphere with a guitar player, high tables, and key concepts printed on cardboard coasters to pitch a beer brand. With a little creativity, you can make your presentation memorable and a bit more fun for the client.

Lastly is the all important element of chemistry. How do you build chemistry with a client you barely know? According to Zach Rosenberg, president of Milner Butcher Media Group, the best way to build chemistry is to do your research on the client, find areas where you may have commonalities, and then weave those touch points into your conversations and presentation. Rosenberg explains

> Do some research upfront on individuals by scouring their social media sites. Gain an understanding of their personal interests, activities, things that make them tick beyond work. Then find a commonality—what passions or interests do you share? What unique capability do you offer that can address their issues? Once determined, find a way to weave those interests into the conversation. Doing this disarms them, brings their shield down and raises the trust factor. (Rosenberg, 2016)

Rosenberg also points out that showing a unified front as a team—that you like each other and can work well together—goes a long way in building client confidence in your agency's abilities. When making your presentation, everyone in the room should participate in the pitch. No one should sit on the sidelines and simply watch. Leave enough time in the presentation to have chemistry-building discussions and conversations. So, if the client gives you an hour to pitch, save 20 minutes for questions and discussions.

One more thing—discretely ask the lead client when they plan on making a decision. Waiting for word can be excruciating for agency members. It helps to know if the decision will be tomorrow or 3 weeks from tomorrow.

After the Pitch—Following Up

As you leave the client presentation, you'll want to give participants a printed document that outlines your proposal and the important information presented in the pitch in more detail (one copy for each participant). This is called the **leave behind**—for obvious reasons. The leave behind allows the client to revisit your presentation as they are making their decision, and to pass it along to others who might not have been available for the pitch. Like the presentation, the leave behind should be graphically appealing and follow your brand identity. Instead of a printed leave behind, some professional agencies create a

Leave behind: A printed document that outlines your agency's client proposal and other pertinent information. The document is left behind for the client to review after the pitch.

website for clients and provide them with the link. A website allows for more graphic animation of the proposal as well as the ability to play any videos from the pitch.

After the pitch, follow up with the client participants via email to thank them for their time and remind them of your enthusiasm for working on their business. If the client asked for any additional information, get it to them as quickly as possible so they can make their decision. Many agencies also find creative ways to remain top of mind with the client. For example, you could send the client a selfie of the new business team with a fun message—"Eager to work on your business." Or, send the client a small gift that creatively reminds them of your presentation —printed coffee mugs, t-shirts, or other "swag."

CONCLUSION

The new business process—from planning to outreach to pitching—is an integral and critical part of any professional agency. It can be the most stressful yet simultaneously the most exciting and fun part of working in an agency. New business can bring together diverse members of the agency to plan and create their best ideas. It involves late nights and cold pizza; inevitable arguments and collective celebrations; metered planning and last minute runs to the print shop. And ultimately, hopefully, it will bring valued new clients into your agency.

REVIEW AND DISCUSSION QUESTIONS

1. What is the difference between an RFI and an RFP?
2. Write down a list of clients you currently have in the agency. Determine if each is a nonprofit client, for-profit client, or on-campus client. Do you have a good mix of each? Based on your agency goals, in what ways (if any) do you need to diversify your roster of clients?
3. Based on your student agency goals, develop three objectives for a new business plan. Think in terms of industry categories (e.g., sporting goods, fashion), geographic regions, or expertise you'd like to gain to further your agency's goals.
4. With a team of agency students, develop a list of 10 "dream clients" you'd like to have in the agency. Once you've developed the list, go back over it and determine what it is about each that makes you want to work for them.
5. Take two clients from your "dream list" in #4 and develop a plan for connecting with each. Walk through your plan in stages from initial outreach to ways you can develop a deeper relationship. Conduct online research to help you develop your plan.
6. As discussed in this chapter, everyone has contacts that could turn into potential clients. Brainstorm ways to collect a running list of these contacts from all members of the agency.
7. Think about a person you know that would be a good contact for your new business pipeline. This may be a person you worked with at an internship, a friend of your family, or someone you met at a professional luncheon. Write down one thing, you could do in the next 24 hours to make an agency contact with this person.

8. Pick a prospect from your "dream list" in #4. What are three capabilities your agency has that could relate to this client? If you have none, what can you do to gain that capability?
9. Imagine you are pitching a local hardware store. Think of ways you can add "style" to your presentation and bring your ideas to life?
10. Spend some time perusing case studies on professional agency websites within your area of expertise (e.g., ad agencies, PR agencies, digital agencies). Write down three things the agencies do that you could adopt for showcasing your own case studies.

REFERENCES AND ADDITIONAL READINGS

American Association of Advertising Agencies/Association of National Advertisers (AAAA/ANA). (2011). *Guidelines for agency search*. Retrieved from https://www.aaaa.org/wp-content/uploads/2011/10/agency_search_white_paper.pdf

Bush, L. (2009). Student public relations agencies: A qualitative study of the pedagogical benefits, risks and a framework for success. *Journalism & Mass Communication Educator, 64*(1), 27–38.

Bush, L., Haygood, D., & Vincent, H. (2017). Student-run communications agencies: Providing students with real-world experiences that impact their careers. *Journalism & Mass Communication Educator, 72*(4), 410–424.

Clarke, A. (2015, March 23). Top ten tips to win new business. *PR Week*. Retrieved from http://www.prweek.com/article/1336668/top-ten-tips-win-new-business

Currie, D. (2016). *Selling less to win more agency new business. Winmo webcast, digital agency day*. Retrieved from https://vimeo.com/153514175

Gass, M. (n.d.). *Fuel Lines blog*. (Site includes many articles on new business). Retrieved from https://fuellingnewbusiness.com

Oetting, J. (2015, March 9). A guide to perfecting the new business pitch. *HubSpot*. Retrieved from https://blog.hubspot.com/agency/guide-new-business-pitch#sm.000004wr21p14dmffzx5m677n69tn

Parekh, R. (2013, October 21). Marketers should take heed as agencies shun low-margin, high-headache biz. *Advertising Age*. Retrieved from http://adage.com/article/agency-news/marketers-heed-agencies-shun-low-margin-biz/244855/

Porter, J. (2012, November 19). Seven secrets to cold calling success. *Entrepreneur*. Retrieved from https://www.entrepreneur.com/article/224931

Rosenberg, Z. (2016, January 24). 5 ways to improve chemistry with your clients. *AdWeek*. Retrieved from http://www.adweek.com/brand-marketing/5-ways-improve-chemistry-your-clients-169129/

Sanders, B. (2017). New business: The winning pitch. *Sanders Consulting Group Website*. Retrieved from http://www.sandersconsulting.com/new-business-the-winning-pitch/

Shedden, D. (2014, October 23). Today in media history: Apple's Steve Jobs introduces the iPod in 2001. *Poynter*. Retrieved from https://www.poynter.org/2014/today-in-media-history-apples-steve-jobs-introduces-the-ipod-in-2001/276301/

Solomon, R. (2016). *The art of client service*. Hoboken, NJ: Wiley.

Chapter 4

Agency Processes

Every organization employs processes to carry out the mission of the organization. Without processes, work in the organization is chaotic and inconsistent. Think of organizational processes as "ways of doing things." By outlining standard ways of doing things, employees know how to operate within the organizational setting, communication between departments and functions is more effective, and the quality of work produced by the organization is more consistent. As a result, clients have far more confidence in the organization's ability to manage their accounts.

Advertising and public relations (PR) agencies employ numerous processes to carry out the day-to-day work of an agency. In a fast-paced business that relies on data and deadlines as much as creativity and collaboration, processes are imperative to keep the agency engine running smoothly. While these processes are similar across the industry, each agency has its "signature" way of doing things based on the goals of the organization, the needs of its clients, and the type of work the agency does. It all comes down to developing processes that improve our ability to do the best work for our clients.

But doing the best work for our clients also means remaining flexible and adaptive. Evolving technologies and continuously changing cultural attitudes require the agencies to manage the chaos while also being adaptive and agile. As Ed Burgoyne, founder of Makr Consulting, states, "Agile at its core is really about ways of working: adapting quickly to changing requirements, environments, client requests, and new learning" (Burgoyne, 2015). Thus, agencies must continually monitor and measure their processes to adapt to their changing environment.

Student-run agencies have become more adept at developing organizational processes in the last decade. With the increase in the number of agencies and the expansion of their capabilities, student agencies have learned to be more structured and measured in how they recruit students, deliver client work, and adapt to changes in the industry. Like professional agencies, each student agency has its own signature processes and ways of doing things. But also like professional agencies, these processes will be similar in scope with the end goal of producing great client work. The key is to develop processes that help you manage the chaos of agency work while being adaptive to changing client needs and industry trends.

In this chapter, we discuss the types of processes you'll want to establish for your agency including

- Recruiting, interviewing, and training the best students
- Effective processes for bringing a client into the agency
- How to manage agency workflow
- Developing internal communication flow and channels
- Measuring agency success

Note: Agency billing and budgeting processes are another crucial part of developing agency processes. These processes will be discussed in Chapter 5 on "The Business Side of Communications."

RECRUITING AND HIRING PROCESSES

Becoming a student agency member should involve more than simply signing up for a class. As discussed in Chapter 2, you will have many different titles and roles in your student agency—from leadership and account team roles to creative production and specialty tactical roles. Thus, you'll want to recruit students with diverse talents and abilities, and you'll need a process for doing so.

While the bulk of your agency staff will likely come from key communications majors (e.g., PR or advertising majors), if your agency structure allows for it, you can also look for talent outside those majors. For example, business schools are a good place to recruit students with marketing and sales expertise. If you're looking for creative design talent, the art department is a good place to start. If your agency has videography capabilities, you might want to recruit students from film or cinema majors.

Before you begin your recruitment efforts, determine the titles and roles your agency needs and write job descriptions for each (see Chapter 2). Then, share short summaries of job descriptions in your recruiting materials where appropriate. Include specific skills or experience, as well as "soft" skills like leadership qualities, attention to detail, or ability to work well in teams. This helps you know the specific abilities you are looking for in applicants while also alerting applicants to the roles they are best suited for and what is expected of them.

Also, remember to develop a timeline for your recruitment efforts. Set a date for when final hiring decisions should be made and then work backwards. Included in your timeline will be the date for distributing materials, deadline for applications, and a timeframe for interviewing and selecting candidates. Some student agencies hire students a semester in advance so they can hit the ground running when the new semester begins. You'll also need to take into account any breaks, like spring break, holidays, and summer vacation, and consider how these will affect your recruitment timeline.

Following are some considerations for recruiting and hiring students.

Candidate Review Criteria

Before you put out a call for applications, think about what you want applicants to submit to help you gauge their qualifications. Having applicants submit resumes, portfolios, and references provide some preliminary forms of qualifications as a part of a student agency hiring process. You can use these tools to help identify where a student would be the best fit and what they can bring to the equation. Preparation of these tools by student candidates is also good practice for eventual application to their first, full time "real job."

As discussed in earlier chapters, many student agencies are taught as a course. If this is the case, course prerequisites are another way to help determine who to hire and who should wait for next semester. Courses your school may offer, like advanced PR writing, introduction to digital design, or even media planning can be established as prerequisites and used to screen out applicants. If you do not have prerequisites for the agency, having students list their previous courses on the application will give you a sense of their level of experience.

This prescreening is important because, depending on your mission, your client base and other opportunities, some students may not be as ready as others. By gauging applicants' experience and status against prerequisites you can identify those who need to "season" before joining your team as well as select those who will move on to the next stage of the hiring process. Also, through early identification of those interested but not-yet-qualified students, there will be a ready pool of students to draw from over time.

Establishing prerequisites is best accomplished with the help of your student services office. Many university registration systems can be set via an automated function to "weed out" those not quite ready for this opportunity. Similarly, there are also opportunities for student services/registration to require permission of the instructor as part of the course registration process, thereby guaranteeing an interview prior to hiring.

Regardless of whether your student agency is a for-credit course, or another type of student activity, you may want to consider developing a standardized test for students to take to demonstrate their acumen and potential fitness for your organization prior to hiring. In the real world, writing tests or skills demonstration tests are often hurdles new applicants must get over to proceed to the next level. Topics for assessment may include demonstrating an understanding of the creative process, fundamentals of client service, basic understanding of PR, advertising and integrated communications skills, as well as a threshold of quality in writing skills, digital literacy, and basic research skills. Also keep in mind that you'll want to hire for diversity—diversity of thought, background, and skills— to have a well-rounded agency. Once these assessments are made, candidates can move on to the interview phase.

Recruiting Students

One of the challenges of student agencies is the recruiting of top talent. As in many areas of life, the quality performers are also the most highly sought after by competing interests. So, how do you rise above the noise and attract the most accomplished, the most talented?

The answer is, have the best message and ensure it gets to the right people. Take a look at resources you have at your disposal to recruit the key people you want.

Classroom visits, student activity fairs, digital signage, flyers, and email/social media blasts are all effective, traditional tactics to get your message out. But why be mundane when you can be memorable? Creativity at this crucial point of introduction is a great opportunity to show off your organization's skills and attract top talent. Consider planning open house events with fun activities or producing short videos. Seek to create an atmosphere of cutting-edge technology and relevant experience. Be sure your messages reflect your agency's desired tone and brand identity. If you are professional and traditional, select a stately approach with sedate colors, traditional professional fonts, and an appeal to professional success. If you are seeking a more hip, cool vibe, consider contemporary looks, fonts, copy, colors, and a "fun" approach to your materials.

Once you have decided upon the approach/appearance of your recruiting materials, you must now craft the message. One of the most compelling message tactics in recruiting is the testimonial. Use your own students or recent alumni to tell positive stories about being involved in a student firm and describe how involvement in your agency led to positive outcomes like a job or internship. Linking positive efforts to positive outcomes is always a compelling argument.

Interviewing

A one-on-one interview with agency leadership should be required before making an offer to a candidate. During these meetings, challenge the applicant to demonstrate commitment, availability, motivation, and ability to work well in teams. Prepare a list of questions ahead of time that will give you more information on the applicant's capabilities, as well as a sense of their personality and work ethic. In Box 4.1, you will find a list of interview questions to get you started.

You can also gauge an applicant's interest and professionalism by how they carry themselves in the interview. Did they dress appropriately for the interview, or come to the session in shorts and tennis shoes? Were they prepared to answer your questions, or did they mumble and have difficulty discussing their qualifications? Another indicator of an applicant's interest is whether the applicant asked you questions about the position and the agency. Applicants who come to interviews well dressed, prepared to respond to your questions, and with a few questions of their own show that they are genuinely interested in the position and not just looking for something to add to their resume.

Commitment and availability are very important assessments that should be made during the interview process. There is a saying, "If you want something done, give it to a busy person." And while that anecdote is often true, experience also shows that one of the key detractors to hiring active, busy students, (those often attracted to student agency opportunities) can be availability. Many students over-obligate themselves or legitimately have multiple responsibilities/demands on their time. These obligations inhibit their ability to maximize the agency experience. Distractions/competing priorities may include outside jobs, leadership in other student organizations, athletic scholarships, and so on.

Be sure to discuss these outside responsibilities during the interview. Having sufficient time to participate in the agency is a key qualifier and something your clients deserve. Pragmatically, selecting the proper person and addressing their ability to commit can avoid situations where a student is selected for a leadership position, but is torn by competing priorities and drops out, leaving the agency with a problem of staffing and adjustment.

Box 4.1   Sample Interview Questions

- Tell me a little about yourself.
- Why do you want to work for the student agency?
- What abilities would you bring to the agency?
- Tell me about a time when you were faced with a problem. How did you approach and overcome the problem?
- If I were to talk with someone who has worked with you in a team setting, what would they tell me about working with you?
- What do you think are your two best qualities or professional abilities?
- What is one area where you would like to improve yourself?
- Tell me about a program or project you worked on (in class, during an internship, in a student organization) that you are really proud of.
- What other activities are you involved with outside of classes? How would you balance your agency work with those other activities?
- What questions do you have for me?

Student Contracts and Compensation

Two ways to stave off the dropout issue are contracting with students and attaching compensation to certain key positions. Depending upon the depth of agency talent, the complexity of the organization, demands on student time by clients and myriad other issues, it may be prudent to draw up an employment contract. The contract with those you hire typically promises favorable outcomes for staying with the program. Rewards may mean the opportunity to return with leadership titles next semester, bonuses in terms of gifts-in-kind for jobs well done, and selection to conferences or additional training opportunities.

Deciding to pay some of your hires in salary is another option for both attracting the right people and ensuring their retention. As discussed in Chapter 2, some student agencies pay key leaders on their staff. Often these compensations are tied to the title or the leadership role within the organization. Deciding what positions to pay is something you will want to establish prior to interviewing and will be dependent upon your student agency organization and client demands.

Student Orientation and Training

So you have successfully recruited your team of students for the semester. Now it is time to train them in the agency's policies, procedures, core competencies, and best practices. Questions new students may have can include simple things like: Where are the closest bathrooms to the spaces? What do we do about work requirements that must be done after hours? Or some of the more complex offerings like: What version of video editing software do you use? What are the technology resources of the agency?

The orientation briefing is also important for bringing in standard operating methodology in client relations. What do we charge? When do we charge? What are our associated research ethics involved in researching a client? And while one-on-one attention is a highly sought approach to getting training started, there are other tactics that can be used to further prepare students for their positions. This can be done through a variety of ways.

- *A student agency PQS guide.* PQS is a military term and stands for personal qualification standards. Each Sailor or Soldier or Marine is required to keep up with these standards and successful completion is usually recognized by a uniform insignia or some other celebration and distinguished piece of gear. Students can be trained using a PQS guide to get oriented on all of the nuances of your agency existence.
- *Assignment of a mentor.* New students can be assigned a mentor—an older student that helps new recruits find their way around. The mentor takes varying degrees of responsibility for the new students.
- *New student orientation briefings.* It may be very useful to host an orientation briefing or series of workshops/briefings for your new students. If done properly, this could also be a helpful review for returning students. Engaging the veteran students to teach these workshops could be very useful. In addition, you can invite guest speakers from professional agencies to discuss agency best practices.

Orienting new students to your agency will also include familiarizing them with your clients. This can be done by developing client background summaries to hand out to students or by giving short presentations on each client. If the client is a returning client, include information on what the agency has done for the client in the past. If the client is new, include what you know about the client's business and the assignment, and encourage students to do more research to fully understand the client's business.

Lastly, don't forget about agency culture when developing your orientation plans. Ice breaker activities or creative brainstorming activities can help students get to know each other and begin the process of working together. The goal of agency orientation is to give students the comfort level that will allow them to hit the ground running when the client work begins.

ONBOARDING A NEW CLIENT

In Chapter 3, we discussed how to develop a new business plan and win new client business. Once you have won the business, you want to transition the client into the agency smoothly. Below we discuss some key components to onboarding a client into your agency and getting your projects underway.

Client Agreements

First and foremost, you'll want to forge some sort of agreement between your agency and the client. This can be accomplished through various meetings and conferences as well as through written documentation. These can range from simple one-page agreements for projects to multipage, multistage marketing plans. Some of these documents are covered in other areas of this text but one of the most important tools for onboarding a client is the **scope of work** document.

Scope of work: Outlines the parameters of a client assignment, such as the type of work to be done, required deliverables and deadlines. If the scope of work is ill-defined, it could result in scope creep or unhappy clients or wasted efforts.

A scope of work document serves to define the initial stages of an engagement and particularly focuses on agency **deliverables**—what the agency will deliver at the end of the project or campaign. This provides a broad-based understanding of the services the agency will provide for the client. For example, let's say a client engaged your agency to develop their

Deliverables: The products and services an agency produces and delivers to a client often as components of a larger project.

social media strategy. The scope of work would outline what that entails. For example, it might include five deliverables as part of the engagement:

1. A content analysis of competitor social media pages and a formal report of the results
2. A content strategy plan outlining the categories of content the client should post and key brand messages

3. A sample timeline of social media posts for 1 month
4. A creative design template for three social media pages: Instagram, Facebook, and Twitter
5. A measurement plan for how the client should measure results

Notice the scope of work does not include executing the social media plan for the client. Outlining the scope of work lets the client know what the agency will deliver, as well as what the agency won't deliver. The document would also include the deadline for the work, the budget for the deliverables, any materials needed and key components that will be included in the process (e.g., client meetings, creative briefs, etc.).

Typically, the scope of work will be a first step generated in support of the larger marketing plan and/or a creative brief. Once the scope of work is developed and approved by the client, the next step is to develop a client contract.

Contracts with clients are an important part of the business of running an agency. They establish what each party will do, specify the deliverables exchanged and provide a legal agreement to refer to should there be any disagreements down the road. Contracts are useful for a variety of reasons including invoicing, managing **project scope creep**, and holding one another accountable. The contract should also address fees, contingencies, terms for completion, and the scope of work. Client contracts can range from a simple, single-page document to a multistage, comprehensive brief. Again, it depends upon the scope of the work and other relevant, situation-specific contracting rules. It is NOT recommended that any client work be started without a contract (Box 4.2).

Project scope creep: When the client engages the student agency to accomplish a specific task but ultimately requests more work be completed without compensation or consideration of hours and resources required to complete the additional tasks. A client contract helps alleviate these issues before they become problematic.

Box 4.2   Sample Client Contract

Client: _____

Account Executive: _____

Contract Period Start: _____ End: _____

The client hereby appoints AGENCY as a (public relations/advertising/strategic communications) consultant. The agency accepts the appointment and agrees to perform the services specified below according to the terms of this agreement.

Below is the project the client has requested the agency to undertake. (If any project has to be completed by a specified deadline, specify mm/dd/yy below). Initial_____

AGENCY is not responsible for the distribution of materials or personal fundraising on behalf of the client (e.g., posters, solicitation of business) unless arrangements are made between the client and firm staff. Initial_____

The agency will plan, develop, and execute public relations and publicity tactics with the understanding that before the release of any materials and/or services provided, the agency will submit materials to the client for specific prior approval. Initial_____

The firm president must approve all project(s) beyond those requested in this contract. Initial_____

The client is solely responsible for the purchase or reimbursement of outside or out-of-pocket expenses relating to the services requested (e.g. printing costs, binders, postage, and mileage). AGENCY will always consult the client before any financial transactions are made. Initial_____

The client reserves the right to cancel or reject the plans or schedules after they have been approved, but, in such an event, the client assumes the agency's liability for expenses or costs involved in the preparation of such canceled projects, but only on plans which have prior client approval. Initial_____

AGENCY also has the right to terminate this contract before the contract length/period is over if the client is not cooperative and willing to participate in activities needed to complete the project requested. Initial_____

AGENCY agrees to return client phone calls and emails within 24 hours of contact with the expectation that the client will return AGENCY contact within 24 hours. Initial_____

Clients will be asked to evaluate the services and satisfaction of the services provided by AGENCY via survey. Initial_____

(Continued)

(Continued)

Billing Rates: For Profit

A. Press Release Writing: $55/hour
B. Media Relations: $35/hour
C. Social Media: $30/hour
D. Website Design and Programming: $35/hour
E. Consulting and Marketing Plans: $55/hour
F. Layout Design (Print Materials): $50/hour
G. Photography and Videography: $50/hour
H. Script Writing: $55/hour
I. Video Direction: $255/hour
J. Client Research: $35/hour

**Nonprofit Rate: 30% Discount   Initial____

Thank you for choosing our agency. We look forward to this project and future projects with you.

Signatures constitute the entire understanding of this contract between AGENCY and the client.

Client: _____ Firm Director: _____
Account Executive: _____ Firm President: _____

Staffing the Account Team

With an approved scope of work document, you can match the needs of the client with agency members who can meet those needs. Depending on the structure of your agency, you'll want to have a lead communicator to serve as the primary liaison between the client and the agency. Then, other team members will help manage and carry out the work.

When staffing an account, think in terms of four qualities: strategic or tactical capabilities, student interests and values, client fit, and team fit. In addition, if you have a wide range of class ranks in your agency, mix senior-level team members with first- or second-year students just starting out. This allows the younger students to learn and develop from the more seasoned juniors and seniors.

Let's take a client scenario as an example of how you might staff an account. Imagine you have just won the business of a local sporting goods store. The scope of work focuses primarily on two things: conducting research with store customers and developing a subsequent social media strategy to engage customer interests. In addition to the client liaison, you've decided this account will require four team members based on the workload.

In terms of strategic or tactical capabilities, you'll first want a team member with strong research abilities. To fill this need, you look at students who have taken one or more research courses or have conducted surveys for other agency accounts in the past.

Next, you'll need a student with experience in developing a social strategy. Looking through student resumes, you find a student who was responsible for social media content in his summer internship. That's a good fit.

With two team members assigned, you need two more. You learn that a junior who worked in the agency last semester is on the women's basketball team. Bingo. This is a team member who can speak the client's language. Her knowledge of sports will also be helpful in developing survey questions and social content relevant to the target audience.

One more team member to go. In looking through student resumes, you spot a sophomore who has expressed a strong desire to learn about social media strategy. That seems like a good fit. However, you remember her interest is in nonprofit work and she currently volunteers with an environmental organization. Maybe she is better suited for one of your two nonprofit accounts. You recall another first-year student who has little experience, but the team leader was impressed with her eagerness to learn the agency business. Okay, there's a better fit with the team.

And so it goes with the remainder of the accounts to fill. Once you've chosen the account team, you'll need to get them up to speed on the client so they can jump in quickly. This will include background on the organization, the scope of work, contact information, and any other information you have on client members.

The First Account Team Meeting

The first account team meeting is one in which most of the follow-on work will be determined. Therefore, communication is essential. The account team meeting is very important to maintaining workflow among the team and ensuring a clear division of labor, accountability, and assignment of tasks. The account team is the most vital single unit contributing to the success of your work. For the first meeting, all members of the account team should be present and the AE or another client point of contact should clearly explain client expectations. If further research is warranted, the first meeting is an excellent place to delegate this. Similarly, if more creative work, specialized copy, websites, or other output is desired, now is the time to inform the creative team. The AE should serve as a facilitator for these assignments but ultimately each member of the account team will set their own schedule and report to the AE.

It is also helpful to develop a team culture in your first team meeting. Set rules and guidelines for how you will work together. Determine how often you will meet, where and when. Spend some time getting to know each other and the strengths and experiences of each student. You want to build a comfort level between team members that everyone is being heard, that you value each team member's contributions and that you trust members to do their best work in a timely manner (see Chapter 10 for more information on working in teams).

MOVING WORK THROUGH THE AGENCY

One of the most challenging aspects of delivering quality client work is managing project workflow. Every agency should have a process for involving the right people at the right time to get the work done on deadline. From preliminary planning and staffing, through preparation, final editing, approval, and implementation there are multiple tools that can be used to help your agency keep clients happy while doing quality work.

How are workflow processes developed? Much depends on the organizational structure of your agency. Some agencies are account executive-centric where all client work is triggered, managed, and approved via an account executive. As discussed in earlier chapters, this arrangement works for small to medium firms. In other organizations, the work is less centralized with account directors, creative directors, and specialty teams all playing a role in ensuring work is completed on behalf of various accounts in accordance with the deadlines, resources, and needs of the clients and the agency. This arrangement works for small to medium firms with a high level of outsourcing or third-party work as well as larger firms with multiple, competing deadlines.

In agencies that have established departments—such as the account team, the creative team, and specialty teams like branding, social media, or media relations—workflow becomes much more complex. This is true not only for student agencies but also for professional agencies. One of the biggest breakdowns in agency communication occurs between the creative and account teams. Creative teams often feel they are in the dark about the larger scope of the project, or don't have the necessary information and materials to complete a project. Conversely, account teams are frustrated when a creative project comes back that does not fit what they felt they had communicated. For this reason, it is critical to develop workflow and communication processes both within a team and between different departments or teams.

Typically, agencies will have three types of agency members involved in client projects: project managers, producers, and agency leadership. Project managers take charge of the master client plan, coordinate all the different agency resources needed to fulfill the plan, make sure work adheres to agency standards and client needs, develop and distribute documentation on the project, and ensure that the project comes in on budget and on time. In smaller agencies, this person might have the role of account executive. In larger agencies, the project manager could be called a team leader or account supervisor.

Producers are agency members who actually produce the work in the client plan. This could include account executives who write news releases, coordinate events, or develop social media content. It could include creative producers who develop websites, design ad campaigns, or film videos. And, producers can also involve specialty tacticians, such as media relations specialists, copywriters, or digital media experts. Producers might all work within one team, or for different agency functions or departments and report to different managers. For example, graphic designers might report to a creative director. Social content creators might report to a social media manager.

Lastly, agency leadership (e.g., agency directors and advisors) will also play a role carrying out client programs. Leadership may need to be involved in providing guidance or strategic direction for a project, and will likely be involved in approvals along the way.

Agency workflow processes will take into account all three types of responsibilities and provide a system for moving work among and between them. In Box 4.3, we have provided an example of an agency workflow process.

Box 4.3   Sample Workflow Process—(Following Successful Client Pitch for Business)

AE meets with client, successful pitch	Work submitted, internal review	Client pitch prepared for new work	Evaluation
AE meets with team	Copy /Art prepared	Work resubmitted to client	Implementation
Scope of work is created	Creative team engaged	Client approves with changes	Client approves work with no changes
Duties assigned via project brief	Research engaged	Changes implemented	Second client presentation prepared

In addition to mapping out your workflow processes, there are several tools that can be used to make these processes more effective.

Working Brief or Project Brief

There is an old joke, "How do you eat an elephant sandwich?" The answer: "One bite at a time." The working brief breaks down the scope of work into manageable pieces. Recorded on paper or living "live" on a google doc or other cloud-based solution, the working brief can prove to be a valuable asset to project managers and the teams and producers associated with the campaign or project. A working brief serves as a master overview of the program, and should capture as much critical information as necessary to complete specific tasks.

Information in the brief should include client name, a brief description

of the assignment, due dates of the deliverables, specific work that needs to be accomplished, and contact information of the primary account team facilitator. Examples of work that needs to be included in a working brief might also include creative items like photography, websites, and other design elements. In other cases, when you may be doing a PR campaign for example, the working brief should include location of pertinent media lists, media materials (like press releases or Q & As) website URLs, and any other information media pitchers might need. In terms of a social media campaign, there should be chosen social media platforms, specific points per social media channel, graphics or other digital art already available, and a timeline for when social media releases should take place.

Regardless of the type of project, the work brief should also include accountability (who is responsible for what) and budget and billing reports (how many hours are authorized and what are our budgeted expenses).

Creative Briefs

The purpose of a creative brief is to guide the work of the creative team in producing a campaign or project for a client. A creative brief will outline the logistics of the project, and give details such as the project format, deadlines, and budget. Most importantly, a creative brief provides insights into the target audience, the client brand and personality, and what the campaign needs to achieve. For example, does the campaign need to build awareness of a client or brand? Change public attitudes about a particular issue? Encourage them to engage with a brand in new ways?

A compelling creative brief will inspire the creative team to do their best work, while providing them with the parameters they need to work within. For example, does the campaign need to include certain messages or use a select color scheme? That information should go in the brief. The brief should also outline the tone of the brand message. This lets the creative team know if they can use humor or cultural trends in their productions, or if they need to be more professional and straight-laced. Creative briefs should be just that, brief, while giving the creative team the direction needed to please the client and address the problem or opportunity. A sample creative/campaign brief is included in Box 4.4.

Box 4.4   Creative/Campaign Brief
TITLE
DATE
VERSION

Background
What is the issue we are facing? Why are we even considering communication plans? What is happening with our clients' business necessitating the need to communicate with our target? What is the competition doing? What is driving the need for the client to do this campaign/tactic?

Assignment
What specifically are we doing? What kinds of media are we considering? What communications delivery vehicles ought to be addressed? How is this supporting our client's overall Marketing and Communications Strategy? How does it align with brand identity, brand history, current or future marketing activity, and short- and long-term business goals? How will our effectiveness be judged?

Communications objectives/outcomes
What is the goal of this campaign? Awareness? Sales increase? Customer traffic? Attitude? Usage shift? How will we know if our campaign meets these goals? How are we going to measure it? How often? How will we know if we are successful?

Who are we speaking with?
Demographics? Primary audience vs. secondary? Geography etc.?

How do they think or act now?
Psychographics? How do they act? Where do they go? What do they do? What do they think of our client/product/service? How can we speak to their human truth?

What do we want them to think/act?
What will people do when they see our campaign? How will they think or feel?

What is the single most important thing to communicate?
One message!!!—Avoid "and's" and ";" and "—"

Why will people believe us
Rationale reasons to believe—the facts.
Emotional reasons to believe—the intangibles, the emotion, the human truth!

Considerations/thought starters/helpful hints
What do you know that might help? Does the client have an idea what they want to see? Have they suggested competitive entities to review to combat or emulate? Should the creative team review last year's campaign, etc.?

Mandatories
What has to be in the campaign? Logo's, taglines, legal marks, call to action, URL?

Timing
Basic timing (not to replace a real timeline). When do we need to review internally? When is the first client meeting? When is the launch date?

Status Reports

Simply put, a status report shows where you are in the process of completing the project, what has been completed and/or approved, and what will be coming up for consideration the following week. Think of a status report like your weekly planner and to-do list. What took place or was completed this week that you can check off the list (e.g., conducted photo shoot at a trade show), and what needs to go on the to-do list for the next week (e.g., second photo shoot scheduled for 2/17). You'll also want to outline any issues you might be having with the project or what you'll need from the client to complete the next phase of the work. Include hard dates for delivery of project elements (final photos to the client by 2/20) and approvals needed (need client approval by 2/26).

Depending on the client and the work, status reports can be burdensome or incredibly helpful. The key is deciding what methodology works best for the client and for the team. For example, the client may want reports "every Thursday afternoon before 3:30." Therefore, the team should ensure all inputs are in earlier that day so the AE or another appointed representative has some time to prepare the report and send it on. Spend some time, early in campaign planning, with both the client and the team(s) to ensure the methodology for reporting to the client is agreed upon, established, and will be adhered to throughout the duration of the campaign.

It is also helpful to use the same format for your status reports from week to week. You can do so by developing a status report template, and then simply fill in the blanks each week. In this way, the client becomes familiar with the format and knows what to look for. It also distinguishes the status report from other emails or communication the client might receive from you.

Traffic Managers

Advertising agencies, or other agencies with creative teams, often employ traffic managers to shepherd work through the agency. Traffic managers work on the production end of the agency to manage the workflow and scheduling of multiple projects and due dates.

Let's say for example you are creating a digital advertising campaign for a client. There are several moving parts to a project like this. You'll need initial client input, team meetings to discuss the project, photography or other visuals, someone to write the copy, layout the ads, and make sure the layout and design meet the production parameters and standards from the digital publisher. For each of these components, you'll also have several drafts of the ads and multiple levels of internal and external approvals, as well as a hard deadline for when the ads needs to go to the publisher/producer.

What could go wrong? One example, if the photo shoot isn't completed by the designated date it will hold up the ability to produce the other components of the ads on time. Or, if the client doesn't approve the copy in time, the designer can't determine how much space she has for visuals. Traffic managers create schedules and workflows to manage all these moving parts and make sure each phase of production is delivered and approved on deadline.

For agencies with only one or two client projects or campaigns per semester, the job of trafficking a project is often managed by the account executive. However, imagine your agency has six account teams, all with similar projects for the creative team. This is where a traffic manager is most beneficial. He or she will develop master schedules for all creative projects and make sure the flow of work is spaced out so as not to overwhelm the creative team with multiple projects at the same time.

Shared Agency Drives

Student agencies are unique from professional agencies in that agency **turnover**—how often agency members leave the organization—is much higher. Your agency may be taught as a class where a new set of students enters the organization each semester. Or, your agency

> **Turnover:** The rate at which student members leave the agency and are replaced by new members.

may turnover staff members every year. This means you'll need to be particularly vigilant in keeping client records. This is especially true with agency-of-record clients where the agency may be working for the same client for several semesters, or even years.

You'll want to develop a system for sharing and archiving semester plans, client reports, creative materials, social media passwords, and so on, so that account knowledge can be efficiently shared between account team members and departments, and subsequently passed on to the next team of agency members. Options for archiving work include the following: Google docs or other online archiving service where information is stored "in the cloud"; hard copy printouts of work (hardly the most optimal in this day and age but possibly important for exceptionally creative or proprietary work); portable jump drives or removable hard drives; or shared intranet drives set up by your university's technology department. In all cases, the work should be organized by client. Optimally the handoff should be done with incoming individuals face-to-face if possible.

INTERNAL AGENCY COMMUNICATIONS

In addition to process workflow, agencies should develop processes for effective internal communications within the agency. Elements to consider include communications flow, communications channels, communications load, and communications activities that support a learning organization.

Communications Flow

Communications flow describes the direction in which message move through the agency. Effective organizations ensure messages are flowing in three directions: top-down (from leadership to members), bottom-up (from members to agency leadership), and side-to-side (between agency teams and members).

In many organizations, communication becomes "top heavy" with most messages flowing from management to workers with very little opportunities for bottom-up or side-to-side communication. With few bottom-up communications opportunities, agency members may feel ignored, taken for granted or feel their voices aren't heard. In addition, agency management might be missing important opportunities to get valuable information and feedback from agency members. Likewise, fewer opportunities for side-to-side communications limit your ability to share important workflow information between members and learn from each other. Too often in student agencies (and in professional agencies, too), account or creative teams become siloed, never communicating with agency members outside their teams. Not only does this prevent the sharing of information, it is also detrimental to agency culture.

Conversely, some agencies may have issues in the other direction—lots of upward communication flow but very little flow from management down to other members of the agency. This can make team members feel in the dark about the agency's progress and abilities, and can cause a loss of trust in agency leadership.

Agencies should assess their communications to make sure messages are flowing in all directions. Do agency members have opportunities to communicate with leadership and voice their concerns or suggestions? If not, you need to create better flow in an upward direction. Are members able to share information between teams and have opportunities to get to know each other? If not, work on side-to-side communications flow. Find ways to build agency culture by creating no-pressure activities where members can converse with each other. This might include serving free pizza in the agency on certain days of the week, or creating more formal communications opportunities like mentoring programs and team-to-team sharing.

Internal Communications Channels

Communications channels refer to the mediums being used to communicate messages within the agency. When teams become busy with client work, the default is often to use email for all communications. While this can be effective in exchanging information, it does little to communicate tone, enthusiasm, or other emotions, and doesn't help agency members build trusted relationships.

In organizational communications, communications mediums are often categorized as either synchronous or asynchronous. **Synchronous channels** are those that "create the sense that all participants are concurrently engaged in the communications event" (Carlson & George, 2004, p. 291). Synchronous channels include face-to-face meetings, telephone conversations, and live chats on mediums such as Facebook. **Asynchronous channels** are those in which there is a delay in response (such as email) and no opportunity for instant feedback.

Synchronous channels: Channels of communication that provide for immediate exchange or interactivity from those participating. Face-to-face meetings or phone calls are examples.

Asynchronous channels: Describes channels of communications for which there are no opportunities for immediate feedback. Email is a good example.

From their study on channel synchronicity and job satisfaction, Cho, Ramgolam, Schaefer, and Sandlin (2011) recommend that organizations employ a diversity of communications channels, with a fair amount of face-to-face meetings to improve organizational identification. While no agency wants to be bogged down with endless meetings, it is recommended agency staff meet weekly to ensure communication is consistent and that members have the ability to provide instant feedback. Occasionally, it may also be necessary for account or creative teams to have twice or three times weekly meetings or in some extreme cases daily meetings. This will likely be the case when campaigns are on deadline and about to launch.

It's also worth noting that phone calls can often eliminate the excessive back and forth communication that happens with email. Remember that your smartphone is not just a way to text; it actually is a phone, too. A 5-minute chat on the phone with a client or team member can accomplish so much more than a day of emailing back and forth.

In addition to meetings and phone calls, assess other ways you are communicating with and between agency members. Are you using a diversity of communications channels? Or are you relying on one more than others. Also consider the amount of communication flowing through the agency. Too little communication and members will be left in the dark. Too much and they will feel overwhelmed. Make sure communications are consistent, frequent, and synchronous without overloading members with agency messages.

Creating a Learning Organization

In his book *The Fifth Discipline* (2006), Peter Senge introduced the idea of the "Learning Organization." From his perspective, learning organizations are

> . . .organizations where people continually expand their capacity to create the results they truly desire, where new and expansive patterns of thinking are nurtured, where collective aspiration is set free, and where people are continually learning how to learn together. (Senge, 2006, p. 3)

What better place to create a learning organization than in the student-run agency? While the biggest benefit of student agency experience is the hands-on work executed for real clients, agencies can provide a variety of ways to increase the capacity for learning.

Many student agencies practice continual learning by inviting guest speakers to address best practices or other professional issues. Maybe the advertising agency down the road talks about new developments in digital media planning. Perhaps a reporter from the local newspaper or television station provides recommendations on the best way to pitch a story. Or, the corporate communications director of the local United Way could give a presentation on efficient fundraising efforts.

One of the best ways to become a learning organization is by truly collaborating with a professional agency to explore market developments and exchange mutual ideas. For example, student agency Live Oak Communications partnered with a content marketing firm to collaborate on client projects and explore new ways of reaching Millennial audiences. The program, called Project ECHO, includes educational sessions with industry professionals as well as joint brainstorms and client collaboration.

Lastly, agency members can learn from each other when the agency creates opportunities for side-to-side communication. Think of the internship experiences that could be shared between members, the "lessons learned" from client mistakes, or the ideas generated from intergroup brainstorms. Not only do these types of activities increase student learning, but also help the agency continually grow and increase its capacity to be a cutting-edge organization.

Agency Resource Library

Another useful tool for a learning organization is to maintain an agency resource library. In addition to utilizing the best practices outlined in this text, resource libraries provide students with reference materials on a wide range of topics pertaining to the agency business. If you have the funds and the space, you can purchase books and trade publications to keep in your agency office. If funding is scarce, consider looking through your library databases and creating a list of reference materials and online resources for agency members to access.

Table 4.1 is a recommended categorical list of books or publications to keep in your resource library.

Table 4.1   Resource Library Recommendations

Resource Library Recommendations	
Branding and/or Brand Positioning	Client Management
Media Law and/or Advertising Law	Digital/Social Media
Creative Thinking and Brainstorming	Communications Design
Search Engine Optimization	Media Relations
Media Analytics	Crisis Communications
Nonprofit Communications	Business Ethics
Qualitative and Quantitative Research Methods	Copywriting and/or Promotional Writing
Public Relations Writing	PR News
Advertising Age (aka AdAge)	Advertising Week (aka AdWeek)

MEASURING FOR SUCCESS

When measuring success there are two metrics that are most important. How successful were the students in the process and consequently, how successful was the agency as a whole? How do you know if your student agency is successful? Agency success depends on many factors. First and foremost, student agencies are successful when they deliver great results for their clients. Important in this process is the use of

360-degree feedback which provides the student (and the faculty advisor) a comprehensive picture of the students' efforts based on multiple input sources.

> **360-degree feedback:** A process in which agency members are evaluated on their work by peers, direct reports, and supervisors.

If you've taken a PR or advertising campaigns course, you know the last step in any campaign is measuring how well the program did in achieving your campaign goals. In Chapter 8, we discuss campaign/program evaluation in detail.

But measuring campaign or program success is only part of the equation. The success of your agency also depends on client satisfaction with your agency's people and processes, how smoothly your processes worked to deliver client programs, the learning benefits students gained from their agency experiences, the effectiveness of agency leadership, and, often, whether your academic department or dean is pleased with the agency.

In Chapter 13, we discuss in detail ways to measure client satisfaction and student performance. Measurement tools can be distributed through formal online or paper surveys, or information can be gathered more informally through client or agency meetings, or discussions with department heads.

Regardless of how you gather measurement information, you'll want to keep records of the agency's progress and include any issues for improvement in the next semester's plans. The goal of any measurement plan should be to identify areas where you are doing well and pinpoint areas for improvement so you can continually make the necessary changes to move your agency and its members to the next level.

CONCLUSION

Agency processes can make or break a student organization's long-term existence. The disciplines and systems in place to manage accounts, satisfy clients, evaluate progress, and determine outcomes are critical to the agency management process.

When done correctly, agency processes should be in place from the beginning to the end of the student engagement. From research to execution to evaluation, the student agency should have understood practices available to everyone.

As we have seen, throughout this chapter, steps for onboarding clients, selecting students, onboarding students, managing workflow, evaluating client progress, and managing productivity are all important things that need to be standardized and taught at all levels.

Following those steps, there also should be a strong evaluation process in place to ensure things are learned, best practices are developed, and mistakes are NOT repeated.

As in every organization, no set of processes fits all organizations. Sizes of organizations, firm core competencies and client requirements/demands will all have an impact on student processes.

Finally, agency processes should be recorded and passed on to other generations of the student agency to permit evolution and refinement of processes, geared toward increasing efficiencies. If the basic processes are recorded and routinely enforced, it increases the ability for a better quality of creative and execution strategies to be developed.

REVIEW AND DISCUSSION QUESTIONS

1. You have narrowed down your selection for a paid leadership role in your agency to two students for one position. One of the students is highly accomplished in many areas with good competence. She is also very involved in the university community and has many beneficial connections in leadership roles within the student body. Her active schedule has many demands on her time.

   The other student is passionate about her craft and has some truly unique skills in the creation of digital media—something your agency has identified as a need. But she also works 20 to 30 hours per week and has been very clear about some other nonstudent, non-work-related responsibilities that may hinder her ability to respond to evolving situations with the agency.

   Given these two choices, whom do you hire and why?

2. In your weekly meeting, one client team reports they are still awaiting client approval for a script. The deadline for the advertising production team is Tuesday. What steps can you take to get this project moving?

3. When preparing a scope of work document, what are some things you must ensure you have in the document?

4. In the initial meetings and client contract, a definitive scope of work is defined and agreed upon. But halfway through the semester, the client keeps asking for more deliverables and additional work. You have not budgeted time or billable hours for this extra work. How do you handle this situation?

5. You have a hardworking, brilliant graphic artist working for you in the agency this semester. The only problem is, they are SLOW, causing the workflow to back up and even miss some deadlines. What can you do to utilize their talents and get production back on track?

6. The creative brief is complete and the team is excited about getting started. But there is a hiccup in the target audience section. You, as the agency director, feel that the client and the team are missing a key demographic. You are convinced you need to tell the team and the client of this oversight. How do you prepare for these two, separate conversations?

7. It is client evaluation time when the client will discuss what they like and did not like about their experience this semester. You feel confident that the overall evaluation will be positive but you are certain that one or two team members may be singled out for poor performance. How do you handle this situation?

8. You and your team are coming up on a hard deadline for a media availability and so far, the client has not approved your messaging—though you feel like they will, based on earlier conversations. The client is also not returning emails and you suspect they are out of town based on earlier conversations. Discuss your options and your actions.

9. The client reviews your work and has some recommendations that you think are seriously off target from the original creative brief. How do you handle these comments and what do you recommend as a solution?
10. It is time to start turning over files for the next semester. What are some things you are sure you must have from the retiring team in order to put the oncoming team on a good footing? List them in order of priority.

REFERENCES AND ADDITIONAL READINGS

Burgoyne, E. (2013). *Ad agency processes and roadmap. AdSubculture.* Retrieved from https://static1.squarespace.com/static/4fd3b8ab84aefc97b18a645f/t/52d8430ee4b093afad199ddc/1389904654530/Ad_Agency_Process_2.01.pdf

Burgoyne, E. (2015). *Understanding agile: The big "A" and the small "a." AdSubculture.* Retrieved from http://adsubculture.com/workflow/2015/8/21/understanding-agile-the-big-a-and-the-small-a

Carlson, J. R., & George, J. F. (2004). Media appropriateness in the conduct and discovery of deceptive communication: The relative influence of richness and synchronicity. *Group Decision and Negotiation, 13*, 191–210.

Cho, J., Ramgolam, D. I., Schaefer, K. M., & Sandlin, A. N. (2011). The rate and delay in overload: An investigation of communication overload and channel synchronicity on identification and job satisfaction. *Journal of Applied Communication Research, 39*(1), 38–54.

Dickson, D. (2009). *The new account manager: Redefining the critical role of account service in the changing business of advertising* (2nd ed.). Chicago, IL: The Copy Workshop.

Schockley-Zalaback, P. (2015). *Fundamentals of organizational communication.* Saddle River, NJ: Pearson.

Senge, P. (2006). *The fifth discipline: The art & practice of the learning organization.* New York, NY: Doubleday.

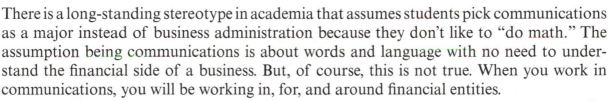

The Business Side of Communications

There is a long-standing stereotype in academia that assumes students pick communications as a major instead of business administration because they don't like to "do math." The assumption being communications is about words and language with no need to understand the financial side of a business. But, of course, this is not true. When you work in communications, you will be working in, for, and around financial entities.

If you plan to work on the client side, you will be expected to comprehend and contribute to the company's **bottom line**. And, when clients hire communications agencies, they seek out agencies that can spend their marketing dollars effectively, providing an adequate return on their investment (ROI). Even if you are working for nonprofit clients, those organizations need to bring in enough donations to keep their nonprofits going, pay their staff members, and be able to afford the important resources they provide to their constituents. The media industry itself, with which agencies work, is a business.

> **Bottom line:** Accounting terminology that describes net profits at the end of a billing cycle. Shorthand for AGI (see definition on page 109).

Ask any owner of an agency or anyone who works for a professional agency, and they will tell you, first and foremost, an agency is a business. While the purpose of the agency is to provide communications services for clients, the end result should be to make a profit. Without profit, the agency doesn't exist. As such, agency members need to have a business-oriented perspective of how their work contributes to the financial performance of both the agency and its clients (Beachboard & Weidman, 2013, p. 33). With all that said, we often do a poor job teaching students the "business side" of communications—in our classes and in student-run agencies (see, e.g., Bush & Miller, 2011). In fact, when asked what they were missing in their student agency experience, graduates most often cite business-related issues such as learning about agency cost structures, creating budgets and estimates, manage the billing process, and understanding a profit and loss statement (Bush, Haygood, & Vincent, 2016). Once graduates have worked in the field, they realize the importance of this knowledge to their positions.

While the aim of your student agency will not likely be to make a profit, you will be creating estimates for clients, developing agency budgets, invoicing clients for expenses, and working within the financial parameters set by your university or department. This is the perfect opportunity to practice business-oriented thinking. In this chapter, you learn

- How an agency does business
- Ways an agency makes money
- How to estimate projects, budget, bill, and make financial arrangements with clients to get paid

THE BASICS

What do we mean when we say an agency is a business?

So, your agency is moving along in its planning stages. You have a good idea of what your mission is going to be. You know what kind of clients you want. You have figured out a leadership model. Now, it is time to manage the business of your agency. This challenge involves answering questions about how you will sustain yourself and continue to operate. Let's start with some fundamentals.

The agency model is like many other consulting services (accounting, law, even some manufacturing) (Figure 5.1).

1. Needs come in from clients (please help me raise awareness for my new product, please help me improve my reputation, please help me restore good feelings about my company, etc.).

2. Solutions are designed and built by a team of experts (ad campaign, public relations [PR] campaign, integrated marketing campaign, new branding, a logo, an event, etc.).

3. Client provides feedback on the solutions proposed.

Figure 5.1   The consulting services pathway to profits.

4. Modifications are made to creative or scope of work.
5. Client approves the modifications.
6. The solutions are implemented by you and your team (advertisements designed, produced and placed/purchased, events are planned and executed, corporate social responsibility obligations are realized, specialty promotions are designed and implemented, crisis PR plan is delivered, social media program is launched, etc.).
7. Evaluations are made and solutions are recommended based on what you set out to accomplish.
8. Results are presented to the client.

9. The client is pleased, the client is billed for the work.
10. The agency gets paid.

In this system architecture, the hope is that at the end of the engagement you get a happy client and you get paid. However, you may encounter some roadblocks or detours along the way that impact this outcome, and often it can come down to payment.

How do you manage these steps? How you steer your agency can make all the difference in whether an agency can live or die, thrive, or starve.

Agency Money Management 101

Let's start with a metaphor. If you imagine an agency's business profile as a robust welcoming campfire, you as the keeper of that fire have certain responsibilities. You want that fire to provide light and heat and be an asset to all of those seeking illumination and warmth. You don't want the fire to ever burn out. In fact, you may well want to make the fire larger and brighter so more can benefit from its existence.

And as any good camper knows, the key to keeping that fire burning is balancing the amount of fuel you have to expend over time. Your challenge, as a manager of our metaphorical fire or, in the real world, your agency, is to balance the depletion of the firewood with the energy and time needed to get more.

Think of the firewood you go out and gather to feed the flame as **revenue**. You spend time and energy gathering that wood so you can put it in the fire and generate more heat and warmth. However, at the same time, the wood, once it is put on the fire, is no longer future fuel but is actually being consumed by

Revenue: Money coming in to an agency.

Expenses: Monies paid to keep an agency working.

the flames. The absence of that wood is called **expenses**. Your challenge, as the keeper of the flame, is to maximize revenue while minimizing expenses, using up your finite resources in the best ways possible to get the most heat and light from the fire.

Switching to reality, what you need to do when managing an agency is to ensure you have a clear path toward gathering revenue, an efficient process for consuming that revenue in a way which maximizes effectiveness, and a sustainable rhythm that allows progress and growth for all involved. This is called having a positive **revenue stream** and it is very important because, for the most part, the larger the fire, the more opportunities you will have to shine

Revenue streams: Sources of the revenue.

brightly and show the world how wonderful your firm is. Larger firms also have more opportunities to pursue larger clients and to attract top-shelf talent.

Financial Terminology

While that was an overly simplistic illustration, it is germane to the discussion of how you manage your expenses in the business of running an agency. Burn through them too fast and your fire is cold and dead. Following is a discussion of some terms you may encounter in your day-to-day operations. Among the items discussed in this area of the business are expenses, revenue, **profit sources**, **core competencies**, and **billable hours**.

Like in our campfire analogy, expenses are what an entity pays to continue to operate—to keep the flames of creativity and industry burning. In some accounting circles, expenses can be interchanged with **liabilities** (what costs I as an agency am liable for before I can show a profit).

Commonly in the industry of agencies there are two categories of expenses. These are usually termed **hard costs** and **soft costs**. Hard costs are things like **payroll costs** (what everyone who works at your agency gets paid), **benefits** (healthcare, retirement savings, etc.—not usually something a student agency encounters), and **overhead** (rent, utilities, equipment, and other things the agency must spend money on to survive and thrive).

Hard costs can also represent other items like capabilities funds. For example, perhaps you want to enhance your selection of tools you can use to solve client challenges. So, you may want to invest internally in something like media relations database software, video editing hardware, social media analytics (like Talkwalker™ or its equivalent), memberships to various websites for stock footage, graphic applications, etc. These are nonspecific hard costs in that they are not tied to a specific client but rather represent an expansion of general client service capabilities.

Soft costs are those things you might do or monies you might spend, specifically for a client like printing, postage, project-based hiring of a subject matter expert, etc. (A good way to differentiate hard costs from soft costs is that soft costs

Profit sources: Where profitable **revenue** comes from (clients, investments, sale of assets).

Core competencies: What an organization or entity does well or is known for doing well.

Billable hours: Hours that a worker completes that can be transferred to specific client accounts, that is, Sherri had 45 billable hours last week for client XYZ. This metric is often used to measure individual productivity and is commonly part of a comparison of what the individual was paid for that same time period. This metric can also be used to conduct side by side comparisons of employees in terms of productivity. Salaries are not usually directly linked to productivity, however.

Liabilities: See hard costs. What an agency owes/pays in order to stay in business.

Hard costs: What you have to pay to stay in business. Often contrasted with soft costs which are traditionally more flexible.

Soft costs: Monies spent by an agency in terms of a specific client or clients.

Payroll costs: A subset of personnel costs, payroll costs describe what it costs an agency to pay someone.

Benefits: What employees are paid in addition to money in the form of discounts, healthcare, retirement, other tangible benefits that do not necessarily include the transfer of cash.

Overhead: Part of what an agency has to pay to do business, see **hard costs**. May include rent, utilities, furniture, and so on.

would likely not be spent if it were not for a specific client). Soft costs can also include **business development expenses**. These expenses are what you spend to secure clients and can include the investment(s) you make in terms of spec/pro-bono work that is done for a client or to "get in the door" with a future prospect. As the adage goes, "sometimes you have to spend money to make money."

For example, say a new account has opened up for a client who manufactures recreational fishing boats. Soft costs for this new business pursuit might include sending someone to attend a boat show where the potential client was participating, developing some creative collateral material for your **pitch** to win the client and/or perhaps engaging a professional angler for a day of research, "picking their brain" about the state of the industry, the quality of the fishing boats, and so on, to better develop your talking points for that new business presentation.

Said another way, expenses are what agencies pay to survive, thrive, find new business, and win it.

In a perfect world, expenses create the infrastructure and the pathway to find revenue-producing engagements, and expenses are always covered by revenue. However, this is not always the case. Often agencies will take a loss or go "in the hole" by authorizing more on expenses short term than they will make in revenue, short term. The idea is, if we invest now, on the **front end**, we may win the business and see more revenue on the **back end**. As your agency ages and grows, however, hopefully there will be lesser need to overspend or "break even" and more of an opportunity to keep a **positive cash flow**, expanding the campfire.

Balancing Revenue and Expenses

In contrast to expenses, revenue is what the agency earns from its efforts. Revenue is of great importance to an agency in offsetting expenses and ensuring the firm's existence. Revenue is also called **receivables** or **assets**,

Business development expenses: Monies and time dedicated to acquiring new clients for an agency.

Pitch: The act of proposing to a client that you work together on a project or ad campaign.

Front end: A term that describes the beginning of a transactional relationship that often includes start-up costs. For example, an agency that is entering into a new relationship with a client may have start-up costs of additional travel, perhaps some space rental, new hires, and so on.

Back end: The net gain for an agency once work is completed. Commonly used with the term front end. Say an agency lost money on the front end servicing a client but it ended up in a profit once all the work was completed by the agency. That would be a profit on the backend.

Positive cash flow/positive revenue stream: Having money/profit to invest or use for development or decompress some salaries, and so on.

Receivables: Receivables are monies owed to you. Receivables and assets are two big factors in describing the financial health of an agency.

Assets: Assets are items of value that you have control over.

depending upon your accountant and/or accounting software programs. Revenues are a very important detail for tracking the **financial health**, **growth potential**, and overall size of your agency. Keeping an eye on this category of the business and contrasting it often with your expense figures can make the difference between a great year and a bad one (a **profitable year** or a **loss year**). And while there are several categories of billings (**gross billings**, **pretax billings**, **posttax billings**, etc.), the term is largely self-explanatory because commonly advertising and PR agencies make most or all of their revenue via gross billings as opposed to **investments** or other financial instruments.

The billing metrics are extremely important because the health of the agency depends upon how these variables are managed/planned for. We will talk in more detail about billing and how to do it later in the chapter. But consider this, your agency loses a paying client for whatever reason. Missing **target goals**, or the smaller goals needed to achieve your larger financial goals, will impact future revenues and change the **ratio of revenue to expenses**.

In most cases, because of this shortfall, an adjustment to expenses might be warranted. If you are watching these changes, and make the adjustments quickly (in rates of spending/expenses perhaps), the consequences may be less painful and less impactful to the overall health of the organization and those who work there.

Similarly, if expenses are too high due to that lost client or failure to take a shrewd enough look at the agency bottom line, the revenue may not be able to keep up and the organization will suffer. For example, you have identified a potential need to hire another employee to handle a specific client who contributes $X of revenue to your

Financial health: How profitable and sustainable a company is. Describes the likelihood of someone doing business with them. Most organizations want to partner with organizations that have strong financial health.

Growth potential: Describes a client's ability to grow in terms of larger market share, more profitability, and so on. Often one of the calculations an agency might use when determining what their fee structure is and/or if they will accept equity in lieu of payment.

Profitable year: When there is positive cash flow at the end of a fiscal year.

Loss year: A year when AGI did not result in a profit.

Gross billings: **Revenues** paid to an agency before taxes, expenses, and other liabilities.

Pretax/pretax billings: money made for work done before taxes are paid (similar to gross profits).

Posttax/posttax billings: Money made for work done after taxes are paid. (similar to net profits.)

Investments: Money that is put aside for growth, typically long term in something or things that show potential to appreciate rather than depreciate. Some examples may include stocks, mutual funds, precious metals, land, or even artwork can sometimes be considered.

Target goals: Smaller goals or targets established as markers to achieving longer term financial goals and business growth.

Ratio of revenue to expenses: Another way of saying, did you make more money than you paid out or did you pay out more money than you made.

bottom line. When you evaluate this new expense of hiring someone against projected revenues for this client, $Y, if $X isn't greater than $Y, you may determine you will actually be losing money by hiring this person. So, you will need to either adjust the fees you are charging the client or find some other way to offset the cost of employing this new person—like perhaps rearranging another employee's workload to accommodate the new client's demands instead of making the hire, or stepping up new business prospecting so a second or third new client's revenues can offset the expenses of the new hire.

Unquestionably, it is better to make these adjustments as soon as they are identified rather than delay. Consider the impact on your agency's reputation and employee morale if in six months you have no choice but to fire the person you just hired because you are losing money on the account you hired them for.

Cash Flow Is King

Another set of terms you might discover while you're establishing the business of your firm involves cash flow. There are two types of cash flow, positive cash flow and **negative cash flow**. Cash flow in general tells you how much **liquidity** you have in your firm and is a quick snapshot of how healthy the firm is or isn't.

In general, positive cash flow tells you that you have some liquidity for investments or **contingencies**, and negative cash flow tells you that you have your revenues tied up in **nonliquid assets**. Get too many nonliquid assets and you run the risk of defaulting on bill payments. Too much in **liquid assets** tells you that you are likely **compressing your payroll**, your ability to work, and so on.

What does cash flow mean for an agency? Positive cash flow means that an agency has money to do what it wants/needs to do in terms of finding new business, hiring new people, offering raises, and so on. Negative cash flow means an agency has tied up all of its revenue in other financial obligations or, more importantly, the agency does not have enough cash to meet future obligations.

Negative cash flow: When an organization owes more than it can pay in cash. Negative cash flows can convert into a credit expense.

Liquidity: A term that describes how much of an agency's holdings can be easily converted into liquid assets.

Liquid assets: Monies that are fluid can be easily converted into cash for any liability of investment.

Contingencies: Unplanned expenses or overages that should be planned for in the event something does not go well.

Nonliquid assets: Assets that cannot be easily converted into liquidity (cash) A good example might be if the agency owned the building it was located in. That would be an asset, certainly, but it would take considerable time to convert it to liquidity, not to mention it would require the agency to move out of its own building.

Compressed payroll: Paying workers less than the market says should be paid. May be done in times of scant resources or in times where the company or organization foregoes awarding raises in favor of other developmental expenses.

It's All About the Numbers

So, how much is too much and how much is too little? Agency consultant Drew McLellan recommends a ratio of 20%:55%:25% (McClellan, 2014) (Figure 5.2). Twenty percent of your revenue should be profit sources, 55% of your revenue should be dedicated to **personnel costs** (salary/wages, benefits, savings plans, etc.), and 25% of your revenue should be spent on overhead (buildings, parking, utilities, etc.). Obviously, you could cut into your profit for a time if you had to, but once you get stuck in a negative cash flow situation—you are running the risk of going under.

Delving further into the workings of those broad categories, profit is the amount of money the agency gets to keep after all expenses and costs are paid. Profit is often broken down into **pretax** and **posttax** or it is often described as **gross profit** versus **net profit**. Meaning that some amount of revenues will have to be dedicated to paying applicable taxes and other obligations (**liabilities**) that will have an impact on the overall number. Talking taxes, most proceeds from an agency are typically subjected to federal, state, and local taxes, so depending upon the applicable tax rate, the pre- and posttax amounts of profit your agency earns can vary widely.

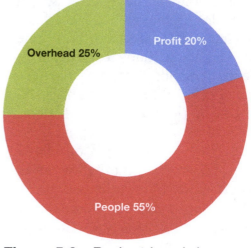

Expense Breakdown for a Typical Agency

Profit 20%

Overhead 25%

People 55%

Figure 5.2   Budget breakdown.

Personnel costs: Payroll costs and benefits including insurance, 401K investments, and so on.

Gross profit/sales: Similar to gross billings, the amount of money an agency is paid prior to taxes, expenses, and **liabilities**.

Net profit: See AGI. It is the money that a financial entity can register as profit after all liabilities are satisfied. Describes a situation where sales figures are specified as profit after expenses are taken out.

Personnel Expenses or Actual Payroll Expense?

While most student agencies will not have payroll expenses, it's an important component to understand for the future. With few exceptions, the largest expense an agency spends is in payroll. Without competent professionals, an agency has very little to leverage and ability to produce profitably. Therefore, it is a very important part of the agency business. However, many business owners make the mistake of calculating only wages as their personnel expenses. In fact, when calculating personnel expenses, you must include vacation pay, insurance (health, long-term disability, short-term disability), retirement plans (401K, pensions, etc.), social security taxes, Medicare taxes, and education/training in addition to wages. You must consider these variables to calculate your actual personnel costs. There are many good software programs out there that can help with calculating true payroll expenses. Once these items are factored in, it is up to you, the business manager, to determine whether to share actual payroll costs with employees. Obviously, it would be in bad form to share employee A's salary/compensation data with Employee B, but sharing a specific employee's compensation data and associated costs with the one who has earned it could be quite instructional for them and you if done correctly.

Overhead is another category that can sometimes frustrate new managers. Overhead figures need to include obvious things like rent and utilities, paid parking (if applicable), and any other fees associated with your building(s). Other pieces of overhead that may not be as obvious include travel expenses, interest paid on equipment loans, cleaning services for your spaces, and expense accounts. For student agencies, it may also be necessary to calculate additional metrics like how much is being paid to the university in overhead costs, and so on.

While we have discussed expenses, it is also important to calculate **income**. Income represents, in large part, the money coming in to the firm. Often this term is correctly interchanged with revenue. However, raw income data tells us very little. Another value growing in popularity for defining an agency's revenue and expenses is the term **AGI** or **Adjusted Gross Income**. Mentioned earlier in the text, AGI is a term very popular with accountants when preparing tax returns, AGI is more precise than gross billings, but less refined than net profit. A simple formula for AGI is

Income: What you make. (See gross income/AGI.)

Adjusted gross income (AGI): Revenue kept by a firm after obligations and liabilities are satisfied. (See net profit).

$$\textit{Gross Billings} - \textit{Cost of Goods Sold} = \textit{Adjusted Gross Income.}$$

Adjusted Gross Income is money that is the small portion the agency maintains discretion over. AGI has to cover all operating expenses including overhead and the most expensive investment, people. As McLellan states: "You may be moving millions through your checking account but you can only make business decisions (on) money that's yours. . ." (McLellan, 2014).

CREATING A STUDENT AGENCY BUDGET

Budgeting is an important practice in agency management and is a good practice to determine how to know where revenue is coming from and where it is going. Much like what most adults (including college students) do for their personal finances, budgeting is one of the first things an agency should do.

Budgeting: The act of forecasting and planning expenditures for a particular client or for the overall financial health of an agency.

Creating a budget helps the agency establish that cash flow balance and can be used to set target revenues and manage future planning. Things to consider when building an agency budget include expenses, revenue, investments, equipment, maintenance, gifts in kind, partnership obligations, charitable contributions, and pro-bono work. There are many good resources out there to help in building an agency budget and/or managing the revenue generating and expense portions of an agency. Many of them live online or are some sort of hybrid cloud-based and locally installed applications. A few prominent ones include Pegasus™, Function Fox™, Function Point™, Workbook™, Clients & Profits™, CURRENTTRACK™, TrafficLIVE™, and AD-IN-ONE™. Each software package has associated costs and platform requirements. Some are built to interface with accounting software and others with chart and/or workflow applications. A good strategy is to contact local sales representatives for each package and see which one is the best fit for your particular needs.

In terms of timing a budget, you can develop your student agency budget by the semester or annually. For example, let's say your academic department gives you $5,000 annually to manage agency expenses. If you don't charge clients for your services, that $5,000 will be the only revenue you have for the year. If you just spend that money whenever the needs arises rather than following a budget, you'll likely run out of money before the year ends.

To avoid this, it is important to plan a budget. For example, how much will you need to spend for office supplies like copy paper, printer cartridges, letterhead, etc.? How much for travel or other new business expenses? Perhaps you want to hold a couple of open houses during the year. How much will you need for food, drinks, or nametags? Or, you might have a monthly fee for a web portal to house your agency website. Think through all of the needs you'll have for the semester or year.

One of the more common ways to illustrate these expenses, in both professional and student agencies, is to develop what is called a **line-item budget**. This document features different categories for different types of expenses—like office supplies, new business expenses, agency events, and so on. Each line

Line-item budget: A budget that breaks down expenses into categories, and groups like expenses together (e.g., travel, office supplies, new business expenses).

item then has a budget for the category—say, $500 for office supplies, $700 for new business expenses, $250 for agency meals, and so on—can then be added up to a total expected figure (like our $5,000). Then, as those expenses come in, you can track them against what you budgeted for each line item. You'll know if you're on track for the year, or if you risk going over budget and need to cut back just by reviewing this budget. Plus, line-item budgets help the agency track expenses over time. For example, maybe last year you budgeted $500 for office supplies but needed $750. Tracking this can help you develop a more accurate budget for the following semester or year.

If your agency charges clients for your services, then those will be added revenues you can add to your budget. But, as the saying goes, don't count your chickens before they're hatched. You can base your annual or semester budget on anticipated client billings. For example, if you know you have three client contracts that will pay "x" amount. However, if you lose one of those clients, as stated above, you'll need to adjust your ratio of revenue to expenses. And, remember that you'll need to manage your cash flow. If those three clients don't pay until the end of the semester, then you can't (shouldn't) spend that money until it's in your account.

To manage cash flow, it's also important to understand the expenses for which the agency is responsible versus those that will be billed back to the client. When that billing will take place is also important. For example, let's say you are printing a brochure to be handed out at a client event. Will the agency pay for that printing cost up front and then bill it back to the client at the end of the semester? If so, you'll need enough cash flow to do so. If you don't have enough cash in your account, you'll need to negotiate with the client to pay the printer at the time of delivery. This might involve what is called a **purchase order**. A purchase order is a document that outlines details like quantities and prices that is signed when the order is made. If the agency were paying for the expense up front, then you would sign the purchase order. However, if the client were paying, then the client would need to sign the purchase order and make arrangements to pay the printer at the time of delivery.

Purchase order: A document that authorizes a vendor to move forward with work. It outlines the scope and pricing of work to be executed (such as printing), and is legally binding for both parties.

As demonstrated in the budget in Table 5.1, you can see the breakdown in real dollars and cents of where the money goes. For example, previously mentioned hard costs are those expenses that you must spend each and every month in order to keep operating. Obviously, these should be incorporated into any budget. In addition to salaries and wages (Box 5.1), other hard costs can include rent/mortgage; utilities (electricity, water, cable, etc.); communications (cell phones, Internet, radios for event coordination, etc.); equipment leases or payments (computers, printers, copiers, video recording and production equipment, audio recording, and production equipment); furnishings leases or payments; taxes; insurance; technology and tech support; transportation, travel, and memberships for stock photography, media databases and other pay for play sites that help you complete your mission.

It is often helpful to consult with an accountant or tax lawyer or both when establishing these costs, projecting these costs, and applying them to your tax liability. Often those professionals you select are savvy to changes in current tax law and are helpful in suggesting strategies for growth and minimizing your tax burden and/or projecting unexpected costs.

Table 5.1 is an example of a basic agency budget. Note the **liabilities** and the **receivables**.

Table 5.1 Agency Budget

Sample Simplified Monthly Budget XYZ Agency—August 2017		
Category—Overhead (Liabilities)	8/2017	YTD
Building (rent/lease)		
Furniture (rent/lease)		
Parking (rent)		
Cleaning services		
Landscaping		

(Continued)

Table 5.1   Agency Budget (*Continued*)

Sample Simplified Monthly Budget XYZ Agency—August 2017		
Category—Overhead (Liabilities)	8/2017	YTD
Utilities		
Internet access		
Electricity		
Water		
Sewer		
Postage/shipping		
Storage		
Taxes (liabilities)		
Federal income		
State		
Local		
Property taxes		
Projected capital gains		
Receivables		
Gross billings		
TV production		
Radio production		
Graphic design		
Digital design		
Media placement commissions		
Web hosting		
Consulting		
Public relations		
Contingency funds in escrow		
Interest earned on balance		

Sample Simplified Monthly Budget XYZ Agency—August 2017		
Category—Overhead (Liabilities)	**8/2017**	**YTD**
Employee contributions 401K		
Other assets/investments		
Commissions on work accomplished		
Payments to vendors (liabilities)		
Television buys		
Radio buys		
Outdoor/out-of-home payments		
Direct mail fees		
Production fees		
Printers		
Photography		
Other freelance vendors		
Personnel expenses (liabilities)		
Salary		
Bonuses		
Insurance: life, health, s.t. disability, l.t. disability, etc.		
Thrift savings		
Matching 401K		
Misc. office supplies		
Meals and entertainment		
Travel		
Profit (Receivables—Liabilities and Taxes yields AGI)		

> ## Box 5.1   People—Your Most Costly and Most Beneficial Expense
>
> In a service-oriented business such as a consulting agency, one of the largest expenses is personnel. In order for your firm to get hired by a client you have to have good people. And, in order to get good people, you have to pay them a competitive wage or salary. Additionally, many employees are motivated by money. So, providing additional revenues or bonuses etc. is often a necessity to retain good people. Mismanaging this expense can lead to lost business, cost the agency the services of quality people, and can make it difficult to free up additional monies for other things like soft costs.

As with any household budget, the devil is often in the details. The more precise you can be in your budgeting, the more accurate a picture you can obtain as to the health and growth potential of your agency.

PROGRAM ESTIMATING AND BUDGETING

In addition to creating agency budgets, you will also be creating client estimates for programming, and managing those budgets throughout the program or campaign. Professional agencies include two elements in client budgets: Time and Expenses. The latter is fairly self-explanatory—expenses are the costs associated with executing a client program. We discuss some of these further on in this section. But expenses are only part of a client budget. Remember, the agency business is a service industry in which clients pay for the communications services agency members perform. But how do agencies determine how to charge for these services? Below, we discuss the concept of billing for agency members' time.

Billing for Time

Most professional agencies have a methodology that revolves around billing for time. In most PR and advertising agencies, each member of the agency has what is called a **billing rate**. A billing rate is how much it costs a client for 1 hour of the agency member's time to work on a project or campaign. Billing rates are established based on experience and expertise, a person's salary range (because those costs need to be recouped by the agency), size and location of the agency, the size and reach of the account, as well as the

> **Billing rate:** How much it costs a client for 1 hour of an agency member's service. Rates vary by experience and expertise, as well as the size and location of an agency and the type of work being executed.

value of the work being done. However, it's important to remember that a billing rate does not necessarily reflect a person's salary. While it should cover a person's salary, it also has to cover other expenses like payroll costs and overhead.

In large professional agencies, billing rates can range from $90 for an entry-level account coordinator to $400 or more for senior-level employees. For example, as a senior vice president in a large international firm, the billing rate for one of the authors was $325 per hour. Local firms working on local or regional accounts will have lower billing rates. And, of course, if you choose to establish billing rates for your student agency, those will be much lower than professional agencies.

Similar to other types of consultancies, most ad and PR practitioners bill their time to clients in 15-minute increments. Their time is tracked via **time sheets/billing sheets** that are filled online by the members at the end of each day or week. Each client and project has a job number. Underneath each client and project number are codes to track specific line-item activities, like client meetings, media pitching, or copywriting on the project.

Time sheet/billing sheet: A document in which agency members record the number of hours spent on each client and project in 15-minute increments. Usually recorded online, time sheets show the financial manager how much time to bill back to each client.

For example, workday of an entry level may look something like the billing sheet in Table 5.2. As you can see here, Cindy Norris spent 2.25 hours on social media planning for the local chain of barbecue restaurants. She also spent 45 minutes or 0.75 hours doing callbacks to media for the upcoming charity 5K and spent 3.5 hours doing reputation management research for a regional energy company and, finally she spent 90 minutes or 1.5 hours preparing focus group questions in preparation for three focus group sessions being conducted next week for a chain of carpet stores seeking to impact Millennials who are shopping for their first homes.

Table 5.2   Corporate Billing Sheet (Student Name: Cindy Norris—Daily Billing Sheet, 28 August 2017)

Client Name	Tasks	Time Spent (in 15-Minute Intervals)	Task Completed (Y or N)	Supervisor Signature
Big Bobs BBQ	Social Media	2.25 hours	Y	
Save the Seals 5K	Media Callbacks	0.75 hours	Y	
Burlington Buzz Windpower	Reputation Mgt. Research	3.5 hours	Y	
Candies Carpets and Interiors	Focus Group Planning	1.5 hours	Y	
Total billing for the day: 8 × $45/hr. = $360 (Total hours worked × billable rate = total billing)				

Note: This form is designed to account for your efforts on behalf of your clients for the benefit of AGENCY. Please be as specific as possible when turning these in.

Adding it all up, Cindy spent 8 hours working for her agency's clients. From this sheet, one might infer that Cindy's work is varied and busy. What you might also understand is these 8 hours should generate $XX in billable time that is passed on to the clients for payment.

You will also notice it is not as simple as 8 hours at a flat rate of $Y. A professional agency will usually adjust the billing rates by the type of work done and the experience level of the person doing the work. This practice allows for more flexibility in servicing the client's needs and opportunities to maximize profitability while ensuring needs are met.

For example, considering our carpet client, multiple people in an account team might work on the account. Each team member might have a specific skill or experience level. So when the client needs some web copy written, they might turn to their mid-level copywriter who bills at $45 per hour for that work. They may also need someone to archive secondary research on carpet companies for $20 per hour and they need some senior-level consultation at $125 per hour. How are these billing rates selected? It is usually a combination of seniority/experience in the teams combined with the difficulty of the work and the rarity of certain skill sets. If you are a young, accomplished social media maven with broad experience reaching Millennials, for example, your skills may be in high demand, there may not be too many of you out there on the job market and you may have worked in a particular industry or a related field that the firm or the client sees as important. Therefore, your individual billing rate may be higher than someone your same age who has a different skill set or is working with a different client.

Should student agencies use billing rates and time sheets to track agency member's time? While the answer depends on the type and set up of agency you are running. It is a good practice to get in the habit of filling out time sheets, even if you are working for non-paying clients. Mirroring your agency as closely as possible to the professional world makes you that much more prepared for getting that internship or entry-level position. Plus, timesheets can help you track your own time and help you learn how much time it takes to execute certain activities, as discussed next.

Estimating Time

Let's say you decide to determine your client fees based on hourly billing rates. How do you estimate how much time it will take to plan, develop, and execute a campaign? The answer is it comes mostly with experience. Might as well start getting that experience right now, right?

The key to estimating time for any project is to remember this: communications activities don't happen in a vacuum. There is teamwork involved, client meetings, research gathering, internal and external approval processes, multiple drafts, and so on. In other words, there are many interactions involved in producing great work.

Let's take a simple news release, for example. As any PR professional will tell you, they aren't so simple. In fact, it's a running game in the industry to count about how many drafts a PR release went through before the client approved a final version. For less important releases, it might be two or three. But for critical news that involves review from multiple people within an organization—from the communications manager to engineers to sales people all the way up to the CEO—it could require 10 or more drafts (we've heard one story of 20). If you only estimated for 2 hours of an account executive's time per page, your agency will lose money.

So, when estimating for a news release, there is much more to estimating time than just writing the news release. You'll need to estimate time for information gathering, how many people in an organization that will involve (both on the client side and agency side), how much time it takes to drive to and from these client meetings, how many drafts will likely be written, internal and external approval processes for each, and so on. That is the TRUE time it takes to "write" a news release.

The second part of estimating time is to then determine WHO in the agency will be involved in the process. For example, an account executive might spend 12 hours meeting with the client, gathering information, writing the release, meeting with the client again for approval, writing a second draft, and so on. But you may also need to estimate time for an account supervisor and/or the agency manager to also attend meetings and approve the release before it goes to the client. Remember, each of these people has different billing rates. So, a time estimate might look something like this:

Account executive	12 hours × $35 per hour	$420
Account supervisor	3 hours × $75 per hour	$225
Agency manager	1 hour × $100 per hour	$100
Total Time		**$745**

And remember, that's just for the "time" part of the equation. You'll also need to estimate any expenses (such as gas mileage, printing, etc.) before you can provide a total for the news release process. Then, you'll go through this estimating process again for each activity involved in the program or campaign.

One big advantage in estimating time is that it helps you determine how many people you need on an account. For example, let's say you have three people on an account. Each will spend an average of 10 hours per week on student agency business. That's 30 hours per week. However, when you estimate the time it will take to execute the client plans you have developed, you realize it will take 40 hours per week of agency members' time. Thus, you know you need to add another person to the account. Conversely, the hours required for another client project may require only 20 hours per week, but there are four people on that account. In this case, you would want to switch two of those folks to a different account.

This is how professional agencies determine the staffing needed for the accounts they have in-house. An agency loses money when members are only 50% billable because they are paying for people who aren't fully billable. The higher up in an agency you go, the less billable you are expected to be. Why? Because you are then doing administrative duties like finding new business, financial planning, managing personnel, and other activities that can't be billed back to the client. But entry-level employees like account coordinators and account executives are expected to be as close to 100% billable as possible.

Estimating Expenses

Costs associated with managing an account are sometimes very predictable and other times, not-so-much. Therefore, it is important in the planning and budgeting phase to anticipate as many expenses as possible prior to launch. Some examples of expenses associated with a campaign follow. These are by no means the only possible expenses campaign planners may encounter.

Stock photography

This term describes the use of existing photography to illustrate a concept or an idea, as well as show off the completed product. Stock photography comes in two broad categories: client-provided stock photography/video and third-party created photography/video. Client-provided stock photography is where the client has already shot or commissioned photos he or she likes for their product or service. When these stock materials are available, it is a huge time saver for the client and can also save money on the budget. For example, Polaris™ industries have a large selection of manufacturer-approved stock photography of their snow machines and all-terrain vehicles (ATVs) that an advertiser can draw upon when composing advertisements for the company. This photography can be downloaded from a secure site and used by graphic artists or creative directors to compose art. Similarly, Carpet One™ floor and home, a large retailer of floor care components, regularly provides video via a downloadable web site for franchisees to use in composing commercials, print ads, billboards etc. Both Carpet One™ and Polaris™ have had **co-op advertising programs**, which reimburse the local advertiser/franchisee much of the cost of advertising but require the advertiser to use their stock video/photography in their communications in order to honor the agreement.

> **Co-op advertising programs:** A common program of paid advertising for franchisees of a large brand where the price of advertising is split between the parent company and the franchise. Advertising accomplished two things: promotes the national brand on a local level, and multiplies the franchisees overall marketing budget so they can grab more reach and/or frequency. Co-op programs are usually highly regulated and carry very specific guidelines for how money is to be spent in terms of an ads final appearance and placement.

Third-party stock photography

In another, similar example, there is also third-party stock photography providers who regularly create generic vignettes and scenarios, which visual designers then use for their final products. This stock photography can also include specialty graphics, templates, and other aids to assist designers with developing a brand look and feel. The photos are typically one-time use or royalty free depending upon the agreement the original providers have with the holding company. Examples of stock photography sources include Istock™ and Shutterstock™ as well as many newer start-ups like Pixabay™ and Gratisography™. The cover of this book and many of the elements inside use stock photography. Similarly, companies are also involved in designing video templates, animations, and other graphics for use in paid media and earned media creations. Some of those digital video sites include Istock™ and Shutterstock™ as well as Adobe Stock™, Motion Elements™, and Videohive™.

Contracting for third-party services

Even with all of the stock images available, ultimately it may be best to contract for your client's own individual photography and/or videography. Nothing sells a brand better than a unique logo, or the look and feel of their advertising (think Target™ Department stores). The downsides to contracting for third-party services is it can be labor intensive and costly. In the case of a student-run firm, you may elect to have your own students or those affiliated

© Kzenon/Shutterstock.com

with your program do the designing/shooting for you. The advantages of using your own students include greater flexibility, lower cost, and good opportunities for collaboration. The primary disadvantage is there may not be enough experience within the pool to deliver the quality you and/or the client desires. In that case, it is perhaps best to contract with either a freelancer or a studio. Often production can be included in a media package by a third party for a nominal fee. But whether you engage a freelancer or an established studio, the critical points to any third-party engagement are the price per image, the level of preparation needed to produce the desired shot, and the concept of royalties/publication rights. Establishing who owns the actual image is something that should be decided prior to the engagement and should be done to ensure no confusion occurs further down the line. See Chapter 12 for more detail about copyright and intellectual property.

Out of pocket expenses

Out of pocket (OOP) expenses are something else that should be included in the initial budgetary plan. Nothing is more frustrating than realizing some monies need to be spent for food, reserving a table, printing, or even poster board only to discover there was no provision in the budget for this expenditure. Therefore, when calculating expenses for a campaign, it is recommended that a **contingency fund** be created to cover just such problems. This fund can

Contingency fund: What is budgeted and used in the event of a contingency.

be built into the budget and billed as necessary throughout the duration of the campaign. Typically, a contingency fund can be between 3% and 5% of the overall budget. In some rare cases, when there are a lot of unknowns, the contingency fund may be as much as 10%. Most professional agencies will include a "±10%" at the end of their budgets, indicating that the estimate could be 10% higher or lower depending on the final execution.

Travel

Compensation for travel is another challenge for student-run firms. Depending upon the relationship of the university to the actual client and/or any events or activities you may be proposing, some funds should be built into the budget to cover reimbursable travel expenses. Reimbursements for personal auto use include the costs of gas for the trip and/ or a cost per mile charge (current business rate is around 54 cents per mile traveled). Or, if renting a car, you'll want to include the cost of rental, as well as any tax or insurance charges. For longer trips that will require daylong or even overnight stays, you'll want to include meals and any lodging fees.

Commission/Mark-ups

Traditionally, in a print, radio, and television world, advertising agencies made most of their money not via time plus expenses, but via media commission on media buys. Typically, a television spot that cost $10,000 would be discounted to agencies by 15%, plus a 17.65% commission on production costs. The client would pay the $10,000 and the agency would keep the 15% difference.

Today, with so many media platforms, many agencies have abandoned the traditional 15% commission model in exchange for an hourly fee or retainer-based model (discussed later in this chapter). However, many ad agencies do still mark up their production costs. Why? Because so much of what an advertising agency does is on the production side. Many smaller, local agencies also still use the 15% commission model on television and radio placements. Thus, if your student agency is placing advertising for clients, you may want to consider this model.

Putting It All Together—Developing Estimates and Managing Budgets

Regardless of which payment model your agency uses, it's a good idea to develop client estimates based on our two categories of time and expenses. If you are charging the client on a retainer basis, estimating time, in addition to expenses, helps you determine if you are putting in more or less time than the retainer entails. Thus, a professional-client estimate would look something like Table 5.3.

Table 5.3   Client Estimate Model

Client Project			
	Time	**Expenses**	**Total**
Program planning	$X.xx	$X.xx	$X.xx
Website development			
Photography	$X.xx	$X.xx	
Shutterstock images		$X.xx	
Design	$X.xx	$X.xx	
Copywriting	$X.xx		
Website Subtotal	$X.xx	$X.xx	$X.xx
Agency travel	$X.xx	$X.xx	$X.xx
Etc.			
Totals	**$X.xx**	**$X.xx**	**Grand total: $X.xx**

As you begin planning and executing the campaign, check back on your budget often. You'll then need to keep track of how much you are spending both on time and expenses. For example, if an Account Executive AE has already spent 10 of an estimated 12 hours on a project and is only halfway through the project, you know you're going to go over budget. Thus, you'll need to adjust your estimate, take a loss on the project, or alert the client that you need more money for the campaign. Likewise, if printing or other costs are more than estimated, you'll need to adjust your budget accordingly.

If your agency does not charge clients for your services, or charges on a retainer basis, the estimates you give to the client will not include the "time" line in your budget. However, you'll want to break out expenses by category and be thorough so the client knows how much each unit costs.

Preparing program estimates takes a lot of research. Don't just ASSUME you know how much it will cost to print a brochure. Instead, call a couple of printers and ask for an estimate. Likewise, when estimating travel, check MapQuest™ or other online mapping tools to determine the number of miles to include in your estimate.

Lastly, as you incur expenses, keep copies of your receipts and vendor invoices and make multiple copies of them. For example, if you need to reimburse for personal travel, you'll have to turn in those receipts before you receive payment from your agency or university (e.g., gas, taxi, meal receipts). Likewise, clients will want evidence that you paid vendors what you said you paid them, so you'll want copies of any receipts for printing, photography, rental fees, and so on, to send along with your client invoices, as discussed below. This is called expense **back up**, or receipts that back up the expenses you incurred.

Back up (for expenses): Receipts for expenses and vendor payments. These are submitted to financial managers for reimbursement and/or attached to client invoices to show proof of expenses incurred/paid.

Projecting Costs and Workflow—Can the Client Afford You?

One of the biggest challenges to the billing process is balancing client service costs with the client's budget. You may design the greatest media plan ever, but if the client can't afford you, what is the point? Similarly, some agencies have great aspirations for their dollars in terms of results yet wish to dispute every task and action with an eye to getting the work done more cheaply.

So, to simplify billing and perhaps mute some of the aforementioned billing objections, some agencies have introduced a blended billing rate—say $75 per hour—which may cost the client more than the going rate for items like clerical work ($35 per hour), but discount the senior consultant rate ($125 per hour). Even with this solution, of a blended billing rate, it is very important that the agency diligently review projected costs.

CLIENT INVOICING

If you are charging clients for services and expenses, you'll need to develop an invoicing system. Again, several online tools are available to help with this process. Or, you can input them into an Excel™ or Word™ document. Regardless of which method you use, there are several issues to consider in developing an invoicing system. Your invoicing policy should be shared with the client at the time you sign the client contract or agree to the work to be done so there are no surprises on either end.

The first invoicing issue is to determine to whom payments will be made. Will they be paid directly to the student agency? Or will the check go to the university or some other entity? Whether or not you are allowed to charge clients for services, and the type of agency account you set up with the university, will determine if you invoice clients and who receives the payments. For example, in some universities, clients make tax-deductible donations to the university. In other universities, the student agency has an account number and client payments need to include that account number when being sent to the university. In still other universities, clients only pay for expenses and the rest of the work is pro-bono.

The second issue is to determine which payment methods you will allow. Can the client only pay by check? Or can the university also accept credit card payments? If you are working for on-campus clients, your university will likely have a system where monies can be transferred from one on-campus department to another without the necessity of cutting checks.

Most service-oriented firms give clients 30 to 60 days to pay from the date of the invoice. After that, they may charge a late fee for payment after the due date. Determine how often you will send out invoices, how long your agency can wait to receive payment from clients, and if you will charge a late fee. Remember, this has everything to do with cash flow. If you need to pay vendors, you need to have that money in your account before you can send out those payments. Thus, you might want to send out invoices each month rather than waiting until the end of the semester. And, you may need the client to pay sooner than 60 days.

Box 5.2   Sample Client Invoice

Invoice Date: May 24, 2017
Due Date: June 30, 2017
Please remit payment within 30 days

Bill To: (Client organization)
          (Client name)
          (Client email)
          Phone: xxx-xxx-xxxx

Item	Description	Cost
Live Oak semester scope	Live Oak scope of work fee	$1,000.00
Travel reimbursement	Gas and meals (Rodeo production day)	$28.72
Prints/disks/drives	Drives and file transfer for print production—summer vintage poster	$44.18
Prints/disks/drives	Prints—summer vintage poster (100 qty.)	$218.00
Production expenses	Props. The Pearl Kitchen—bottle of Grove wine	$31.85
Snapchat filter fee	Client Snapchat® filters	$21.51
Total		**$1,344.26**

Please make check payable to
Live Oak Communications—Elon University
and mail to:
Hal Vincent
Elon School Communications
2850 Campus Box
Elon, NC 27244

Thank you for your business!

When creating your invoices, make them look professional. You might want to use your agency's letterhead logo at the top of the invoice. Then, include the client company name, contact information, and the person who contracted the work on the invoice. Clearly put the date of the invoice at the top of the page, as well as the due date and include any late fee policies or other terms at the bottom of the invoice. Also include to whom the payment should be made and any account numbers to be designated on the payment.

In the body of the invoice, itemize the costs and services being charged to the client. For this, it's helpful to go back to the original estimate and insert the actual costs where before you had estimated costs. Rather than just putting one overall total, the client will want the invoice categorized by line item, with costs clearly broken out and explained. This is extremely important for client financial managers. For example, certain categories of expenses are often taxed differently, or paid through different budgets, and thus the client will need to have them itemized on the invoice.

In addition, clients usually require that you include back up for any expenses. A copy of any invoice that your agency has paid or will pay on behalf of the client needs to be attached to your agency invoice. Not only is this important to prove the credibility of your invoice, it is often an Internal Revenue Service (IRS) requirement.

Lastly, make sure account or agency managers have ample time to prepare invoices. Invoicing is often the LAST thing that takes place each semester. You don't want students leaving for break before you have thorough and professional invoices prepared to send out to clients.

REVENUE MODELS: HOW AGENCIES GET PAID

Now that we have discussed budgeting, expenses, billing and so on, it might be useful to discuss some of the ways agencies actually get paid. There are several billing models for agencies. Some of the more popular are

1. **Retainer**
2. **Project work**
3. **Fee for service**
4. **Outcome or performance-based compensation**
5. **Equity in lieu of payment**

Retainer

This is a popular model for consultancies. **Retainer** means you are paid a flat fee every month or every year to be at the client's disposal when they need you. A typical retainer relationship involves upfront negotiation for the amount, a 60-day out clause and a rough plan of how the monies will be allocated.

Retainer: A relationship with a client where the agency is paid a flat fee every month for work. Some months there will be more work done than the retainer supports, and there will be other months when there will be less work accomplished than the retainer supports. A retainer supports stability and growth in a client/agency relationship and evens out cash flow through both parties.

The retainer model is very popular among those in the legal and accounting professions as well. It basically gives the client peace of mind and gives the firm some stability in their monthly revenues. The smart account executive in a retainer relationship will provide status reports weekly to the client and billing sheets/running tally of hours spent to date. By monitoring these, it will become easier to schedule programs, campaigns, and events when you know you have enough time "on the books." See more about scheduling and planning under billing.

Project Work

One of the best ways to "get your foot in the door" when it comes to starting agency/client relationships is the project. By pursuing **project work** with a client, you get to see how they operate and they can do the same for you. Project work is especially appropriate for student-run firms because it allows for the turnover of personnel as students move through your program; engagements have a defined start and stop point that allow for student evaluation; they have a specific goal in mind, which helps the students build goals, strategies, and tactics around the objective(s); they allow for ease of billing and clear evaluations for success; and they are often the stepping stone to larger innovations or more comprehensive efforts.

Project work: One way for an agency to generate **revenue** is by projects. May include graphics, logo, media relations, and so on.

Projects can be as simple as a new logo design or as complex as rebuilding a graphic identity, creating a website, or generating publicity. Project work can often require various touchpoints that students have to navigate for success. This approach allows students to develop networking ties, for example, or other opportunities for jobs/collaborations.

Fee for Services

This is similar to the project engagement. However, in most cases, a **fee for services** reflects a specific specialty that a firm or agency offers. For example, if you want to have a contract drawn up, you could call an attorney, but you

Fee for services: Describes a transactional relationship where an agency is paid for a service rendered to a client.

would want to call one who has experience in contract law. Similarly, if a client wants to engage millennials or other young demographics in a social media campaign, who better to call than a group of their peers who are experienced in that form of communication? Very often student-run firms are approached by clients who want a specific task accomplished by experts in the student or young adult demographic and for that they are willing to enter into a fee for services engagement.

Outcome or Performance-Based Compensation

This is a slightly different arrangement that is popular with start-ups or those clients who are sure of their desired outcome but unsure who to trust to deliver it. It is an acceptable arrangement for a student-run firm if it is one of several engagements the team is working on. Outcome-based engagements can pay big dividends if successful. If not, well, therein lies the risk.

An outcome or performance-based engagement is much like it sounds: when the agency hits or exceeds the bar the client and the agency previously agreed to, they get paid in full or sometimes paid in full with a bonus. If they miss the mark, they get nothing or a very reduced compensation for their time. With the advent of new analytics, particularly in social media and the growing disciplines of big data and outcome analytics, this engagement is becoming more and more popular. Before deciding to take your firm in this direction, ensure you have a clear, specific contract; a trusted method of analysis; a clear understanding of the objectives and confidence in a solid, results-oriented team. It is also recommended that you negotiate, up front, some form of compensation in case you miss the mark so all of your efforts do not go to waste.

> **Outcome or performance-based compensation:** An arrangement where an agency is paid by a client for hitting certain performance marks. For example, perhaps an agency would be paid double its original asked for a fee if it exceeded in getting 2 million Facebook likes in 60 days. If the agency hits the mark they may make hundreds of thousands of dollars, but if they miss they may only make a few hundred.

Equity in Lieu of Payment

Not too popular with student-run firms because of compliance issues and challenges to universities accepting stocks or shares in lieu of revenue, the arrangement is often quite lucrative, particularly in the start-up community or in an aggressive new product launch or rebrand. As the name implies, **equity in lieu of payment** means an agency gets a "piece of the action" that can translate into stock options, stocks or perhaps a dividend payment for work instead of cash. If you have the revenue from other sources that you can forego immediate payment for a client offering equity, it is a win-win and students can learn a lot about investor relations and financial relations by entering into and managing this compensation.

> **Equity in lieu of payment:** An arrangement where an agency is paid in company stock or other equity instead of up-front money. Common in low budget or start-up companies.

CONCLUSION

The business of the agency is a very broad and comprehensive process that, when followed correctly, can help your organization reach a towering pillar of success that lights up your capabilities and triumphs like a signal fire. In contrast, if executed poorly, your bare embers may extinguish, never to reach the robust, illuminating glow you intended for your firm to become.

Running the business of the agency requires a lot of hard work, a proactive approach to soliciting new clients, some foresight and planning in preparation for the future, and some diligent stewardship of resources. Good luck and keep the fire burning.

REVIEW AND DISCUSSION QUESTIONS

1. Explain the difference between liabilities and assets.
2. In most cases, which is more: gross revenue or net revenue?
3. Explain some considerations the text mentions when considering hiring a person.
4. Explain hard costs.
5. Besides salary, can you name other expenses associated with hiring personnel?
6. Hiring a golf pro to provide insights into PGA golf courses for a pitch to a country club is considered what type of expense? Hard cost or soft cost?
7. Flying one of your employees to a trade show to accompany a client debuting a new product at that show would be considered a hard cost or a soft cost?
8. Paying the rent on your corporate office in Hilton Head, SC is a hard cost or a soft cost?
9. Explain what a retainer is.
10. Explain the use of contingency funds.

REFERENCES AND ADDITIONAL READINGS

Arens, W., Schaefer, D., & Weigold, M. (2015). *M advertising* (2nd ed.). New York, NY: McGraw Hill Education.

Beachboard, M. R., & Weidman, L. M. (2013). Client-centered skill sets: What small IMC agencies need from college graduates. *Journal of Advertising Education, 17*(2), 28–38.

Bush, L., Haygood, D., & Vincent, H. (2016, October 4). Student-run communications agencies: Providing students with real-world communications experiences that impact their careers. *Journalism & Mass Communication Educator, 72, (4)* 410–424.

Bush, L., & Miller, B. (2011). U.S. student-run agencies: Organization, attributes and advisor perceptions of student learning outcomes. *Public Relations Review, 37*, 485–491.

Cision. (2015). *The American Association of Advertising Agencies issues new best practice guidelines recommending that agencies 'transform' compensation model*. Retrieved from http://www.prnewswire.com/news-releases/the-american-association-of-advertising-agencies-issues-new-best-practice-guidelines-recommending-that-agencies-transform-compensation-model-300109115.html

Docur8ed. (2017). *Advertising agency tools: The 54 best software tools to run and scale your ad agency*. Posted on docur8ed.com. Retrieved from http://www.docurated.com/top-50-tools-run-scale-ad-agency

Functionpoint. (n.d.). *Is your creative agency billing enough?* Functionpoint Productivity Software (weblog). Retrieved from https://functionpoint.com/blog/is-your-creative-agency-billing-enough/

Hameroll, E. (1998). *The advertising agency business: The complete manual for management of operation* (3rd ed.). Lincolnwood, IL: NTC/Contemporary Publishing Company.

McClellan, D. (2014, May 22). *Financial metrics that matter to agencies.* Message posted to *Medium.* Retrieved from https://medium.com/@DrewMcLellan/financial-metrics-that-matter-to-agencies-d909a85b968c

Quora. (2016). *How do ad agencies charge their clients? How do they justify their rates? What are the typical rates/fees of a big name agency (e.g. JWT; CP+B) vs. a small rising boutique firm?* Posted to Quora.com. Retrieved from https://www.quora.com/How-do-ad-agencies-charge-their-clients-How-do-they-justify-their-rates-What-are-the-typical-rates-fees-of-a-big-name-agency-e-g-JWT-CP+B-vs-a-small-rising-boutique-firm

Sempo. (2014). *Retainer vs hourly billing: How do you design a pricing model that works for both agency and client?* Retrieved from http://blog.sempo.org/2014/03/retainer-vs-hourly-billing-how-do-you-devise-a-pricing-model-that-works-for-both-agency-and-client/

Sherman, F. (n.d.). *What percentage of gross sales should a company payroll be? Small Business/Chron.* Retrieved from http://smallbusiness.chron.com/percentage-gross-sales-should-company-payroll-be-17416.html

Smith, R. (2017). *Strategic planning for public relations* (5th ed.). New York, NY: Routledge.

Suggett, P. (2016). *How does an advertising agency work?* Published on thebalance.com. Retrieved from www.thebalance.com/how-does-an-agency-work-38447

Two Hats Consulting. (n.d.). *Guidelines for effective advertiser/agency remuneration.* Retrieved from https://twohatsconsulting.com/fee-structures-in-advertising/

Woolley, D. (2016). *Managing marketing: The changing economics of the advertising agency business.* Trinity P3 podcast. Retrieved from https://www.trinityp3.com/2016/07/changing-economics-advertising-agency-business/

Diversity and Inclusion

"Ridiculous ad," . . . "Shows no awareness," . . . "Feels completely dishonest and contrived." These were a few of the words Edward Boches, former advertising executive and professor of advertising at Boston University, used to describe a controversial Pepsi commercial in 2017 (Monllos, 2017). The ad in question depicted Kendall Jenner handing a police officer a Pepsi in the midst of a nonspecific street protest. The spot was released on April 4, 2017 and the backlash was swift and severe. Thousands took to Twitter to ridicule the tone-insensitive ad. Many felt the spot attempted to co-opt the Black Lives Matter movement while trivializing the seriousness of protests against police brutality and other societal issues. By April 5, Pepsi had pulled the ad and issued an apology.

Later in 2017, Dove launched a 4-second gif ad for Dove Body Wash. In it, a young black woman is shown removing her dark brown shirt and underneath is a young white woman in a white shirt, who then removes her shirt to reveal a woman of color in a tan shirt. While marketers intended to send the message that Dove Body Wash is for all women and skin types, for many the ad came off as implying only white or light skin is clean (Associated Press, 2017). Dove quickly pulled the gif and apologized for "missing the mark," but not before a screenshot of the black woman transforming into a white woman went viral. Film producer/director/writer Ava DuVernay tweeted: "You can do better than 'missed the mark.' Flip + diminishing. Deepens your offense. You do good work. Have been for years. Do better here." Others were more pointed: "Lol did this even look right to y'all? I mean your whole team sat down and cleared this … How?" tweeted Musimbwa, a South African designer.

Search the Internet and you'll find dozens of other examples of advertisers releasing ads or PR campaigns and then having to pull them and apologize. How do advertisers and their agencies so spectacularly miss the mark?

Companies often miss the mark because of what is termed **cultural reductionism**—the inability to see situations from a cultural perspective other than one's own (Krownapple, 2016, p. 131). According to crisis communications expert Mike Hatcliffe, a moment of cultural reductionism in your organization "can create lasting damage to your brand and weaken trust with stakeholders" (Hatcliffe, 2017).

Cultural reductionism: The inability to see situations from another's cultural perspective. Often, our cultural upbringing blinds us to the fact that there is more than one way of looking at a situation.

When we unpack "cultural reductionism," however, we see a larger, more systemic issue at work in the industry—a lack of diversity and inclusion. The less diverse and inclusive our organization is—both in its employment and its businesses practices—the better the chances of missing the mark when communicating with diverse target audiences.

The term **diversity** refers to the ways in which people differ from one another, or what makes us unique. Diversity can be described in relation to demographic characteristics such as race and gender, or nondemographic characteristics such as our skills, work experiences, or ways of thinking. The term **inclusion** refers to creating an environment in which diverse groups of people all feel welcome and respected as equally valued members of the organization. When inclusion is reflected in an organization's culture and practices, the organization works more effectively and is more innovative and competitive.

> **Diversity:** The ways we differ from each other. Diversity can be described in terms of demographic characteristics such as race and gender, or in terms of varied experiences and ways of thinking.

> **Inclusion:** Creating an environment in which people from all social and identity groups feel welcomed and respected.

Interestingly, a study funded by the Billie Jean King Leadership Initiative (Smith & Turner, 2015) showed that Millennials view diversity and inclusion in the workplace differently than their older peers. While Gen X and Boomer generations tend to define diversity as demographic representation and equality, Millennials tend to focus more on **cognitive diversity**, or the blending of different individual perspectives and experiences. In other words, Millennials focus more on individuality; older generations focus more on diverse demographic groups. While the Millennial perspective seems like progress, experts caution that we can't move forward with a false sense that we have suc-

© Gustavo Frazao/Shutterstock.com

> **Cognitive diversity:** Differences in mental reasoning or ways of thinking.

cessfully tackled issues like race, gender, or LGBTQ discrimination in the workplace and in society at large. Ample evidence shows that we haven't. Thus, considering both demographic and cognitive diversity is necessary.

In Chapter 4, we discussed ways to recruit students with diverse perspectives in your hiring practices. Beyond recruitment, however, it's important to understand what you can do to create an inclusive environment and produce work that accurately reflects the target audiences with which you are communicating. In this chapter we

- Outline the diversity issues facing the advertising and public relations (PR) industry
- Discuss how the industry is addressing these issues
- Summarize ways to create an inclusive environment
- Discuss approaches to developing multicultural content

UNPACKING THE INDUSTRY'S "DIVERSITY PROBLEM"

For decades, the advertising and PR industries have lamented what is often referred to as the "diversity problem." According to the Bureau of Labor Statistics (2016) African Americans, Asians, and Hispanics make up only about 21% of those employed in the industry. While women make up about half of those employed in advertising, the industry suffers from what some call a *MadMen* world of gender bias and discrimination. In 2016, the global CEO of J. Walter Thompson resigned amidst allegations of racist and sexist behavior, sparking new calls for diversity and inclusion initiatives. In the PR industry, women outnumber men by almost two-thirds, but fewer women hold leadership roles at the top. Only 10% of all PR professionals are African American or Hispanic (O'Dwyer, 2014).

Solving the industry's "diversity problem" isn't just a matter of recruiting a more diverse community of employees. It requires changing industry culture, as well. In 2009, a watershed study (Bendick & Egan, 2009) benchmarked the systemic barriers for African Americans in the industry, including wage inequality, lack of representation, occupational segregation, and the inability to advance. The study pointed out that recruiting wasn't the issue; industry scholarships, internships, and work by multicultural associations have created a fairly diverse pipeline of employees (see Box 6.1). Rather, creating an environment where employees feel welcomed, respected, and treated fairly was at the heart of the problem. Yet in a 2016 survey by the American Association of Advertising Agencies, "nearly 50% of industry professionals believe industry culture is still discriminatory," (Stein, 2016).

BOX 6.1 Industry Association Diversity Initiatives

Industry associations have many programs and awards in place to increase diversity in the industry. These include the following:

ADCOLOR	Champions diversity and inclusion in creative industries
AHAA: The Voice of Hispanic Marketing	Annual conference, seminars, and Rising Stars Award
American Advertising Federation	Most Promising Multicultural Students Program
American Association of Advertising Agencies	Multicultural Advertising Intern Program
Asian American Advertising Federation	3AF Excellence Awards, and Asian Marketing Summit
Black Media Consortium	#INTHEBLACK Consortium educating agencies on the economic power of the black consumer market

(Continued)

Hispanic Public Relations Association	¡BRAVO! Awards
International Association of Business Communicators	Global conferences and workshops
LAGRANT Foundation	Scholarships, mentoring, job placement and career development programs
Marcus Graham Project	iCR8™ Boot Camps
Organization of Black Designers	Hosts DesigNation conference
PR Council	Diversity Distinction in PR Awards
Public Relations Society of America	PRSA Chapter Diversity Awards, Chapter Diversity & Inclusion Toolkit
Public Relations Society of America Foundation and Education (PRIME)	PR internships, mentoring
She Runs It	Champions women as leaders in advertising and marketing

In her *Advertising Age* essay, "Why the Ad Agency's Diversity Strategy Needs a New Brief," Rochelle Newman-Carrasco (2016) stressed that the term "diversity and inclusion" may be doing our industry more harm than good. "The words have become rather meaningless, even dangerous. They lull us into a false sense of security, providing a feel-good mantra that checks all the right boxes but does none of the heavy lifting," Newman-Carrasco said. She cautions that recruiting more people of color into an entrenched corporate culture will do little to change the outlook of the industry. The industry must also make a commitment to recognize and respect cultural differences, and change the dialogue about issues such as unconscious bias, **microaggressions**, and gender identity.

Microaggression: Casually putting down a member of a socially marginalized group (e.g., "You are good at math, for a girl.").

Clients are driving agencies to pay attention to diversity—in recruiting, in corporate culture, and in branded content—and are taking steps to lead by example. In 2017, 150 corporate CEOs—including companies like Proctor & Gamble, Accenture, PricewaterhouseCoopers, Deloitte, Target, Walmart, and Johnson & Johnson—launched C.E.O. Action for Diversity and Inclusion™, an initiative described as "the largest CEO-driven business commitment to advance diversity and inclusion in the workplace" (ceoaction.com website). The initiative includes a commitment by CEOs to three goals: encouraging workplace dialogue about diversity and inclusion, expanding bias education, and sharing best practices. Large agency conglomerates Omnicom, WPP, and Interpublic Group are part of this initiative.

CREATING AN INCLUSIVE WORKPLACE

By educating students on workplace diversity and inclusion now, student agencies can ensure that graduates become part of the solution to the industry's "diversity problem" when they enter the field. This may involve enlisting university experts in diversity and inclusion training. Many universities train faculty, staffs, and students on working in a diverse and inclusive environment. We suggest you invite university administrators and faculty into your agency to talk about these initiatives and/or host diversity workshops with agency members. This will help you to develop a plan and subsequent actions for creating an inclusive agency, as well as provide guidance for agency members on practicing inclusive actions every day.

Simply being aware of diversity and inclusion is not enough. Your agency needs to practice sustained efforts to make inclusivity an embedded part of your agency's culture. To talk the talk you have to walk the walk. This requires being fair and unbiased in your hiring and promotion practices, creating inclusive client teams, and developing agency practices that invite and welcome diverse viewpoints.

Below are a few actions individuals can take to foster a welcoming and inclusive environment.

Recognize Unconscious Bias

We are hardwired to divide the world into categories based on our background and experiences. When we are faced with processing millions of pieces of information every day, our brains take shortcuts. This often helps us make sense of the world and generate quick decisions, but it can also lead to stereotyping individuals or groups of people. This is particularly true if you have had limited contact or connections with people different than you.

Unconscious bias is when we make assumptions or **stereotypes** about people based on our own background, cultural socialization, and personal experiences without even knowing it. For example, one of the authors was shocked to realize one day that, when she needed to move a large table or heavy chairs from one classroom to another, she automatically asked students who identified as men to help. This was based on her own biased cultural socialization that men are strong and do the heavy lifting, while woman are stereotyped as more delicate. This assumption is unfair, and also ignores research that shows gender is a continuum, rather than a binary.

Unconscious bias: Holding prejudice against or for one group of people without realizing it.

Stereotype: An assumption that all members of a social or identity group behave, think, or feel the same way.

While an example like the above may seem trivial, when you extrapolate this perception to the workplace, it can cause great harm. It leads to assumptions that certain genders of people can only do certain jobs. It is an assumption that kept women out of STEM fields for generations, kept men out of caregiving jobs such as nursing or teaching preschool, and prevented transgender and genderqueer individuals from getting jobs at all.

You can recognize your own unconscious biases by paying attention to your assumptions about people or groups of people, or by using online tools, such as Project Implicit® found here https://implicit.harvard.edu/implicit/. Then, ask yourself where these biases come from? Were you raised with them? Did you form your opinion based on what someone else said rather than your own experiences? Or, did you have a negative interaction with one person and generalize that experience to all members of the group? Perhaps you read or heard something that went along with your opinion. This is often called **confirmation bias** where our brain seeks out information that confirms our biases and ignores all other information.

Confirmation bias: Seeking out information that confirms our preexisting beliefs and ignoring information that might conflict with those beliefs.

Once you have recognized your unconscious biases, you can monitor them and work to avoid making decisions based on bias. Getting to know people within the group for which you have an unconscious bias is also helpful. For example, if you have never had a conversation with someone from a religious faith different from your own, look around your university for speaking engagements, scholarly lectures, or events where you can learn more about other faiths and meet people

© Gustavo Frazao/Shutterstock.com

who practice them. The more cultural "cues" you load into your brain, the more information your brain will have to make decisions. And, the best way to deal with unconscious bias is to treat people as individuals rather than making assumptions based on group identity.

Understand Intersectionality

One way to focus more on the individual, rather than the group, is to understand intersectionality. The term **intersectionality** was coined by Kimberle' Williams Crenshaw, law professor and leading scholar of critical race theory. To understand a person's identity, we must recognize that identity is a construct from several overlapping—or intersecting—social groups,

Intersectionality: Identities are constructs of several overlapping—or intersecting—social groups or identities, such as race, gender, age, economic status, geography, and physical or mental ability.

including race, ethnicity, gender, sexual orientation, age, mental and physical disability, socioeconomic status, and so on (see Luther, Ringer, & Clark, 2012). For example, a white LGBTQ woman is a member of the dominant white culture, but also shares aspects of her identity with groups that have been marginalized. Similarly, a black man may share some of his identity with all men, but his identity has also been shaped by experiences unique to his race, socioeconomic background, geography, and so on.

Intersectionality helps us understand how individuals process and react to different situations. For example, gamers often identify with what is called "geek" culture and feel a deep **in-group** bond—or shared identity—with other gamers. If a gaming company decided to change the way gamers logged in to a system, making it more difficult, gamers might protest the move as one cohesive group. However, if the aim of the new system was to cut down on online harassment, gamers who identify as women and/or people of color—identities that often face harassment in the gaming industry—might feel very differently than their other gaming peers.

> **In-group:** A group with which you share an identity or interest.

In addition, intersectionality shows how overlapping identities can create other distinct identity groups. Crenshaw often tells the story of General Motors and five African American women who sued for discrimination in 1976 (Adewunmi, 2014). The case was unique at the time because it addressed two different areas of law—discrimination based on race and discrimination based on gender. However, there was no area of law that overlapped race and gender. Not all women at General Motors were discriminated against, and not all African Americans faced discrimination. Because it was a situation unique to those two overlapping identities, the courts didn't have a way to address it and the women lost the case.

Intersectionality helps us avoid stereotypes and assumptions. Instead, we can focus on the individual, appreciate their unique identity and better comprehend where they are coming from in various situations. In addition, it illuminates areas of workplace policy or practice that may not be inclusive of overlapping identities.

Use Inclusive Language

There is a long-standing riddle that is often told to demonstrate our unconscious biases. And this riddle can also show how our language reflects those biases.

> A father and his son were in an automobile accident. Both were injured badly and taken to the hospital. While doctors were working on the father in another room, the son was taken into surgery. The surgeon walked in, looked down at the boy and said, "I can't perform surgery on this boy because he is my son."

The question to the riddle is: Who is the surgeon? If your initial reaction is to ponder how the father can be in two places at once—injured in another room and also standing over the boy in surgery—you are not alone. Based on cultural socialization, we often assume the surgeon is a man. The answer to the question is: the surgeon is the boy's mother. However, there are other possibilities. Perhaps the boy has two fathers. His fathers could be married to each other, or one could be a stepfather. Because of this socialization, we often use the pronoun "him" when referring to doctors or surgeons. Or, refer to "her" when talking about nurses.

Inclusive language is language that avoids stereotypes, biases, or assumptions and doesn't exclude people as members of the group. For example, many universities use the term "first-year" students rather than "freshman" to include all genders. And, universities have been criticized as being "overly sensitive" for doing so. Why does it matter?

> **Inclusive language:** Language that avoids assumptions, biases, and stereotypes and includes every potential member of a referenced group.

It matters because words matter. Language reflects and shapes our society. When we continue to use outdated terminology that assumes gender, race, ability, and so forth, we are essentially eliminating wide swaths of people and perpetuating stereotypes and unconscious bias. In fact, research has shown that, when we use a term that favors men (such as "chairman,") people automatically assume the person is a man even when it was intended to be universal (Kassab, n.d.). Yet we often continue to use sexist terminology without a thought. Using inclusive language signals to agency members, potential members, and clients that we are a welcoming and inclusive agency.

Pay attention to the use of pronouns in your work and interactions. If you are writing advertising copy, a press release, or social media content, rephrase or rewrite sentences that use "he" or "she" when they don't refer to a particular person. Alternatively, as society becomes more aware of the gender continuum, it has increasingly become acceptable to use the singular "they" by editors and journalists (as we often do in this text).

Another area for consideration is ableist language. Often without thinking, we use terms like "crazy," "insane," or "lame" to describe thoughts or ideas. However, this perpetuates a stigma, one that people with mental or physical disabilities are working hard to eliminate. Instead, consider alternatives, such as outrageous, intense, or uncool. When referring to a person with a disability, focus on the person first, rather than the disability (e.g., student with a disability, rather than "disabled student").

It is also important to understand the broad range of terminology used to describe different races or ethnicities. For example, the words Latino (men), Latina (women), and Latinx (gender inclusive) refer to people of Latin American decent, whereas the word Hispanic is "of or relating to Spain." These terms are often used interchangeably (though they shouldn't be). In marketing, the term "Hispanic marketing" is used to refer to marketing programs that target Spanish-speaking people, regardless of ethnic origin. Still, some Latinx prefer to be identified by their ancestral country of origin, dispelling the stereotype that all Latinx are Mexican.

Likewise, there is widespread personal choice in whether one chooses to be identified as African American or Black. The term African American usually identifies Americans of African descent, while Black often refers to people from a wide range of countries including the Caribbean and the Americas. "People of Color" is an umbrella term that refers to people who identify as non-white. For a list of inclusive terminology, refer to Table 6.1 or check out this guide from the University of Missouri: https://diversity.missouri.edu/education/handouts/inclusive-language.pdf

Table 6.1 Inclusive Language

Don't Use	Instead Use
mankind	humankind
man the phones	staff the phones
businessman	business person
chairwoman	chair
congressmen	members of Congress
himself/herself	oneself
he/she	rephrase or use the singular "they" (not referring to a specific person)
girls	women (if over 18)
you guys	you all
disabled person	person with a disability
handicapped	person with a disability
tone-deaf	tone insensitive
transsexual	trans or transgender
homosexual	member of the LGBTQ community
minorities	refer to the specific group (e.g., African Americans), or use other terms such as "people of color"
illegal immigrant	undocumented immigrant
old people, elderly	seniors, older adults

Talk About It

In 2016, a sniper killed five police officers in the midst of crowds protesting police shootings of black citizens in Louisiana and Minnesota. The following week, the CEO of PricewaterhouseCoopers received an email from an employee saying the silence after returning to work was deafening. No one was talking about it, and this created a tense and stressful work situation. As a result, CEO Tim Ryan brought employees together to have open discussions about race, which led to a more relaxed environment and greater employee trust.

© ESB Basic/Shutterstock.com

We are often afraid to talk about our differences for several reasons; we fear we might offend someone, we don't know how to approach it, we're socialized NOT to talk about it, or we're afraid talking about it will only make things worse. But NOT talking about it can let issues fester and make employees feel that we don't care about their concerns. Talking about our differences can help us unearth issues we didn't know were there, and create a common language for ongoing discussions.

The nonprofit workplace leadership company Catalyst (2016), developed a list of "Conversation Ground Rules" for having difficult conversations about our differences. Their recommendations include approaching conversations with positive intent, with the mindset that something good will come out of them; engaging in dialogue rather than debate; truly listening and understanding where someone is coming from by asking questions and clarifying; being willing to admit mistakes; analyzing our assumptions; and, being okay with feeling a little bit uncomfortable.

By engaging in these conversations, we create a more trusting atmosphere where we can foster genuine relationships. If you are apprehensive about having these conversations in your student agency, enlist the help of an experienced facilitator to get you started. Once you learn the "language" of conversation, it will be easier to incorporate these discussions into your agency culture.

MULTICULTURAL IS THE NEW MAINSTREAM

Changing an entrenched, dominant system does more than simply avoid cultural pitfalls. It is critical at a time when communications audiences are becoming more diverse. Currently, 40% of the U.S. population identifies as Hispanic, Asian, Black, or mixed race, and by 2055, Pew Research predicts there will be no majority race in the U.S. (Lacy, 2017; Cohn & Caumont, 2016). In some states, like Texas and California, white, non-Hispanics comprise less than 50% of the population.

In addition, Millennials—the largest and most racially diverse group in U.S. history — wield tremendous consumer and voting power, and will continue to do so in the coming decade. Add to the mix other population trends identified by Pew Research: women are taking on greater leadership roles in both the workforce and the household, marriage rates are declining and blended families are on the rise, the middle class is shrinking, the religious landscape is changing, and, as a whole, the world's population is aging (Cohn & Camount, 2016). Taken together, these shifts point to a need to be more diverse and inclusive in our thinking to produce branded content that accurately reflects our multicultural society.

Multicultural agencies and industry associations are helping to lead the charge. In 2016, the Association of National Advertisers launched the Alliance for Inclusion and Multicultural Marketing with the goal of mapping out best practices for the industry. The Alliance brings together large national advertisers like Wells Fargo, Coca-Cola, Kellogg, and Procter & Gamble; multicultural associations and agencies like AHA: The Voice of Hispanic Marketing, Lopez Negrete Communications, and Burrell Communications; and media companies like NBC Universal, Univision, and the Video Advertising Bureau.

Mass media, including advertising and PR, play a significant role in both shaping and reflecting U.S. culture. This can be seen in the words and phrases we pick up from television or advertisements (e.g., Just Do It), the clothing styles we adopt, the discussions we have on social media, and the views we have about ourselves and others. Thus, when we create communications content, we have a responsibility to accurately reflect those we are representing or engaging with in our communications.

There is always the risk, however, of "missing the mark" when developing advertising and PR campaigns. Because we "segment" audiences into different groups for efficiency and economy of scale, there is the potential to leave someone out or create a message that doesn't relate to intersectional identities within a subgroup. However, there are also practices you can use to avoid making mistakes or perpetuating cultural reductionism. Some of these are outlined below.

Avoid Stereotypes

The concept of intersectionality helps us understand that all people in a social subgroup are not alike. Yet the media industry often stereotypes based on social groups, such as all women love shopping, all men are obsessed with football, all black people live in the inner city, all gay men like show tunes, and so on.

For example, when consumer packaged goods companies outline their target audiences, they frequently use the standard target of "Women, 18–54," as if women are one monolithic group. As we learned in discussing intersectionality, the values and issues of women will differ based on overlapping identities. When we target "women" in advertising, we often default to white, heterosexual women and assume that all other women have had similar experiences. In a nutshell, this is lazy marketing. Not only does this leave many women out, it also creates the potential for our communications to misrepresent our audience and further harm underrepresented groups.

As another example, Millennials are perhaps one of the most researched generational cohorts in history. Yet advertisers often make broad generalizations when targeting this cohort. While many Millennials do share some common experiences (growing up with technology, for instance), there are profound differences based on intersectional identities. For example, the Hispanic Millennial Project (2015) found that Hispanic Millennials contribute more to household expenses, place more emphasis on getting an advanced degree, and are more likely to consider owning a home and a business as indicators of success than their non-Hispanic Millennial peers. Further, the project found significant differences in foreign-born versus U.S.-born Hispanics.

When communicating with target audiences, stay away from broad generalizations and stereotypes. Do your research—online and by talking to others in person. Don't assume you understand a target audience because you share one aspect of their social identity.

Avoid Cultural Appropriation

Katy Perry wearing cornrows in her video "This is How We Do;" college students donning sombreros at a Cinco de Mayo party; film actors wearing blackface to depict African Americans; festival-goers wearing Indian headdresses at a Coachella concert—these are all examples of cultural appropriation. At its core, **cultural appropriation** is when members of one culture adopt, or "appropriate," aspects of a culture that is not their own. This often involves a power dynamic, when the dominant culture appropriates aspects from cultures that have been marginalized or discriminated against, frequently by the very people who are doing the appropriation. This could include appropriating dress, music, fashions, food, cultural symbols, or other cultural traditions. Cultural appropriation differs from assimilation, where members of a culture adopt aspects of the dominant culture to fit in (and sometimes, to survive), or cultural exchange, where two cultures share aspects of their cultures with each other equally.

> **Cultural appropriation:** When members of one culture (particularly the dominant culture) adopt or "appropriate" aspects of a culture that is not their own.

Cultural appropriation is problematic for several reasons. First, it often ignores, dismisses, distorts, stereotypes, exploits, or erases the history and traditions of marginalized cultures, many of which have faced violent oppression from more dominant cultures. For example, when a festival-goer wears a Native American headdress to a Coachella concert, it disrespects the symbolic and sacred tradition of tribal headdresses while ignoring the genocide of Native peoples by white colonization (Keene, 2010).

Appropriation often allows the dominant culture to inappropriately benefit from the labor of a marginalized culture. For example, when a fashion designer profits from appropriating traditional Native designs, many see this as stealing the intellectual property of the Native culture. Further, white designers can use their privilege to sell Native designs in a dominant system where many Native Americans might (and do) face discrimination and lack of access.

Lastly, cultural appropriation can also perpetuate racial stereotypes. In some cases, this takes the form of mocking diverse cultures. In others, members of the dominant culture are praised or rewarded for appropriating cultural traditions where members of the other culture would be criticized. For example, many black women face discrimination in the workplace for wearing traditional African American hairstyles, while white entertainers are often lauded as "trend setters" for appropriating the same styles.

Many dismiss claims of cultural appropriation as being "overly sensitive," but smart advertisers know to avoid cultural appropriation. Take, for example, the Pepsi spot mentioned earlier in this chapter. Toward the end of the spot, Kendall Jenner faces off with a police officer, offering him a peace offering of a Pepsi. To many, this was disconcertingly similar to a widely publicized photo of Ieshia Evans, a young black woman who stood firm when rushed by police in riot gear at a protest in Louisiana. A great deal of the backlash over the Pepsi spot focused on this image, which many felt appropriated an icon from African American culture.

Be Genuine; Don't Play the Numbers Game

We see it on historically white college campuses all the time. The university brochure shows a picture of a diverse group of students—a black student, a white student, a Latino student, a Muslim student, a student in a wheelchair. Yet when we walk across campus we're hard pressed to find the diverse group pictured in the photograph. This is often a Catch 22 for marketers. While clients want to appeal to a diverse group of consumers—be it for a college or a car company—oftentimes they do not yet represent the

diverse audience they hope to recruit. Thus, they force the look of diversity in their marketing materials. While the aspiration is to attract diverse identities, forcing diversity can have the opposite effect.

This is perhaps one of the most misunderstood aspects of "diversity" in the industry: throwing in a few different identities does not make an advertisement diverse. The cultural insights of those identities must be represented as well. While clients and agencies should be cognizant of diverse representation in their marketing materials, Derek Walker, owner of Brown and Browner Advertising, says diversity should be genuine. "I think it's better to have an authentic story than forced diversity," Walker said in an interview with The Drum News. "I think we minorities have been wrong in not helping define what we mean by diversity. It's more than just the number of faces. It's about the insights," he said (Lacy, 2017).

In the interview, Walker also said advertisers should own up to diversity issues within their organizations. He gives the example of an Airbnb Super Bowl spot aired in 2017 with the hashtag #WeAccept. The ad touted the company's values of global diversity. However, in the year leading up to that spot, many Airbnb guests had experienced racial discrimination on the company's platform and in its bookings (see, for example, Dickey, 2016). Though the company had instituted several policies to resolve the issues, Walker said the Super Bowl spot itself sidestepped the problem. "Airbnb said, 'We're diverse,' [in the Super Bowl] without acknowledging they have a problem . . . This is one of those times where the ad may seem empowering, but the reality is the brand doesn't live up to the hype" he said in the interview (Lacy, 2017). As a result, many consumers saw this as being disingenuous.

Marketers and agencies must approach diversity from a perspective of authenticity and honesty. Storylines, as well as casting, should reflect the cultures, experiences, and insights of the audiences you want to reach. And, marketers should be honest with the public about diversity issues that are being addressed by their organizations and work to achieve real change, rather than using advertising to paper over them.

Pay Attention to Cultural and Religious Traditions

In 2017, NC Pride found itself in a dilemma soon after it announced the date for its annual festival and parade. The date, September 30, was also the date of the holiest Jewish holiday of the year, Yom Kippur. Those who observe Yom Kipper fast for 24 hours and attend services, so Jewish LGBTQ members and supporters wouldn't be able to attend the festival. After backlash from the community and several media reports, NC Pride vowed to solve the issue by picking another date (Lynch, 2017).

Dates, numbers, colors, and idioms have different meanings in different cultures. For example, in some Asian cultures certain colors of blue designate mourning, and the number "4" implies death, just as the number "13" is considered unlucky by some in the United States. When Pepsi launched in China, its phrase "Pepsi brings you back to life" was loosely translated as "Pepsi brings your ancestors back from the grave."

In addition to testing content (see below), a quick Internet search can help educate you on numbers, colors, and word meanings in different cultures and languages. And, before you select a date for that big event, check the calendar for religious holidays or other cultural events.

Test Content Before Launching

On the surface, the most obvious reason for "missing the mark" is that advertisers don't check in with their audiences, effectively testing spots before they air. As often happens in the advertising industry, we come up with a clever idea and are convinced others will see it as we do. Hubris, plain and simple, can prevent us from seeking out potential pitfalls to our ideas. As business consultant Liz Strauss says, "Clever is risky because it gets us looking at ourselves not the people we're talking to" (Strauss, 2011).

© Roobcio/Shutterstock.com

When an advertiser or agency spectacularly misses the mark, you will often hear other agency professionals exclaim, "WHAT WERE THEY THINKING????" The answer is that perhaps THEY (and their clients) were doing the thinking instead of letting the target audience drive the storyline. Every ad and PR program should be tested with targeted consumers before it is launched, preferably through focus groups, online consumer panels, or other research methods. While this is not always possible with the limited budgets of student-run agencies, there are other ways to "check in" with audiences. Universities have a diverse group of programs, including African American studies, women and gender studies, foreign language studies, multicultural and LGBTQ centers, as well as diverse student groups on campus. Check in with some of these programs and students to make sure your communications are not missing the mark.

Practice the "Total Market" Approach

A fairly new approach to communicating with diverse audiences is called **Total Market Approach**. Traditionally, advertisers have segmented their markets into the "general market" (mostly white consumers) and the "multicultural market" (everyone else) (Canfield, 2016). The Total Market Approach combines these segments in totality, taking a cross-cultural approach to marketing by researching and integrating diverse segments early in the process and throughout execution. By looking at

> **Total Market Approach:** A cross-cultural approach in which marketers research and integrate diverse segments into their marketing processes early in the planning and throughout execution. Rather than segmenting audiences by the "general market" and "multicultural market," this approach considers all cultural segments as one market.

the market in totality—including every cultural segment—marketers can then determine if they need to execute a segmented approach to marketing communications (e.g., a separate Hispanic marketing component) or one cross-cultural approach that includes "cultural cues that have universal appeal" (Odell, 2015).

For example, in 2015, Wells Fargo took the Total Market Approach in developing a TV spot targeting Millennials called "First Paycheck." The spot featured a young Latina woman receiving her first paycheck. While the spot was bilingual and included cultural cues like showing a multigenerational family, the concept of getting your first full-time paycheck was a universal concept that could appeal to many Millennials.

Total Market Approach is gaining steam with advertisers and agencies. Companies like Toyota, McDonald's, Coca-Cola, Clorox, Walmart, and Procter & Gamble, to name a few, are experimenting with this approach. Many advertisers are bringing together their agencies of record with their multicultural agencies to develop Total Market strategies, and are realizing cost benefits as a result.

However, if not done right, Total Market can end up ignoring multicultural audiences, leading to loss of market share. Pepper Miller, author and president of Hunter-Miller Group, points out several issues with integrating ethnic markets into a general market approach. These include the lack of diversity in marketing departments that would lead to greater understanding of multicultural audiences, a lack of accountability for Total Market, no understanding of multicultural media, and the need for analytics that can measure cultural relevance and resonance across segments. "Total Market . . . is not a diversity initiative. It is a concept of how marketing could work. It should be inclusive and CMOs should keep minority-focused agencies and media in the mix to continue to address the specific needs of these segments," Miller said (Miller, 2016).

CONCLUSION

Diversity and inclusion may seem like a complex web of "do's" and "don'ts" that create a minefield for advertisers and their agencies. But in the end, it's really just about people. And as we know, people are complex.

Gone are the early days when everyone watched the same three television channels and agencies took a scattershot approach to reaching target audiences. Thank goodness. These are much more exciting times in the advertising and PR business. It's a time of staggering technological change when marketers can learn more about consumer values and preferences than at any other time in history. It's a time when stakeholders have more of a voice in how companies behave, the products and services they create, and how they treat people both inside and outside of their organizations. If we listen to those voices, chances are we'll get it right.

Lastly, it's a time when we can work together with people from all backgrounds and perspectives to create new possibilities and innovative ideas. Millennials are making their mark on the industry, and soon they will welcome a new generation of advertising and PR professionals—those working in student agencies right now (often called Gen Z). You will have your own ideas about diversity and inclusion. Perhaps you'll move the industry beyond its current culture, and usher in a day when differences are not just accepted, but are also valued and celebrated.

REVIEW AND DISCUSSION QUESTIONS

1. What is the difference between the terms "diversity" and "inclusion?"
2. Make a list of demographic characteristics (such as race, gender, age, religious affiliation, social economic status, geography, ability). As you walk through each demographic, are there any unconscious biases you might have about a particular identity group within those demographics? If so, list three ways you can work to overcome those biases.
3. Describe your own intersectional identity based on the demographic groups you listed above. How might your intersectional identity shape your perspective or view of the world? Are there any times when you identify more strongly with one part of your identity than another?
4. Based on the intersectional identity you described in #3 above, what are some stereotypes people may have or have had about you? Discuss these with your teammates.
5. Imagine you are developing an advertisement for a hearing aid company. What are some assumptions you might make about people who wear hearing aids? After listing these assumptions, discuss ways you can become better informed about the target audience for hearing aids?
6. Read through the following paragraph:

   "When a campus doctor examines a patient, he should determine if his symptoms require further tests. If so, he should direct the student to the urgent care clinic, which is just a short walk down the road. The student should speak to the nurse on duty. She will make an appointment for the student to see a specialist. Students can use their parent's insurance to cover the costs."

   Can you spot any inclusive language issues with this paragraph? How could you rewrite it to be more inclusive?

7. Imagine you are developing a website to increase applications to your university. How might you go about taking a Total Market Approach to content development?
8. Brainstorm with your teammates three ways you can make your student agency more inclusive.

REFERENCES AND ADDITIONAL READINGS

Adcolor (n.d.). *Our goal is to create a community of diverse professionals who are here to support and celebrate one another*. Retrieved from http://adcolor.org/

Adewunmi, B. (2014, April 2). Kimberle' Crenshaw on intersectionality. *New Statesman*. Retrieved from http://www.newstatesman.com/lifestyle/2014/04/kimberl-crenshaw-intersectionality-i-wanted-come-everyday-metaphor-anyone-could

AHAA (n.d.). *The voice of Hispanic marketing*. Retrieved from http://www.ahaa.org/

American Advertising Federation (n.d.). *Most promising multicultural students program*. Retrieved from http://www.aaf.org/AAFMemberR/Awards_and_Events/Awards/Most_Promising_Multicultural_Students/About.aspx

American Association of Advertising Agencies (n.d.). *Multicultural advertising intern program*. Retrieved from http://www.aaaa.org/home-page/your-career/maip/

Asian American Advertising Federation (n.d.). Retrieved from http://www.3af.org/index.htm

Associated Press. (2017, October 8). Dove apologizes for Facebook soap ad that many call racist. *ABC News*. Retrieved from http://abcnews.go.com/US/wireStory/dove-apologizes-facebook-soap-ad-call-racist-50359756

Bendick, M., & Egan, M.L. (2009, January). *Research perspectives on race and employment in the advertising industry*. Bendrick and Egan Economic Consultants, Inc.. Retrieved from http://www.bendickegan.com/pdf/2009/Bendick%20Egan%20Advertising%20Industry%20Report%20Jan%2009.pdf

Black Media Matters Consortium (n.d.). *For info on #INTHEBLACK*. Retrieved from http://www.blackmediamatters.org/intheblack/

Bureau of Labor Statistics. (2016). *Labor force statistics from the current population survey*. Retrieved from https://www.bls.gov/cps/cpsaat18.htm

Canfield, C. (2016, April 21). *Multicultural marketing: Have you considered a 'Total Market' approach?* Pace Communications website. Retrieved from http://www.paceco.com/insights/strategy/multicultural-marketing-total-market-approach/

Catalyst. (2016). *Engaging in conversations about gender, race and ethnicity in the workplace*. New York: Catalyst. Retrieved form http://www.catalyst.org/knowledge/engaging-conversations-about-gender-race-and-ethnicity-workplace

Cohn, D., & Caumont, A. (2016, March 31). *10 demographic trends that are shaping the U.S. and the world*. Pew Research Center. Retrieved from http://www.pewresearch.org/fact-tank/2016/03/31/10-demographic-trends-that-are-shaping-the-u-s-and-the-world/

Dickey, M. R. (2016, September 8). Here's Airbnb's plan to fix its racism and discrimination problem. *TechCrunch*. Retrieved from https://techcrunch.com/2016/09/08/airbnb-plan-fix-racism-discrimination/

Dishman, L. (2015, May 18). *Millennials have a different definition of diversity and inclusion*. Fast Company. Retrieved from https://www.fastcompany.com/3046358/the-new-rules-of-work/millennials-have-a-different-definition-of-diversity-and-inclusion

Elliott, S. (2000, March 6). Ads speak to Asian Americans. *New York Times*. Retrieved from http://www.nytimes.com/2000/03/06/business/the-media-business-advertising-ads-speak-to-asian-americans.html

Ember, S. (2016, May 1). For women in advertising it's still a "Mad Men" world. *New York Times*. Retrieved from https://www.nytimes.com/2016/05/02/business/media/for-women-in-advertising-its-still-a-mad-men-world.html

Grillo, G. (2015, April 23). The advertising industry needs diverse leadership to thrive. *Advertising Age*. Retrieved from http://adage.com/article/agency-viewpoint/advertising-industry-diverse-leadership-thrive/297998/

Hatcliffe, M. (2017, April 25). *"Cultural blindness" may be your next crisis*. Rock Dove Solutions website. Retrieved from https://www.rockdovesolutions.com/blog/cultural-blindness-may-be-your-next-crisis

Hispanic Millennial Project. (2015). *Wave 1: Introducing Hispanic Millennials*. Research conducted by Sensis and ThinkNow Research. Retrieved from http://www.hispanicmillennialproject.com/

Hispanic Public Relations Association (n.d.). Retrieved from http://www.hpra-usa.org/

Kassab, M. (n.d.). *Inclusive language in four easy steps. Harvard university division of continuing education website*. Retrieved from https://www.extension.harvard.edu/professional-development/blog/inclusive-language-four-easy-steps

Keene, A. (2010, April 27). But why can't I wear a Hipster Headdress? *Native Appropriations*. Retrieved from http://nativeappropriations.com/2010/04/but-why-cant-i-wear-a-hipster-headdress.html

Khazan, O. (2014, August 8). Why are there so many women in public relations? *The Atlantic*. Retrieved from http://adage.com/article/agency-viewpoint/advertising-industry-diverse-leadership-thrive/297998/

Killerman, S. (n.d.). *Breaking through the binary: Gender explained using continuums*. Retrieved from http://itspronouncedmetrosexual.com/2011/11/breaking-through-the-binary-gender-explained-using-continuums/#sthash.4OJIdZ7i.QFuFCiNH.dpbs

Krownapple, J. (2016). *Guiding teams to excellence with equity: Culturally proficient facilitation*. Thousand Oaks, CA: Corwin Press, a division of Sage.

Lacy, L. (2017, February 16). In advertising, as in culture, the US still struggles with diversity. *The Drum News*. Retrieved from http://www.thedrum.com/news/2017/02/16/advertising-culture-the-us-still-struggles-with-diversity

Luther, C., Ringer Lepre, C., & Clark, N. (2012). *Diversity in U.S. mass media* (1st ed.). Hoboken, NJ: Blackwell Publishing Ltd.

Lynch, H. (2017, July 6). NC Pride says it will solve LGBT festival conflict. *Raleigh News & Observer*. Retrieved from http://www.newsobserver.com/news/local/counties/durham-county/article159971034.html

Marcus Graham Project (n.d.). *iCR8™ methodology and boot camps*. Retrieved from http://marcusgrahamproject.org/mg-rebuild/bootcamp/

McCarthy, A. (2016, September 9). Diversity in advertising: Social media demands that brands pay attention. *eMarketer*. Retrieved from https://www.emarketer.com/Article/Diversity-Advertising-Social-Media-Demands-that-Brands-Pay-Attention/1014454

Miller, P. (2016, August 23). The promise and reality of 'Total Market' and how CMOs need to address it. *Forbes*. Retrieved from https://www.forbes.com/sites/onmarketing/2016/08/23/the-promise-and-reality-of-total-market-and-how-cmos-need-to-address-it/#716265555e9c

Mindtools. (n.d.). *Avoiding unconscious bias at work*. Retrieved from https://www.mindtools.com/pages/article/avoiding-unconscious-bias.htm

Monllos, K. (2017, April 5). How Pepsi got it so wrong: Unpacking one of the most reviled ads in recent memory. *Advertising Week*. Retrieved from http://www.adweek.com/brand-marketing/how-pepsi-got-it-so-wrong-unpacking-one-of-the-most-reviled-ads-in-recent-memory/

Newman-Carrasco, M. (2016, August 30). Why the ad industry's diversity strategy needs a new brief. *Advertising Age*. Retrieved from http://adage.com/article/agency-viewpoint/ad-industry-s-diversity-strategy-a/305638/

Odell, P. (2015, February 6). Wells Fargo's total marketing approach journey. *Chief Marketer*. Retrieved from http://www.chiefmarketer.com/wells-fargos-total-marketing-journey/

O'Dwyer, J. (2014, October 13). Capozzi outlines efforts to boost minorities in PR. *O'Dwyer's*. Retrieved from http://www.odwyerpr.com/story/public/3323/2014-10-13/capozzi-outlines-efforts-boost-minorities-pr.html

Olson, E. (2017, June 12). 150 executives commit to fostering diversity and inclusion. *New York Times*. Retrieved from https://www.nytimes.com/2017/06/12/business/dealbook/work-racist-sexism-diversity.html

Organization of Black Designers (n.d.). *Welcome to organization of black designers*. Retrieved from http://obd.org/

Porter, J. (2014, October 6). You're more biased than you think. *Fast Company*. Retrieved from https://www.fastcompany.com/3036627/strong-female-lead/youre-more-biased-than-you-think

Public Relations Society of America Foundation (n.d.). *PRIME programs*. Retrieved from http://www.prsafoundation.org/

Richards, K. (2016, October 10). The ANA's new alliance wants to provide the blueprint for multicultural marketing. *Advertising Week*. Retrieved from http://www.adweek.com/brand-marketing/anas-new-alliance-will-work-provide-blueprint-multicultural-marketing-173973/

She Runs It (n.d.). *Formerly advertising women of New York*. Retrieved from http://sherunsit.org/

Smith, C., & Turner, S. (2015). *The radical transformation of diversity and inclusion: Millennial influence*. Deloitte in collaboration with the Billy Jean King Leadership Initiative. Retrieved from https://www2.deloitte.com/us/en/pages/about-deloitte/articles/radical-transformation-of-diversity-and-inclusion.html

Stein, L. (2016, September 27). 4A's survey: Nearly half of industry professionals say agency is discriminatory. *Advertising Age*. Retrieved from http://adage.com/article/special-report-advertising-week/working-4a-s-survey-half-industry-professionals-agencies-discriminatory/306016/

Stout, J. G., & Dasgupta, N. (2011). When he doesn't mean you: Gender-exclusive language as ostracism. *Personality and Social Psychology Bulletin, 37*(6), 757–769.

Strauss, L. (2011, February 7). Groupon super bowl ad: When being clever offends and how to win one for Tibet. *Successful Blog.com*. Retrieved from http://www.successful-blog.com/1/groupon-when-being-clever-offends-and-how-to-win-one-for-tibet/

The LAGRANT Foundation (n.d.). *For scholarships and programs*. Retrieved from https://www.lagrantfoundation.org/Programs

Toro, A. (2016, September 30). A commitment to diversity and inclusion. *Public Relations Tactics*. Retrieved from http://apps.prsa.org/intelligence/tactics/articles/view/11659/1132/a_commitment_to_diversity_and_inclusion#.WVAgJ452rNR

Victor, D. (2015, April 5). Pepsi pulls ad accused of trivializing BLM. *New York Times*. Retrieved from https://www.nytimes.com/2017/04/05/business/kendall-jenner-pepsi-ad.html?_r=0

Part II

Program Planning and Management

Client Relationship Management

Clients are the lifeblood of a student-run agency. Without clients, there would be no agency. The term **client relationship management** consists of three parts: the client, your relationship with the client, and effective management of that relationship. Once you've recruited the right clients for your agency and won client business, your goal is to build and maintain a positive, successful relationship with those clients. To do so requires proactive, ongoing management.

> **Client relationship management:**
> Building and maintaining ongoing, positive relationships with clients through consistent and effective communication.

In business, the term **client** describes those who purchase or utilize a professional service such as legal aid, accounting services, or advertising and marketing services (like a student-run communications agency). In the communications industry, client can refer to both the organization for which your agency is working, as well as the specific people within that organization with whom you are working. Thus, when we say "the client," we are often referring to a collective "they."

> **Client:** An organization and the people within it who purchase or utilize a professional service.

> **Account:** A client organization with which an agency has a financial relationship.

Agency professionals also refer to clients as **accounts**. This represents the financial relationship between the two; agencies provide services for clients and clients pay them for those services. Thus, account executives or account managers are those in the agency responsible for overseeing client accounts. It's important to note, however, that everyone in the agency plays a role in developing and maintaining successful client relationships.

Littlejohn and Foss (2011) state that relationships are comprised of "interactional patterns" which are "connected to one another over time and create communication contexts that extend beyond any single communication event" (p. 229). They are dynamic, rather than static, meaning that they change over time based on how we "continually adapt our behaviors to the feedback we receive from others" (p. 230). The key ingredient to this ongoing change is communication—"relationships are formed, maintained, and changed through communication" (p. 255).

Client/agency relationships have often been described as partnerships or even marriages. In a communications agency, the relationship you have with the client is both interpersonal (the relationship between an account manager and members of the client team) and organizational (the relationship between the client and the agency as an entity). The two are intertwined. Thus, the relationship one person has with the client is often the perception the client has of the agency as an organization.

Sometimes, relationships go smoothly. Other times, there are tensions or miscommunications that make the relationship rocky. The purpose of this chapter is to help you

- Understand the client/agency connection
- Discover communications techniques to negotiate better client relationships
- Explore how to be a good client counselor
- Learn how to manage ongoing client relationships
- Communicate consistently and effectively with clients

© michaeljung/Shutterstock.com

MAKING A GOOD FIRST IMPRESSION

You've likely heard first impressions are critical in a relationship and are often hard to reverse. The same is true for your first impression with your new client. You want the relationship to get off on the right foot from the get-go. Once your agency has secured a new client, the account team will schedule a client meeting to discuss the client's challenges and goals for a communications program. This meeting can be held at either the agency or your client's place of business, depending on the client's preference. It's helpful to have your first meeting at the client's offices. This gives you a chance to see the client's environment first-hand, meet employees, and tour any facilities that are part of the client's organization. Before you do so, you'll want to prepare yourself for making a good first impression.

Do Your Research

While the client will brief your team on parts of their business, they will expect you to do some preliminary research on your own. As Jean Aukerman, global brand manager for Dow Fiber Solutions said in an interview with *Advertising Age* (Maddox, 2005), she wants agency members to be "students of my business." Immerse yourself in the client's world—consume the product, visit the client's place of business, review the website, join social media pages, and study the client's competitors.

Conduct a Google or database search (e.g., Lexis Nexis) of the client, the industry in which they work and their competitors. For example, if you are working for a local insurance company, you can find information online about the insurance market (e.g., the size of the market, the major players in the market, etc.); what has been written in the media about the company, its executives and competitors; how the company presents its brand on websites and social media; as well as how the target audience interacts with the company. If you are working for a local resource center that caters to the Hispanic community, you can find U.S. Census data about the size of the Hispanic community and research some of the concerns that the NGO addresses.

Pay close attention to the terminology the client uses to talk about its organization, its brand/s and target audiences. You can also determine the tone of the client's communications through websites and social media pages. Are they casual and fun in their communications or is their tone more professional? Also, sign up for any email blasts or join the organizations online membership if these options are available. Understanding as much as you can about the client will save both you and the client time, leaving more time to discuss the client's goals and challenges.

Lastly, find out what you can about the people you'll be meeting. Know their titles and roles in the organization. Connect with them on LinkedIn and follow them on Twitter. Find out their professional interests outside of their work. For example, you might find a client is on the board of the local animal shelter. This will give you more touch points for connecting with that client.

Ask Meaningful Questions

In classes you've attended, you've likely heard a professor say, "There is no such thing as a stupid question." Not so in the professional world. Uninformed questions waste your clients' time and communicate a lack of informed interest in their business. Let's say you are working for a grocery store chain. At the first meeting you ask the client how many stores they have. This is something that could easily have been found on the retailer's website and will signal to the client that you didn't care enough to do your research.

Rather than addressing topics easily found with a little research, spend your limited time with the client asking questions to help clarify the client's goals, clear up any confusion about their business, and help you develop a communications plan. Think through questions with your team ahead of time, write them down, and be prepared to discuss them in the meeting. It is also helpful to organize your questions by topic (e.g., brand, competition, communication) for easier reference during the client meeting.

In addition, you'll want to understand the larger context of the client's business, even if you're only working on a particular project. Understanding the big picture can help you determine where your project fits with the whole. In Box 7.1, you'll find a list of 15 meaningful questions to get you started. Although these are some suggested questions, like any other conversation your discussions with your client should be fluid, interactive, and informative for both you and them.

Box 7.1   Meaningful Client Questions

1. What is your "elevator speech" about your business? In other words, how would you describe your business/organization to a new customer/client/donor in just a few sentences?
2. On the curve of growth, maturation, or decline, where would you say your organization is? Why?
3. What keeps you up at night? OR What are your top three challenges with your business or organization?
4. We noticed there are several companies in this space. Which of these would you consider to be your top competitor? What do they offer that you don't and vice versa?
5. In terms of overall communication: What would you say you do well? What would you say you don't do well/need to improve?
6. In terms of a 1, 3, and 5-year plan, what are some communications goals you would like to accomplish? (How can communications help)?
7. Who is your target audience? What is your biggest challenge with this audience? What do you feel is your best opportunity with the audience?
8. Have you done any audience research that you can share with us?
9. What types of communications are you currently using, or have you used in the past, toward this target audience? What has worked well? What hasn't worked well? Why?
10. What are your goals for this assignment/campaign/project?
11. What does success look like? In other words, what results would you be happy with?
12. What is your budget for this campaign/assignment/project?
13. Who will our primary client contact be?
14. What else do I/we need to know?
15. What else would you like to know about us?

Listen and Clarify

As humans, we tend to think about what we'll say next instead of listening to what the other person is telling us. While we want to impress the client with our knowledge, it's important in this first meeting to listen to what the client is telling us about their business. Listening is critical in client meetings.

Think of it like a doctor's appointment. The doctor must gather information about your symptoms, past medical history, and the medications you are taking before making a diagnosis. Similarly, you need to understand the client's background and challenges before you can make an intelligent diagnosis and prescribe solutions. Hear what

© Antonio Guillem/Shutterstock.com

the client is saying about their organization and how they are saying it. Also, listen to what they are NOT saying. Ask clarifying questions to make sure you understand. This will provide important clues for how you should tackle their challenges.

Write It Down, Start a Record

It doesn't do much good to listen if you forget what the client said as soon as the meeting is over. Don't assume you will remember what the client told you without writing it down (you won't). Your notes from the first meeting will become an important part of your research and a guide for brainstorming strategies and creative tactics.

Many students take notes on laptops or tablets. This is appropriate unless the technology becomes distracting. For example, if every team member is clicking away on a laptop, the noise can overpower the conversation. The design of laptops can also set up physical barriers between your team and the client. In this case, you may want to take notes with pen and paper, and then type them up later to file and share with team members. Notepads or tablets are also helpful when touring client facilities where it isn't feasible to take notes on a laptop. Everyone in the meeting should take notes, but you might want to designate one team member as the "official" scribe. Others can then fill in the blanks with their own notes later. Another option is to record the conversation using a smartphone. Be sure to ask the client first if they mind being recorded. By recording the conversation, the review can be very useful and comparatively effortless compared to compiling a series of notes from others.

Dress Appropriately

Gone are the *MadMen* days of advertising where everyone dressed in suits, ties, and dresses. While some clients may still have a more formal dress code, others will be **business casual** (dressed nicely, but more informally). There are two ways to determine the

Business casual: A manner of dressing that is less formal than wearing suits, but still conveys a sense of professionalism.

appropriate dress for a client meeting. The first is to take your cues from the client. If the client environment is more formal, you'll want to dress accordingly. Or, if the client is business casual, then you can dress the same. The second cue is to follow your agency's employee handbook. Your agency may require that you always dress in professional attire even if the client is business casual. Consider your schedule and prepare ahead of time for the appropriate dress. If you know you'll be in gym class immediately before a client meeting, take a change of clothes with you to save time. Dressing as a professional means you will be seen as a professional.

COUNSELOR VERSUS ORDER TAKER

If you've done your research and listened closely to your client's challenges, you're ready to be a **strategic counselor** rather than just an order taker. An order taker delivers exactly what the client asks and no more. A strategic counselor thinks deeply about client challenges, and brings new insights and ideas to the table to achieve results.

In Box 7.2, you'll find an agency conversation with a nonprofit client and the difference in the conversation when the agency is an order taker versus a strategic counselor. Take a minute to read through both conversations.

© ESB Professional/Shutterstock.com

© szefei/Shutterstock.com

Strategic counselor: An agency member who thinks deeply about client challenges and brings new insights and ideas to the table to achieve results.

Box 7.2	Counselor Versus Order Taker Conversation

Order Taker

Client:	We want you to produce a video of our annual meeting and place that video on our website.
Agency:	Okay, great. We can do that. When is the meeting and what do you want us to film at the meeting?
Client:	It's on March 18. We'd like you to get footage of our keynote speaker and all of the breakout sessions afterward.
Agency:	Okay, can you get us a schedule of the events? We'll make sure to have videographers set up at each of the sessions. How long do you want the video to be?

Client: In the past, the video has been about 10 minutes long.
Agency: Okay, we'll produce a 10-minute video.

Here's how the conversation might go differently if the agency were a strategic counselor.

Strategic Counselor

Client: We want you to produce a video of our annual meeting and place that video on our website.
Agency: Okay, we can certainly do that. Let me ask you a few questions to get more information. What is the purpose of doing a video?
Client: Well, many of our members can't travel to attend the annual meeting. We put a video of the meeting on our website every year so they can at least see some of the highlights of the meeting.
Agency: What results do you want to achieve with the video? In other words, for those who can't attend the meeting, what do you want them to take away from the video?
Client: Ideally, we want them to feel like they're there, to engage them in the conversations. We hope they will send us their input on the contents of the meeting.
Agency: How well has the video worked in the past to achieve this objective?
Client: Marginally well. Some of the members view it, but they rarely send us their thoughts or input. And, by the time they do, it's often too late to include their input into our programming.
Agency: Have you thought of other ways of engaging these members in the meeting?
Client: Like what?
Agency: I know most of your members are on social media. You could live tweet the meeting on Twitter, and ask nonattending members to tweet their input and questions during the sessions. I also read an article recently about a nonprofit that used Facebook Live to engage members who couldn't attend their event. The live feed worked particularly well because viewers' comments were also live. In fact, even those who were at the meeting logged in and commented.
Client: Hmm, that's interesting. I'd like to hear more about this.
Agency: Sure. If you can give us a few days, we'll look into it more and develop a plan for how you might better engage your nonattending participants in your meeting. Would next Friday be okay?
Client: Yes. That would be great! I look forward to seeing your thoughts.

What differences do you notice between the two conversations? You may have noticed the first conversation was very tactical—how long the video should be, when it will be filmed, and so on. What about the second conversation? Did you notice the agency dug deeper to find out why the client wanted a video and the results the client was trying to achieve?

Strategic counselors are results-oriented rather than simply tacticians. They focus on the end goal and bring to the table ways in which the client can more effectively achieve desired results. You may also have noticed that the agency provided an example of how another nonprofit had engaged its members. This lets the client know that alternatives are both available and realistic.

Being a good counselor requires that you stay abreast of trends in the industry. Reading case studies of other campaigns is a good way to fill your knowledge bank with great ideas, and then reapply them to your client's specific situation. Agency counselors are also proactive. They don't wait for clients to come to them with problems. Instead, they are proactive in alerting clients to alternative ways of achieving results.

Some resources that will help you include regularly reading advertising and public relations (PR) publications such as *AdWeek*, *Advertising Age,* and *PR Week*. While these publications require subscriptions, you can usually gain access to them through your library's database. Stay abreast of your client's industry, as well. Follow industry news on Twitter, read industry trade publications, and remain vigilant about your client's competition. You can use **Google Alerts** to receive regular updates on your client's industry.

Google Alerts: A service that searches the web for predetermined keywords and notifies you when they appear in news or other online sources.

When you see something that relates to your client's challenges, shoot them an email: "Hi Deb. I saw this article today in *PR Week* and I think it relates to the situation you were discussing yesterday." In sharing this information, your client will see you as a valuable partner.

Being a good counselor is a mindset. Be curious. Dig deeper than what the client has told you on the surface. Ask, "Why?" Think in terms of results and be proactive in bringing your client new ways to address their challenges.

"My industry has probably transformed again just since we started the session."

© Cartoon Resource/Shutterstock.com

MANAGING CLIENT RELATIONSHIPS

Take a minute to think of a personal relationship you have with a friend or partner. What makes that relationship a "good" relationship? You may have thought of factors like trust, time spent together, shared values, common interests, or loyalty. Over time, you've gotten to know that person's likes and dislikes, what makes them tick, and what makes them happy or frustrated. You've adapted your behavior in response to this knowledge. You've also likely had your differences. You've disagreed, let each other down, took each other for granted, or even grew apart. In all, you've learned that relationships don't just happen. They take time, nurturing and even hard work to keep them going.

Professional relationships share many of the same characteristics as personal relationships. They are built through interactions, grow and change over time, and require ongoing management of interpersonal tensions (Littlejohn & Foss, p. 230). The difference between professional and personal relationships is the context in which they take place. Personal relationships are built around our personal lives; professional relationships are centered in a business environment and the work that takes place therein. Much like a personal relationship, the key to a successful client relationship can be summed up in one word—communication.

> **Professional relationships:** Relationships built through interactions in a business environment that require effective communication to manage continual change and interpersonal tensions.

Poor communication is one of the top complaints by clients about their agency relationship. Clients often feel "in the dark" about what their agency is working on, and then are frustrated when they find a project doesn't follow the direction they had given. Miscommunication occurs when account leaders don't outline agreed upon goals and direction, present a clear plan of action to achieve those goals, and then keep the client updated on the progress. But agencies are not the only ones responsible for a "good" relationship. Clients are the other half of the equation.

The Association of National Advertisers (ANA) conducts surveys of its members and of advertising agencies to determine the strength of the client/agency relationship. In past years, agency concerns have included dissatisfaction in terms of client briefings, client approval processes, and agency compensation. Likewise, the American Association of Advertising Agencies (2007) in a joint AAAA-ANA study reports key agency "value drivers" include providing fresh creative ideas and multichannel execution, working collaboratively with the client, integrating agency functions, putting the best people on the client's business, and providing new media and technology solutions (p. 3).

Clients want agencies that are responsive to their needs, consistent in their communication, and solve problems quickly. Below, we will discuss several ways to develop a more successful client relationship.

Manage Client Expectations

Have you ever gone to a movie that you heard was "awesome" but were disappointed that it didn't live up to those expectations? Likewise, have you ever heard a movie was terrible and then found that you thoroughly enjoyed it? Similarly, clients have preconceived notions of student agencies and often either over- or underestimate what students can accomplish. It is your responsibility to manage client expectations from the first meeting throughout the project. In other words, you need to align what the client thinks you can deliver with what you can actually deliver.

Let's say, for example, your client asks you to develop a "viral" video for a new product launch. When you attend the client briefing, the client keeps using this term —viral—to describe the video. A good account manager should stop the client at this point and clarify what is meant by "viral." Does the client expect the video to garner a million views on

YouTube and become a trending topic on Twitter? If so, you need to realistically outline the results you can accomplish and manage your client's expectations. Not doing so sets up the agency for failure.

Client expectations can be unrealistic in the areas of quality of work, quantity of work, program results, or the type of work a student agency can deliver. For example, the client may think the agency can launch a national social media campaign within just a few weeks. They may think a video will have the quality of an award-winning director. Or, they may think you can significantly increase their SEO when you don't have anyone on the team who understands how to do so. Clearly communicate with the client your **agency's capabilities**, the timeline for executing the work, and the results they can expect.

> **Agency capabilities:** The type of work an agency can perform for clients, such as branding, research, website development, and video production.

Conversely, clients can also UNDERestimate what students can accomplish, holding students back from achieving their full potential. A client may ask you to help with media relations for an upcoming event, but then you find they only want you to serve drinks to the press. With this type of client, show them work you've done for other clients as examples. This is effectively done through what are called **case studies**—reports that outline a campaign you've done from start to finish, including the goals, research, strategy, execution, and results.

> **Case studies:** Reports that outline the work you've done for a client including goals, research, strategy, execution, and results.

To show a client what your agency can do creatively, you can also do a project on spec—or speculation. **Spec** work means that an agency develops creative without being paid for it to demonstrate the agency's creative skills. Case studies and spec creative work can be used with both types of clients to help realistically set expectations for the agency's work.

> **Spec (speculation) work:** Developing creative work to demonstrate an agency's capabilities without being paid for it under the "speculation" that the client will be impressed enough to hire you for the job.

Don't Overpromise

One of the ways we set up our agency for failure is overpromising what the agency can realistically achieve. It's easy to get caught up in the excitement of a potential campaign and want to do everything the client asks, especially when we want to win the client's business. However, we do a disservice to both our clients and ourselves when we don't set realistic boundaries. So, don't promise the client you can create 10 videos over the course of the semester when you only have one videographer.

Agencies are particularly vulnerable to overpromising when it comes to creative work. As is often the case, account managers attend client meetings and agree to move forward with a project without first checking with the creative team. They then find that the creative team is working on several projects and can't take on another in the same timeframe. Internal communications between creative and account teams is critical before making a promise to a client.

In Chapter 8, you will learn how to develop a strategic semester plan and outline the scope of work the agency will deliver for your client in a given timeframe. It's essential for the client to sign off on this plan so both the client and the agency know what will be accomplished by the end of the semester. When other client requests come up during the semester outside of this scope of work, make sure to communicate with other members of your account and creative teams before agreeing to do additional work. If you can't do the work, tell the client why.

© ibreakstock/Shutterstock.com

Share the Process

Another way to manage client expectations is to share your agency processes with the client. Every agency has processes to ensure that quality work goes through the right channels and is delivered on time. Sharing these processes can help the client understand what to expect of the agency, what is expected of the client, and the timeline for when different stages of the work will be completed.

Let's say you are working on a new logo for a client. Logo development goes through many stages before a final graphic is produced. For example, you'll have an initial meeting to obtain client input; you'll write a creative brief and discuss it with the creative team; the creative team will develop several initial concepts, and these will need to be approved through both the creative director and the account team; then those concepts will be shared with the client before moving forward with subsequent designs. The client will then have its own approval before the work can be executed. There may be three or more rounds of creative design, each needing approval, and this takes time. Share this process with the client and give them a timeline for each stage. Not only will this manage client expectations, it will also signal to the client when they should be available for creative reviews.

Communicate Consistently

Too often, an agency receives client agreement on a semester plan and then disappears into a "black hole" without any communication with the client. During this time, the agency may be working feverishly on the campaign or project but the client isn't aware of this. They think nothing is being done and become disillusioned with the process.

A good account manager will keep the client informed with regular **status reports** on the agency's progress and solicit input and agreement from the client along the way. This may be done through weekly or biweekly meetings, through regular emails or through periodic phone calls. The client may also be open to text messages for quick questions or immediate updates.

Status report: A report that updates your client on the status of work in progress, that is, where you are in the process of completing a certain project, program, or campaign.

To determine the best way to communicate with your client, simply ask them—What is the best way to communicate with you? Some clients prefer short emails; others want detailed weekly reports; others prefer to meet with the agency in person. How you communicate with clients depends on the form of communication most convenient and effective for them—and each client's preferences may differ. You may also make suggestions. For example, you might tell your client that you would like to update them through email every Friday on the agency's progress. Ask them if this will be sufficient or if they would be prefer a different method.

Consistent communication between the agency and client has several benefits. First, it lets the client know that the agency is progressing on the work and not slacking off. Second, communication allows the client to provide input and feedback along the way. Clients know their business and may be able to make the process easier for you. For example, a client may have just completed a photo shoot. Seeing your weekly update reminds him to tell you—"BTW, we have some new photos you could use on our Instagram page." Third, consistent communication lets you know you're on the right track. Some clients want to be more involved in the process than others. Find out how often the client wants to see your work along the way, rather than waiting until it's finished and finding out you're way off base.

Lastly, and perhaps most importantly, regular updates signal to the client when you need them to review your work. It's never a good idea to wait until your work is completed to ask the client for a review date. Clients are busy, busy people. They have dozens of other tasks to attend to in addition to working with your agency. If you wait until the last minute, you may find the client is out of town or has back-to-back meetings scheduled, and this could delay your work. Here is an example of giving the client a "heads up" via email when you need their input:

Hi Sarah,
The creative team is finalizing the edits to the event video, and they expect to be finished early the week of March 27. Please let me know your schedule for that week and when you will be available to review the link. As a reminder, our timeline is to have final approval no later than **April 7**. This will give us time to send the video to your production team before the event.

Best,
Jordan

Communicating consistently also means determining WHO will communicate with the client. Traditionally, account teams designate a point person to handle all communication with the client (usually the account executive). This ensures that communications are not fragmented and the client is not communicating different information to different team members. However, it is not always feasible for the point person to handle every contact. For example, a creative team member may need to ask the client questions about an upcoming photo shoot when the account manager isn't available. In this case, you'll need to devise a system to make sure all information communicated by the client is shared with everyone on the team. The best way to do this is through a contact report, which is outlined later in this chapter.

One last point of caution—be careful of OVER-communicating with the client. As mentioned above, clients are busy people. Receiving a dozen emails from the agency every week can become tedious and the client may end up ignoring them. Stay organized, keep a running list of what you need to communicate with the client and do so in regular updates, rather than firing off an email every time something comes to mind. Then, share client responses with the team so everyone has access to the information and is on the same page.

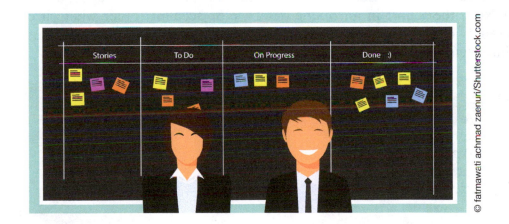

© fatmawati achmad zaenuri/Shutterstock.com

Utilize Contact Reports

A **contact report** is a report generated by account team members each time you have significant contact with the client, such as a meeting or phone call. Each professional agency may have a different template for contact reports, but the purpose is the same—to summarize the discussion that took place during the meeting or phone call; report any key decisions that were made; and outline next steps, the person or persons designated to complete those steps, and the date by which each task should be completed. Contacts reports are then distributed to those who attended the meeting and others who are working on the program or need the information—usually within 24 hours of the client contact.

Contact report: A report generated by account team members after a client meeting or phone call to summarize the discussion and any important decisions made, and to outline a timeline and responsibilities for next steps.

The top of the report should include the date of the meeting and list everyone who attended the meeting or phone call from both the agency and client side (list clients first). The introduction of the report should include the purpose of the meeting—for example, "The purpose of the meeting was to discuss the client's input for redesigning the website." Beneath the introduction, create subheads for each project or topic discussed, and end each section with a timeline for next steps and the designated person to complete each step. Be concise in writing your reports. Rather than writing a transcript of the meeting, just hit the highlights.

Contact reports are a way to manage information between the agency and the client, to keep the timeline progressing, and to "cover your bases" if there is ever a dispute with the client. For example, if the client asks why the agency changed the website banner from green to blue, you can refer back to the appropriate contact report where that decision was made. They are also a good way to keep team members "in the loop" to ensure each client and team member has the same information.

Taking good notes during the meeting or phone call, as mentioned earlier in this chapter, is key to writing a thorough contact report. Once you distribute the report, ask participants for any corrections or additions and then amend the report and redistribute it. Then, keep the report in an online database or account folder where it can be easily accessed by current team members, and by student members in subsequent semesters. You'll find a template for a client report in Box 7.3.

Box 7.3   Sample Contact Report

Date: Tuesday, October 17, 2017
Time: 10:30 a.m.–12:00 p.m.
Place: Agency office
Participants: (Name)
                        (Name)
                        (Name)

Purpose
Purpose of the meeting was to ...

1. Topic #1
(Summary of what was discussed on the topic, any updates, and key decisions made.)

Next Steps	*Date Due*
(Who is responsible for what)	(Date it should happen or be completed by)

Example:	
Hal to move forward on obtaining media list	w/o 10/23
Client to send photos for brochure to Lee	10/19
Lee to contact supplier to determine printing costs	10/20

2. Topic #2
(Summary of what was discussed on the topic, any updates, and key decisions made)

Next Steps   *Date Due*
(Who is responsible for what)

3. Topic #3
Next Steps   *Date Due*
(Who is responsible for what)

Don't Air the Agency's Dirty Laundry

Imagine if one of your professors complained to you about another student or professor. How would that make you feel? Likely it would make you question the professor's loyalty, or lose confidence in the professor. You might even think—what are they saying about ME to others?

In a professional setting, we need to walk a fine line between being personable with our clients, but remaining professional and loyal to our agency. This means not complaining or moaning about others in the agency or the agency as a whole in front of the client. The result of doing so can come back to haunt you and can damage the agency's reputation with that client or potential clients the person may talk with.

Let's say, for example, the client is unhappy with a website design and feels the team didn't understand the client direction. In the face of an unhappy client, our instinct might be to throw the creative team under the bus. The reverse can also be true where the creative team blames the account executive for the lack of direction. Instead, remain professional in front of the client and sort out issues between the two teams when you get back to the agency.

This is a good time to remember that agency relationships are both interpersonal (one-to-one relationships) and organizational (agency to client). The client will likely not care whose "fault" it was, and won't likely remember who was to blame. Instead, they will lose confidence in the agency as a whole.

Stick to Your Commitments

Overpromising, not communicating consistently, not managing client expectations, airing dirty laundry—these are all ways to lose the client's trust. Another way is simply failing to meet the reasonable commitments that you have made to the client.

If you're the agency that always misses deadlines, the agency that never gets results, the agency that always delivers less than you promised, you will quickly damage the reputation of your agency. This can have long-term effects. Remember, there are students waiting in the wings to take on your position in the months and years ahead. What you do today affects what they can accomplish next semester or even next year. Clients talk and word gets around. You want the word of mouth on your agency to be positive.

Follow your agency's processes, do your best to meet deadlines, and always try to delight the client with your work. Yes, there will be times when you don't meet those promises, but those times should be rare (Box 7.4). Aim for, "Wow, I never expected students could do this great work!" rather than "Well, this is the most I could have expected from a group of students."

Box 7.4   Client Relationship Tips

While discussing client expectations and meeting deadlines, there are key concepts that may assist you in planning your client relationship. These recommendations offer general opportunities to enhance/reinforce the client/agency relationship and suggest a starting point for cementing a positive relationship.

1. *Under promise and over deliver*. This phrase refers to setting goals for your agency in a timeline you know you can deliver on and then providing what is desired EARLIER than advertised with excellent quality and a little bit extra. For example, your client asks for a video of a sales meeting, with edits and graphic support. You agree to provide the product 3 weeks after the event. But, in the spirit of over delivering, you provide the requested product in 2 weeks AND use the footage to prepare two, 15-second teasers about the event that the client can email to their list of contacts and post on their website/social media.

2. *Create raving fans*. In 1993, authors Ken Blanchard and Sheldon Bowles introduced the concept of creating raving fans. In summary, a raving fan is someone so pleased with your service they can't wait to tell others about what you did for them. The best way to do this is to make client engagement as easy as possible for them. For example, if a client provides you with a digital file of an average photograph for their brochure, take the initiative to improve or reshoot the photo, correcting the problem. Provide the edited/reshot photo to the client as an option for their brochure.

3. *Focus on outcomes/success, admit shortcomings*. Always think in terms of providing evidence of the agency listening and providing what the client expected and wanted. But also, focus on outcomes and strategic goals met. Admit any shortcomings before they are pointed out and speak in terms of "lessons learned" for next time.

Check In With Clients Often

One of the best ways to determine if clients are satisfied with the agency's work is to ask them. A client survey at the end of the semester can give you a more complete assessment of the agency's work (see Chapter 13). But, don't wait until the end of the semester to determine if the client is satisfied.

A few times during the project or campaign, ask your client how it's going. Ask them if they are pleased with the work so far, what they feel is going well in the relationship and project and what could be improved. Doing so will help you make adjustments in the process along the way and will signal to your client that you care about their business. And, ask your clients if you may visit them as often as possible to present work or simply check-in. Clients respond very favorably to a student team who embraces, embodies, and lives the client business. Many experts in client relationships point out, "you can't manage a relationship from a desk."

WHEN THINGS GO WRONG

Mistakes are a fact of life in the agency business. As much as we try to control situations, mishaps will occur during the campaign or program that will need to be addressed with the client. Typos in printed material will appear, projects will go over budget, deadlines will be missed, video footage will be lost—and so on. One of the authors recalls a situation when a TV film crew accidentally set off smoke alarms in a hotel where a client artist was being interviewed. Hotel guests were evacuated—including the artist—resulting in the client missing an important interview with the television station.

When something like this occurs, the first thing to remember is—Don't panic! Easier said than done, but if you call the client in a panic, the client will become panicked as well. Instead, good account leaders will approach a crisis in the following way:

1. *Remain calm.* When a crisis occurs, our first instinct is often to berate the person who made the mistake. But, yelling at an account or creative executive won't help solve the problem and will make the situation tenser than it already is. Remain calm and think what to do next.

2. *Gather the troops to assess the situation and formulate alternative solutions.* This should occur as soon as you know of the problem. Call an emergency meeting of the key players to assess the problem and develop at least two alternatives for how it can be rectified. You may need to access other resources in this process. For example, if there has been a misprint in a brochure, call the printer to ask how soon they can reprint the material and how much it will cost. In this step, you will need to determine the cost of the mistake and who will pay for it. At times, the agency may have to take the hit. Other times, such as in the case of going over budget, the client may have to come up with the costs. Or, if a third party was responsible, you'll need to negotiate the financial cost with that supplier. Know this information before calling the client.

3. *Call the client.* Unless the situation requires immediate client attention (e.g., something's on fire), call the client as soon as possible AFTER you have developed alternative solutions and additional costs. Never hide mistakes or wait several days or weeks before telling the client. Doing so will make them lose trust in your agency. Be honest and straightforward with them. Tell them a mistake was made, own it, and then present your solutions for how it can be rectified. Clients will not be happy, but they will be much less panicked—and feel much more confident in your team—if you present alternative solutions for how you'll make it right. For this step, it is better to have a phone call with the client if possible. Email is not a good way to deliver

bad news because it doesn't allow for a one-on-one discussion with the client. Clients may also have their own solutions to the problem, so be open to discussing these.

4. *Debrief with key agency members.* This final step is critical to making sure both the team and the agency as a whole learn from mistakes. This is the time to determine what went wrong and how to prevent it from happening again. Was it a problem with communication? If so, how can that gap be closed? Share this information with others in the agency so they can learn from the mistake as well. For example, if a camera malfunctioned, others on the creative team will want to know how to prevent this in future film shoots. By sharing with the agency you can also determine if agency processes need to be adjusted.

Remember, mistakes are bound to happen. Remain calm, gather the troops, deliver the news honestly to the client with alternative solutions, and then debrief with the team to determine the steps you can take to preventing it from happening again.

© iQoncept/Shutterstock.com

DEALING WITH DIFFICULT CLIENTS

The ultimate goal in client/agency relationships is mutual respect. However, agency professionals often face challenging clients who make the job more difficult. In an article in *PR Week* (Murphy, 1999), PR professionals outlined different types of difficult clients, including "the alarmist," "the bully," "the unresponsive client," and "the client new to PR." You may face a client with these types of challenges, or even a combination of them. Many of the points already outlined in this chapter will help in dealing with these difficult relationships. Below are more specific ways of dealing with the four most common types of difficult clients.

The Alarmist

This type of client is often called a "Nervous Nelly/Ned." They lack confidence in other's abilities and try to micromanage your work. Take time to have a conversation with them early in the relationship. Let them know you have their best interests in mind and ask how you can reassure them that the account is in goods hands. Alarmists may need more updates than other clients to build their trust. Be proactive in providing updates before they ask for them. This will go a long way in helping them feel more confident in your abilities.

Alarmists may also prefer more collaboration on their projects. Include them in brainstorms or strategy meetings. When clients are involved in program development, they are less likely to be worried about the end result.

In addition, it's best to provide one point person on the account who deals with the Nervous Ned/Nelly on a regular basis. Alarmists tend to take over account management, contacting every member of the team separately. This can quickly devolve into chaos. Ask team members to direct these calls or emails back to the point person to manage the client's issues and direction.

The Overzealous Client

This type of client shares some of the characteristics of the alarmist in that they may want excessive contact. Unlike the alarmist, however, overzealous clients have *so* much confidence in your abilities they want to dump all of their projects on you. Set boundaries. If you make a habit of always accommodating an overzealous client, you'll establish an unhealthy pattern. This can set up a vicious cycle. The client asks for something unreasonable, the agency tries but can't deliver, which quickly erodes the client's trust. It's okay to say "no" when the client asks you to perform beyond your capabilities or the time you have available. Say no, and then tell the client why you can't accommodate their request.

With overzealous clients, it's critical to outline the parameters of the relationship up front, let them know when and how you will communicate with them throughout the semester, and then stick to it. You can also give them choices when they approach you with additional work. Tell them you could accommodate their request but will have to replace a project already in the semester plan. They can then determine which project is more important.

The Bully

Bullies tend to excessively complain and intimidate the team at every curve, and will often become combative. Stay as positive as possible with these types of clients. Never become combative. Bullies will find enough to complain about—no need to give them more. Stay positive, but confident, and try to determine the underlying reason for the client's attitude. You may find something is bothering the client that they had not previously revealed.

Some clients are combative simply because they have a negative outlook on life or a mindset that always looks for problems. Stand up to the client's challenges and address their issues directly. You will find these types of clients appreciate straight talk rather than someone who folds under pressure.

Although it's hard, don't take a client's negativity personally. Keep in mind that it's not about you as a person; it's about the work. Rather than becoming defensive, it's often best to let the client vent their frustrations, then bring the conversation back to the work and what you can do to address the client's issues.

In this type of situation, focus on the future rather than rehashing what went wrong in the past. See if you can achieve mutual agreement on a way forward. One way to do this is to ask questions and clarify. For example, "I hear what you're saying. It sounds like you want us to focus more on the product attributes and less on the price. Is that a correct assessment?" Sometimes, clients have difficulty pinpointing the specific issue that is bothering them. You can help by listening for underlying causes and weed out what is merely complaining versus legitimate issues that you can address. Assuring clients that they are being listened to is often enough to soften their attitudes.

The Unresponsive Client

Some clients are enthusiastic when the relationship begins, but then disappear when you need them to provide feedback or approval. Unresponsive clients make it difficult, if not impossible, to move projects forward. Clients may be unresponsive because they are just too busy, or they may have lower priorities for the projects you're assigned.

These types of clients need structure and strict timelines for approval processes. However, be prepared for them to ignore that structure. Account managers may have to be the "enforcers" when it comes to getting clients to respond. Padding timelines with ample time for the client to respond will help. As outlined earlier in the chapter, it is also helpful to give unresponsive clients a "heads up" when work is coming their way for approval, and remind them of your deadlines.

Unresponsive clients will likely want less contact than alarmists or overzealous clients, and will want contact to be shorter and more to the point. You can establish a system with these clients to flag work that needs their immediate attention, versus work that can wait. For example, agree to flag emails needing immediate attention with "PLEASE RESPOND" or something of that nature. You may also want to text the client to alert them to something waiting in their inbox.

Lastly, enlist others in the client organization to help you enforce client deadlines. An administrative assistant or even the receptionist can remind the client to respond to your email or take your call. Someone who works closely with the client can walk into the client's office and tell them in person—"Hey, the agency needs your approval on that copy by the end of the day."

Even if you do everything possible to deal with difficult clients, it may not be enough. If the relationship is no longer beneficial to the agency, you need to let the client go. In an article in *Advertising Age*, Ilise Benun, founder of Marketing Mentor, identified four "red flags" to look for: "chaos, no budgets, cluelessness, and disrespect" (Morrison & Bruell, 2014).

If the client relationship has become too difficult to manage, it's time to bring in agency management and your faculty advisor. Discuss the pros and cons of the relationship with them and enlist their guidance. It's helpful in these meetings to keep a list of

© Antonio Guillem/Shutterstock.com

issues needing attention. Sometimes, a call to the client from the agency advisor can smooth over the situation. However, if a mutually agreeable relationship is impossible, devise a plan for how to let the client go in a positive way that maintains your reputation in the industry.

CONCLUSION

Throughout this chapter, we have discussed ways to establish, develop, and maintain effective client relationships. Much of what is established in the first week or so of the relationship will determine the success of the relationship going forward. Make sure to be well prepared, listen to client concerns, share your agency processes, and develop an agreed upon plan for what you will accomplish. Then, keep the client informed of your progress, own up to mistakes, and work to develop a mutually beneficial relationship.

Over time, you will acquire your own "tricks of the trade" for effective relationship management. Pass these down to others to make your agency a learning-centered organization. Most importantly, don't be afraid to take risks and make mistakes. The student agency is the place to experiment with different styles and techniques that you can then master in the professional world.

Lastly, rely on agency management and your faculty advisor when things get tough. They can help you think through difficult situations and guide you in developing effective solutions.

REVIEW AND DISCUSSION QUESTIONS

1. Describe the difference between a personal/interpersonal relationship and a professional/organizational relationship.
2. What are five techniques you can use to build successful client relationships?
3. Name three ways that trust might be eroded with a client.
4. Your agency is developing a new website for a local nonprofit organization. Discuss ways you can manage client expectations on this project.
5. You are planning an event at a local country club to launch your client's new product to key stakeholders and the media. The event is in 1 week and the invitations have already gone out. The manager of the club calls to say they have had a wiring problem and cannot hold the event. Discuss with your team ways to manage this situation and inform your client. What steps would you take?
6. Your client is unhappy with the progress of a video shoot. While you feel the footage is good, the client says it is grainy and unprofessional. Role play with another student; one student playing the role of the agency account executive and the other playing the role of the "bully" client. How would you manage the conversation? Afterward, review the conversation and discuss ways to improve it. Then, switch roles.
7. Practice writing a contact report. The next time you meet with a team for a class project, take notes during the meeting and write a contact report afterward. Send it to your team and ask them for feedback. Were you a good listener during the meeting? Did you miss anything? Was the report clear and concise?

8. What is the difference between a counselor and an order taker?
9. Describe three ways to be a good client counselor.
10. Imagine that the local United Way has asked your agency to develop an advertising campaign to increase donations. Using databases available through your university library, conduct research on the client to prepare you for the first client briefing. Then, review the list of meaningful questions in Box 7.1 and develop your own set of questions to ask the client at the first meeting.

REFERENCES AND ADDITIONAL READINGS

American Association of Advertising Agencies. (2007). *Report on the agency-advertiser value survey. Report conducted by Ignite consulting group on behalf of the American association of advertising agencies and the association of national advertisers.* Retrieved from http://www.ignitiongroup.com/wp-content/uploads/ana-aaaa_agency-advertiser_value_survey.pdf

Association of National Advertisers. (2015). *Enhancing client/agency relationships.* Retrieved from http://www.ana.net/content/show/id/enhancing-relationships

Blanchard, K., & Bowles, S. (1993). *Raving fans: A revolutionary approach to customer service.* New York, NY: William Marrow.

Davies, M., & Palihawadana, D. (2006). Developing a model of tolerance in client-agency relationships in advertising. *International Journal of Advertising, 25*(3), 381–407.

Dickson, D. (2009). *The new account manager: Redefining the critical role of account service in the changing business of advertising* (2nd ed.). Chicago, IL: The Copy Workshop.

Hines, K. (2011). *8 Tips for creating a great case study. Kissmetrics blog.* Retrieved from https://blog.kissmetrics.com/creating-a-great-case-study/

Kealy, C. (2014). How to make yourself invaluable. *Communication World, 31*(3), 24-26.

Littlejohn, S., & Foss, K. (2011). *Theories of human communication* (10th ed.). Long Grove, IL: Waveland Press.

Maddox, K. (2005, September 12). ANA survey: Client agency relationships strong. *Advertising Age.* Retrieved from http://adage.com/article/btob/ana-survey-client-agency-relations-strong/261624/

McMains, A. (2008, December 15). New study reveals what a client wants in an agency. *AdWeek.* Retrieved from http://www.adweek.com/brand-marketing/new-study-reveals-what-client-wants-agency-97785/

Morrison, M. (2016, May 2). How account management was reborn: The account manager is more powerful than ever. *Advertising Age.* Retrieved from http://adage.com/article/agency-news/dad-s-account-man/303804/

Morrison, M., & Bruell, A. (2014, July 28). Five best practices from small shops. *Advertising Age, 85(16), 12.*

Murphy, C. (1999, September 27). PR technique—Client relations: Dealing with the difficult client. *PR Week.* Retrieved from https://www.prweek.com/article/1231629/pr-technique-client-relations-dealing-difficult-client-agencies-them-clients-tough-work-with-deal-situations-claire-murphy-takes-look-variety

Schultz, E. J., & Parekh, R. (2013). The best client-agency marriages. *Advertising Age, 84*(17), 1.

Solomon, R. (2016). *The art of client service.* Hoboken, NJ: Wiley.

Writing a Strategic/ Semester Plan

It is hard to argue that the sole reason a professional or student-run agency exists is to create the tactics, tools, and communications programs that accomplish specific goals that benefit clients. Whether it is a large-scale advertising campaign to instill brand loyalty, a media relations effort that garners coverage from the press or other influencers, or even a tactical banner ad that drives clicks to a website that gathers leads for sales purposes, agencies use communications to drive organizations' success. But how does an agency consistently deliver these creative, strategic, and innovative efforts with physical outputs like advertising or media kits? How in an ever changing world of technology, skeptical publics, emerging media platforms, and evolving wants and needs of a population can an agency deliver the old time-tested mantra: On time, On strategy, and On budget? The answer is, "with a plan."

Legendary baseball player and team manager, Yogi Berra, famous for his "yogisims," said, "If you don't know where you're going, you might not get there" (Berra & Kaplan, 2003). How appropriate. In this gem of a saying, we learn the importance of both *defining* what is the end goal or big picture, and *developing* a **plan** to accomplish that goal. You hear it all the time: you have to plan. Plan for retirement, plan for college savings, plan for a vacation, plans while on vacation, making plans for the weekend, 3-year plans, 5-year plans, and so on. So why do we casually toss around the words plan, planning, and even strategy? Because it is a natural human act to make plans but then not always follow through on them.

Plan: A detailed articulation of the steps needed to accomplish and reach a desired outcome.

So planning, and having a plan, are generally regarded as absolutely necessary to achieve goals; at least to do that consistently, efficiently, and effectively. Some have modified a statement by the venerable Benjamin Franklin to say, "If you fail to plan, you plan to fail."

In this chapter, we'll explore

- The nature and importance of plans and planning
- Characteristics and elements of a good plan
- Types of plans a student-run agency encounters

- Strategic communications planning and the plan
- The tactical communications plan and/or the "semester plan"

THE NATURE AND IMPORTANCE OF PLANS AND PLANNING

Humans by nature tend to be planners. Time and again, we have seen the importance of developing a plan in order to make progress. Whether it is sketching blueprints to ensure a new building is sound and does not collapse or mapping a destination and choosing which roads to take to avoid tolls and arrive on time, we plan consciously and unconsciously numerous times a day. As early as the story of Noah and the arc, humans make plans. The desire and need for plans are numerous, and relevant to our life as people and to fulfilling our personal needs and desires.

Plans, often the tangible output or creation from the planning process actually fit into a larger picture of how an organization might deliberately and methodically think and act to achieve its mission and provide value or relevance to potential customers, constituents, stakeholders, or beneficiaries. One useful model to recognize the role of plans and planning in communications is the **PIE** Planning Process (Bobbitt & Sullivan, 2014). Its three steps generally are the following:

> **PIE process:** Planning, Implementation, and Evaluation—the three-step model for developing a communications program/ campaign.

1. *Planning*—Research to analyze a problem and explore opportunities in order to determine the most effective response or proactive steps to secure success in the future.
2. *Implementation*—Execution of the plan. Which is also vital because the plan does not live in a vacuum and must be created by determined, talented individuals, and teams.
3. *Evaluation*—Measure the effectiveness as communications occur and afterwards to determine what needs to be done next.

Plans very generally might be created to

- *Improve*—Your grades or your health and fitness, or relationship with a loved one.
- *Avoid impending hardship*—To avoid hunger if the power goes out after a storm or secure a good job so as not to live on a parent's couch.
- Be more *efficient or successful*—Finish all necessary studying to do well on multiple examinations at the end of the term or burn more calories per workout.

Even when planning in business or communications, at its core, planning helps us to do things better, avoid problems, and be more efficient with time, money, and effort to achieve the best outcomes.

As a student, how many times have you begun a new school year or semester and said, "This time I will . . . " So planning as a process is often either unconscious **intuitive planning** or conscious **deliberate planning**. Intuitive planning is an absolutely valuable skill and should be fully embraced and appreciated. And while using intuition or simply creating necessary objectives and steps to achieve them can yield positive results, it requires a high level of confidence and experience from the plan maker to be successful. For instance, you plan to cook lasagna tonight. You have done it 50 times before. You likely don't need a formal written list of ingredients, nor cook time reminders, nor clear articulation of what successful lasagna will look or taste like. Your experience cooking lasagna and other Italian-inspired dishes will very well likely lead to something scrumptious. But, imagine you are planning to cook lasagna at a rental house, on spring break, in a strange town that you flew in to yesterday, for 20 guests only five of which you know well, in a kitchen with a different stove. Now, perhaps some deliberate planning is needed, maybe a plan of ingredients since you're shopping in a new grocery store, in a different community. A plan to address different culinary desires and preferences of your guests. A different plan of cooking in a strange stove with a different burner in a kitchen with different cooking pans.

© marekuliasz/Shutterstock.com

Intuitive planning: Natural, unconscious action of most humans to think through the steps needed and possible barriers to accomplishing goals even when not formalized in writing.

Deliberate planning: Systematic and thoughtful process of identifying objectives or desired outcomes and identifying the needed steps to achieve them.

© garagestock/Shutterstock.com

Planning is both natural as we intuitively map out courses of actions to get where or what we want, and unnatural to sometimes write out needs, action steps, outcomes, and an evaluation process. But the undeniable fact is that with a plan we have an increased likelihood of bringing about desired outcomes.

CHARACTERISTICS AND ELEMENTS OF A GOOD PLAN

What is a good plan you ask? We'll talk about types or kinds of plans next, but first, let's look at universal characteristics that all good plans share. Very simply, a good plan is one that brings about desired outcomes. Or, a good plan is one that helps you achieve the goal or reach the objective you wanted to accomplish. But not all plans are created equal. In fact, often times humans accomplish great things with bad plans or no plan at all. Delightful accidents and fortuitous turns of events or just plain dumb luck are great. But you don't want to bet the agency's future or future of your clients' businesses on a crapshoot. So good plans become more like great plans when they are goal-oriented, realistic, and measurable; essentially, all the things outlined in Box 8.1.

Box 8.1   **Characteristics of Great Plans**
1. Achieve a goal(s)
2. Are understandable
3. Are doable
4. Are flexible
5. Are measurable
6. Are disposable "single use plans" (relevant to the situation at hand)
7. Are enduring "ongoing plans" (potential to become templates or baselines for future plans)

So planning, any planning, really ALL planning shares some similar elements or components. These necessities must be present to not only devise a good plan, but also ultimately execute (i.e., make) and implement (i.e., launch) it. These elements include the following:

1. Identification of end goal(s) and/or objective(s)
2. Research and/or past experience
3. Determination of needs to achieve goal
4. Timing and/or sequencing of needed steps to achieve goals
5. Execution of steps
6. Evaluation of plan for timely efforts (tweaking) while its being executed and implemented
7. Evaluation of plan for future efforts upon completion

TYPES OF PLANS A STUDENT-RUN AGENCY ENCOUNTERS

A quick search of the Internet reveals a staggering number of types of plans. It seems that virtually every aspect of our lives can be and are possible planning experiences. Healthy eating plans, parenting plans, spirituality exploration plans, financial plans, holiday gift giving plans, and so on. Then if when we focus on areas of interests such as "watching streaming videos" we can even find plans for how to watch eight seasons of a show in one weekend (complete with a nutrition plan and bio-break plan, i.e., when and what to eat and when to schedule bathroom breaks). Who knew you could make binge watching more effective and efficient? So, it should come as no surprise when we think about advertising, public relations (PR), strategic communications, social media strategy, web design, customer promotions, email marketing, and all of the other various functions student-run agencies perform for their clients, we are blindsided with many plans, structures, and even worse, names for all of these plans.

Should we be concerned with tactical plans, strategic plans, marketing plans, operational plans, contingency plans, managerial plans, or staff training and development plans? The real question is less about what all of these plans mean and which plans we should concern ourselves with. Rather, let's aim to understand what is a plan, why we need a plan, what goes into OUR needed plan(s), and how do we execute a plan. Then the semantics tend to work themselves out.

In business planning, there are generally three major of types of plans. Broadly speaking, they allow flexibility for a myriad of other more specifics plans that encourage smart planning. Interestingly, just as an individual plan is supposed to help detail and organize multiple steps to reach goals, multiple plans should also work together to reach a common goal, objective, or desired outcome.

Major Types of Plans

1. *Long-term plans.* Sometimes these are called standing plans or ongoing plans. These plans tend to be a bedrock or foundation for an organization to both operate its needed business functions and to proactively plan for future opportunities and threats to success. As we'll see, strategic communications plans tend to be long-term plans. They tend to have broader or, some might say, more visionary goals and have longer lengths of time to reach goals. These goals might be something like "be recognized as a leading student-run agency by industry executives within the next 5 years." We'll need a strategic communications plan to accomplish that. Long terms are sometimes called "steering plans" such as an employee development plan to ensure proper onboarding of new staff with systematic review periods and training for recently promoted supervisors. It's likely your student-run agency has some of these plans in place, say an operational plan discussed in Chapter 2 or a client onboarding and financial plan discussed in Chapter 4, or even an agency brand identity and new business acquisition plan discussed in Chapter 14.
2. *Short-terms plans.* Sometimes called tactical plans or targeted plans. These plans tend to focus on more immediate and often concrete goals and objectives. They tend to have more specific action items and often try to address an immediate issue and are anchored in a finite amount of time something must occur. Such as, develop a media kit for a promotional event within 4 weeks or organize an agency end-of-year open house party for current and prospective clients.

3. *Contingency plans.* Sometimes thought of as *"if* this, *then* this." The U.S. government has probably one of the most recognized contingency plans. If the president is unable to serve, then the vice president becomes president. You can imagine there are many action steps needed to make that official. When is the swearing in? Who becomes vice president? Many companies have contingency plans if say the needed raw materials to make their products become unavailable, or the classic **crisis communications plan** detailing how the organization will respond internally to employees/stakeholders and outwardly to the media/public in the event of an emergency. Often there are triggers or defining events that prompt the implementation of contingency plans into motion.

Crisis communications plan: A specific contingency plan in public relations that is established well before a crisis occurs. It outlines steps and processes to address audiences, and identifies who and how they will engage the media regarding the issue.

Broadly speaking, the plans you will likely encounter may be first addressed as one of these three plans. Most likely your agency will develop and execute long-term plans, such as operational plans, administrative plans, financial plans, development and training plans, or short-term plans, like create a new agency logo this semester or plan the promotions of a guest speaker for next week.

© Dusit/Shutterstock.com

A Strategic Plan Is NOT a Strategic Communication Plan

When working with clients, they likely have a plan that tends to shape their identity, their business practices, and their mission. This is their **strategic plan**. WHOA! Notice we are not saying their strategic COMMUNICATIONS plan. Let's be clear we are not talking about strategic communications yet.

Your agency and your clients probably all have strategic plans that may or may not include anything about communications in them. Margaret Rouse, writing for *Information Technology*, points out how a strategic plan emerging from a strategic planning process captures, "[a] vision for the future as well as identify their goals and objectives for the organization. The process also includes establishing the sequence in which those goals should fall so that the organization is enabled to reach its stated vision" (Rouse, 2017). What we see is that in business planning terms, a strategic plan is concerned with vision for an organization and how to get there.

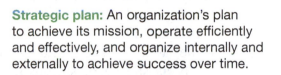

Strategic plan: An organization's plan to achieve its mission, operate efficiently and effectively, and organize internally and externally to achieve success over time.

Legendary marketing professor Philip Kotler describes the process of a strategic plan maintaining a "fit between the organization's goals and capabilities and its changing marketing opportunities" (Kotler & Armstrong, 2006). For instance, how can your local nonprofit arts council client be the source for arts education and enriching programs in public spaces to drive intellectual curiosity and economic sustainability? Quite a challenge, huh? That is what their strategic plan tries to address including topics such as what kinds of business partners to solicit for donations, what kinds of artists to fund for public projects, what traveling theater companies to hire to perform plays in the park this summer. Notice they are not talking about how to COMMUNICATE these activities . . . yet.

The Client's Marketing Plan

Next up and most closely linked to our jobs as strategic communicators who employ an array of communications solutions for clients is the **marketing plan**. The marketing plan turns strategy into action because of its nature to deliver value to people (Kotler & Armstrong, 2006). Like any good plan, it has a strategic vision or articulation of what the organization does or provides to people. It outlines steps to take that are grounded in the **4Ps of marketing**—product, price, place, and promotion—to ensure that an organization

Marketing plan: A comprehensive plan to address how to create, distribute, and sell a valuable product or service to intended constituents.

4Ps of marketing: Product, Price, Placement, and Promotions; Promotions being the most relevant and applicable to the strategic communications business.

provides a good or service (product), at an appropriate price, with efficient opportunity for people to access/get/use the organization's offering (place) and finally, that it is communicated accurately and effectively so people know the organization's product is available and valuable (promotion). This final P, promotion, is the foundation from which strategic communications emerge. While agencies don't always write marketing plans, they often have input and nearly always (or should always) use them as the guide for addressing their main role: the promotions P.

Many professional markers will define the most basic role of promotions as "AIDA," Attention, Interest, Desire, Action. The thinking goes that if people know, notice, and want, then they will act. For marketers and communicators this is a great starting point but not nearly as simple or simplistic as it seems (Bendinger, 2017). We still have to answer to whom, where, when, about what and how we should communicate on behalf of our client.

So, say your client is a nonprofit environmental group. Their marketing plan indicates they will provide public events to attract new supporters and earn as much as 50% of their yearly revenue from donations. You now translate that need into a plan that strategic communications can achieve. In general, **strategic communications** can be defined as the deliberate and purposeful use of communications to achieve an organization's goals (Holtzhausen & Zerfass, 2013, p. 284). In the case of your environmental client, your job will be to develop a **strategic communications plan** to successfully promote the clients marketing need from their marketing plan, that is, communicate these events so the client can provide environmental protection and accomplish their company strategic vision.

It is likely then you might have some **tactical communications plans**, or you may call it a **semester plan**, to make sure the student-run agency executes and implements the strategic communications plan to achieve the outcomes described in the client marketing plan. The tactical plan might often be akin to a timeline or schedule covered in Chapter 9.

Strategic communications: The purposeful use of communication to achieve an organization's goals.

Strategic communications plan: A plan that address the objectives, strategies, and tactics needed to resonate with intended audiences, delivered most effectively and efficiently grounded in evaluation for optimizing the best results to achieve an organization's business or mission oriented goals.

Tactical communications plan: A plan that often complements the strategic communications plan to be more specific about a particular communication tactic and tends to focus on very purposefully short-term priorities and specific outcomes as opposed to board strategic vision.

Semester plan: A time-bound, usually in a semester, action, or tactical plan that details the agency's deliverables and steps and strategies to accomplish them. Deliverables may span multiple semesters but this plan is aimed at focusing agency energy toward accomplishments during this set time.

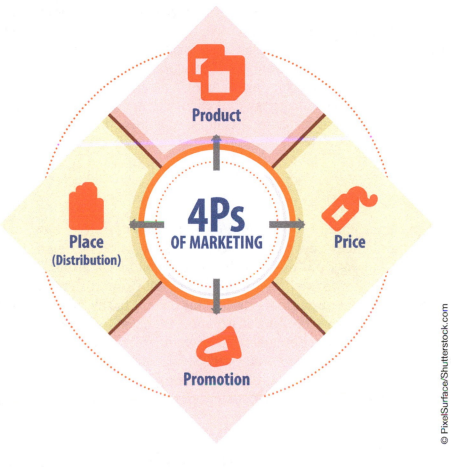

© PixelSurface/Shutterstock.com

STRATEGIC COMMUNICATIONS PLANNING

Developing a strategic communications plan might be the most important thing an agency does because it determines what we make and why we make it. It determines if your clients and ultimately your agency are successful. Of course it is vital to execute plans flawlessly, creatively, strategically, and beautifully. And the delivery of innovative communications solutions is much more difficult if not strategically planned. It becomes more of dumb luck and good fortune versus the deliberate act of formalizing and codifying steps to ensure efficiency and effectives to reach not just good, but great outcomes. Start broadly and follow the guideposts of the planning process to develop the ideal plan to achieve your desired end results.

So let's briefly break down the strategic communications planning process and needs. Essentially, the planning process is the work you do to develop a strategic communications plan, the elements of which we discuss later in the chapter.

Step 1—Information Gathering

Research takes place at every step of the planning process. But it's particularly important to gather information at the beginning of the process to inform your team about the client's organization, its market, category, competitors, target audiences, brand positioning, and so on. In essence, research is the input that will help you make sound, strategic decisions.

There are numerous ways you can gather information, as outlined in the Professional Practice article on research. Depending on the scope of the assignment and the client's budget, research might include interviewing people at the client organization, conducting online research on the market category and client competitors, monitoring social media feeds to determine consumer/customer attitudes, or conducting primary research such as surveys or focus groups.

Step 2—Goal Setting

Articulate goals of the client business and/or marketing plan. Or, why are we even communicating with audiences anyway? We need to know where we want to end up so we not only get there, but we do it as smoothly as possible. Remember the marketing plan and the company's vision for delivering something of value to its constituents. What is the business objective of communicating for this client? Is the outcome increased sales? From new customers or from current customers? Increased visitors to a location or the capturing of prospect customer emails from a website offer? Encourage trial of the company? Encourage usage, first time or repeat? Steal market share? Penetrate an existing business category? Offer new or improved goods or services? Compete on lowest price or highest quality available? Replace lost customers or retain current ones in the face of competition?

© chsherbakova yuliya/Shutterstock.com

target audience

Step 3—Target Audience Selection

Out of all the possible audiences or publics, which audience will you target with this particular program? What do you know about this audience? What do you need to know about this audience (research)? Avoid trying to be all things to all people. Your target audience should be narrow enough to affect real change, but broad enough to make an impact on the client's business. Read further along in the chapter for more on target audience selection.

Step 4—Set Communications Objectives

Translate business/marketing objectives into strategic communications objectives. This is broadly speaking what the goal of the overall strategic communications plan is. Or, said differently: "The overarching reason we need to communicate with our target audience is because of X." Communications objectives generally fit into one or more of four categories: awareness, understanding, attitudes, and/or behaviors. While not an exhaustive list, perhaps the goal of the strategic communications plan is to

1. Introduce or raise awareness of the client organization
2. Inform or educate about the client organization
3. Reach and appeal to a new audience for the client organization
4. Increase frequency of messages or stimulate engagement with audiences of the client organization
5. Instill a brand identity and positive reputation or shape perception of the client organization
6. Redefine or clarify or battle current perception of the client organization
7. Instill desire and prompt action among the audiences of the client organization

One helpful model to begin the planning process and embark on writing the strategic communications plan is called S.M.A.R.T. This model was popularized in the 1980s and often credited to George T. Doran (1981), a consultant and former Director of Corporate Planning for Washington Water Power Company. According to this model, objectives should be the following:

Specific (some say significant)
Measurable (some say meaningful, manageable, maintainable)
Attainable (sometimes achievable, sometimes assignable)
Realistic (sometimes relevant)
Timely (sometimes time-bound)—the point is to have a deadline or answer . . . by when?

Some have even added the "-er" to make this model Smarter (Yemm, 2013):

Evaluate or Ethical
Review or Reassess, Re-evaluate

Step 5—Develop Strategies and Tactics

In essence, outline how you are going to achieve your goals and objectives. If you think of the planning process as a trip, the goals/objectives are the destination (where do we want to go?), strategies are the route you'll take to get there (in essence, the map), and tactics are the vehicle/s you'll use (bus, train, plane). We'll talk more about strategies and tactics in the next section. Important points to remember are that strategies and tactics must (a) be based on research insights, (b) connect with your target audience, and (c) achieve your goals and objectives. In essence, tactics stem from strategies, which stem from goals. Make sure they link together.

Step 6—Execute Plan

This is what the agency does every day and is covered in your work processes Chapters 4, 7, and 9.

Step 7—Measure Your Progress and Results

There are two basic ways to measure your campaign as the product of the specific plan: **ongoing evaluation** (while the campaign is in progress) and **summative evaluation** (what were the end results?) (Bobbitt & Sullivan, 2014).

Ongoing evaluation: An evaluation of a specific plan that seeks to analyze how the plan is working towards meetings its objectives so that it might be revised or tweaked to be even more efficient or effective.

For ongoing evaluation, determine methods and processes to measure whether or not your goals, and your client's goals, are being met as you begin to implement your communications efforts and tactics. Prepare for shifts or changes to try to reach those goals.

For summative evaluation, will you look primarily to business results such as sales lifts or increase customer traffic? Or will you also look to communications-specific measures like increases in awareness, message recall, mes-

Summative evaluation: An evaluation of a specific plan that seeks to analyze if the plan was successful in meeting its stated objectives, and report on the specifics of how success is evident.

sage believability, intent to purchase, and so on? Will you look to social media engagement numbers, or sentiment levels of audience feedback? How can you measure people's attitudes or feelings toward your client organization? Will you conduct pre/post surveys to ask people? Will you count the number of mentions and level of support you see from the media or influencers?

Also include a **formative evaluation** so you can use those learnings later on. This evaluation is *what we learned,* whereby the agency can embrace lessons about itself including its talents, processes and procedures, and even its strengths and weaknesses in delivering strategic and creative solutions for clients in the future.

Formative evaluation: A holistic evaluation that seeks to analyze how the plan as a process worked, or its repective parts, to determine any learnings for how a person or organization might embark on a similar challenge in the future.

Box 8.2   What is a Strategic Plan

WHAT IS A STRATEGIC PLAN?

VERY SIMPLY IT IS THE WRITTEN RECOMMENDATION ON HOW OUR AGENCY WILL

1. SAY THE RIGHT MESSAGE
2. TO THE RIGHT PEOPLE
3. IN THE RIGHT WAY
4. AT THE RIGHT TIME
5. WITH THE RIGHT OUTCOME/RESULT

LET'S BREAK THOSE DOWN

THE RIGHT MESSAGE

What are we saying literally and figuratively? Are we educating people, raising awareness, changing beliefs, positioning against the competition, offering rational benefits, emotional benefits, instilling an immediacy/call-to-action, brand building or promoting a product specific or uniqueness or an event or a cause, etc. How do we get Attention Interest Desire Action (AIDA)

THE RIGHT PEOPLE

Primary, secondary, and outlier audiences. Demographics. Psychographics (hopes, dream, wants, fears, attractions, repulsions). Brand awareness, trust/reputation, beliefs, perceptions, drivers and barriers to usage or believability

THE RIGHT WAY

How do we deliver the message? An ad? On TV? A blog writer, a newspaper journalist writes a story, a BuzzFeed quiz, at an event, in the mail or email? On Facebook? Via re-tweet? YouTube video? A coupon? Website? What is the purpose per message delivery method independently and how do they all work together?

THE RIGHT TIME

How often do they hear/see our message? What frame of mind are they in when they receive our message? What time of day, week, season?

WITH THE RIGHT OUTCOME/RESULT

What do we want people to Think, Feel/Believe, Act/Do? How do we measure it? What will happen to prove our communications ARE working and DID work? How will we measure that people see our communications, believe our message, and then act accordingly?

DEVELOPING THE STRATEGIC COMMUNICATIONS PLAN

Before we even contemplate writing one word of a strategic plan we must, must, must conduct research. It is hard to ever overemphasize the need for quality research and understanding as a determinant of an effective strategic communications plan. It has been said that research is the alpha and omega, the beginning and the end of the strategic planning process. Others have noted it is really more of an omnipresent force driving our strategic and creative outputs at all times. It is why many academic classes, majors, and even graduate degrees are offered in research, not to mention countless books, blogs, and articles for in depth study. It is why we included a professional article in this text on conducting research.

Now we can get down to the arduous yet important and rewarding task of writing down specifically how we will create communications that yield success. You'll notice that some of this needed information has already been addressed in the planning process. So, let's get to the plan (Box 8.3).

Box 8.3   The Components of the Strategic Communications Plan

1. Situation analysis
2. Target audience(s)/publics(s) profiles
3. Marketing/communications problems and opportunities
4. Insights and challenges/opportunities redefined
5. Strategic communications goals and objectives
6. Strategic communications strategies
7. Strategic communications tactics
8. Message delivery plan (media plan)
9. Measurement and evaluation—budget, timing and approvals

Define the Landscape—The Situation Analysis

Before you determine where to go, you need to know where you are. Presenting all the research and relevant information you can acquire in one place becomes the situation analysis. This important first step for clients and students can reveal how much you already do know and don't know (Avery & Yount, 2016). This is an important revelation in itself helping you realize the complexity or simplicity of messages you may need to create for audiences.

The primary importance of this step is to begin to articulate (i.e., write it down, it is a plan, after all) the current realities and perceptions surrounding this client, their business category, competition, current, and past communications activities and success, customers/users/stakeholders, business mission and profitability/sustainability model, and so on. Understanding the brand, its value, and how people perceive it, respect it, engage with it, communicate with it, communicate about it, and interact with it are vital. Similarly, knowing its business model, user interaction seasonality, geography, category challenges and innovations, purchase or customer interaction cycle, and so on, all may influence the what, when, and to whom you ultimately develop communications tactics. Reading the Professional Practice articles in this book on branding and research will help.

The most important part is to cover all your bases and be realistic. It might be helpful in this section to conduct a **SWOT analysis**—analyzing the Strengths, Weakness, Opportunities, and Threats of your client, particularly framed in relation to the business or marketing goal you plan to address with communications. The **7Cs of strategic communications research**—the Client, Consumer, Competition, Category, Culture, (Media) Convergence, and (Brand/Service) Delivery Channel all need to be explored, analyzed, and reported on. The good and bad. As the saying goes, don't put lipstick on a pig.

SWOT analysis: Strengths, Weaknesses, Opportunities, and Threats.

7Cs of strategic communications research: Broad areas of research that often yield insight to develop messages and message delivery strategies. Client, Consumer, Competition, Category, Culture, media Convergence, and brand delivery Channel.

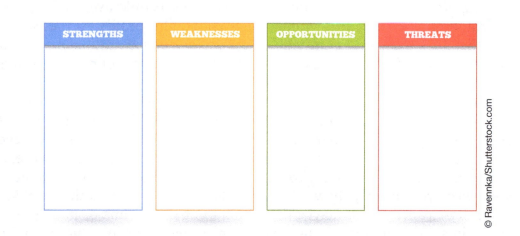

© Ravennka/Shutterstock.com

Define the Target Audience(s)/Public(s)

This possibly is the most important factor that will determine if the programs contained in your plan will be successful. If you wanted to convince three friends to take a road-trip to see your favorite band this weekend, you know you will likely need to tailor your message, its delivery, and its timing to persuade them. Each of your friends has a busy schedule. Each has desire for what to do this weekend. Each of them has different opinions of the band. Each has different opinions of you and how much they care about seeing you happy.

In her seminal work detailing a human-centered communications approach, *Hitting the Sweet Spot*, Lisa Fortini-Campbell breaks down audience **segmentation**. This approach, based not surprisingly on vast amounts of research, helps not only to identify to whom we should speak, but also why and how. By analyzing our possible target or intended audiences/publics we can use the six bases of segmentation to better understand them literally, abstractly, and emotionally (Fortini-Campbell, 2001). Creating an audience profile or persona or even a narrative or collage are common ways to accurately identify complex audiences, whether they be primary, secondary, or even tertiary audiences. Segmenting audiences includes looking at

> **Segmentation:** The act of creating clearly delineated target publics defined by demographics, psychographics, behaviors, usages, geography, and loyalty.

1. *Demographics*—Physical observable traits such as age, ethnicity, gender identification, income, education, habitation characteristics, religious affiliation, and so on.
2. *Psychographics*—Attitudes, values and lifestyles. Or hopes, dreams, wants, fears, attractions, and repulsions. This is more of an emotional determination about the psychology and sociology of why we value or desire or reject or associate with other people, and with brands and organizations.
3. *Geographics*—Geography is more than just where people live. In fact, it is often indicative of a person's demographic or psychographic profile. As they say, birds of a feather flock together. For instance, there is a high concentration of senior citizens in the Sarasota, Florida area; or people tend to value environmental sustainability and protection in the Portland, Oregon area.

   Moreover, within each location, different neighborhoods and even streets exhibit differences in demographic and psychographic characteristics. This is especially important if your client's business footprint is very local (hence why knowing this in the situational analysis was so important). For instance, a family-run dry cleaner really needs to raise awareness and be first choice in the affluent area where presumably the working population is wearing clothes likely needing to be dry-cleaned. And, maybe they should not spend time or money communicating in areas with lower household incomes, and deemed "blue collar." Unless, perhaps, that neighborhood exhibits a high volume of "church-goers," especially in the Southeastern United States and especially in more suburban-to-rural communities.
4. *Behavior*—Does your intended audience or public eat out regularly? Do they enjoy local parks or drive 50+ miles regularly to attend concerts or theater? Do they download movies to buy or just rent? Do they use their email or IM or Facebook Messenger most often to communicate with friends? What do they use when they

want to wish their grandmother a happy birthday? Behavioral characteristics will help us as we think of "cues" in our messages that show we understand their life. Not to mention where they go and what they do will have direct impacts on the where and when we attempt to reach them and influence them with our message delivery efforts.

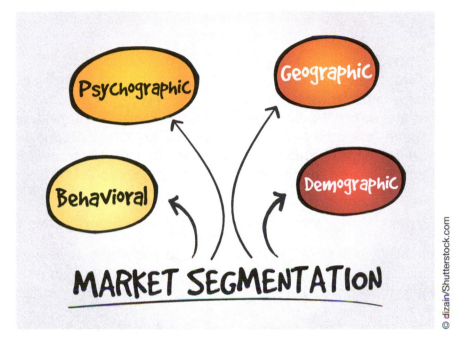

5. *Brand/Product Usage/Loyalty/Perception/Reputation*—Now we can get even more specific to how audiences feel/think/act in regard to the client brand or organization. A **reputation analysis**, again based on research, can answer questions such as how visible or known (awareness) your client is, how are they perceived and if this is the correct and desired perception, and how that reputation has changed or is likely to change over time (Smith, 2017). People's usage and engagement reveal enormous implications as you begin to think of your strategic communications plan objectives and desired

> **Reputation analysis:** Research to determine the reputation of an organization as voiced by influencers, media, and publics often through social media.

outcomes. Brand identity and loyalty are also important to determine if you are seeking new brand engagers or trying to deepen the involvement with those who have low degrees of loyalty. Or maybe your hope will be for those with a high degree of loyalty and strong perception to engage others via their social media platforms to advocate (and advertise) for your client.

6. *Benefits*—Let's admit it. Don't we all at least subconsciously ask ourselves, "What's in it for me?" As we develop any strategic communications message or hope to influence how a person thinks, feels, or acts, we have to be honest about why they would do that. Maybe you prefer 5-hour Energy to coffee because it is small, fast-acting,

long-lasting, and portable; unless it is Starbucks with that really cool logo on the cup for all your classmates to be envious of in that morning class. Maybe you prefer PC to MAC because the price is lower and it performs well for your needs. Maybe you are wearing that pair of shoes because you can't help but feel more stylish or maybe they are just the most comfortable. And that food truck just somehow feels more authentic and it somehow feels more like a cultural experience then visiting a major chain restaurant.

Benefits to a person often operate on our heads; they are rational, they are functional, and they work for us. And they operate on our hearts; it makes us feel beautiful, a good community citizen, better for the planet, helpful to people in need, a better parent, a smarter shopper, and so on. Rarely does a brand or organization appeal, or cause people to be repulsed, purely on a head or heart level. More often than not, appeal sits on a head–heart spectrum and is relatively different for each person. Do you feel as cool as I do when wearing Ray-Bans? You have your heart and I have mine, it's cool.

Define the Business/Marketing Problems (Needs) and Opportunities (Wants)

This is where a client's business/marketing plan is so important. Realistically, if you are working with smaller campus organizations and nonprofits, they might not have a written business plan. But what they do have are stated needs and wants, or problems and opportunities. This is why a client kickoff meeting or briefing or on-boarding each and every semester coupled with regular business evaluation and check-in discussions must happen (see Chapter 4). It is the unstated or even the unknown problems and opportunities that the student-run agency identifies and prioritizes that really propel it from just an order taker and doer, to a strategic partner that provides real value. This earns client trust and dependence and leads to more great clients and great opportunities to learn and create (Chapter 7).

Clients have concrete needs and wants, such as to increase social media followers or click-throughs by 4%, or increase first time trial by new customers by 10%. And they have more abstract ones, like redefine heavy loyalists' brand perception from one of traditional to innovative and distinct from the competition; or convince those who are disinterested in donating money that your client is the most effective at using charitable funds for community good. The point is to recognize that even if your communications efforts are creative and widely seen, and appreciated, and compelling, if they don't solve a business/problem or take advantage of a business opportunity/want then they are simply not effective and truly a waste of time, effort, and money.

Define Insights and Redefine the Challenges and Opportunities

Much has already been said about insights in the professional article on research. A true insight is not some obscure piece of trivia or simply identifying facts or realities, like students stream more movies digitally on devices than play DVDs. Rather, it is a revelation of a hidden truth that we all know but often are not able to articulate or acknowledge (Dru, 2002).

The classic example of the 1990s Got Milk Campaign stemmed from the insight that people purchased milk because they need it for specific occasions like with cookies or with a cereal, rather than the perceived health benefits of calcium. Just as important as uncovering an inherent human truth and arranging the data to reveal the obvious, yet previously unarticulated reality of what makes a brand, product, or organization special, is the need to then redefine the client's business challenge into something that strategic communications can solve or bring about. Rather than create communications to sell more milk, communications can remind people of the horrific shock of not having milk at that time they need it most, like with cookies or cereal. The insight rested in the true, but not spoken feeling people get when they run out of milk when they have something that really needs milk (Quesenberry, 2016).

So maybe your client needs to solicit new donations from first time donors (marketing objective). To redefine the challenge, maybe you can say in reality they need to "emerge as the umbrella charity seeking money to provide opportunities for all the others." Therefore, people should donate to the only nonprofit that allows others to help people. This redefinition of problem and potential opportunity leads you directly to goals and objectives.

Develop Goals and Objectives

Much is written about the differences between a goal and an objective. In general, a goal is the destination, what you want to achieve overall with your business, marketing, or communications plan. Objectives are the measureable milestones you will reach on the way to achieving that goal. For example, a goal might be to become the top-rated school in the district by 2020. An objective to achieve that goal might be to increase math scores in the district by "x" percent.

But, for our purposes, it is advised that goals and objectives be treated as the same general idea. In professional agencies, it is less important what you call them and more important that you have them. So, let's define an objective as the desired end of an action; what one expects to accomplish (Parente, 2006). Fortunately, marketing or business objectives have likely been determined and described in the situation analysis. Now you have to translate those into strategic communications objectives.

So, if the client needs to increase sales of milkshakes, the communications objective might be to "educate customers that the client's milkshakes are made with whole milk and compliment most food on the menu." If the client's business necessitated an increase in the number of attendees at a fundraising event, then the communications objective might be, "reach possible first time attendees with message of affordable family fun for a good cause."

Maybe it is like this; a basketball coach's goal (client business) is to win the game, and the point guard's (agency communications objective) is to hit at least 90% of free throws. The player's objective is different and only one piece of a bigger picture that may lead to the coach winning the game. They both ultimately have the same goal (or objective), they

© NicoElNino/Shutterstock.com

just use their special talents differently to get the desired outcome. So objectives give us the endpoint of why we communicate with audiences or publics in the first place.

In communications, we often breakdown objectives into mental objectives (what do we want the target audience to think or believe?) and behavioral objectives (what do we want the audience to do?). Here comes a bigger question. How do we get there?

Develop Communications Strategies

To get to those endpoints or accomplish communications objectives we need strategies. Strategies are targeted audience approaches to structure and deliver messages through specified communications channels or platforms (Wilson & Ogden, 2015). One of the first strategies to consider say, "when developing interest and desire for our client's product," in possibly the broadest sense, is deciding between paid media (advertising) or earned media (PR). Really though, the strategy is much more specific such as, "generate interest in our client's product through beautiful food photography." Perhaps another strategy to reach that objective of piquing interest and instilling desire might be, "engage or incentivize current customers to share their favorite menu items on their social media feed."

Broadly speaking, strategy is the bucket of "how's" by which you accomplish your objectives. It is not uncommon to have several strategies to reach a single objective (but not too many). Remember our basketball coach and her desire to achieve her goal of winning the game? Her strategies might include double teaming the opponent's best shooter, or driving toward the basket to draw fouls and put the opponent in jeopardy of fouling out, or maybe having her team sprint down the court in hopes of tiring the opponent who does not have as many players resting on the beach. All of these strategies aim to accomplish the goal of winning the game. Now your tactics will be even more specific. Such as, who on our side will form the double team. Which player will pass the ball so we can sprint most effectively to tire the other team? What kind of incentivizing do we plan to do so customers will share their favorite menu items on their social media feed?

A subset of developing communications strategies is to develop your creative strategy (i.e., creative concepts) and messaging (what you want to get across in your communications). A creative concept is the centralizing theme or "brand defining idea" around which a campaign is built. Creative concepts you probably recognize are Nike's Just Do It!, Susan G. Koman's Pink Ribbon campaign, or Dove's Campaign for Real Beauty. Let's take the Dove campaign as an example of how a strategic communications plan plays out.

For Dove, marketing insights told them that the health and beauty market was oversaturated; Dove could not compete unless they did something that was a complete departure. Audience insights told them that women don't feel good about the way they look—the unrealistic idea of beauty depicted in fashion magazines is unattainable. The business goal for the campaign was to increase sales and market share. Given the audience insights, the communications objective might have been something like "Develop a campaign that makes women feel good about themselves." How would they do that? Redefine beauty, facilitate a dialogue about "true" beauty, and align Dove with this new definition (strategy). The creative strategy then was to portray "real" women in all communications. Thus, the Campaign for Real Beauty was born. And, the key message the campaign conveyed to the target was that all women are beautiful.

In essence, communications strategies provide direction for your campaign. Without them, you'll get lost. And though your campaign strategies will not seem as straightforward and obvious to you as the Dove strategy, keep working at it. With the help of research, audience insights, creative brainstorming, and your eye on the destination, you'll get there.

Define Communications Tactics

So this is it. This is what agencies do and why they get hired. Tactics are what make success happen for clients. Was that obvious enough? These are the specific communication tools and instruments agencies craft creatively, beautifully, artfully, and strategically to reach the right person the right way with the right message. This cannot be covered in all its glory in these pages. That is why you are likely majoring in communications, marketing, advertising, PR, or similar studies. At its core we must simply ask that the tactics, whether printed, emailed, coded, or even spoken on a telephone are grounded in the strategy that the strategic plan has provided, to reach people, affect them, and achieve desired business outcomes.

So very broadly speaking tactics may be

- *Advertising*—Broadcast (video, digital preroll, radio satellite or terrestrial or podcast), print (newspaper, magazine, direct mail, brochure, catalog, newsletter), outdoor (billboard, public transit, wall murals), digital (display ads, native content), or even a hybrid magazine ad that only appears on a tablet or mobile phone.
- *PR*—Press releases for news stories or mentions, public appearances, media kits, blogging, fam tours, events.
- *Social media*—The client's own feeds, and/or promoting and steering publics' use of their feeds to promote the client.
- *Influencer marketing*
- *Strategic alliances and co-ops*
- *Email*
- *Sales promotions*
- *Contests*
- *Loyalty/frequency programs*
- *Point of purchase (POP)/Point of sale (POS)*

Have we missed anything? Surely so. One student-run agency even paid fellow students who lived near campus to wrap their vehicles with a sales message for a local restaurant to be 24-hour advertising in apartment and campus parking lots. Not a bad way to reach fellow students.

Going back to the Dove campaign example, some of the tactics they used included the "Evolution" video showing how makeup and photoshopping create a false sense of beauty, sponsorships of self-esteem workshops, partnerships with Girls, Inc. and Girl Scouts of America, billboards, print ads, and so on. All tying back to the creative theme of "Real Beauty."

Communications tactics are so varied we couldn't possibly list them all here. But, developing tactics is the fun part of the profession. You and your agency team now get to brainstorm all the possible ways you might construct messages to resonate with your intended audiences/public, in places, and times, and ways that work. And, it will now be "strategic." That magic word batted around so frequently will be true because each action, message, and message delivery will indeed be grounded with a purpose to achieve your communication objective which should then achieve your clients' business/marketing objective that should then help solve problems and maximize opportunities for success.

Define the Message Delivery Plan

When talking about audience segmentation, we said, "birds of a feather flock together." Likewise, when deciding where to place messages in the media we should, "fish where the fish are." In other words, if you want to reach younger Millennials, placing a message in a daily newspaper is likely not going to work. There are few fish (Millennials) there. Message delivery is addressed in more detail in the professional article on Media Planning.

In the strategic plan, the timing of communications tactics being implemented must have resonance and impact your identified target audiences. For instance, a manufacturer of sunscreen most likely will communicate March through August (when more people are in the sun) rather than in December and January. A coffee shop will likely want to reach people in the mornings as they begin their day, or perhaps even late afternoon as classes are slowing down to reach the student crowd with a "great place, great pick me up," message. Maybe reaching a parents-of-young children audience might be early morning as they are packing up the kids and dropping them off at school, or at approximately 8:00 to 11:00 p.m.; the time they have put the kids to bed and are trying to unwind with their preferred media.

In the strategic plan, we often think of this as the "when we should communicate." The advertising business tends to call this the **media plan**, but more widely in all strategic communications it is referred to as the **message delivery plan**. For most agencies, it is really not a

Media plan: Traditional term for the plan of the where, when, and how much to pay to place a message in through media vendors such as a magazine or billboard.

Message delivery plan: Modern term for the plan as to where messages are received by audiences including such social media, email, or influencers' blogs.

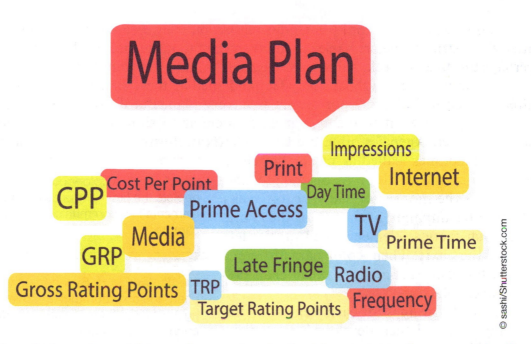

separate plan. It is a plan-within-a-plan; a plan in the bigger strategic communications plan. It is very specific to when and where messages are transmitted or distributed, and with what frequency, to reach the intended recipient. Essentially there are just a few key questions to ask.

- What time of year, week, day is most needed?
- What media platforms is the audience using when we need to reach them?
- What message delivery method is most effective to accomplish the communications goals (and are they different per target audience and at different times)?

Ask yourself when is email most effective in communicating information to you? How about Snapchat? And what about a podcast? They are used at different times and for different purposes, and the type of message and timing matters if people are to notice the communication message and care and act.

Develop the Implementation Plan—Phasing, Timelines, and Budgets

This section outlines how and when you will execute each of your tactics. Implementation elements include phasing, timelines, budgets, and any other elements that are crucial to program execution.

Phasing, or sequencing, involves laying out when the tactics in your campaign will launch, how long they will last, and how they integrate with each other. In essence, think of this as a master schedule. For example, perhaps the website launches at the beginning of February. Advertising drops 2 weeks later in mid-February and goes through the end of April. You launch your social media contest at the beginning of March. The contest is up for 3 weeks before entries are closed (end of March). Judging then takes 2 weeks and winners are announced in early April—in a press release, on the website, and on social media. And, after you distribute the press release, you then want to make media calls to pitch the story— perhaps this takes a week. All of these elements would go in your master schedule.

If your campaign ONLY includes paid media, these phasing elements may have already been included in your message delivery plan. But if you have multiple tactical elements, you'll want to create a master calendar to show how all of these elements come together. Agencies often use **Gantt charts** to illustrate program phasing. A Gantt chart, sometimes called a **media flowchart** in advertising to include media weight and costs, lists the months of the year (or weeks of the full campaign) at the top of the chart, with each tactical element listed on the left side of the chart. Then, color bars (different colors for each tactic) show when each element takes place.

Gantt chart: A color-coded bar chart that depicts the timing or phasing of all tactical elements in a communications program or campaign.

Media flowchart: Synonmous with Gantt chart, the common term in advertising agencies and often includes media weight and/or pricing information.

Detailed timelines for each element of the phasing plan are then developed. For example, you'll want a timeline for the website with specific dates for developing concepts, designing the layout, writing copy, internal and external approvals, photography, and so on. You should have a timeline for every tactic in your campaign.

Finally, you'll develop budgets for each of these tactics (see Chapter 5). A website budget, a budget for advertising, social media, media relations, and so on. Your budgets may include both time and expenses. For some plans you may start with ballpark budgets, and then develop final budgets once the

Example of Gantt Chart

program is approved. The implementation plan is essentially your roadmap for execution, and serves as your guide for bringing the campaign in on time and on budget.

Define Success—Evaluation Plan

So how do you know if strategic communications tactics worked? Or if they worked after the plan has been executed and implemented? You develop measurement/evaluation plans. Evaluation plans must be developed BEFORE a plan is executed so you'll know *what to measure, how to measure it, when to measure it, and what to do differently* if it is not working or did not work.

You may look to business-related goals and ask if the agencies communications efforts help to bring about the clients' business goals, wants, and needs. And/or you may also look to communications-specific goals to see if your efforts brought about desired outcomes. Did that email blast achieve a 30% open rate with a 7% click-through for a 2% sales conversion? Did unaided brand awareness increase over the life of the campaign? You may measure and evaluate the campaign or strategic communication plan as a whole or maybe by specific communications tactics.

Evaluation plans are often segmented by inputs, outputs, and outcomes. **Inputs** are what went into the campaign—for example, five print ads, two press releases, a social media contest, and so on. **Outputs** are what were generated from those inputs. For example, the five print ads may have reached one million people; the two press releases may have generated 10 media articles and five blog posts that reached 350,000 people; the social media contest may have garnered 2,500 entries, 5,000 Facebook likes, and 200 retweets.

Inputs: What was produced during the campaign, for example, five Facebook ads, two videos, a new website, and so on.

Outcomes are the impact of the campaign on the target audience or business. Just because you reached one million people with ads doesn't mean anything resulted from it. What did the target audience DO as a result of seeing the ads? Did the ads change attitudes? Increase sales? Improve brand perceptions? And, how do we know?

Outputs: What was generated as a result of your campaign tactics. Outputs might include number of website hits, reach of an ad campaign, or the number of people who submitted contest entries.

Outcomes: The impacts of your campaign on your target audience or the client's business. Outcomes might include changes in perceptions or attitudes, increases in sales or donations, or improved brand loyalty or customer relationships.

While outputs most often relate to measuring the results of our *tactics*, outcomes most often relate to measuring our overarching *goals and objectives*—for example, building awareness, changing perceptions, increasing sales. Outputs can be measured fairly easily by counting the number of website hits, monitoring the number of retweets, tallying how many people attended an event, and so on. Outcomes often require more complex measurements such as pre- and post-campaign surveys or adding up sales receipts compared to the same period last year. Your student agency may not have the capabilities for conducting these measurements, or the client may not have the money. Still, both outputs and outcomes should be considered in developing your evaluation plan.

DEVELOPING A SEMESTER PLAN

Student-run agencies tend to think of delivering strategy and execution in the time frame of a school semester. This makes sense and it is a natural "time-bound" element we discussed in S.M.A.R.T. planning. If you are developing a strategic communications plan for your client, chances are you won't be able to complete all the steps in the planning process

Box 8.4 **How a Semester Plan Fits into a Strategic Communications Plan**

Strategic Plan

Semester Plan

Tactical Plan (Research)
• Target audience
• Business catagory
• Reputation Analysis

Tactical Plan (Communications Tools Development)
• Print Ad
• Media Kit
• Email Template
• Social Media Content

Tactical Plan (Message Delivery)
• Rate cards / prices
• Editorial calendars
• File delivery requirements

in just one semester. So, you might develop the plan or parts of the plan in the first semester, and execute it the following semester.

For instance, what do you need to do in order to complete Step 1 (situational analysis) in a strategic communications plan? Well, you need research and probably a good bit of it. So who is going to investigate the client's current communications efforts? When will you investigate the trends in their business category? How will you gather information about the competition and their strengths' and weaknesses? This is but one part of the tactical, semester plan you need to accomplish for just the first step in your overall strategic plan.

Now imagine you have many steps and many different timing needs in order to learn about your target audience and then gain client approval on your objectives. Say you recommend a grand opening event as a key communication strategy or even a contest/raffle drawing at that event as a tactic; then you might need research on best practices for such a tactic like researching legal ramifications for a contest in your county/state. These are the nitty-gritty steps within the strategic plan that need tactical communications plans (Box 8.4). The tactical plans are then encompassed in everything you will do this semester in your semester plan.

Just remember, it is entirely possible you and/or your agency has been working with the client for several semesters and are already executing the strategic plan, or that you are working with your client on a project basis and don't have or even need a strategic plan. Some clients may simply need social media content and a trade show banner this semester. Or maybe even a product sell sheet and a corporate "about us" video for their website. The point is, sometimes the semester plan is a tactical plan where the focus is on the steps to deliver a communications instrument (like media pitch emails) or even a point of view or a research findings report. But for all of these scenarios, you'll often create a semester plan, or a plan that outlines what you will work on and accomplish THIS SEMESTER.

© iQoncept/Shutterstock.com

What to Include in a Semester Plan

What you include in a semester plan will largely depend on your timeframe and the type of work you are conducting for your client. However, there are three key elements that will likely be included in every semester plan: deliverables (what you will deliver to the client by the end of the semester); a timeline (what will be accomplished, when); and a budget (what it costs to executive the deliverables, including any time and expenses).

Your semester plan may also include other elements that are important to the work. Let's take a video as an example. To create a video for the client, you'll want to know why the client needs the video. What is the purpose of the video? What are they using it for? Is there a challenge they need the video to overcome? What does the client want to accomplish with the video? The answers to all of these questions might go in a brief situation analysis (e.g., a paragraph or two), and maybe a "Goals/Objective" section that outlines the goal for producing the video.

It's also important to know the audience for the video. Who are we targeting? What are their demographics, psychographics, geography, and so on? These answers to these questions would go in a "Target Audience" section of the plan. And, you might have a "Strategy" section that briefly outlines how you will go about producing the video to accomplish the client's goals, as well as outlining the key messages and/or brand positioning that needs to come across in the video.

Then, you would have a tactical plan and timeline. This would include a plan for scriptwriting, recruiting talent, travelling to film locations, filming, editing, reediting, uploading, and so on. And, of course, you'll need to include time for client approvals. Accompanying the timeline would be a budget. How much will talent cost? Are there any materials you need for editing? Props? And so on. Finally, you may have an evaluation section on how you will evaluate your work and/or the results of your work.

The point is that every semester plan will be different. Some will be similar to scope-of-work documents (see Chapter 4), whereas others will be a hybrid between a strategic plan and a tactical plan. It all depends on your agency processes, the client and the type of work you are doing.

A Word About Client Approvals

- They must happen
- Time must be accounted for to secure them. Clients are not always "in the office"
- Time for revisions must be planned in order to secure them
- They need to be clear and formal and ideally a written agreement, especially if you are spending the client's money

All too often agencies get so caught up in brilliant strategy and creative execution they forget that clients might not agree or they might want to tweak your work. So plan ahead and be diligent about getting the client's buy in on every step of the process lest you create a bunch of killer concepts that unfortunately do not address the client's marketing communications need. In fact, client approval is a hallmark of establishing good relationships seen in Chapter 7.

CONCLUSION

A strategic plan is a culmination of all of the activities the agency does. It is the codified unification of the steps needed to create and implement communications campaigns. It is a combination of a research plan, a message content strategy, a message/media delivery plan, and a budget plan. It is brought to life through various tactical plans to achieve all of the steps. Perhaps it is best to think of it as the master plan for a client's success that directs people to all of the other plans to achieve its parts. It is deliberate and written down for all to see, all to follow, all to revise and shift as necessary, and all to evaluate as you execute and implement tactics.

Planning is natural to humans, but the discipline of stating objectives and really planning action steps while anticipating timing and other curveballs takes skill and practice. But just like baking perfect lasagna even as the variables change of where, when, how many, the available ingredients and cooking utensils, the more you do it, the more the unanticipated hurdles and windows of opportunities become clearer and you sail smoothly toward your goals.

REVIEW AND DISCUSSION QUESTIONS

1. Why do humans have a natural tendency to embrace and eschew planning as a process? What are the broad purposes or main reasons that people make plans?
2. What is a plan? What common characteristics do effective plans tend to share?
3. Why is the inclusion of measurement and evaluation so important in a plan?
4. Describe the three major types of plans? How can a student-run agency create and implement each of them?
5. How do marketing plans, strategic plans, and strategic communications plans complement one another and differ from one another?
6. What are some common objectives of strategic communications plans? How are they similar or different than the marketing plan objectives?
7. Why is segmentation so important for developing strategic communications plans? How does your agency conduct research and make recommendations based on segmentation?
8. What are objectives, strategies, and tactics? How do they relate, yet differ when your agency creates a strategic communications plan for your clients?
9. How does a semester plan differ from and complement a student-run agency's strategic communications plan?
10. Why is a message delivery plan often a component of a larger strategic communications plan? Why does it deserve such special attention?

REFERENCES AND ADDITIONAL READINGS

Avery, J., & Yount, D. (2016). *Advertising campaign planning: Developing an advertising-based marketing plan* (5th ed.). Chicago, IL: The Copy Workshop.

Bendinger, B. (2017). *The A to B shift in Readings in account planning* (2nd ed.). Chicago, IL: The Copy Workshop.

Berra, Y., & Kaplan, D. (2003). *What time is it? You mean now? Advice for life from the Zennest master of them all.* New York, NY: Simon & Shuster.

Bobbit, R., & Sullivan, R. (2014). *Developing the public relations campaign: A team based approach* (3rd ed.). Boston, MA: Pearson Education/Allyn and Bacon.

Doran, G. T. (1981). There's a S.M.A.R.T. way to write management's goals and objectives. *Management Review, 70*(11), 35–36.

Dru, J. (2002). *Beyond disruption: Changing the rules in the marketplace.* New York, NY: John Wiley & Sons.

Fortini-Campbell, L. (2001). *Hitting the sweet spot: How consumer insights can inspire better marketing and advertising.* Chicago, IL: The Copy Workshop.

Holtzhausen, D., & Zerfass, A. (2013). Strategic communication: Pillars and perspectives of an alternative paradigm. In K. Sriramesh, A. Zerfass, & J. N. Kim (Eds.), *Public relations and communication management: Current trends and emerging topics* (pp. 283–302). New York, NY: Routledge/Taylor & Francis.

Kotler, P., & Armstrong, G. (2006). *Principles of marketing* (11th ed.). Upper Saddle River, NJ: Pearson Prentice Hall.

Parente, D. (2006). *Advertising campaign strategy* (4th ed.). Mason, OH: Cengage Learning.

Quesenberry, K. (2016). *Social media strategy: Marketing and advertising in the consumer revolution.* Lanham, MD: Roman & Littlefield.

Rouse, M. (2017). *In SearchCIO/Techtarget.com.* Retrieved from http://searchcio.techtarget.com/definition/strategic-planning

Smith, R. (2017). *Strategic planning for public relations* (5th ed.). New York, NY: Routledge.

Wilson, L., & Ogden, J. (2015). *Strategic communications planning for public relations and marketing* (6th ed.). Dubuque, IA: Kendall Hunt Publishing Company.

Yemm, G. (2013). *Essential guide to leading your team: How to set goals, measure performance and reward talent* (pp. 37–39). New York, NY: Pearson Education.

Chapter 9

Project Management

To the uninitiated, the advertising and public relations (PR) worlds can seem impossibly glamorous, replete with big ideas, dramatic pitches, brilliant campaigns, Hollywood-level production and extravagant, star-studded galas and parties. Although it's certainly an exciting career, it isn't exactly the life of Don Draper from AMC's *MadMen* or Olivia Pope from ABC's *Scandal*. Well, maybe just a little bit. After all, it's the glamor and excitement that initially draws many students to consider a career in communications in the first place.

It's important, however, to remember that behind the big impact from big campaigns, you will find big budgets and even bigger stakes. You've probably heard, "the devil is in the details." It's those details that can derail otherwise big ideas from being implemented and generating successful outcomes. Incredibly high client expectations, tight timelines, unforeseen glitches, necessary revenue targets, and shareholder expectations all ratchet up the pressure to create very little room for error when it comes to the flawless execution of strategic communications campaigns. For this reason, agencies must constantly improve their mastery of an underappreciated, yet mission-critical component of this business: **project management**. After all, if we don't have solid client relationships founded on trust earned from delivering effective and successful campaigns and communications programs time and again, then we are out of business. Many clients will tell you they would rather have average ideas delivered smoothly and timely as opposed to brilliance that is a headache to launch.

> **Project management:** The use of established processes and procedures to ensure a project is planned and executed within budget, on time, and in line with the client's strategic objectives.

As a new employee in your first professional job in the communications business, one of the most significant challenges you will encounter is to learn and understand your agency's project management process. Moreover, the more junior you are in your career, the more you will work internally at your organization to deliver the strategies and concepts needed for client success. As you become more seasoned, your focus will likely shift toward more client and other external big picture planning issues rather than the actual execution of plans.

Every agency has its own proprietary way of managing the milestones, checkpoints, and myriad of details that go into a successful project or campaign; work at 10 different agencies and you'll likely see 10 different approaches. The timelines, templates, terminology, and team members may vary from agency to agency and even from account to account within agencies. Whether you become an art director or a media buyer, a social media content producer or a crisis communications professional, familiarity with and understanding of the fundamentals of project management will enable you to quickly begin working in lockstep with the other members of your team, making you indispensable to both agency leadership and to your client. It's essential. It's an unavoidable part of the strategic communications agency business. And, it's job security for those who appreciate it and master it.

In this chapter, we discuss and explore

- The origins of project management
- Defining project management
- Strategic communications project management
- Project management: beginning to end
- Project management in "the real world"

Regardless of your role in the student-run agency, or really wherever your post college path takes you, appreciating, understanding, and adhering to project management principles will be an invaluable skill for you, your colleagues, and the organizations that you work for or lead in the future.

THE ORIGINS OF PROJECT MANAGEMENT

As a student embarking on the lifelong strategic communications educational journey, it is not important at this time for you to try to anticipate and master the specific and nuanced project management approach your future employer may use. Instead, let's focus on the bigger picture of project management so you might help your student-run agency develop its own unique process to ensure that you make the kind of communication programs that benefit your clients and help you launch your career.

Despite their many differences, effective project management processes all contain the same essential fundamentals. The specific tactics and techniques really don't matter much, and they are relatively interchangeable anyway. Moreover, every project is different and will likely call for tweaks in the process, so it can't be too rigid or inflexible. Rather, it is most important for you to understand the *value* of solid project management, the *fundamentals* of successful project management approaches, how to *work effectively* within an established project management framework, and how to *improve and support* the project management process within your agency team. With a rock-solid foundation of universal project management skills developed during your time at a student-run agency, you'll be prepared to hit the ground running in your professional career, regardless of the specific "system" used. But first, a little history.

The Traffic Department

In the earlier days of advertising specifically, project managers were often housed in the **traffic department** and likely held titles indicating levels of experience or seniority ranging from traffic coordinators, to traffic mangers, to traffic supervisors, to the director of traffic. Traditionally, PR agencies, which didn't produce ads or the same types of creative materials as ad agencies, did not have traffic departments. Instead, account executives or account coordinators were responsible for shepherding any work through agency processes. As the complexity of PR deliverables increases, so emerges the existence of the project management specialist in today's larger PR firms.

© Kaesler Media/Shutterstock.com

Traffic department: Now replaced by project management in many agencies, this department was responsible for moving projects through the agency process and out the door.

In ad agencies, before the creation of and near universal adoption of email, cloud servers, and web-based tools, it was necessary to physically move layouts, creative briefs, planning documents, high resolution proofs, match prints, copy decks, and many other materials around the agency from department-to-department and person-to-person so that each team member could complete his or her work. Traffic coordinators were responsible for keeping these materials moving, literally, in accordance with timelines so that all the aspects of a project were completed on time and with the proper approvals, or **signoffs**.

A person successful in the traffic department had to be systematic, exact, farsighted, and keenly aware of all of the processes that go into ensuring an agency delivered its outputs and outcomes for clients. They not only know who does each job in the agency, but how it is done, and how long each step takes (Hamerhoff, 1998, p. 181).

Signoffs: Synonymous with approval. Indicates that a person has agreed the existing stage and materials are approved to proceed with whatever the next step in the process might be.

The traffic department closely monitored agency staff's time and the client's money, or even more specifically, how much profit the agency would make. As we have seen in Chapter 5, timesheets and time accounting are critical elements of many agencies' revenue structures. Being efficient with one's time and that of others leads to account profitability (Davis & Dickinson, 2017), which ultimately leads to receiving a paycheck and maybe even a raise one day.

Traffic managers also helped keep project costs within budget. Before a team could begin working on a new project or campaign, it was the traffic manager's responsibility to "open the job" so that work could begin and all of the billable hours and costs relating to each project could be estimated, tracked, accounted for, and ultimately billed upon completion or when they "close the job." Large manila expanding pocket folders called **job jackets** held all the important papers related to each **job**, and the edges of the folder were often mysteriously coded with a long string of letters and numbers signifying the client, project, component, and date: the job number. It was not unheard of for one campaign to have dozens of job numbers, one for each version of a TV spot, size of a print ad, length of a radio spot, and so on. Avery and Yount, in their chapter *Working Procedures* refer to this as "the box" (Avery & Yount, 2010).

Job jacket: Literal, physical folder or envelope or digital file where all important and necessary documents related to the job/deliverable are kept and accessible for all parties that need them.

Job: General term for a project name or deliverable that the agency is working on; often will have an associated number or other marker to help track time and expenses.

> It can be a physical box, in which case it should be wide and tall enough to hold a file folder. It can be a file drawer, a fruit box, or a plastic or cardboard box designed to hold files. Or it can be a folder on an internet site like Google docs…. Make certain it is has enough capacity to store some large file and of course, be sure you have a back up in place.
>
> (Avery & Yount, 2010, p. 13).

The traffic coordinator position was typically an entry-level job with long hours, high stress, and sometimes, little respect. Coordinators had to be excellent problem solvers and likeable, confident motivators. And, they had very little control over the deliverable specifics or seniority or clout with other team members. They had the unenviable job of trying to corral some creative geniuses that had difficulty with and sometimes despised traditional business hours, accountability to procedures, or office communication methods. In fact, it was not unheard of for creative teams to hide from their traffic coordinators as critical deadlines approached—often decamping at their favorite out-of-office hangout to brainstorm. At the same time, traffic coordinators answered to the account team, who took the brunt of client complaints and crises and often relied on the traffic coordinator to perform minor miracles on a daily basis. Even before it was common to see tennis shoes in the work place, the traffic department might have been one of the first places where it made sense to wear sensible shoes because staff were literally moving all day long between people and departments. Sometimes, yes, they were actually running. As if all this wasn't stressful enough, traffic coordinators would often end each day by spending hours waiting around for final outputs of the day's work to be ready to ship out via FedEx or bike messenger so they would arrive at a client's office for approval first thing the next morning. Miss the last pickup, and they'd be driving to the airport to get that package on the FedEx plane. In fact, it was not entirely unheard of for an account manager to purchase a last-minute airline ticket and fly the work there personally, if the circumstances warranted.

Don Dickinson, in The New Account Manager said it well that,

© Stokkete/Shutterstock.com

> "[T]raffic managers are the circulatory system of the agency," and that traffic is "… a thankless job … But a good traffic manager is a life saver, deserving regular recognition and appreciation for riding a tough project through the agency production maze. Chocolates are always nice."
>
> (Dickinson, 2009, p. 40)

One final aspect of traffic is noteworthy. Not only were they the experts in the agency work-flow processes and knowledgeable of the people and time needed to complete tasks to route materials internally, but also they had the final job to make sure that the work, usually advertisements, actually left the building. They were the ones who had to understand the final delivery instructions on sizes, formats, and due dates to make sure a TV station received the beta tape or the newspaper received the film or disk with the ads sized accordingly. One author of this book fondly remembers the traffic manager jogging across Central Park to make sure NBC had the newest TV spot in time to run the following day on a major primetime sitcom.

Eventually, "traffic" became both a noun, as in "Call Michael in traffic to check on the deadline," and a verb, as in "I'm going to traffic this layout before lunch." So you could certainly, "ask traffic to traffic the outdoor billboard file."

The Birth of Project Management

The traffic department and traffic manager didn't become extinct, but they did evolve. Two dramatic shifts in the communications industry heralded the reformation of traffic and ushered in modern **project management**: the digital revolution and agency integration. Over the past 20 years, these two factors have catapulted businesses and organizations forward, sparking massive shifts in how they operate, seemingly overnight. As a result, the communications industry as it existed in 1950, or really even in 2000, bears very little resemblance to the present.

The digital revolution rapidly streamlined the flow of information and materials among departments within the agency, to and from the client, and ultimately to the media outlets and publications or other intended audiences. No longer did bulky job jackets need to be moved from desk to desk, and rushing to make the FedEx pickup time became a thing of the past. With a few keystrokes, even large, high-resolution images and videos could be easily posted and shared for collaboration, client approval, and publication. Can you believe the disks for file transfer common in the late-1990s could barely hold 1 MB of data?

Although these technological advancements resulted in significant savings in costs and time, it also had the effect of dramatically increasing the speed of the business; clients now expected revisions in hours, rather than days or weeks. And, as in many other industries, the workday's time-on-the-job limits vanished. Clients no longer waited to open a package and approve layouts when they arrived at the office in the morning; they expected to receive the revisions at 10:00 p.m., provide feedback from their couch while watching *Law and Order,* and then find the updated layouts in their email early the next morning. No longer was a traffic coordinator needed to move physical materials from place to place. The art director could just text the latest files to the account executive, who could send them on to the client. Inserting an extra person into the process just slowed things down. After all, who needs a traffic coordinator if you have self-driving cars?

The digital revolution also brought big changes to the type of work that agencies began to produce. No longer were agencies outputs primarily physical advertising executions and faxed press releases. Back in the days when print ads and television spots ruled, it was relatively easy to learn how to move ideas and concepts through the creative process and ultimately turn them into ads. The production steps and specifications were consistent from job to job, and a high level of technical understanding by the traffic manager wasn't needed. When agencies began to produce complex digital communications such as websites, mobile apps, and online advertising, all that changed. When PR firms began to manage social media content and complex corporate social responsibility efforts, the level of detail and technical knowledge that needed to be shared between teams dramatically increased, and it was no longer feasible to have a "middleman" like a traffic coordinator relaying this information, especially when they didn't always fully understand it. Traffic coordinators had difficulty making the shift, as well; many a traffic coordinator drove herself to insanity trying to print out 200 pages of a website for the proofreading department to review and mark up with a red pencil. Quite clearly, the old model didn't work anymore.

Agency integration also brought a new level of complexity and fragmentation to the communications business. As the overall business needs of clients evolved in the age of email, social media, and numerous media platforms from which people received and shared communications, the landscape became increasingly multifaceted. Clients found they could not typically rely on one large agency to handle all aspects of their strategic communications. When the options were TV, radio, direct mail, print and outdoor advertising, coupled with press releases to earn positive press coverage, things were simpler. But now, we have advanced social media, complex customer loyalty programs, paid search, search engine optimization (SEO), website development, mobile marketing, content generation and curation, viral marketing, event and experiential marketing, sampling, and an endless list of new and emerging communication channels; naturally, no one agency can truly claim to be an expert at all of these. So, clients must engage with a variety of creative and media partners, and they're expecting these partners to coordinate seamlessly with each other. Agencies have tried to address this need by purchasing smaller agencies and combining them into holding companies, or other affiliated networks or agencies-with-in-agencies models that can offer a range of services (see Chapter 1).

Thomas Richie of Chicago-based "craft agency" Tom, Dick, and Harry writes on the agency's blog, "Thanks to the laws of entropy and capitalism, the world is becoming increasingly complex, and there's no going back. Clients have legitimate and urgent needs for teams of specialists that can actually work together. But it's not easy. It's super hard, and it turns out that a monolithic holding company has no advantage in figuring it out vs. a collection of unaffiliated agencies. Here's the capital 'T' truth—for 'Agency Integration' to work, it takes real work" (Richie, 2016).

© PixelFractor/Shutterstock.com

So, where does that leave the old notion of a traffic coordinator in today's world? One word: obsolete. No longer needed for his or her skills in moving things from place to place, yet asked to coordinate increasingly sophisticated and complex projects with a variety of external agencies and partners, the traffic coordinator was put out to pasture and a new, Ninja-sleek, digitally savvy team member was born: the project manager.

DEFINING PROJECT MANAGEMENT

Now that you better understand the history and significance of project management's rise in the communications industry, let us further delve into the specifics of the project management's characteristics and role. It is important to note that project management, at its highest levels, is an extremely detailed, disciplined, and technical skill. In highly complex businesses you might see job descriptions requiring applicants to possess "Six Sigma" or PMP (Project Management Professional) certification. These professional certifications are generally reserved for project managers within highly technical or regulated industries such as engineering or manufacturing, while advertising and PR agencies require more industry-specific expertise and "on the job" training. Therefore, the term project management itself is flexible and has different meanings depending on the industry in which it is applied. One author remembers the agency traffic department reorganizing as the department of content deployment. Nonetheless, some fundamentals are consistently found across all business sectors. Even more important to note, everyone, particularly PR executives and advertising account managers, must possess some skill in project management to ensure they deliver clients' expectations and needs on time and on budget.

The Project Management Institute (PMI), a professional learning organization for project managers, defines project management as the "expert application of knowledge, skills, tools, and techniques in order to meet project requirements," in this case to deliver the on-time, on-budget results, learning and integration that organizations need (PMI, 2017). You can find the discipline of project management in nearly every professional industry, from construction, to disaster relief, and of course, communications. Although each industry's specific requirements differ, there are many fundamental elements of project management that transcend industries, making good project management skills an excellent life asset no matter where your career may lead you.

According to the PMI website (2017), successful **project managers** are change agents. They are flexible, disciplined, goal-oriented people who can "inspire a shared sense of purpose" and build trust with a diverse group of stakeholders. They can see the big picture, while identifying and managing the details. They possess many of the problem-solving, resourcefulness and resilience skills discussed in Chapter 10. For a more detailed discussion of project management skills, visit the PMI website at https://www.pmi.org/about/learn-about-pmi/who-are-project-managers.

Project manager: The individual or team responsible for creating, maintaining, and ensuring a project team's work aligns with project timelines, budgets, and specifications.

© Rawpixel.com/Shutterstock.com

STRATEGIC COMMUNICATIONS PROJECT MANAGEMENT

Project Managers Within the Communications Agency Structure

Within advertising and PR agencies, project managers shoulder a significant amount of responsibility. While other agency staff members generate the creative ideas, plan the media placements, cultivate relationships with the media or other influencers, or manage the client, it is the project manager who unifies the activities of many to make it all come together. It is not enough for an agency to develop a brilliant concept if the deadline is missed and the campaign doesn't launch before the date of the event it is designed to promote. Ultimately, the project manager (or the account management team if a dedicated project manager is not in place), armed with a great strategic and semester plan (Chapter 8), is arguably the single most important factor in driving an agency's profitability, more so even than the account executive or a creative director. After all, this role ensures that agency resources are used in the most efficient way possible, reducing wasted time, costly mistakes, agency–client disputes, and all of the other factors that can make an account profitable ... or not (Box 9.1).

Box 9.1 The Orbital Role of Project Management

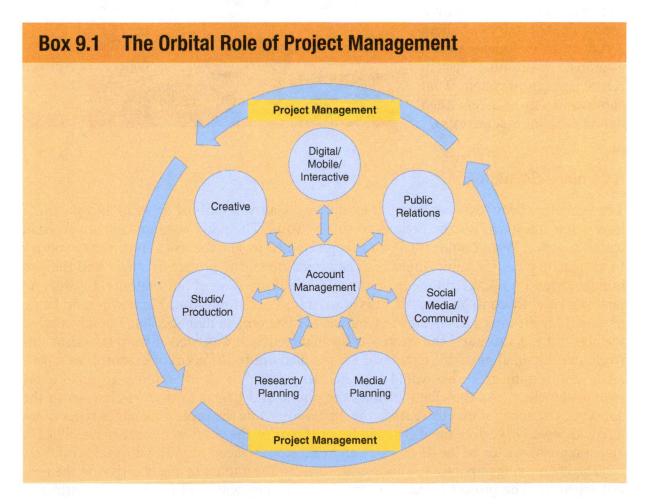

Functions of the Project Manager Role

So, what does an agency project manager do, exactly? Let's examine a moment in the life of an agency project manager. It is important to note that if there is no specific project manager or project management department, SOMEONE, regardless of their title, must be the project manager or else all team members are working without an understanding of how the multiple elements of great agency work intertwine. And, if there is not a project manager or project management team, then often the agency director or someone who is in charge of the whole agency and is aware of the workflow of all of the projects must manage the process to avoid dumping an insurmountable amount of deliverables on the agency at the same time. Without a project manager you may have a great ship, but it does not have a rudder, or in today's world, a global positioning system (GPS) navigation system. That someone is most likely then an/the account executives(s).

© AYA images/Shutterstock.com

A Common Scenario

The agency's client texts her account executive. "Can you call me as soon as you can? I have a few questions and something to run by you." The good account executive's head starts to spin, "What could it be?" and they begin to review the work in progress and try to anticipate what the topic might be. They track down the project manager and the two huddle around a speakerphone with any and all information about ongoing, future, and possibly, recently completed tasks. This is an example of doing your homework and being prepared for meetings, as covered in Chapter 11. The project manager had already alerted the account executive and the creative team that feedback was needed from the client this week, per the timeline; if the client had not reached out to the account executive as scheduled, the account executive would have had to gently "check in" midday to proactively remind the client. As the client answers the phone and begins to discuss changes to the concepts, the account executive leads the discussion while the project manager types notes into a Google Drive document that will become part of the conference report available for all team members to see the discussions and next steps to keep this job/deliverable on task.

The client hangs up, and the discussion turns to the impact of the changes on the project schedule. The project manager points out that they will need to revisit the estimates and add another day to the photo shoot, and the retouching date for the photographer may be problematic. This will also require another round of legal reviews in order to approve the updated copy suggested by the client. Based on this information, the account executive updates the Google Drive document to finalize a conference report, quickly summarizing the changes requested. She then emails this report to the client along with a revised timeline and project estimate, and quickly receives an approval for the changes to proceed. The project manager then shares the information with the agency creative and production teams, and relays any questions or challenges to the account executive for further clarification with the client. The project manager then thinks about how these changes may affect staff time and availability on other jobs for other clients and makes necessary recommendations and changes to those schedules as well.

Project Manager Versus Account Executive: Two Sides of the Same Coin

It is important to understand the difference between the role of project manager and that of account executive. At first, it may seem as if these functions are quite similar, and in many ways, they are. Both roles are populated by individuals who are primarily concerned with the timing, cost, details, and client satisfaction with the work the agency produces. Both roles tend to attract detail-oriented, strong personalities with tremendous leadership potential. They differ in several important ways, which may be important for you to consider as you first structure or work in your student-run agency, and second, parlay your student agency experience to prepare for a career in the advertising and PR industries. Often, the subtle distinctions between these roles can make the difference between job satisfaction and burnout. This is a comparison with similarities and nuances of the project manager versus account executive role in the agency:

Responsibility	Account Executive	Project Manager
Communication	Primary client contact; responsible for building and maintaining an overall relationship with the client. Relaying strategy and client needs with positive motivation to all agency team members	Primary agency team contact; responsible for communicating all details, specific steps and managing updates to projects with all team members; may serve as backup client contact if account executive is not available, especially for quick day-to-day details
Agency Function	Drives strategic direction of communications messaging (the "big picture"), ensures work is aligned to client's brand identity and strategy, responsible for overall financial growth of the account	Manages day-to-day project details within the agency to ensure on-time, on-budget project delivery to adhere to strategic and semester plans/scope of work

(Continued)

(Continued)

Responsibility	Account Executive	Project Manager
Document Production and Management	Produces brand or organizational steering documents, research reports, creative briefs, conference reports, creative presentations	Produces and manages estimates, timelines, budgets, work plans, scope documents, version control of scripts, layouts, copy decks, and agency resource (time and money) allocation
Media Planning/ Buying	Works with media planner/ buyer to develop and gain client approval for media plans that are aligned to client's objectives and budget	Using media plan, develops list of creative deliverables needed to fulfill plan based on specs from media outlets (dimensions, file sizes, color, etc.)

The account manager often thinks of the project manager as their right hand in helping the agency do all of the needed things to make great communications efforts. They rely on them to help with the minute details of each step independently and interdependently as they build toward single jobs, which build to overall strategic plans and their many parts for clients' success. The project manager looks to the account manager for important, **drop-dead deadlines**, **client mandatories,** and nuances of client preference or needs that only the account manager who spends so much time on the client's business can offer. The project manager also expects timely feedback from clients about the work via the account manager and a sense of team work and flexibility to address the inevitable hurdles the agency will face when producing so many complex communications solutions on deadline for many clients.

Drop-dead deadlines: Very important, do-or-die deadlines with no wiggle room for extension such as a media start date or the date materials must be received by.

Client mandatories: "Must-haves" as indicated by the client or the account team, such as URL addresses, certain logos, inclusion of an existing tag-line, date of an event, and so on.

Again, if you don't have a specified project manager in your student agency, account executives or account managers may likely be playing both roles. Or, the tasks of a project manager might be split between members of both the creative and account teams. Or, everyone in the agency may play a role in project management. However you staff the role, it's critical to make sure project management tasks are covered.

PROJECT MANAGEMENT: BEGINNING TO END

Before your agency takes on its first client, it is essential to have a defined process for doing so. More information about developing your agency processes and can be found in Chapters 4 and 5. If your student-run agency has been in business for a while, these processes may already be established and it will not be necessary to reinvent the wheel. The successful project manager, however, continually analyzes the process to look for improvements and efficiencies; if these prove viable, they may become a formal part of the agency's process for all clients. After all, processes are not set in stone, but are able to evolve, grow, and streamline as circumstances require and new tools become available.

Project Management Technology Solutions

As mentioned in Chapters 4 and 8, your student-run agency may create the working brief as a static Word document printed and revised in a physical job jacket, or opt to use a **cloud-based sharing** platform such as Google Docs or other specific **all-in-one workplace collaboration system**. The main point is that plans, timelines, conference reports and the like are available somewhere for many people to review, revise, and adhere to. You might consider whether an all-in-one project management system, such as Basecamp, Asana, or Podio, may better meet your needs. Transitioning to a comprehensive project management system has many benefits, but is also a big decision with cost and workload implications. Therefore, the decision to research, select, and implement such a system may be driven by your agency's student leadership in conjunction with your faculty advisor.

Below is a brief comparison of several of the most-used technology tools for project management. They generally fall into two main categories: file sharing/collaboration and comprehensive project management. You may find that your agency needs more than one solution, or that a comprehensive tool would work best. As new features and capabilities are added, and new products are developed, this information will change over time. Therefore, it is important to do your own detailed research and take advantage of trial subscriptions to "test drive" various solutions when considering adoption of new agency tools.

Cloud-based sharing system: A secure online server space for saving, sharing, and revising files and folders related to a project; team members and clients may view and edit shared items.

All-in-one workplace collaboration system: A secure online system for tracking and collaborating on all aspects of projects, including budgets, timelines, schedules, approvals, and revisions.

© lucadp/Shutterstock.com

It is not a bad idea to suggest your student staff ask around during their internships what programs, if any, the professionals use. This is also a good question to ask anytime you host guest speakers or visit professionals on your Ad Club or Public Relations Student Society of America (PRSSA) trips. You will be astounded at the number of options available. You might even find that some fellow student entrepreneurs or computer science majors might want to design a tailor-made solution just for your agency. Many of the platforms in use today were created by entrepreneurs who wanted to improve the wheel and create a system that addressed their specific needs and challenges of agency life and business.

Cloud-Based File Sharing/Document Collaboration		
Google Docs/Drive • Cloud-based shared document drive • Access through your Google account • Quickly create and share text documents, spreadsheets, and slide presentations using Google Docs, Sheets, Slides, etc.	**Dropbox or OneDrive** • Cloud-based shared document drive • Access through separate login • Quickly share, sync and update documents generated on your computer using PC or Mac programs	**RedPen or GoVisually** • Cloud-based shared document system • Access through separate login • Quickly share and comment on designs and layouts
Advantages: • Free (up to 15G) • Quick and easy to use • Includes productivity apps (Docs, Sheets, and Slides). Changes and comments can be viewed in real time and made by multiple individuals, simultaneously	Advantages: • Enhanced security • Automatic upload/ synching • More file space for minimal cost • Maintains original file formats (MS Office, Mac, Photoshop, etc.)	Advantages: • Free trial • Specifically designed for sharing and commenting on visual creative work • Strong version control process
Disadvantages: • Formatting documents can be limited; does not maintain original file formats from MS Office or Mac • Can be difficult to organize and find documents (new "team" feature makes this easier)	Disadvantages: • Does not include productivity apps such as Google Docs, Sheets, and Slides (with the exception of "Dropbox Paper" for taking notes)	Disadvantages: • Designed for sharing visual work (layouts, etc.) not content, scripts, press releases, etc.

To Share or Not to Share?

Shared documents and drives such as Google Docs, Google Drive, Dropbox, and so on have obvious benefits, such as the ability to be viewed and updated by multiple team members over time as information changes. They eliminate the need to print out or email updated versions of documents as they are updated, reducing the amount of paper or email each staff member must review. And who wouldn't rather check their computer at midnight to review agency work rather than go into the office to look at a piece of paper? It is important, however, to consider the following safeguards if you opt to use these systems (Box 9.2).

Box 9.2   Considerations When "Sharing"

1. Security
2. Version control
3. Reliability
4. Accountability (sign-offs/approvals)

- *Security:* Shared documents are only as secure as the accounts of each of the sharing participants. Confidential client information can be easily viewed by anyone with access to an account with sharing privileges. Although this is unlikely to be a significant concern with most student-run agency clients, it can have critical implications in the real world, as was seen in the investigations regarding classified information on government officials' private email servers. At a minimum, your agency staff should access shared resources using login credentials based on their official university student email/network accounts, not personal accounts. You may also consider requiring agency staff to create more secure passwords for their accounts. Finally, caution staff members not to let others access their accounts or to open agency/client documents over unsecure Wi-Fi networks. Client information databases, budgets and expenditures, or customer mailing lists should be handled with extra caution.
- *Version control:* The benefit of shared documents—the ability to quickly access and make updates from anywhere—can also be a significant risk when many team members are editing the same document. It is easy for critical details to be deleted or changed, and information can be lost with no way to retrieve it. Therefore, you should carefully consider with whom the document is shared and whether they will be able to edit the documents or only view them. You can also consider requiring each edit to be saved as a new document or version (e.g., CLIENTNAME_ DATE_VERSION, i.e., Kelloggs_09-17-17_a). Or, you can require team members to "comment" when suggesting changes, rather than editing the document content itself. Lastly, you will want to make sure to "lock down" an approved version of any client documents once finalized by the client, whether by changing the editing

permissions, replacing a Google Doc with a PDF file that cannot be edited, or adding the word "FINAL" to the file name. One author fondly remembers trafficking an advertisement to *Parents* magazine titled, "REALLYFINAL_final_final ver 3" because someone named the file final a little bit too early in the process.

- *Reliability:* It is important to note that Google Drive and other cloud-based solutions are reliant upon Internet access. If the network is down, so is your agency. Therefore, expected network outages or severe weather circumstances may require a backup plan or policy. In many cases, changes can be made offline and uploaded later when access is restored. If you are travelling and know you may not have access to client documents when you need them, you may wish to print a copy or download a copy to your computer or tablet for offline access.

- *Accountability:* How do we officially and with 100% confidence know that the creative director or faculty advisor has signed off or approved the version to go to the client? In the old days, layouts often had a sticker on the back with the names or titles of all of the people who must approve a document or design whereby they would initial or sign it. If one letter changed in the copy or the photo moved one millimeter to the left, then it had to be reprinted, a new sticker attached, and then rerouted for all to re-sign. As laborious as this was, it ensured that everyone knew what they were agreeing to and if it came back with a typo, well, it was signed off on. Cloud-based systems don't usually have this capability and thus, anyone can grab a version and send it off to a client or to a media outlet.

As you can imagine, many of these issues are addressed and accounted for in professional, and student versions, of project management software. All-in-one workplace collaboration systems have been developed over time often by those who became frustrated with aspects of their present system in use. For every type of business and every type of agency, there are many choices for these systems, and there are new ones being developed every day. In fact, your student agency just might get a new system for low to no cost from a new provider who wants to pilot test their system. So if someone emails or calls and says they have a better system for you, it is often worth a listen. Here are some basic pros and cons of these types of systems:

Project Management "All-In-One" Systems		
Basecamp	**inMotionNow**	**Scoro**
• Comprehensive online project management system • Includes messaging system, discussion boards, document sharing, timeline management tools	• Comprehensive creative workflow management system • Includes tools for developing creative brief and other agency-specific documents	• Comprehensive online project management system • Includes campaign metric tracking tools, billing, and more

Advantages:	Advantages:	Advantages:
• Engaging and appealing user interface • Replaces multiple tools (Dropbox, Google Docs, Slack, Hipchat, email calendar, email) • Free 30-day trial	• Designed specifically for advertising, PR, digital and social media agencies • Strong review/approval management tools for use by client and agency	• Includes time tracking, billing, and customer relationship management (CRM) reporting tools
Disadvantages:	**Disadvantages:**	**Disadvantages:**
• Requires some work to understand and use all the tools • May not facilitate development of face-to-face conversation and problem solving skills • Not designed specifically for advertising creative development; may be more suited to digital, social media, or PR agencies • Best for internal team collaboration; client involvement may still require traditional communication tools • Fee based	• Requires training and ramp-up time for agency and clients • Fee based	• May be more complex and feature-heavy than necessary for a student agency • Fee based

This is just a sampling of the many solutions available on the market. For a more comprehensive overview of various project management tools, visit https://www.scoro.com/blog/marketing-agency-project-management-tools/ or https://blog.hubspot.com/agency/agency-project-management-tools

A Walk Through Project Management at the Agency

Project Kickoff

As discussed in Chapter 8, a strategic plan likely outlines all of the many jobs or deliverables that the agency needs to develop. The semester plan broadly informs the agency and the client of the what, how, and when deliverables will be created within a time-frame on a generally agreed-upon budget. In Chapter 4, we saw that new projects (per the strategic plan) will generally begin with a client kickoff meeting at which overall client input, project deliverables, research considerations, and budget/timeline constraints will be discussed. Once this information is received, the agency team can then develop a number of items for client approval, including a scope of work, timeline, estimate, creative brief, working brief, and media plan.

Now is when project management kicks into full swing. They take all of the information provided by the client and the account team and strategists with important details on timing and budget, and begin to assemble the internal work plan to coordinate all of the agency team members needed to complete the job. To borrow an example from the military, it is as if the generals have developed the battle plan and now the officers begin to brief their troops on the steps needed to accomplish the mission. The project manager is responsible for the development of many of these items and it is well worth spending the time to get them right, in writing, and formally approved by the client. This will not seem important when all is going well, but it can make all the difference when a client relationship turns sour, there is a billing dispute, or a deadline is missed. Investing time up front to think through all aspects of the project and eliminate as many "unknowns" as possible can make the difference between success and disaster. In many cases, you will uncover information that the client has not even considered, which has the added benefit of helping the client clarify their strategic objectives and improve their overall satisfaction with the value of the agency role in their business.

Working Brief (or May Be Known as the Action Plan or Timeline)

The account executive is primarily responsible for developing the creative brief and scope of work and semester plan, which inspires the agency team members to address the communications challenges of the client and provides insights into the target audience, the client brand and personality and what the campaign needs to achieve. Likewise, the project manager is responsible for developing the working brief.

The working brief, often contained in or synonymous with a semester plan, should include a detailed timeline, cost estimates, a list of available assets and their locations (logo, photography, etc.), as well as an itemized list of final deliverables (print ad sizes and specs, social media placement word counts, pixel requirements, and upload links, video formats, etc.). In short, it should include all of the details team members need to know in order to successfully complete the project. If you are using an online project management system, setting up a new client or project in this system may or may not replace the development of a working brief. You may need to develop a working brief for client approval and then import this information into your agency's system. Some project management systems will generate a project overview document that you can use for client review/approval. Whatever the case, it is essential for you to work with your account executive to generate a formal written document and obtain client approval of key project details before investing agency time and resources on the project.

Timeline Development Considerations

Your agency's timeline can be as simple as a text document or spreadsheet with dates and deliverables, or as complex as a colorful flowchart from your online project management system. Whatever the format, there are some key considerations that must be included.

- *Agency revision turnaround times.* Have you included enough time for revisions? Have you considered weekends, school holidays, and other important events (homecoming, exams, etc.)?
- *Client/agency revisions deliverable dates.* There are two kinds to consider: when the agency will deliver to the client, and, when the client will deliver feedback to the agency. Be mindful of client schedules and plan for realities—they might be out of town for a week. Consider whether there are "mission critical" client deliverables without which the project cannot proceed, and establish dates by which they must be delivered to the agency. It is unfair for clients to hold the agency to deadlines when the agency is waiting on materials back from the client that it should have received weeks ago, but it happens often. So plan for it.
- *Internal and client approval dates.* Establish dates by which the internal account team and the client must review and approve work. Make sure your account executive has time to review and comment. If your agency's faculty advisor must provide approval, build in time for that as well. In particular, give working professionals a reasonable review turnaround time. They may not work weekends or nights, and they may have to gain feedback from several team members on the client side. Be respectful of this.
- *Drop-dead launch dates.* If there is an event or media launch by which deliverables must be provided, note this. You never want to push back a scheduled media start or say to the client you won't have their materials ready for a grand opening or key investor meeting that has been planned months in advance. Be aware of any shifting of earlier dates (revisions, approvals, etc.) that may jeopardize this date, and address accordingly.
- *Creative lockdown dates.* If you are launching a campaign with multiple versions of the same creative big idea or there is somehow another source template from which all other smaller executions or other programs will be developed, you will want to establish a creative lockdown date and then allow time for development of different versions or sizes of the creative based on the approved final layout. This avoids the need to make many last-minute changes to multiple versions if the client makes a last minute revision.
- *External partner dates.* Are you contracting with any outside suppliers like a print shop for postcards or posters? Do you have a supplier printing custom items for an experiential event where you need t-shirts or a large vinyl banner or a table tent? If so, recognize everyone has different timelines and production needs to deliver those materials, so make sure you connect with them on due dates for files, approvals, proof reviews, and so on.

- *Traffic date.* Note that dates for layouts and content delivery to media outlets are several days to several weeks prior to the publication date and build this into the timeline. It is vital to know if the school newspaper needs materials three weeks or three days before publication. It is painful to learn that the poster you thought would only take four days to deliver will take over a week because the print shop is backed up.

- *Proofreading.* Be sure that proofreading is part of your process. If possible, this should be done by someone who has not reviewed the layout many times during the creative process. For digital campaigns, you will also need to build in time for Quality Assurance (QA), prelaunch testing, email campaign testing, and so on.

© demarcomedia/Shutterstock.com

- *Legal approvals.* In some industries (financial, healthcare, insurance, etc.), the client must conduct a legal review of the creative to ensure that it meets industry requirements. Professional agencies may also conduct their own legal review to make sure they comply with copyright and broadcast guidelines. If needed, include this in your timeline.

Timesheets and Job Tracking

The project manager has two key roles: (1) they must be the one knowledgeable enough to identify all the agency team members to be involved with each deliverable, and (2) determine how much time is reasonably required from each person on each aspect of it. Then they have the unenviable tasks of helping agency team members complete their work within the time estimate or alerting management when projects might exceed the forecasted amount. Then finally, they must make sure everyone tracks their time correctly and relay that information to management or accounting to be billed and collected from clients. That is important or no one at a professional agency gets a paycheck.

As discussed in Chapter 5, agency cost estimates may be generated based on a per-project fee, yearly retainer, or hourly rate. Regardless of how your student-run agency is compensated, you may wish to use timesheets to track the time team members spend on each project and compare it to budgeted time and costs for your clients. This can help your agency streamline processes, improve profitability, and better develop accurate timelines and estimates for future projects. This effort may be excellent preparation for the "real world" in which an agency's time and out-of-pocket costs are almost always tracked and managed carefully to avoid the dreaded **non-billable expenses** or **write-offs**. In fact, it could be argued that a student-run agency experience without this aspect does not fully prepare students for the realities of an agency career.

If you choose to track your agency team's time, you can set up a simple shared timesheet spreadsheet or use an off-the-shelf timesheet management system. This may be created by your faculty advisor or developed by an agency leadership team. You will start by establishing a rate for each staff role (copywriter, creative director, account executive, media planner, etc.) and then estimating the number of hours each staff member will need to complete the "job" or project. The rate can then be multiplied by the number of hours to generate a total cost in hours for the project, and added to any "out of pocket" costs (travel, printing, shipping, etc.) to generate a total project cost. Don't forget to include time for the project manager's work too! Staff members will then log their time daily via a timesheet, and this can be compared to the estimated number of hours periodically, in order to determine whether a project remains on budget and within the scope of the estimate.

> **Non-billable expenses:** Costs associated with a job that are necessary but not able to be directly or separately billed to a client; the "cost of doing business."

> **Write-offs:** A dreaded occurrence when money has been spent that should be legitimately billed or otherwise collected from the client, but the agency is unable to do so usually because of a mistake or breakdown in proper procedures. For example, paying a printer for 200 copies before the client approved the final version, and now changes are needed.

PROJECT MANAGEMENT IN THE "REAL WORLD"

If you find the role of project manager challenging and enjoyable in your student-run agency, you may want to consider pursuing a career path in project management after graduation. In fact, the experience as a successful project manager is desired by nearly all hiring managers in any type of business. It demonstrates your attention to detail, ability to manage many different types of people on varying timelines, and possession of a keen eye for the nitty-gritty steps that help companies earn a profit and deliver on their mission. In the future, you may be able to leverage these experiences to launch a successful career, as discussed in Chapter 15.

Once you have successfully mastered the project management system used within your student-run agency, you will find it relatively easy to quickly get up to speed with the process used at any agency or other organization at which you might work in your future career. However, if you do not respect or take the time to learn how to work within such a system while in a learning environment like the student-run agency, you will find it incredibly difficult to magically transform yourself into a disciplined, process-oriented team member in the real world. You may even find that you no longer enjoy working in the strategic communications industry when real-world process constraints are imposed upon your creativity; if so, it's best to find that out now rather than later. The fact is that every business is just that, a business, and your student-run agency is trying to replicate the same business processes and challenges you will face in the future. Process and project management breakdowns are often the downfall of many a great campaign, idea, or communications plan. In short, the mastery of project management makes the difference between consistent and profitable results, and losing accounts.

© nd3000/Shutterstock.com

CONCLUSION

The perks that entice many students to pursue a career in advertising and PR—creativity, fun, freedom, and a little bit of glamour—are in relatively short supply in your early years in this industry. Much of the real work at the agency is in the trenches, masterfully pulling minor miracles that the world never hears about as you save a project from being hopelessly ineffective, or worse, killed due to timing or budget overruns. Therefore, if you can find motivation and enjoyment in being part of producing great work within timeline and budget constraints, under pressure, and with demanding clients, then you will find a career in strategic communications to be tremendously challenging and rewarding.

If you enjoy the idea of the traffic cop ensuring that people and vehicles move through crowded streets with safety and ease, or imagine the life of an air traffic controller would be cool, then project management may just be for you. In other words, let project management become part of your professional DNA from the very start, and you will find yourself at a significant advantage down the road—wherever it may lead you.

REVIEW AND DISCUSSION QUESTIONS

1. What is the traffic department? Why was it traditionally called this?
2. What forces led to a reshaping and reorganizing of the traffic department?

3. How does a project manager differ from a traditional traffic manager? What is needed from a project manager in today's professional strategic communication environment? How is that the same or different than at your student-run agency?

4. What are the major responsibilities of a project manager? How many of them are relevant to the type of jobs your student-run agency engages in?

5. If project management or a project manager does not exist in your agency, who assumes responsibilities for their role? Why is this important?

6. What is a job jacket? What kinds of materials do you think your agency will likely create that will go into them?

7. What are the characteristics of a good project manager?

8. How are a project manager's responsibilities similar to an account executive's? How are they different?

9. What is the difference between cloud-based sharing systems and all-in-one collaborative systems? Which might make the most sense for your student-run agency?

10. What are the major considerations when deciding on the best project management system for your agency? What is the biggest concern and need for your agency from its project management system or process?

11. When developing the deadlines for a job, what are the major types of dates that a project manager should pay special attention to?

12. How might project management prowess help any agency staffer in their skill development for a professional career in strategic communications?

REFERENCES AND ADDITIONAL READINGS

Avery, J., & Yount, D. (2010). *Advertising campaign planning: Developing an advertising-based marketing plan* (5th ed.). Irvine, CA: Melvin & Leigh Publishers.

Davis, C., & Dickinson, D. (2017). *The advertising and PR account management workshop*. Irvine, CA: Melvin & Leigh Publishers.

Dickinson, D. (2009). *The new account manager* (2nd ed.). Chicago, IL: The Copy Workshop.

Hamerhoff, E. J. (1998). *The advertising agency business: The complete manual for management and operation* (3rd ed.). Chicago, IL: NTC Business Books.

Project Management Institute (PMI). (2017). *Who are project managers?* Retrieved from https://www.pmi.org/about/learn-about-pmi/who-are-project-managers

Richie, T. (2016). Agency integration is easy. Just kidding. *Dick's soapbox: News and views you can use.* Retrieved from http://tdhcreative.com/news/detail/agency-integration-is-easy.-just-kidding

Sanders, B. (2017). New business: The winning pitch. Sanders Consulting Group website. Retrieved from http://www.sandersconsulting.com/new-business-the-winning-pitch/

Developing a Professional Identity

In one of the first studies on the learning benefits of student-run agencies, agency advisors outlined three levels of student learning: applying classroom learning to real client situations, understanding business processes and protocols, and developing a professional identity (Bush, 2009). It is this third category—professionalism—that we will cover in this chapter.

In a professional working environment, there are two skill sets employers look for when interviewing applicants—hard skills and soft skills. **Hard skills** are the quantifiable skills associated with the knowledge and abilities needed for the specific industry and/or position. In the agency environment, hard skills might include things like knowing how to pitch stories to the media, understanding how to research and write a strategic communications plan, or knowledge about how to measure a social media campaign. The professional articles in this textbook and many of the chapters relate to agency hard skills.

> **Hard skills:** Quantifiable skills related to the knowledge and abilities needed for a particular job (e.g., corporate lawyers have knowledge of corporate laws).

Soft skills are the more intangible skills that employees display when working in a professional environment. These include abilities such as being a good communicator, working well within a team, being a good listener, and displaying motivation and passion for the work. Increasingly, employers look for applicants who have a good balance of both skill sets. And, if all hard skills are equal, soft skills give you a competitive advantage and can lead to promotion within the organization.

> **Soft skills:** Intangible skills related to your ability to interact with other people and display positive attitudes.

What's more, student agency graduates themselves have highlighted the importance of soft skills to their current positions. In a series of interviews in 2016 (Bush, Haygood, & Vincent, 2017), graduates cited soft skills such as people skills, organizational skills, and communications skills as abilities learned in the student agency that are critical to their current careers.

In this chapter, we touch on these types of soft skills and how you can practice them in your student agency tenure. Chapter 7 will also help you apply these soft skills when working with clients. This chapter covers

- The agency working environment
- Beneficial soft skills in such an environment
- How to give and get feedback
- Creative thinking and problem-solving
- Manage the stress of working in an agency

AGENCY WORKING ENVIRONMENT

To understand how to display professionalism in your day-to-day work life, it is helpful to understand what it is like to work in an agency environment. Some of the terms that describe an agency work environment can be found in Table 10.1.

Table 10.1   Agency Work Environment—The Good and the Bad

Positive	Potentially Negative
Fast-paced	Stressful
Collaborative	Long hours
Innovative	Pressure to be "billable"
Creative	Always on deadline
Exciting	Difficult clients
Variety	Often lacks diversity

Whether working for an ad agency, public relations (PR) agency, or specialty agency, the agency environment is fast-paced, innovative, and collaborative. Members work in teams and with people across departments to develop and execute communications programs for clients directed at a variety of target audiences. Because of the creative nature of campaigns, the business is exciting and imaginative, where "big ideas" and innovative ways of doing things are welcomed and encouraged.

Unlike "desk jobs" or positions where one does a similar job day-in and day-out, agency employees often work on a variety of accounts and programs and repeatedly face new and unique challenges. For example, you might be asked to determine if a coconut can be mailed across the country and arrive intact with nothing but an address label attached to it (true story), or asked to ride in an 18-wheeler to better understand the life of a truck driver (also true). Or, at the extreme end of the spectrum, have to perform the Heimlich maneuver on a client choking at a luncheon (believe it or not, it happened—twice).

The agency business is people-focused and collaborative. Agency members work with people at every level of a client organization—from engineers to plant workers to CEOs—each of which speak a different organizational language and have different organizational concerns. And, an agency employee might shift roles and communication styles several times in one day, from meeting with a dairy farmer in the morning to an investment banker in the afternoon. Within the agency, while members may work independently on certain tasks, they most often work in teams where the work benefits from a diversity of ideas, talents, and experiences. They may also work with outside suppliers to pull together or execute programs.

© Sukanya White/Shutterstock.com

Though the business is exciting and innovative, it can also be extremely stressful. Agency members work long hours under demanding deadlines to serve client needs, bring their ideas to life, and respond to crises or outside events that could effect the client's business. Strenuous travel schedules and odd working hours may also be involved. For example, when one of the authors needed to film a grocery store scene for a client video, the shoot had to take place at 2 a.m. after the store was closed. Finally, agency professionals face pressures to constantly be "billable" and contribute to the financial success of both the client and agency organization (see Chapter 5).

Given this culture, what are the soft skills needed to succeed in an agency environment? In the next sections, we discuss many of these skills and how you can improve upon them during your student agency experience.

COMMUNICATIONS COMPETENCY

In the business world in general, and the agency world specifically, every employee strives to be a competent communicator. Simply put, **communications competency** means that you have the ability to understand and interpret the feelings and messages of others, and can in turn develop clear messages and strategies that are understood by others, while taking ethical responsibility for the outcomes of your communication (Shockley-Zabalek, 2015, p. 6).

Communications competency: The ability to understand and interpret the feelings and messages of others and in turn communicate messages and feelings effectively with others.

As part of its communications' training course for executives, U.K.-based Making Business Matter has identified seven essential qualities to being an effective communicator. These include under-standing the needs of others; clearly communicating messages; adapting your communication style to the situation and people involved; being able to use a range of communications methods (such as email, face-to-face, etc.); building an influential network; being self-aware of your own emotions, actions, and respect toward others; and being able to appro-priately deal with and manage conflict (Making Business Matter, n.d.).

As a communications major, you will spend your entire college career learning how to be an effective communicator. There are many courses, textbooks, research arti-cles, and extracurricular programs that cover a variety of the competencies listed earlier. For the purpose of this text, however, and your work in the student agency, let's take a closer look at two of them.

Self-Awareness

There are essentially two parts to being self-aware: outward self-awareness (or how your actions affect others) and inward self-awareness (your motivations and working style).

When around close friends or family, we seldom have to think about how we're coming across or how they will respond to a joke or quirky behavior. We know them well, they know us well, and we've developed a familiar language. In a professional setting, how-ever, we have to practice more **outward self-awareness**, recognizing how our behaviors will impact and be interpreted by others. For example, a student team was conducting a focus group for a class assignment. The professor checked in with the group midway through and noticed that one of the student facilitators was standing directly behind several of the participants, taking notes with his laptop propped on a bookcase. Not only were the participants uncomfortable that he was hovering directly behind them, the tapping on his laptop was so loud that it was disrupting the conversation. Yet this student was concen-trating so deeply on taking notes that he was completely unaware of how his actions were affecting others.

Outward self-awareness: Being aware of how our actions and behaviors will impact and be interpreted by others.

Working in the student agency gives you many opportunities to practice being outwardly self-aware. Make it a point to pay atten-tion to your behaviors, responses, and emotions when interacting with others. For exam-ple, when you enter a meeting, do you greet others in the room and introduce yourself? Or do you just plop down in a seat and start checking your text messages? The first says,

"I acknowledge and am interested in you," while the latter says, "Meh, it's all about me." Do you pay attention to what others are saying and engage respectfully in the conversation? Or are you loudly digging in your backpack and then interrupt someone because you haven't been paying attention? Little behaviors can make big impressions. Strive to be professional in all interactions with others, including face-to-face meetings, email, voice mail, or telephone conversations.

When interacting with others, also notice when you become agitated or frustrated and what triggered it. Ask yourself, "What am I feeling at this moment and what is making me feel this way?" Then, think about how you usually respond in such situations and if that response is appropriate. Sometimes, simply pausing and checking in with ourselves can help us respond to a situation more appropriately. Also, if you are a more introverted person, you may have to push yourself to speak up and interject your ideas and opinions into conversations. Saying nothing can give the appearance that you don't have anything of value to say when that is not true.

The other type of self-awareness—**inward self-awareness**—relates to your working style and motivations. Are you a big picture person or a detail person? Do you like to collaborate with others or work more independently?

> **Inward self-awareness:** Understanding our own working styles, personality traits, and motivations.

One way to become more inwardly self-aware is to take a personality test such as the Myers–Briggs Type Indicator® (MBTI®). Tests such as these not only tell you your dominant personality traits, but can also identify how you access information, what motivates you, and how you can be more effective in the workplace. For example, under the MBTI test, an INTP personality type loves theories and abstract ideas, can think deeply about solving a problem, and often likes to work independently. Conversely, an ESTP is bored with theories and concepts, focuses more on immediate results, and is motivated by working with other people. Many universities give the MBTI test and others through their career or professional development centers.

Box 10.1   Professional Attributes

10 Attributes of a Professional

Respectful
Trustworthy/dependable
Honest
Adaptive
Takes responsibility for actions
Dresses appropriately
Ethical
Conscientious
Supportive
Positive

Awareness of Others

Hand in hand with being self-aware is being able to read others and interpret their needs and feelings. This requires paying attention, setting aside judgment, and stepping into another person's shoes. It's also means respecting a person's individuality and adapting our communications styles to a diversity of people and situations. In a nutshell, being aware of people and situations is about being perceptive.

A perceptive person is observant. They pick up cues about people and situations by paying attention to both verbal and nonverbal communication, as well as their external surroundings. For example, a perceptive person would notice that the client ordered a vegetarian meal at lunch, has a picture of their dog on their desk, or drinks coffee from a Kansas City Royal's mug. All of these things tell you something about that person. A perceptive person would notice when a teammate is getting a little hoarse during a presentation, and would quietly fetch a glass of water for them. A perceptive person can tell by a client's body language if they are interested in the ideas being presented. A furrowed brow might mean you should stop and ask if something needs to be clarified. Raised brows might show surprise and intrigue at what you're presenting.

Being perceptive is a priceless soft skill to learn for your professional work life. As Loren Minor, COO of recruitment firm Decision Toolbox says, "Perceptive people are always more successful in life and in work. Top performers aren't always the smartest people; they're the ones who connect with others and have a higher emotional quotient" (Vozza, 2015).

You can learn about others by asking open-ended questions that show your interest in their lives and experiences. For example, a simple question such as "Tell me about your weekend," can help us learn about a person's interests, values, and motivations. Likewise, asking a colleague "What are you working on these days?" can open up a conversation about their professional interests and challenges.

Finally, learn how to be an active listener. Too often we pretend to listen when someone else is speaking, but our minds are really elsewhere. **Active listening** allows you to be an active participant in the conversation, and leads to fully understanding another's meaning. You can practice active listening by acknowledging you are listening (e.g., with a nod of the head); repeating, or rephrasing to help clarify the sender's meaning (So, if I hear you correctly, what you're saying is . . .); and inviting the person to go deeper by asking questions, (You mentioned "x"—tell me more about that).

Active listening: Technique for actively engaging in a conversation by acknowledging what the other is saying and repeating or rephrasing their messages to ensure clarity and shared meaning.

PROBLEM-SOLVING, RESOURCEFULNESS, AND RESILIENCE

In addition to being a competent communicator, there are other attitudinal and behavioral skills that professionals practice in the agency workplace. Next we discuss three of these.

Problem-Solving

As mentioned earlier, agency members face new and unique situations every day. Communications agencies are essentially in the business of solving client problems or capitalizing on market opportunities. Clients come to agencies with a set of circumstances that need attention, and the agency's role is to come up with solutions that will move the client's brand or organization forward. Problem-solving is the nature of the business.

In addition, numerous problems will crop up in the day-to-day operations of an agency, whether it is a mistake made by the agency, by the client, or an outside force that requires attention. As such, agency members need to think quickly on their feet, come up with solutions—be problem solvers.

When faced with a problem, there are two types of people: those who panic and say, "Oh NOOOOO, there's a problem. I HATE problems!" and those who say, "Oh YAY, a chance to put my skills to work." So, be the latter. Whether you're tasked with developing a client plan to address a market situation, or something has gone wrong that needs fixing—work with a problem-solving mindset. But, what does that mean?

First of all, it means not only accepting problems, but also EXPECTING them. Treat problems as a normal course of business. Second, it means setting aside your anger or annoyance that a problem has occurred. If you don't, all your energy will be focused on your annoyance rather than the possibilities for solutions. Third, treat the problem as an opportunity. Yes, we know, we know—that's a tired cliché. But it's true. For example, did you know that Post-it Notes were the result of a problem? In 1968, a scientist at 3M was trying to develop a super strong adhesive, but instead developed a product that would stick, but only temporarily. Oops. But, wait—someone might NEED an adhesive that sticks but doesn't stick. Voila: Post-it Notes.

When faced with problems, we often revert to what is called **learned helplessness**. We use phrases like "I can't . . ." or "I don't know how . . ." that set us up for

Learned helplessness: The feeling that you are powerless to solve a problem or change a situation (either because of past experiences or because the problem seems impossible to solve), and you give up before trying.

failure. Instead, practice phrases like "What if . . ." or "Wouldn't it be nice if we could . . ." (see, e.g., Treffinger, Isaksen, & Stead-Dorval, 2006). These phrases will switch your brain to solution-generating mode rather than getting stuck in whining mode.

Problem-solving requires using two types of thinking: critical thinking and creative thinking. Use your critical thinking and analytical mindset to define and analyze the problem. Ask questions such as What's the problem? How did we get here? And, "Have we seen this same type of situation before?" Use research and information gathering to assess the nature of the problem: What happened? Why did it happen? Who needs to be involved in the solution? and so on. Then, use creative thinking to generate possible solutions. This is where brainstorming comes in. There is usually more than one solution to a problem. Brainstorming helps you develop dozens of possible solutions that can then be weighed against criteria later on.

Resourcefulness

According to Merriam Webster's dictionary, resourcefulness is defined as "able to meet situations: capable of devising ways and means, clever in dealing with problems—a resourceful leader." Resourceful people make things that seem impossible, possible. They make phone calls, search the Internet, talk to friends and family—turn over every rock to find a "ways and means" to accomplish something (like mailing a coconut).

For instance, a homeowner was recently remodeling her kitchen. To save money, the homeowner wanted to use her old faucet in the new sink. But when the plumber came to install the faucet, the connections were too short to go through the countertop and hook up to the water lines. The plumber called three suppliers but none had an adapter to solve the problem. Thus, the homeowner would need to purchase a new faucet—a fairly costly purchase. But when she went to Home Depot to look for one, she thought, "Hmmm. I wonder if . . ." She tracked down the store's plumbing expert, explained the problem and, yes, he had a solution: two plastic adapters that cost around $8.00. Resourcefulness pays off.

To be a successful agency member, you need to be resourceful. Being resourceful means you don't wait for someone to task you with something, but instead go searching for solutions before problems occur. It means you don't ask your supervisor to answer every question, but instead find the answers on your own. It also means you are the one who answers the question, "I wonder if we could . . ." with "Yes! And here's how." Resourceful employees manage up—instead of presenting a problem to their supervisors, they present the problem AND a solution.

According to leadership coach John Baldoni (2010), resourcefulness requires being open minded to new possibilities, optimizing what you have to work with, reworking processes with an eye toward simplicity, and finding ways to do things that might seem impractical. Being resourceful feels good, builds confidence in your own problem-solving abilities, and makes you a valued professional to both your client and your agency.

You can practice being resourceful by learning new things and improvising when the exact tools aren't readily available. For example, instead of eating out or going to the grocery store, prepare a meal with only what is available in your cupboard. If your shoelace breaks, how might you hold the shoe together without purchasing a new lace? Learn how to change a tire, sew a hem, or think ahead for what you might need or do if the power goes out.

If you are from a lower income background, you likely have a lot of practice being resourceful. Those skills will be highly valued at the student agency and when you enter the workforce.

You can also create a small toolkit of helpful items to use in a pinch. For school, this might include a miniature stapler, a thumb drive with backup copies of a presentation, and extra pens or pencils. Think like a parent. Parents are often great at being resourceful. When you were little, your parent or guardian might have had a "kid toolkit." Dad had extra hair ties in his pocket, or used his jingling keys to distract a fussy baby. Auntie carried small bags of snacks in her purse or had games loaded on her phone to keep kids engaged. Nana kept safety pins and tissues on hand—just in case. As the saying goes, necessity it the mother of invention. Practicing resourcefulness now will help you go to work with a problem-solving mindset later.

Resilience

When interviewing for internships or entry-level positions, many interviewers will ask candidates to describe a challenging situation or disappointment and how they dealt with it. Agency life gives you plenty of examples. Clients will not buy every idea you present, programs will get canceled or significantly altered, some campaigns will fail, mistakes will be made—in general, things will not go as planned or desired. The mark of a professional is how you bounce back from adversity and make the best of difficult situations.

Being resilient requires all of the skill sets discussed earlier—problem-solving, resourcefulness, good communications skills, and being self-aware and adaptive. And it includes another quality—optimism. Resilient people don't give up at the first sign of adversity, or take their ball and go home. They accept the situation for what it is and are optimistic they'll find ways to overcome it—even when it feels impossible.

One of the reasons we get sidelined in the agency world is because we become too emotionally attached to our ideas. We spend hours, days, or even months coming up with the perfect headline or developing that awesome social media campaign. It's our baby. So when a client or colleague poo-poo's it, it's hard to let it go. But any agency professional will tell you that they wrote an even better headline, or came up with an even more awesome social campaign the second or third time around.

© iQoncept/Shutterstock.com

Vent, redirect, and then move on. It's frustrating and difficult to let something go. Before we can move on, sometimes we just need to vent (to the appropriate people) and redirect our thinking. Rather than becoming dramatic in the workplace or in front of a client, turn to your support network to vent your frustrations—a friend or family member, for example—or take your frustrations out at the gym. Vent, but don't dwell. Give yourself a timeframe for venting, and then redirect your thinking to the new reality. "Okay, this didn't work. What needs to change?" When the goalposts are moved, we need to get our bearings and determine what needs to happen next to achieve our goals. Then, with our new goals clearly in mind, we can move on to using our resourcefulness and problem-solving skills.

One critical thing to remember—don't take it personally. If a client says, "This is crap!" (which they sometimes do), remember it's not about you. It's about the work and the client's own goals and preferences. Yes, it is about YOUR work, but part of your work as a professional is being adaptive and rolling with the punches. When you know your work is battle worn and time tested, the victory will be that much sweeter.

WORKING IN A TEAM

There is a funny meme online that reads, "When I die, I want my teammates to lower me into the grave so they can let me down one more time." LOL. We've all been there. We've worked on a team where we feel we're the ONLY one doing the work, and then the "slackers" get equal credit. In a student or professional agency, it's critical for everyone to contribute, not only to share the load, but also because diverse contributions are essential and valuable. The majority of organizations today operate under team-based structures. Thus, organizations can't afford for those teams to be dysfunctional.

There are many reasons people don't participate equally in groups. When dominant group members push their ideas as the best, others may feel their contributions aren't valued or necessary. A team member may be more introverted and feel uncomfortable speaking up in a team environment. Or, some team members may not have enough confidence in their own abilities. It's important to understand how teams work, the skills needed to develop effective teams, and your own role in contributing to cohesive teams.

Group Communications Roles

Roles within a team are generally classified into three categories: task-oriented roles, maintenance-oriented roles, and self-centered roles (Shockley-Zalabek, 2015, p. 198). **Task roles** relate to the work itself and the process by which the group achieves its goal. Those who focus on task roles concentrate on what needs to get done, by when and who will do it. **Maintenance roles** relate more to social cohesiveness and the ability of the group to work together. Those

Task roles: Describes group roles associated with tackling the task at hand, such as making a plan and outlining the steps and timing to achieve it.

Maintenance roles: Group roles associates with group cohesiveness, such as effective communication and conflict management.

who concentrate on maintenance roles are concerned about group participation and conflict management. They want to make sure everyone is heard and gets along.

Finally, **self-centered roles** relate to what we, personally, want to get out of the group. All of us have our own goals in participating in a team. These can be positive if they are supported by the task and maintenance roles of the group, but destructive if our personal

Self-centered roles: Describes our personal goals and what we want to achieve when participating in a team.

goals are incompatible or override the goals of the team. For example, if our personal goal is to have OUR ideas implemented without concern for collaboration, this will be destructive to both group cohesiveness and the quality of the final product.

Teams need to pay attention to all three roles to form cohesive and effective teams. If all team members are focused on the task and no one notices that a more introverted team member is not speaking up, then you'll be missing out on that team member's talents. Likewise, if everyone is focused on group cohesiveness, but no one is focused on getting the work done, then the team's goals will suffer. And, if team members' personal goals are not being met, they will be less likely to participate in team efforts.

Storming and Norming

In 1965, psychologist Bruce Tuckman identified four stages of group development: forming, storming, norming, and performing. In the forming stage, groups are new and just coming together. Members are motivated, but not sure what to expect from others in the group. At this stage, it is helpful to define both the group's goals as well as individual goals to make sure they are compatible. It's also important to identity individual team member skills to help assign tasks. For example, one team member may be a big-picture person with strong strategic thinking capabilities, whereas another is more detail-oriented and loves to do research and timelines.

The second stage—storming—is where teams often face their first conflicts. As team members start to complete tasks, differences in working styles become apparent, and team members may push back against team goals or question the team's approach. In this stage, it is important to focus on maintenance roles. Concentrate on building trust between team members and reducing group conflicts. While it can feel time consuming to focus on social cohesiveness rather than the tasks at hand, if all team members aren't on board it will be difficult, if not impossible, to produce quality work. And, if team members are conflict avoidant, or in disagreement with the process, they may figuratively drop out of the group entirely, leaving others with more stressful workloads.

It's also important for group members to understand that disagreements, when presented respectfully and with good intentions, are healthy and can lead to a better quality product. Groups who simply aim for quick agreement and avoid conflict often fall into what is called **groupthink**, where teams make

Groupthink: When a group is so cohesive that members cannot perceive potential conflicts or negative outcomes of their decisions. Groupthink discourages dissent and individual thinking.

bad decisions and ignore potential consequences of their decisions. Groupthink can be avoided by making sure dissenting opinions and alternative viewpoints are heard. Sometimes, it's helpful to appoint a **devil's advocate** in each team meeting. Devil's advocates are given permission to shoot holes in the team's ideas to help the team think through all of the potential downfalls or consequences of their decisions. By giving a team member permission to play devil's advocate, other team members will more accepting when that person questions their assumptions. And, it helps the team identify potential pitfalls to their programs.

> **Devil's advocate:** Giving a group member permission to shoot holes in the team's plans or decisions to identify potential pitfalls and avoid groupthink.

The third and fourth stages—norming and performing—are where the team begins to feel comfortable with the process. Teammates understand each other better and know their strengths and weaknesses. Conflicts have been resolved and the work begins to fall into place. At these stages, team members can work on tasks more independently and know when to ask for help or guidance from the team. It's important to check in with members from time to time to make sure one team member is not overloaded, and that others know when they need to step in.

Holding Effective Team Meetings

Effective team meetings don't just "happen" on their own without preparation and agreed upon processes. You wouldn't get in a car and just begin driving without knowing your destination and the route you'll take to get there. And you certainly wouldn't invite others to come along without telling them where they're going, how long the trip will take, and what they should bring to prepare for the trip. So, think of the following as your GPS for holding effective team meetings.

© Monkey Business Images/Shutterstock.com

Identify Your Deliverable

It is helpful to start out every meeting by identifying the deliverable/s—what needs to be accomplished during the meeting. Too often, we attend meetings where no deliverable or agenda has been identified, and these meetings tend to wander off course and end up being a waste of time.

So, for example, if you are holding a meeting on an upcoming client event, the deliverables might be (a) decide on two venue options to present to the client, based on the available five and (b) determine how to best present the venue options to the client. Then, everyone in the meeting knows where the meeting is headed. Pay attention to verbs in identifying your deliverables. For example, "discuss venue options" is much more ambiguous than "decide on two." Discussions can go on forever, but decisions must be made in a timely manner.

Determining deliverables also helps you know what to send to teammates before the meeting to help them prepare. For example, if team members have been researching the five options, send that information to all team members ahead of time to review before the meeting. Team members will then know the scope of the decision, and can prepare questions they may have for the meeting.

Determine the Process for Achieving Deliverables

Once a deliverable has been identified, together with the team, take 5 minutes or so to determine the process for achieving the deliverable. For example, each team member could give a summary of the venue they researched and then discuss them as a group. Or, you could start off by identifying a list of criteria for the best venue (e.g., fits the client's budget, hosts at least 200 people, is easy to access, etc.) and then weigh each venue against the criteria. By letting the team jointly decide on a process, you make sure everyone is on board and knows each stop along the route. Conversely, if the meeting facilitator dictates how you will arrive at the decision, you may have to stop along the way if team members aren't feeling comfortable with the process.

Put a timeframe to each part of the process (e.g., develop criteria—10 minutes, review each venue—20 minutes, etc.). By doing so, you can keep the group on track with your given meeting timeframe.

Assign a Scribe

As the saying goes, the group has no memory. Assign someone to write down what happens during the meeting, summarize discussions, and record the key decisions made. We often assume that we'll remember what happened in a meeting or that others are taking notes. Even if others are taking notes, they are recording what is important from their own perspective and not that of the team. The group has no memory, and if an official scribe is not assigned, key information will be lost and you'll come to the next meeting forgetting what was previously decided. Assigning a scribe also makes it easier to develop a contact report later on.

Determine Next Steps

After the deliverable has been achieved, determine the next steps needed to keep moving the program along. For example, now that you've decided on the two venues and how you will present them to the client, what happens next? Do you need to take pictures of the venues to present to the client? Who will do that? Determine the next steps that need to happen, when they will happen, by whom and when the team needs to meet again. Too often we make good decisions in a meeting but they go nowhere because we haven't determined the next steps.

Critique the Process

This may seem like a waste of time, but if you get in the habit of doing this at the end of every meeting, you'll be surprised at how much more productive the team becomes. Spend 5 minutes at the end of the meeting critiquing the meeting itself. What worked well? What didn't work well? How might we do it better next time? Did everyone feel included? Were all ideas heard? Keep in mind both task roles and maintenance roles, as well as personal goals.

For example, someone might say, "I thought it worked really well for each team member to do research before the meeting." Great! You'll know to utilize that technique for the next meeting. Or, someone might say, "Well, I had some ideas to share, but we never got to the point where I felt comfortable expressing them." Okay, maybe next time we go around the table and ask for each person's input separately. Another team member might say, "This time worked really well for me, but I got hungry because this is normally the time I have dinner. Maybe we could each take turns bringing snacks. I'll be happy to bring them for our next meeting." OHHHH. That's an AWESOME idea. Meeting adjourned.

Follow Up

Within the 24 hours after the meeting (or sooner if possible), follow up with a contact report (see Chapter 7) and any other materials or information promised during the meeting. The scribe can write up and distribute the report, or can give notes to the facilitator for developing the contact report. Keep the contact report simple and scannable, and make sure to include the all-important next steps and the person responsible for each. At the next meeting, you can then check your list to make sure all next steps have been accomplished or are in progress.

THE GIFT OF FEEDBACK

Take a minute to think of a lesson you have learned in life. Not something you have read in a textbook, but something you have experienced. We'll wait.

Okay, now that you've thought of a lesson, think about how you learned that lesson? Chances are you learned it firsthand—by doing it right, or, more than likely, by doing it wrong. A teacher or caregiver can tell us what we should or shouldn't do, but it often isn't until we experience the lesson firsthand that we truly learn it. For example, Nana might have told you not to touch the burner on the stove because it's hot. But your curiosity got the best of you and you touched it anyway. OUCH! Yep, one shouldn't touch a hot burner.

The most memorable lessons in life are often learned by making mistakes. By doing things the wrong way, we learn to do them the right way. And, sometimes we don't even know we're making mistakes. We may be oblivious of how our actions or behaviors are affecting others until someone tells us. Conversely, we may not know we did something *right,* or that it had a positive effect on the client or our coworkers. That's why we often need others to point out what we're doing—right or wrong—how we might do better or how we can continuing doing what we're doing right. It's important to remember that the purpose of feedback is both to improve negative behaviors as well as to reinforce positive behaviors.

But why is it so hard to hear feedback from others? Simply put—humans have egos. We like to think of ourselves as perfect, and it's hard to hear when we're not. We love to be praised. Anything short of that feels like criticism. But in his 2000 book, Nigel Bristow gave us another way to look at feedback: as a "gift." It's a gift given by others who have taken the time to impart their knowledge and experience. It's a gift to receive because it helps us become better and stronger individuals. It's something we need, and something we desire—and it's a gift that keeps on giving throughout our professional lives.

Professional workplaces have both formal and informal ways of giving feedback to employees. Most workplaces give formal feedback, such as performance reviews, either annually or semiannually, and task supervisors to give informal feedback on an ongoing basis.

Below we outline a few ways to both give and receive the gift of feedback:

1. *Invite feedback:* Studies show that your generation—Millennials and Gen Z—want lots of feedback. However, in the fast-paced agency work environment you may have to ask for feedback from your supervisor or colleagues. You can invite feedback by simply asking: "How am I doing? Is there anything I can improve upon?" Inviting feedback shows your eagerness to learn and your openness to hearing how you can do better.

2. *Give/get feedback regularly:* Feedback should be given regularly, in person, and as soon as possible after a particular behavior is noticed. People have a better chance of recognizing and correcting/reinforcing their behaviors soon after they have taken place. If you wait a few weeks to get/give feedback, the person could repeat negative behaviors again before having a chance to correct them. Also, it is best to give feedback in person rather than via email or some other means. Feedback should be a two-way conversation rather than a missive from one person to the other.

3. *Praise in public, correct in private:* Praising someone in public for positive behaviors not only makes them feel good, but it helps others see what praise-worthy behavior looks like. Conversely, it can be embarrassing to be corrected in front of others. If you need to correct a colleague's behavior, do so in person and in private. An exception to this rule would be an inappropriate behavior that needs to be called out on the spot, like sexual harassment or a racial slur. In this case, call it out immediately and then have a more detailed conversation in private—for example, "(Name), that is inappropriate behavior. Let's go into the hall and talk about it."

4. *Focus on the behavior, not the person:* We often view corrective feedback (wrongly) as, "I'm a bad person." Feedback is not about who you are as a person; it's about

your actions. So, feedback should focus on the "what," not the "who." If you are giving feedback, provide examples of the behavior in question and focus on how it can be corrected in the future. When getting feedback, ask for examples of behavior that needs to be corrected, and then jointly discuss ways you can more effectively handle similar situations.

5. *Determine your intent:* Feedback should be given and received in an atmosphere of mutual respect and learning. When giving feedback, your intent should be to help the person learn and grown, not to "get back" at someone or make them do things your way. Likewise, when getting feedback your intent should be to learn how to improve, rather than argue about who is right or wrong or rationalize your behavior. Focus on the content of the message and try not to get defensive. If you feel yourself reacting poorly, ask to be excused for a moment to gather your thoughts.

6. *Take action:* Feedback doesn't do any good if you don't act on it. After getting feedback, take some time to think about it (but don't dwell on it), and devise a plan for putting the feedback into action. Then, follow up with your supervisor/colleague to see how you've progressed. If you're giving feedback, notice when the person has made progress and praise them for it. Remember, feedback is about progress, not perfection.

© Francesco83/Shutterstock.com

In summary, think about how your student agency can create a culture that invites and delivers feedback on a regular basis. After all, that's what student agencies are about—learning to progress as professionals and as communications experts.

CREATIVE THINKING

How do you avoid all the economic costs of owning and maintaining a car, but still keep your mobility? Robin Chase had the answer—Zipcar, now the world's largest car-sharing business. How do you use the spare room in your apartment to make money? You set up a couple of air mattresses and loan them out to convention-goers who can't find an empty hotel room—which was how Airbnb started. Wouldn't it be great if you could cook a gourmet meal every day of the week without all the hassle of grocery shopping and searching for recipes? Now you can with Blue Apron home delivery meal kits. All of these are examples of people who used creative thinking to solve a problem or capitalize on an opportunity.

While we may not think of it as a "soft" skill, creativity is an essential skill for working in the agency business, and really, in most businesses. Creative people develop imaginative campaigns and find innovative solutions to client's communications challenges.

In the past few years, one of the authors taught a creative thinking and problem-solving course. The question she had before launching the course was: Can creativity be taught? Or, more specifically, can creativity be learned? After extensive research and teaching the class for the first semester, the answer she came to was Yes, it can.

While some people are naturally creative, others have to work at it. But that doesn't mean that anyone—and everyone—can't be creative. It just takes a creative mindset and a few tools to switch from your left brain (where analytical thinking takes place) to your right brain (where more creative thinking resides). More accurately, creative thinking often occurs by switching back and forth between the two. Critical thinking and creative thinking go hand in hand.

But what do we mean when we say someone is "creative?" Being creative doesn't necessarily mean you are "artsy," though it can. Agencies rely on artists, designers, and filmmakers to develop creative campaigns. But even those are "hard skills" that come from having both a natural ability as well as being taught techniques such as effective layout and the use of color. When we talk about creativity or creative thinking in the agency business, we are usually referring to a creative perspective or way of looking at the world. Creative people see things differently. They notice things that others don't, or look at situations in ways that might not be the "norm." They're curious. They contemplate the "What if . . ." They break the rules.

Breaking the Rules—Overcoming Barriers to Creative Thinking

Developing a creative mindset requires setting aside the assumptions we have about ourselves and the world around us. The first of those being: I'm just not creative. How do you know? Did someone tell you that? Or are you comparing yourself to someone else? Comparisons can be deadly because someone will always be better, stronger, faster, and this prevents us from seeing our own talents and abilities, or the skills we can learn.

Another barrier to creativity includes sticking to what we've been taught is the "right" or "only" way to do things based on our upbringing and our culture. For example, in America, we put cheese in the refrigerator to keep it from going "bad." But in France, cheese is seen as a living thing. Living things don't go in the refrigerator. A big part of creativity is simply unlearning what we've been taught and rejecting that there is only one way to do things.

In the book *Deep Survival* (2017), Laurence Gonzalez contemplates why some people survive when lost in the wilderness and others don't. He found those most likely to survive are those who break the rules. For example, a firefighter was lost in a national park and might have been rescued sooner had he built a fire that could have been spotted for miles away. But he didn't, because it was against the rules to build a fire in that section of the park. The author found toddlers also have a pretty high chance of survival when lost in the woods. Why? Because they don't yet KNOW the rules. Toddlers are curious and can spend hours surveying every little stick or rock around them, staying in a fairly small space while doing so. In addition, toddlers simply don't know they're lost—"I'm not lost. Mommy and Daddy are lost."

When we say, "break the rules," we don't mean doing something unethical or unfairly taking an advantage of a situation. Society has rules for good reason. They help things go smoothly, make sure everyone has the same advantages and keep us safe. What we mean by "breaking the rules" is questioning the way things are always done and contemplating ways to do things differently.

To break the rules, we need to question our assumptions about the way things "are" and contemplate the way they "could be"—no matter how outrageous or impractical. For example, think about the brand positioning of Snickers candy bars. Our assumptions about candy bars are that they are sweet (a dessert, perhaps) meant for kids, or maybe an occasional indulgence for adults. But Snickers reversed those assumptions and broke the rules. To Snickers, candy bars are for young men, not as a dessert, but as a way to satisfy their hunger. The well-known Dove campaign is another example of breaking the rules. The assumption in the fashion industry was that models sell beauty products, and that women "aspire" to be like those (often unrealistic) models. But Dove said: "What if . . .?" What if we could make every woman feel beautiful? Dove abandoned the use of professional models and used real women instead. Thus, the Campaign for Real Beauty was born.

Where Creative Ideas Come From

Have you ever attended a brainstorm where the facilitator asked, "Does anyone have any ideas?" and then there were crickets? Chances are, not much came from that "brainstorm." The misperception about creative ideas is that they come from nothing—like pink unicorns, imaginative ideas just suddenly appear out of nowhere. But that's not the case, especially in the agency business.

When it comes to creative ideas, a familiar saying is, "There are no new ideas under the sun." That's because new ideas don't come from a blank sheet of paper; they come from synthesizing, evolving, or reapplying old ideas into something new (Harris, 1998). In the agency business, you will often see the same type of campaign reapplied for different clients and brands. For example, we're not sure where the idea originated of letting consumers "vote" online for a winning flavor or contest entrant, but look how many brands use this technique in their campaigns.

To be a creative thinker and develop innovative ideas, you have to fill your brain with as many different "old" ideas as possible. Be curious. Look around you. Read industry trade publications on new campaigns. Look at winning campaigns on awards' websites. In his book, *Thinkertoys*, Michael Michalko (2006) recommends building what he calls a **brain bank**. A brain bank can be physical, like

Brain bank: A bank of objects and ideas collected for future brainstorming. Brain banks might include clippings from magazines, memes from the Internet, photos from your phone, or lyrics from a song—items or ideas that could spark creative thinking.

a shoebox filled with ideas, or more intangible, like simply filling your brain with ideas. For example, when you read a magazine, cut out a picture that might spark an idea and put it in your brain bank. Or, if you see a funny meme online that relates to your client, save it in an online brain bank. Then, when it comes time to brainstorm, you'll have a bank full of unicorns to stimulate your thinking.

And speaking of brainstorms, they require more than just getting a group of people together. Use creative tools such as Brute Think (see Sachs, 2016), Cherry Split (see Brain Guide, n.d.), Lotus Blossom (see Michalko, 2016), or the many other techniques outlined in *Thinkertoys* to help generate off-the-wall ideas. Or, devise techniques of your own. The key to brainstorming is to generate as many ideas as possible (like 100), in the first session or two. Don't judge or evaluate ideas until you've generated as many as possible. Then, you can go back to evaluate and develop the best ideas further based on your program criteria. In addition, use tactile objects in the brainstorm like Play-Doh, Legos, Slinky, stress balls, and so on. Tactile objects help get you out of the left brain and into the more creative right brain. It's helpful to keep a brainstorming toy box in the student agency filled with these items for brainstorming use. You'll find an example of a brainstorm facilitation guide in Box 10.2.

Box 10.2   Brainstorming Session Facilitator's Guide

Facilitator: (Name)

Recorder/scribe: (Name) Keep track of your ideas on large easel pads or on whiteboards (Tip: you can photograph them and transcribe later). Remember, you want to generate as many as 100 ideas, so make sure you can record them.

Timeframe for brainstorm: How much time will you allot for the brainstorm? A good timeframe for a first brainstorm is 1 to 1½ hours. After that, brains start to get tired.

Where will you hold the brainstorm and how will the room/space be set up? The room should be casual and comfortable. What creative props will you use? (e.g., Play-Doh, Legos, pipe cleaners).

What is the challenge? Write the challenge out for participants. For example, the challenge might be "In what ways might we differentiate our product from the competitor?"

How will you open/set up the brainstorm? What rules will you set for the group? No ideas are bad ideas, everyone participates, reserve judgment for later, etc.

How will you get the creative thinking started? Use a warm-up exercise like, "What would get us fired?" Brainstorm all the things you could do in a campaign that would make the client fire you. Then, see if there are any that spark creative ideas.

Summarize the brainstorming techniques you will use during your session. You can use techniques from creative thinking books or develop your own techniques. Summarize at least three techniques you will use in the brainstorm session and describe how you will use them. For example, you might use Brute Think, where you choose a random word, write down all the assumptions about that word, and then brainstorm ideas related to your problem/challenge.

(Continued)

(Continued)

Example:

Challenge: In what ways might we differentiate our frozen waffles from the competitor?

Random word: Flamingo

Things associated with flamingos:
- Pink
- Tropical
- Stand on one leg

Creative ideas:
- Make our waffles different colors
- Give away a tropical vacation
- Challenge consumers to eat waffles standing on one leg; videotape it for social media

Outline a timeline for the brainstorm based on your techniques:

Example:
- State the challenge and rules: 5 min
- Warm-up exercise: 10 min
- Brute think: 15 min
- Cherry split: 15 min
- Etc.

What are the criteria by which you will judge creative concepts? This is the "convergence" portion of the brainstorm. Remember, don't evaluate until AFTER you've generated ideas. How will you know you have a "good" concept? List 3-5 imperatives that each concept should include, do, or involve?

For example, ideas must
- Differentiate the product
- Be realistic within our budget
- Integrate the client's brand positioning
- Etc.

What are obstacles you could face in the brainstorm and how will you overcome them? (e.g., if one technique doesn't work, move on to another).

© ESB Professional/Shutterstock.com

Michael Michalko's book *Thinkertoys* (2006) is a treasure trove of tools and examples of creative thinking and brainstorming. Keep a copy of this or other creative thinking books in your student agency for reference.

So, is creativity a soft skill, a hard skill, or a bit of both? We'll let you decide. But what we know from our years of working in the industry is that creative thinking is an essential skill for being a valued agency member.

MANAGING STRESS: CREATING A STUDY–WORK–LIFE BALANCE

We live in a workaholic American culture, both in the academic and professional worlds, where being busy has become somewhat of a status symbol (Pinsker, 2017). Often, we participate in what leadership development specialist Rachael Simmons calls the "Stress Olympics" (Bennett, 2017). "You think YOU'RE busy. Listen to MY to-do list." We tend to equate being stressed with being successful. We take on too much. We think we have to do it all—perfectly. And we end up being less productive because our bodies and minds are chronically overloaded.

If you aren't aware, chronic stress can cause not only mental health issues but also physical ones. According to the American Psychological Association, stress can lead to increased blood pressure, headaches, insomnia, depression, and many other health-related issues. In short, stress is bad. Yet, it is often unavoidable. Life is stressful. Jobs are stressful. And, as you are well aware, college is stressful.

But rather than going for the gold in the "stress Olympics," studies show that we are more productive and successful when we learn to manage stress levels and strive for a study–work–life balance. That means that we learn to be more focused and mindful when we're studying or working, and balance our time with enough rest and recreation to reenergize both our bodies and our minds.

While the following is not meant to be a comprehensive list, below are a few ways you can strive for a study–work–life balance while working for the student agency. Consult with your university for more techniques.

Don't Take on Too Much

Here's a phenomenon we've noticed in our years of managing student agencies: the most passionate, motivated students apply. Which is great, because we get excellent talent. But, those motivated students are also involved in 10 other on-campus organizations or communities for which they are equally passionate, as well as working at part-time jobs or internships. As the semester progresses, students get frustrated and stressed because they just don't have the time to devote to all of them. Their work suffers, their stress level suffers, and the student agency suffers. Most importantly, their academic grades suffer.

So, instead of signing up for EVERY exciting thing on campus, pick two or three that you can really sink your teeth into and do the best job possible. Make a list of all the activities you want to be involved with, and then evaluate which ones will benefit your long-term goals the most, and which ones will benefit from your own talent and abilities. Then, set a schedule based on the time you need to devote to your academics, work, and recreational activities. Being realistic is a beneficial soft skill to develop. Working 40 hours a week, plus taking five classes, plus being involved in 10 extracurricular activities just isn't realistic. We have to learn to say, "No, I just can't take on any more."

Power Down

In the 21st century, we are an "always on" society. We're connected to our workplaces and each other 24/7. Millennials and Generation Z are multitaskers—doing homework, listening to music, texting a friend, and watching a video all at the same time. But this means your mind is being pulled in a dozen different directions, with no chance to just "turn off" from the stresses of being digitally connected.

At times it may be necessary to (GASP) turn off your phone and power down. Take some quiet time for yourself or converse one-on-one with friends and loved ones. For example, you might make it a point not to check email or texts for 2 hours during the dinner hour. Or, give yourself an hour of power down time when you wake up in the morning. It's awfully hard to go from a deep sleep to "OMG—there are a million things happening on social media!!!!" At first, you might feel disconnected or as if you're missing out on something. But that Snapchat story will still be there later on. And, your withering psyche will thank you for decluttering and focusing on what's important—if only for a little while.

Take a Break

If you find yourself reading the same sentence over and over again and not comprehending a single word, it might be time to take a break. Walk outside (without your phone), get some fresh air, do stretching exercises, and refocus your mind on something other than work. When you return to the project, your mind will feel rested and ready to engage. Taking a mental break is different than procrastinating. Procrastinating is a work avoidance strategy; taking a mental break is like hitting the reset button to make your work more productive.

This technique is also useful in the midst of a tense group discussion. Give the group a 5-minute time-out to walk outside for a minute or chat socially about something other than the task at hand. When the group returns, you'll notice a drop in the tension. If you are in the middle of a tense client meeting and can't take a physical break, try taking a mental break. Sit back in your chair, take deep breaths, and remove yourself mentally from the conversation for a few minutes. A short mental break can keep you from saying something you might regret, and will help you see the situation from a calmer perspective.

Practice Mindfulness

Mindfulness has become both a buzzword and a programmed activity on college campuses in the past few years. But what does it mean? Simply put, **mindfulness** means to live fully in the present moment. It comes from the practice of meditation, where those who practice it focus on the breath and center their minds and bodies on their meditation.

Mindfulness: Being fully engaged in and conscious of the present moment, rather than thinking of what happened in the past or what might happen in the future.

Being mindful not only keeps your attention focused, it also lessens your stress level. Instead of worrying about ALL the things you need to get done, focus on what is happening right now. A good phrase to practice in any situation is Be Here Now. So, when you're at your job, instead of thinking about that monster research paper that's waiting for you, just concentrate on your job. Be—At Your Job—Now. Worrying about the paper is useless because you can't do anything about it at the present moment.

Likewise, when you're in class, instead of checking social media or texting a friend, be—in class—now. You'll be amazed at how much more engaging the class is—and how much more you learn—when you concentrate on just being a part of the class experience. And, when you're in a client meeting, focus on what's happening in the meeting. Notice the client's body language, listen to their words, and watch how they react to what's happening in the meeting.

© racorn/Shutterstock.com

You can practice mindfulness techniques on your own, or take a yoga or meditation class. Many colleges offer these as part of your student activities fund.

Give Yourself Permission to Fail

Here's a little secret. One of the authors failed the first year of college, dropped out for nearly 2 years, returned to a different major and went on to become a successful agency executive and now a college professor. That's a positive failure story.

In a society where our social media feeds make it seem like everyone's life is perfect, we are often terrified of failing. When we do fail, we berate ourselves endlessly and allow our self-esteem to be damaged. Sometimes, we don't even have to fail to feel like a failure (Like, "OMG I got a B!" Nope—not a failure). Many of us (many, MANY of us) go so far as to experience **imposter syndrome**—the feeling that you're a fraud, that you don't belong here,

Imposter syndrome: When we lack confidence in our own talents and abilities, we can feel like an imposter—a fraud—and worry that someone will find us out. Many successful people experience imposter syndrome.

and any minute someone's going to find you out and expose you. It's a real thing (see, e.g., Eschenroeder, 2017).

We're here to tell you to stop. Just STOP. We're all frauds. We're all faking it until we make it. Failing doesn't make YOU a failure. It just makes you human. And, you can't progress as a human OR a professional without failing. We hope you've noticed throughout this textbook our emphasis on not only succeeding, but also on failing. The student agency (and college, and life in general) is essentially a lab for taking risks, making mistakes, learning from them, and bouncing back to try again. So, go ahead. You have our permission to be human.

Ask for Help

When you're stuck, stressed, or at the end of your rope—ask for help. You are surrounded by people willing and eager to pull your head above water. Asking for help can take on many forms. You can ask a professor for help with your classwork. Ask a friend to pick up some takeout when he's headed off campus for a bit. Or, ask a campus counselor to listen when you are feeling stressed or depressed. Sometimes, we are hesitant to ask for help because we feel we should be super heroes who can handle it all. But guess what? We ALL need help. Asking for help shows that you are . . . wait for it . . . RESOURCEFUL.

The student agency has a structure in place to guide students through their agency experience and help them along the way. Use those resources. When you're on deadline and know you just can't get it all done in time—ask your student supervisor, agency advisor, or another team member for help. Agencies are built around an ebb and flow of work. When you're cranking away at midnight on that PSA script, another team might have downtime before the next client project. That's the nature of the business. And it's good practice for teammates to learn how to "share the load" and step into help when another team is in a pinch. Then, when you have downtime, you'll return the favor.

CONCLUSION

As you work your way through the student agency, and through your college career, you'll develop your own professional identity. Just like your personality, your professional identity will be unique to you; what works for others may not work for you and vice versa.

The important thing to remember is to be aware of it. Understand that the student agency is not just a place to learn hard skills; it's also a place to practice being a professional. Get to know your own working style and how you react to diverse professional situations. Practice different communications skills like active listening and group roles. Be mindful of where you are and what is happening around you at any given moment. Learn what motivates you about the work—and what doesn't.

Most importantly, don't be afraid to take risks, make mistakes, and know what it feels like to be a resilient problem solver. You'll be able to carry these skills forward into your career.

REVIEW AND DISCUSSION QUESTIONS

1. What are the differences between hard skills and soft skills?
2. What are the differences between inward self-awareness and outward self-awareness?
3. Think of three ways you can practice being outwardly self-aware?
4. With a partner, practice active listening. Have your partner tell you about what they did last weekend. Practice repeating, rephrasing, and asking questions to understand their meaning and show you are fully engaged in the conversation. Then switch and tell your partner about your weekend.
5. Think of something new you could learn to increase your ability to be resourceful. Then, learn that skill.
6. Your client has an event on Thursday for 200 people, for which your agency is developing the programs. The printer calls you on Wednesday to say there has been a mix-up and they won't be able to have the programs printed until Friday. There is no other printer in town. How would you handle this situation? Use both critical and creative thinking in developing a solution.
7. Walk through Question 6 with a team. As you are discussing possible solutions, pay attention to both task and maintenance roles. Are both being covered? Also, use the exercise to practice holding an effective meeting, starting with defining your deliverable.
8. Write down two failures you have experienced and how you dealt with each. Discuss them with your team.
9. Think of a time when you had to be resilient by facing a difficult situation and bouncing back. What did you learn from that situation that you could apply to your work at the student agency?
10. Take a 5-minute walk around campus. Turn off your phone and just take in your surroundings without thinking about anything. Be mindful of where you are and what is occurring around you. Don't think about anything but what is happening at the moment. Use all of your available senses. What do you notice? How do you feel? Discuss the experience with a teammate or group.

REFERENCES AND ADDITIONAL READINGS

American Psychological Association. (n.d.). *Coping with stress at work*. Retrieved from http://www.apa.org/helpcenter/work-stress.aspx

Baldoni, J. (2010, January 13). The importance of resourcefulness. *Harvard Business Review*. Retrieved from https://hbr.org/2010/01/leaders-can-learn-to-make-do-a

Bennett, J. (2017, June 24). On campus failure is on the syllabus. *New York Times*. Retrieved from https://www.nytimes.com/2017/06/24/fashion/fear-of-failure.html?linkId=41390630&_r=0

Boitnott, J. (2014, September 24). 10 Longtime brainstorming techniques that still work. *Inc.* Retrieved from https://www.inc.com/john-boitnott/10-longtime-brainstorming-techniques-that-still-work.html

Brain Guide. (n.d.). *Brainstorming technique 3: Cherry split*. Brain Guide. Retrieved from https://brain-guide.org/brainstorming-technique-3-cherry-split/

Bristow, N. (2000). *Where's the gift? How to achieve phenomenal success by discovering the gift in all feedback.* Lindon, Utah: Cascade Press.

Bush, L. (2009). Student public relations agencies: A qualitative study of the pedagogical benefits, risks and a framework for success. *Journalism & Mass Communication Educator, 64*(Spring), 27–38.

Bush, L., Haygood, D., & Vincent, H. (2017). Student-run communications agencies: Providing students with real-world experiences that impact their careers. *Journalism & Mass Communication Educator, 72*, 410–424. First Published 2016, October 4.

Gonzalez, L. (2017). *Deep survival: Who lives, who dies, and why.* New York, NY: W. W. Norton & Co.

Hansen, D. (2012, January 24). 7 steps to increase self-awareness and catapult your career. *Forbes.* Retrieved from https://www.forbes.com/sites/drewhansen/2012/01/24/7-steps-to-increase-self-awareness-and-catapult-your-career/2/#20e002695f09

Harris, R. (1998, July 1). Introduction to creative thinking. *Virtual Salt.* Retrieved from http://www.virtualsalt.com/crebook1.htm

Making Business Matter. (n.d.). *Competency framework communications skills.* Making Business Matter.co.uk. Retrieved from http://www.makingbusinessmatter.co.uk/training-courses/communication-skills-training/

Michalko, M. (2006). *Thinkertoys: A handbook of creative thinking techniques.* New York, NY: Ten Speed Press, a division of Random House.

Michalko, M. (2013, February 13). Creating thinking technique: Lotus blossom. *Creative Thinking.* Retrieved from http://creativethinking.net/creative-thinking-technique-lotus-blossom/#sthash.CfpgUWef.nxTCLjGi.dpbs

Mindful Staff. (2014, October 8). What is mindfulness? *Mindful.* Retrieved from https://www.mindful.org/what-is-mindfulness/

Pinsker, J. (2017, March 1). 'Ugh, I'm so busy:' A status symbol for our time. *The Atlantic.* Retrieved from https://www.theatlantic.com/business/archive/2017/03/busyness-status-symbol/518178/

Sachs, H. (2016, July 6). Uncage your ideas with brutethink, a highly effective creativity technique. *Remember Everything.* Retrieved from https://remembereverything.org/brutethink-creativity-technique/

Shockley-Zalabek, P. (2015). *Fundamental of organizational communication.* Upper Saddle River, NJ: Pearson.

Treffinger, D., Isaksen, S., & Stead-Dorval, K. (2006). *Creative problem solving: An introduction* (4th ed.). Waco, TX: Prufrock Press.

Tuckman, B. (1965). Development sequence in small groups. *Psychological Bulletin, 63*(6), 384–399.

Vozza, S. (2015, August 24). Five ways to read someone. *Fast Company* https://www.fastcompany.com/3049746/five-ways-to-read-someones-mind

Woodcock, A. (2016, April 5). Working conditions in a creative advertising agency. *Medium.* Retrieved from https://medium.com/@AdamWoodcock/working-conditions-in-a-creative-advertising-agency-89af2548a97d

Selling Your Ideas

Too often in our hyperdigital world, we tend to overlook or bypass the most persuasive form of communication—face-to-face. A big part of working in an agency is selling your ideas to the client or potential client in face-to-face meetings and formal or informal presentations.

Presenting face-to-face has several advantages over other forms of communication. First, it helps you establish and build trust with the client, which is more difficult to do via email or other digital platforms. Second, it allows for synchronous communication, or communication in which the client can provide feedback and students can respond to that feedback in real time. Because of this, it can be more productive. Rather than sending a series of emails where there are delayed responses and questions that need additional explanation, holding a meeting allows you to cover a broad array of topics, discuss them in detail, and achieve consensus.

Face-to-face communications can also be more persuasive than other forms of communication. Because you are meeting in person, you can show more energy and enthusiasm for your programs, appeal immediately to the client's stated concerns, and read the client's nonverbal reactions to your content. Bohns and Roghanizad found that face-to-face requests are 34 times more effective than requests made via email (Bohns, 2017). Lastly, face-to-face communication can eliminate the confusion of trying to read intent or emotions in texts, emails, or even phone calls. Words and meanings simply translate better when given in person.

But there is more to selling your ideas than simply making a presentation. It takes preparation, knowledge, and practice to persuade your supervisor or client that your proposal or creative piece is the best way to address the client's challenge. In this chapter, we discuss the following:

- Use of persuasive appeals in making presentations
- Developing content that tells a story
- Delivering an effective presentation
- Scheduling and presenting client meetings

TYPES OF PERSUASIVE APPEALS

The ancient Greek philosopher Aristotle outlined three types of persuasive appeals that are still appropriate today, particularly in the field of advertising and public relations (PR): Ethos, Logos, and Pathos.

Ethos relates to the credibility and character of the presenter. Outlining your credentials and expertise in a field can establish strong credibility with your audience. You've likely noticed that when you attend a presentation

> **Ethos:** An appeal based on credibility, character, and ethics.

or lecture on campus, the program will include a biography of the presenter's credentials. This tells you the speaker is well qualified to talk about the topic. For example, as the chief operating officer of Facebook, a former vice president of Google, the first woman to serve on Facebook's board, author of a book on business leadership, and founder of an organization to promote women in business, Sheryl Sandberg has a great deal of credibility to talk about a variety of issues in the technology field. But what if you don't yet have that kind of experience and expertise?

One way to build credibility is to do your homework. Research the client's business, the industry, and the types of programs you are presenting. If you are asking the client to take a risk they have never tried before, research other companies that have been successful with this type of program. By showing you know what you're talking about, you will have more credibility with the client.

And, realize that there likely ARE areas where you have expertise. For example, while clients have been using social media as a branding tool for several years, they may not be as well versed in some of the newer platforms and applications such as Snapchat, Instagram Stories, or Facebook Live. If your client is targeting Millennials or Gen Z, you will have unique insights into those generations to share with your client. Or, perhaps your background, experiences, or identity can provide the client with a different way of looking at the world. There are always areas where you have expertise.

Other ways to show ethos include being ethical in your business practices, honest in your dealings with the client, and enthusiastic about learning. If a client finds you are not being upfront in what you are presenting, or are hiding information from them, you can quickly lose credibility. But when you are honest and show a commitment to doing a great job, the client will be more comfortable letting you handle the business.

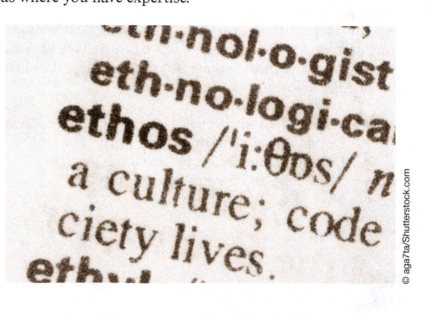

© aga7ta/Shutterstock.com

The second type of persuasive appeal is **logos**, or logical appeals. As we have stated throughout this text, clients manage organizations, which rely on sound business practices.

> **Logos:** An appeal based on logic and reasoning.

Rather than simply saying, "We think this will work," you need to back up your statements with sound logic—"We're convinced this will work because x, y, z." Build a strong rationale for every program or idea you present to the client. Building an argument requires, again, doing your research. Programs work when you fully understand the organizational challenge, when you know what the target audience needs and wants, and when your execution is based on solid strategies and tactics.

Let's say your client is a study abroad organization that wants to increase student participation in its programs through a social media campaign. You present a campaign to your client that utilizes Snapchat. But the client doesn't use Snapchat; they only use Twitter and Facebook. To convince the client that Snapchat is the right platform, you might introduce data that shows 78% of high school and college students use Snapchat, more so than Facebook or Instagram; 70% log on at least six times per day; nearly 44 million Millennials use Snapchat; and, Snapchat is a growing advertising platform for all types of Millennial brands (eMarketer, 2017). That is a logical appeal, and a stronger rationale than, "Well, we use Snapchat, so we think others will, too."

A part of building a strong argument is to think through all the potential holes in your idea, or questions the client will ask. Put yourself in the client's shoes. What will logically convince them that your idea is the way to go?

The third type of appeal is **pathos**, or emotional appeals. While logical arguments appeal to a client's head, pathos appeals to the client's heart. This is true in producing

> **Pathos:** An appeal based on emotions.

advertising and PR content, as well as in making presentations. Why do you think animal shelters show pictures of sad, neglected animals, accompanied by moving music, when asking for donations? They could just give you the horrifying stats of how many animals are abandoned or abused each year, and often they do. But it's those sad pictures of neglected animals that tug at our heartstrings and make us want to DO SOMETHING about it.

Pathos includes appeals that make clients laugh, give them something they can personally relate to, appeal to their ego, or make them feel an urgent need to act. In other words, pathos makes a connection with the client that goes beyond data and statistics.

Let's return to our Snapchat scenario. You've given the client the logical reasons they should use Snapchat. Now, what will get them to act? Perhaps you found that no other study abroad program has used Snapchat before. Your client could be the first—a leader, a pioneer, seen as forward-looking and "cool" in the eyes of their target audience. But, they need to act now before a competitor beats them to it. That's a pretty compelling appeal to the client's ego.

Most often your creative will be the emotional appeal that moves the client, and your consumer, to action. So, perhaps you present a Snapchat campaign where study abroad participants tell emotional stories about how their experience changed their view of the world. When you present these stories, they make the client laugh or say "Awww" or "Ahhhhh." That's the appeal that will drive them to action.

A good example of the importance of using all three types of appeal in both your campaigns and your client presentations comes from a campaign one of the authors worked on for a company that makes store branded products (like Walgreens' brand of aspirin or Walmart's brand of lotion). The company used pharmacists to deliver the message about the efficacy of store branded products and it had worked well for several years. But, now their sales had hit a wall and the client wasn't sure why. He delivered a box of research to the agency that showed in survey after survey consumers KNEW store brand products contained the same ingredients as national brands for less money (logos), but they were still purchasing national brands. The agency held a series of focus groups to determine why. They found the decision was not a logical one; it was emotional (pathos). Consumers believed in the efficacy of store brands, but they simply trusted name brands more (ethos) because name brands had built a strong brand image over the years.

The agency subsequently tested different categories of spokespeople—pharmacists, celebrities, and professional athletes—to determine who would move consumers to purchase. They found that pharmacists could deliver the efficacy message, but that didn't move consumers to action. Celebrities simply weren't believable, because they make lots of money and probably have assistants who make these purchases. It turned out that athletes, and more specifically, women who are athletes, were the most believable and credible. These athletes likely need the types of products the company was marketing, but don't make as much money as celebrities or professional athletes who are men. And, consumers admired their grit and determination. Thus, the agency built a campaign around supporting girls' and women's sports, using well-known athletes from the Women's National Basketball Association (WNBA), and women's softball and soccer to build trust in store branded products.

STORYTELLING

In his book *11 Deadly Presentation Sins*, actor and corporate communications consultant Rob Biesenbach outlines the importance of storytelling when giving a presentation.

> Storytelling is one of the most powerful forms of communication there is. If you want to make an impact, if you want your points to stick, nothing beats a well-told story. Stories lend context and meaning to your ideas. They lift people up and inspire them. They elevate your presentation to a higher plane. (Biesenbach, 2014, p. 37)

Biesenbach defines a story as, "a character in pursuit of a goal in the face of an obstacle or challenge" (Biesenbach, 2014, p. 37). Stories humanize concepts and ideas. Which, after all, is what we want our programs to do.

Pro Tip

Think of three personal stories that relate to the client's situation, challenge, or organization. Keep them in the back of your mind to use during presentations or small-talk with the client before or after the presentation.

Like a well-told story, your presentation should have a beginning, middle, and end. The beginning of a story grabs our attention, introduces us to the characters, and engages us enough that we want to read more. Without an engaging beginning, we'd put the book right back on the shelf. Likewise, you want the beginning of your presentation to grab the client's attention and make them eager to flip to the next page. This is where you want to show excitement, enthusiasm, and gratitude for the client inviting you to present; introduce the people (characters) who will be presenting and provide their credentials; and give clients a taste of what they'll hear as you move forward.

For example, you might tease the client with a key insight you learned from your research that begs to be addressed in the rest of your presentation. Advertising executive Jon Steel outlines this kind of teaser in a story he tells about a presentation to Porsche (Steel, 2007). After telling the client they had spent many hours researching the challenge, the agency put up a cartoon that introduced the heart of the problem. The cartoon showed two cars: a Porsche and a "regular" car. A thought bubble above the driver of the regular car revealed what he thinks about the Porsche driver in a single word: Asshole. Though the client was taken aback, the agency disclosed that consumers who could afford a Porsche were embarrassed to purchase one because they thought they would be seen as snobs. Then, the rest of the presentation told the client how they could overcome this challenge.

While we don't recommend using inappropriate language in a student agency presentation, you get the point. Reveal something in the introduction that makes the client want to hear more. This could include stating your vision for the client—"Today we're going to show you how you can become the leader in study abroad"; telling a personal story, "When I studied abroad, the thing that stood out most was how it changed my view of the world"; or teasing a creative theme they will see later in the presentation.

The middle of your presentation then tells the rest of the story and how the client will overcome the challenge and achieve their goals, or how your program will help the target audience overcome a challenge. It should include the bulk of your research, strategies, tactics, and creative. But remember, instead of simply presenting information—tell the story. Use both logical and emotional appeals. Tell smaller stories within the bigger story. Use analogies and metaphors the client can relate to.

In addition, think about the flow of how the story unfolds. Just as a storyteller wouldn't talk about the wedding before revealing how two people met, you wouldn't want to present your creative before discussing the research that led you there. Your creative ideas or materials are the climax of the story. If you build the story of how you got to those ideas (through research, strategies, critical and creative thinking), then the client will understand how and why you developed the creative solution you did, and will be more likely to buy in to the program. Remember in math class when the teacher said, "Solve the problem and show your work?" The same is true for client presentations. You want to show the path you took to arrive at the solution so the client will arrive there with you.

Once you have presented your solutions and the details of how they will be executed, end with a big finish. Too many times we end with, "So, that's our proposal." But that does a disservice to our story and leaves the reader/viewer flat. Endings to stories circle back to the beginning and tie up any loose ends. Show the client how the story has come full circle by restating key themes, reinforcing how your program will resolve the conflict, or using an interesting quote that sums up the key takeaway.

Lastly, end with a call to action. What do you want the client to do as a result of what you just presented? In a new business presentation, you'd ask them to choose your agency. For existing clients, it might include approving your proposal, discussing it with you and deciding on a creative option, or making some other type of decision. Whatever your call to action may be, you don't want the client to just sit on what you presented—you want them to do something.

© Trueffelpix/Shutterstock.com

CREATING CONTENT

Think of a presentation you've attended that was memorable—one that intrigued you and stayed with you long after the presentation. What made that presentation special? Maybe it had an interesting theme that was carried throughout the presentation. Perhaps the speaker used props or other visual aids to illustrate key points. Or, they asked the audience to participate by asking questions and then writing the answers on a flipchart or board for everyone to see. They might have used multiple forms of media—audio, video, text, and graphics—to illustrate their points and keep your attention.

What they likely DIDN'T do was read through slide after slide of nothing but words and long paragraphs. Chances are you've sat through that kind of presentation. You noticed the speaker open a PowerPoint with 50 slides and you wanted to bolt from the room. Not only was it boring, it lost your attention and didn't involve you in the presentation.

When giving a presentation, we want our ideas to shine—our ideas are the main characters in the story. But they don't shine when we bore the audience or give them so much detail that they don't remember the key takeaways. So, your task as a presenter is to distill your ideas into a few key points and then make those points as memorable as possible. Following are some ways to do that.

Take Time to Prepare Content

Whether making a new business pitch or presenting a program or creative treatment to an existing client, give your team enough time to develop the presentation content. To present a good story, you first have to write it. And writing a good story takes time.

> ### Pro Tip
>
> Set up a "War Room" in your student agency for ideation and content preparation. This is a creative space where you can display ideas on a wall, brainstorm, mock up your boards, meet with your team and rehearse while surrounded by all the elements of your presentation.

Waiting until the last minute to prepare materials means we often throw a generic PowerPoint together, or worse, cut and paste long paragraphs into our slides. We spend so much time developing our ideas that we leave little time to prepare our presentation. But remember, a great idea will go nowhere if the client doesn't buy it. So take the time to think through the best ways to sell your ideas to the client. This applies equally to existing client presentations as well as new business presentations.

Always Think of Your Audience

To know when and where to effectively use persuasive appeals, you need to understand your audience. Too often, presenters focus on what THEY want to say, instead of what the client is most interested in hearing. When developing your content, as well as when presenting that content, always keep the audience in mind.

As discussed in Chapter 3, determine who will be in the room for the presentation. Will you be presenting to engineers, sales people, communications professionals, or a combination of organizational positions? Each of these positions will be interested in how your plan affects them. Sales people, for example, may want to know how they can gain customers. Communications professionals will be interested in the organization's reputation and how the program affects a variety of stakeholders. Financial executives will want to know how the program contributes to the bottom line.

> ### Pro Tip
>
> Print out pictures of the clients attending a presentation with a short bio of each and hand out to your team members. Team members can memorize the faces and titles and know whom they are talking to during the presentation.

The people in the room will determine not only the content you present, but also how you present it. For example, engineers often think in terms of flowcharts and production stages, rather than words on slides. Communications professionals will be interested in how your ideas come to life in the quality of your creative themes and materials. Tailor both your presentation and your materials to the audience.

Condense Your Content

A key point to remember in developing your content is that a written proposal is not the same thing as a presentation. If you walk into a client meeting and hand out a 10-page proposal with nothing but long paragraphs, the client will read what's on the paper instead of listening to you present it. Instead, you want to condense the content of your proposal into a few key talking points and then support those points with graphics and illustrations.

Even if you have a great deal of research and insights to present, distill the content into a few main points (e.g., "The three key insights that came out of our research were . . ."). You can then include the detailed research report in the **leave-behind** for the client to read through later.

Leave-behind: A printed document that outlines your agency's client proposal and other pertinent information. The document is left behind for the client to review after a pitch or presentation.

Whether you use Google Slides, PowerPoint, or some other tool, your slides should support and highlight what you are saying rather than saying it for you. You want the client to pay attention to YOU, rather than simply reading through your slides. So, instead of long, complete sentences, highlight three of four words that convey the heart of the points you are trying to make. You can fill in the blanks as you explain them.

So, for example, this

Focus group participants said they seldom use the program because they find it confusing. They especially thought there were too many emails to open about the program and weren't sure whether those emails were deals just for them or if everyone got the same ones. They would prefer if the deals were particular to their purchases. They also said they'd prefer to log into the program when they want instead of getting so many emails clogging up their inboxes. A couple of participants said an app would accomplish this rather than emails, and the rest of the group agreed.

Becomes this

- Keep it simple
- Make it personal
- An App???

We often err on the side of too much information in presentations because we find it all so fascinating. But the client won't remember 10 key points; they will remember two or three. Presentations, like any written content, are about making choices of what to keep and what to toss or include in the leave-behind.

© Georgejmclittle/Shutterstock.com

Bring Your Ideas to Life

Rather than just "telling" the client your story, you also want to "show" your story by bringing it to life for the client. And, you want to do so in ways that imprint your agency's signature brand on your presentation. As entrepreneur and business developer Thomas Stovall puts it, you want to "leave your scent behind." Stovall says, "Make 'em smell you . . . Present yourself and your business in ways that are so compelling and creative that you are forever imprinted on the memory of your prospects" (Stovall, 2014, p. 188). There are several ways you can bring your ideas to life. They include the following:

Create a custom slide template and theme

Rather than using the templates provided by PowerPoint or Google, create a signature template that relates directly to the client and their situation. For example, when a Strategic Campaigns class presented to client Biscuitville, one of the teams created a template in the restaurant's color scheme, took photos of the team eating the client's product, and included the client's rolling pin logo at the bottom of every slide. In addition, instead of the typical "Goals, Strategy, Tactics," titles, the team used creative titles like "Taking Your Order" (goals), "Meal Prep" (research), and "Now Serving" (strategy).

In another example, a student team presenting to Lowe's Home Improvement used splattered paint on their slide template with text written on paint roller graphics. Make sure the creative theme relates to the client, its products, services, or challenges. It's also a good idea to incorporate the client logo and color schemes into your presentation, but do so in an original way that will set you apart from other agencies.

Use graphics and other visuals

To accompany your main points, use graphics, photos, illustrations, or other visuals on your slides. So, in the above example of "An App?" you could include an image of a mobile phone. Or, for "Keep it simple" you might show a picture of a consumer looking confused.

Avoid using clip art and instead use stock photography, screen shots, or take your own photos. For example, if you are presenting to a grocery store, take pictures of your team shopping in the store (with the manager's permission, of course). This shows your commitment to the client, personalizes your presentation, and can help clients visualize your team as part of their organization. When presenting a social media plan, show the Snapchat and Facebook logos as you talk about those platforms. Visuals do just that—they help us visualize a word, a phrase, or an idea.

Mock ups

Traditionally, professional agencies mock up any creative materials and mount them to boards for presentation. Why boards? There are several reasons. First, putting creative material on boards separates the creative from the "logos" part of the presentation, making it stand out as something special. Second, mock ups look more like what an ad or other creative material would actually look like instead of just a picture on a slide. Third, after being introduced, boards can be propped on ledges or easels in the room for the client to view for the rest of the presentation. This is particularly helpful if you are presenting a campaign with a series of ads or other creative elements that go together. It helps the client to see them laid out together instead of having to remember the previous ad as you flip to the next. Because creative is often the star of the show, it's helpful to keep the creative visual displayed as you talk about media placement, budgets, and so forth.

Storyboards: A graphic way to depict a commercial or video treatment. Each scene of the commercial is illustrated on a board with accompanying copy.

When presenting commercials, public service announcements (PSAs), or videos, professional agencies use **storyboards**. Storyboards show each scene of the commercial or video using illustrations or photos, with the accompanying copy at the bottom of each clip. This helps bring the ad concept to life. Presenters then explain each scene to the client and read the copy aloud. You can find numerous examples of storyboards online through a simple Google search.

Storyboard Example

© Mila Basenko/Shutterstock.com

Pro Tip

Print out copy and paste it to the back of your board. This way, the presenter can read the copy without having to flip the board away from the client.

You can mock up and enlarge examples of any ads, apps, website designs, or other creative materials. When mocking up boards, there are a few things to remember. First, you don't want your board to look like a fifth grade art project. Use foam core or other sturdy board instead of flimsy poster board. Print out the material and place it evenly on the board with a spray mount instead of glue (which tends to create bumps). Or, have your boards professionally printed. Make sure your visuals are large enough to be seen by all clients in the room. If there is small type, read it out loud. It's also a good idea when presenting boards to walk up to the client so they can clearly see the storyboard instead of staying at the presentation screen. After presenting the concept, boards can also be passed around the room so each client can see them up close.

Props and premium items

Using props or items you are proposing as part of your plan can also bring your presentation to life. For example, when one group of students was pitching a statewide campout to an environmental client, they set up a tent, sleeping bag, and other camping equipment in the room. If you are proposing a water bottle giveaway as part of your program, mock up enough water bottles for every client in the room and hand them out when you present that idea. You can do the same with t-shirts, pins, shopping bags, and so on.

Use multimedia

Using multimedia in a presentation can keep the client engaged and help them experience what the target audience will experience. It also breaks up the monotony of viewing slides and can illustrate your hard work and commitment to the client and the challenge.

If you are proposing a video, other than a storyboard, you could record a video using a collage of pictures with appropriate background music while someone reads the script. This is often a good way to bring the commercial or video to life before you've shot the footage. It's particularly helpful to get across emotional or humorous material. If you are proposing a radio spot, record the script, and play the audio at the appropriate time. On the slide, you could have a picture of a car radio while the audio is playing so the client gets that they are hearing this on the radio.

Think of other ways to use multimedia. For example, if you are presenting research, you might have a compilation of short clips from your focus group. It's helpful for the client to hear consumers or customers speak directly on their product. Or, if you haven't conducted focus groups, you could shoot a "person on the street" video asking consumers what they know or think of the client's organization or product. For example, when a PR agency pitched a client that sold brats (sausages you eat like hot dogs), they set up a grill outside their office building, offered free brats to passersby, and then videotaped them eating and talking about the product (of course, they also had participants sign release forms). This was a great intro video for the presentation and teaser to the agency's strategy and ideas.

A word of caution: Don't let technology become the story. Sometimes, our presentations can become so flashy they distract from the story instead of supporting it. Make sure any multimedia materials amplify and illustrate the story instead of becoming the story itself. Remember, your ideas should be the main characters, not the technology.

Audience Participation

Another element to consider when developing your content is how you will include the client in your presentation. Remember, you want to present TO and WITH the client, not AT them. Here's a good client participation example. When one student agency was presenting logo designs to a client, they created "Hot or Not" sheets, much like the Tinder swipe left/swipe right concept. As each logo design was revealed, client members rated the logo on their "Hot or Not" sheet. Not only was this a fun way to engage the client, the sheets were also a great discussion starter to determine which logo best fit the client's criteria.

You could also engage the client in creating a collage that illustrates their target audience or strategies. For example, if you are working with a client to increase social media followers, you could hand them a stack of photos and ask them to select those they think are most likely to follow their brand on social media. Lay these photos out on a table or pin them to a board. Then, ask the client to tell you something about the people in the photos—their likes/dislikes, interests, activities—and what would incentivize them to follow the brand (e.g., coupons/discounts? friend recommendations? charitable activities? etc.) Write these points down on your collage. By the time you have finished the exercise, the client will have played a role in identifying your target audience and strategies.

Determining how to engage the client through participation takes creative brainstorming and depends on the type of client. If you have a more informal client, you can be more informal, asking the client questions or for input throughout your presentation. In a formal presentation, you can engage clients by asking more rhetorical questions or having them write down key thoughts and insights as you are presenting.

© Constantin Stanciu/Shutterstock.com

DELIVERING THE PRESENTATION

There are myriad things to think about when giving a presentation: how much time you have to present, where you'll present, what the setup of the room looks like, who will be in the room, and so forth. First, you need to determine who from the agency will present the content.

If you are presenting logos, website designs, or other creative material, you'll want to have the creative director and/or designer in the presentation. If you're presenting a media relations campaign, the account member who developed the media plan should present. And, of course, the account manager and those who will be executing the campaign should also be in the room. When determining who should be in the presentation, think about ethos, or which agency members will lend the most credibility and be able to accurately respond to client questions.

Once you've determined who will be in the presentation, decide how each member will contribute. You shouldn't have people in the room who don't contribute in some way to the story.

Let's think back to our storytelling scenario. In stories, characters deliver dialogue, insights, and narratives that contribute to the overall arc of the story. Likewise, each agency member will deliver dialogue and narratives that shape the story of your proposal. Throughout the presentation, those characters interact with each other, as well as the audience, to tell the story. And they do so using visuals and props that illustrate key storylines. In essence, when delivering a presentation you are delivering a script. Below are several ways to shape that script.

Run of Show

A helpful way to map out your story and which characters will deliver each storyline is by creating a **run of show**. Run of show documents are used by event planners to map out how an event will unfold, and are also used to map out how presentations unfold. They include who is responsible for presenting content, which content they will pres-

Run of show: A document that outlines the order of the presentation: who speaks when, for how long, with which props/slides/boards, and the purpose of their section of the presentation.

ent, what they need to accomplish when they present, how much time they have and which slides, props, or other materials they will use to illustrate their storylines. In essence, the run of show is your script for the story. You can find an example of a run of show in Table 11.1.

Table 11.1   Run of Show Example

Who	What	Time	Goal	Prop/Visual
Dwayne	Introduction	2:00	Build rapport, grab attention	Slides #1 and#2
Jasmine	Challenge	2:00	Show we get it!	Slide #3
Jasmine	Research	5:00	Build case for "leadership" strategy	Slides #4–#7
Dwayne	Client check in	1:00	Make sure client is on same page—gauge reaction so far	None
Tameka	Strategy	2:00	Set the stage for creative	Slide #8
Tameka and Tyrone	Small World concept	8:00	Sell the concept, WOW them!	Slide #9 Boards #1–#4
Tameka	Around the Globe event	3:00	Bring concept to life	Globe market bag Board #5, Map

(Continued)

Table 11.1   Run of Show Example (*Continued*)

Who	What	Time	Goal	Prop/Visual
James	Media plan	3:00	Why outlets will work	Slides #10–#13
James	Social media	3:00	Show how it engages audience	Slides #14 and #15 iPhone mock up
Jordan	Timeline	2:00	Show logical flow	Slide #16
Jordan	Budget	2:00	Big reach but cost-effective	Slides #17–#18
Dwayne	Wrap-up	2:00	Reiterate key themes; reinforce how responds to client challenge; ask for business	Hand out t-shirts
All, emceed by Dwayne	Q&A	5:00	Build trust and confidence in agency	None

Run of show documents help you map out the flow of your presentation and remind members when they are to present and who comes before and after them. They are also helpful in making sure your team sticks to the timeframe allotted for the presentation.

As part of the document, determine whether you will have one agency member serve as an "emcee" for your presentation to introduce the story and each character as they appear in the presentation, or whether agency members will introduce themselves and the person presenting after them. Think of a show like the Oscars. At the Oscars, an emcee gives an introduction to the program, subsequently introduces each category and the celebrities who will present the categories, and then appears again at the end of the show to bring the program to a close.

An emcee in your presentation (such as the account manager) would play the same role. However, you may find when you rehearse the presentation that this format is too bulky for what you have to present. In this case, you may decide the account manager will provide the introduction and the big finish, but other agency members will hand the platform over to each other throughout the middle of the presentation. Also, make sure your presentation doesn't jump around too much from person to person. If each member is up for only a minute, you will lose the coherency of your story.

Meaningful Transitions

Whichever format you choose, you'll need to work on meaningful transitions from one person to another. What is a meaningful transition? Well, let's first start with what is NOT a meaningful transition. "Jasmine is gonna talk next," is not a meaningful transition. Remember, you are telling a story, and thus you don't want to lose the flow of your narrative. Transitions are the glue that holds the story together and helps the client move from one chapter to the next. So, instead of thinking of transitions as throwaway lines, consider how you can use transitions to reinforce the story.

As an example, let's go back to our study abroad client. You have a vision that your client can be the leader in study abroad, and your proposal will show them how they can do that. How can you reinforce that leadership theme in your transitions? One way might be to introduce a leadership quote that is reinforced in other transitions. It might go something like this

> **Jackson:** Entrepreneur Lisa Haisha once said, "Great leaders don't set out to be a leader. They set out to make a difference. It's never about the role, always about the goal." We know you ARE making a difference. However, in the research I just showed you, your target audience doesn't always know about it. Through our creative concepts, Jasmine is going to show you how we can make sure that they do. Jasmine?

> **Jasmine:** Great leaders set out to make a difference. I'd like you to keep that quote in mind as we present our creative concepts. We thought a lot about that quote and what it means to study abroad students. As Jackson said, the goal for our creative is to show students the difference you're making. We think the best way to do that is to show how your programs help THEM make a difference.

Instead of just tossing out a throwaway line, you've now reinforced your leadership theme, reiterated the main point from your research, and set up your creative concepts. And, you've given the client something valuable to think about as they view your creative, which makes them participants in your presentation rather than bystanders. Your transitions can play a role in "leaving your scent" and focus the audience on the next presenter. For example, when a group of students presented to Ford Motor Company for the Public Relations Society of America Bateman

© Alan Poulson Photography/Shutterstock.com

Competition, their transitions included tossing a set of car keys from each presenter to the next. This left a memorable impression with the client, and the students won the competition.

Transitions also do something else: they show cohesiveness between team members. In his book on client service, Robert Soloman says we should, "Fight about work with colleagues; fight for work with clients" (Solomon, 2016). In other words, everyone needs to be on the same page, fighting for your ideas together, and selling them in a cohesive storyline to the client. Referring to another team member's content during the presentation shows that you're a united front that works together and believes in what you're selling.

Blocking the Presentation

If you have ever worked on a play, you might be familiar with the term **blocking**. Simply put, blocking is about choreography, or laying out where actors will stand and move throughout a scene. Similarly, blocking a presentation means figuring out where team members will stand, whether you stand together or separately, and where you place props, boards, or other materials in relation to the speakers and the client.

> **Blocking:** To block a presentation means to map out the movement of the presenters, where they stand/sit, and the location of any props/boards in relation to the client.

To block a presentation you first need to know the layout of the room where you'll be presenting. Where will the screen be? Where will the clients sit? Is there a ledge or easel available for boards? Is there a table or lectern in the room? What about lighting? Is it a well-lit room or rather dark? Does the room have a projector? Or will you need to bring one? If you are presenting at your own offices or classroom, it's easier to figure out the layout of the room. If you are making a new business pitch to a client, you might consider asking them if one member can come take a picture of the presentation room. Clients will often allow this, and it gives you the opportunity to see the space before you present.

Once you have the layout of the room, map out how your team will interact with the client in that space. In more informal presentations, team members might be sitting at a conference table with the client. But even in this scenario, you want to determine if the client is at one end of the table and the agency team at the other end, or if you intermix your team with the client team. You'll also want to determine where you'll set your props, boards, or other materials in relation to the client.

In more formal presentations, your team will likely be presenting standing up near the screen. In classroom presentations, all students usually stand at the front of the room together when making the presentation. However, in professional settings, this can be awkward because the client doesn't know which team member to focus on. Instead, consider having only one or two people stand at a time with others sitting at the conference table. Think about where each team member should sit for easy transitions. Also, where will you place your boards, both before and after presenting them? You want to place them where you will have easy access to them without interrupting the flow of your presentation. And, if you are displaying boards, you want to display them where the client can easily see them without having to turn around.

> ## Pro Tip
>
> Number your boards on the back in order of how they will be presented. Then, turn them toward the wall with the first board to be presented on the outside. Presenters will know which board is theirs and can easily pick it up without having to fish through the pile.

Another consideration is who controls the computer and/or projector during the presentation. It's best to have a "clicker" where those presenting can flip through their own slides. But if one is not available, you'll need a team member to flip them and to determine how they will know when to flip to the next visual.

All of this takes choreography. Map them out and rehearse them so there are no awkward transitions or team members bumping into each other.

Rehearse, Rehearse, Rehearse Again

This point cannot be overstated. You may have the best ideas in the world and have spent time developing your content to tell a compelling story. But if you flub the delivery, you'll lose credibility and your client won't buy those ideas. Rehearse multiple times. Rehearse individually so you have your part down pat. And rehearse as a team so you know how all those parts fit together.

Rehearsal can happen in several phases. The first rehearsal will be rough, where your team walks through what each person will talk about in general, when, which props/boards/materials they will use and how much time they have. Then, team members should take some time to develop their own section of the presentation. When you come back together for a second rehearsal, you'll be able to hear the talking points each member has prepared and make sure they fit together. There is nothing worse than getting up to present your part and realizing that someone else has already covered it. Here is where you can also work on transitions from one team member to the next and work out any kinks in the content.

Then, again, team members should rehearse individually to memorize their part of the presentation. You want to come as close as possible to presenting without notes. It's okay to have notecards to refer to during the presentation. However, write keywords on the notecards rather than complete sentences. You want your presentation to be natural, like having a conversation with the client. Thus, instead of memorizing sentences, memorize key points, and then talk conversationally around those points. Each time you give the presentation the wording will be a little different, but your key points will come across authentically.

What you DON'T want to do is to read directly from your notes like reading a bedtime story to the client. And that's what reading from notes will do—put the client to sleep. You lose eye contact with the client when reading from notes, and thus lose your passion and enthusiasm. Reading from notes shows you didn't prepare and don't believe enough in your ideas to be able to sell them naturally. And if you can't sell them, the client won't buy them.

Pro Tip

Rehearse in front of a mirror. When you look at yourself in the mirror, you are looking at the client. Practice eye contact, facial expressions, and hand gestures while you present. Eliminate distractions like playing with your hair or continually adjusting glasses.

In a third team rehearsal, you should have all your slides, props, and other materials fully prepared so team members can practice with them. This is where you work out the kinks in your blocking, polish your transitions, and work on your delivery. It's also where you can clock your presentation to make sure you are not going over the allotted time and practice Q&A (see below).

Don't be afraid to get and give feedback between team members. It's also a good idea to have a couple of other people—professors, other agency members, or your advisor—sit in on the presentation at this point. They can give you impartial feedback on how the full presentation is coming across. Sometimes, we can be so close to our content that we don't see what is missing. Having third parties give feedback helps fill those gaps.

Rehearsing in front of others can also help you practice making eye contact with the client. Too often, presenters talk to the screen instead of talking to the client. Practice what is referred to as touch, turn, and talk. Touch the screen (or point to the word or graphic you are discussing on the screen), and then turn BEFORE talking about your point. If you talk before turning, you're talking to the screen.

In your third rehearsal, walk through the presentation twice. Or schedule a fourth rehearsal if you don't have time. You should walk through the fully prepared presentation twice to put polish on your delivery and choreography. This is where you get excited. You see all your hard work come together in a dynamic presentation, and are confident and eager to sell your ideas to the client.

Pro Tip

Pay attention to excessive use of "and" or "um" in your speech. Replace them with pauses instead. Practice this in everyday conversations.

Q&A

An important component in preparing for a presentation is preparing for client questions and how you will respond to them. Think through all of the questions the client might have about your program. Will they want to know how it fits in with their other communications programs? Will they have questions about the budget? Will they ask if you are sure the program will work with their target audience? Will they want to know who will work on the program? How will you respond to these questions? You should prepare and practice responses for each potential question.

In addition, you should determine WHO should respond to each question. And, of course, the "who" is determined by who is most qualified to respond to each type of question. Though you can't predict every question the client will ask, you can assign categories of questions to each presenter. For example, if Darnell worked on the budget, Darnell should answer any questions about budget. If Jillian worked on the research, Jillian should answer any questions about research. Each team member should prepare for any questions relating to their assigned categories. Then, the emcee can direct client questions to the appropriate team member.

One-build rule: When responding to Q&A, only one person should add on to the initial teammate's response.

You should also practice what is called the **one-build rule**. Sometimes, agency members want to add on to a response given by another agency member to clarify or elaborate, and that's fine. But then another team member adds to that, and another and another and by the time everyone chimes in the answer has become confusing and muddled. Instead, make it a practice that only one team member should add to any response, and then stop. In other words, only one person is building on the first response. The question has then been answered and elaborated on enough that you have adequately responded to that question.

© Trueffelpix/Shutterstock.com

Technicalities

In addition to developing content and practicing delivery, you also need to think about technical issues. Will you need to bring your own projector? If so, who will reserve and pick it up? Who is making sure the boards are printed and delivered to the presentation? Whose laptop will hold the master presentation? Is the battery fully charged? Are you carpooling to the client office or taking separate cars? Does everyone have directions and a phone number in case they get lost?

And what if the technology fails? In the "old" days, we copied our presentations onto transparencies to use with an overhead projector as a backup. Today, you might have the presentation copied to a backup computer or thumb drive, or print out copies of the presentation if you need to hand them out. Be resourceful and think of ways you can present your main points if something goes wrong. For example, one of the authors presented to a client where both the digital projector AND the overhead projector failed. Luckily, she had markers in her brief case and drew out the main points on an easel pad. It was one of the best presentations she had ever given. Why? Because she rolled with it and adapted, and the client was impressed with her quick thinking.

Or, what if the client changes rooms at the last minute. Or one of the main clients can't join the presentation or will be an hour late? Communications professionals could fill a book, if not a library, with both humorous and horrifying stories of presentation mishaps. Be prepared for anything and ready to adapt to the situation.

Reading the Room

There is one more element that is as critical, if not more so, than all of the concepts presented in this chapter—reading the room. This means paying attention to what is going on around you and listening to the feedback you are getting throughout the presentation.

Feedback doesn't just come in the form of verbal comments; it also comes in the form of the client's posture, facial expressions, and whether or not they are paying attention. Is the client checking email on his phone instead of paying attention to your presentation? It might be he's waiting for an important email. Or, it could mean you are boring him. When you made a certain point, did one of the clients turn to her neighbor and bring up another example? That might mean your point struck a chord.

As pitch expert Peter Levitan says, "Be prepared to make subtle adjustments to your presentation based on what you are seeing. I have been in pitches where I know that my colleague is failing by watching the audience's reaction . . . All of your presenters must be aware of how they are being received and make adjustments" (Levitan, 2014, p. 114).

What might those subtle adjustments be? It might be adding more enthusiasm and passion to your presentation. Or, it could mean cutting your section short because you see the client isn't responding. A good way to find out what those facial expressions mean is to check in with the client. This could be as simple as asking something like, "Is this making sense?" If the client says, "Yes, but I know all this already," then that might be a good indication to cut the preliminaries and jump to your solutions.

Checking in helps us know if we are reading the room correctly. One of the authors experienced this when presenting a campaign to an industry-wide audience. There were more than 200 people in the audience. The agency had just spent about 20 minutes presenting its creative concepts. The next speaker coming to the podium noticed the audience was silent. No response. The room was dead. The CEO of the company sponsoring the campaign noticed it too, and he looked worried. So, before presenting her part, the next speaker checked in with the audience by simply asking, "How do you like it so far?" The response? Wild applause. Okay, so we're good. That let the speaker know she could proceed with the execution phase, but to engage the audience a little more as she was presenting.

HOLDING EFFECTIVE CLIENT MEETINGS

We often think in terms of a "presentation" when doing a new business pitch, but tend to forget about visuals and storytelling when meeting with an existing client. Instead, we should treat every face-to-face with the client as an opportunity to present and sell our ideas.

As we discussed in Chapter 10 on holding group meetings, effective meetings don't just "happen." They take a lot of preparation and skill. You want to make sure your client meetings are effective and efficient for both you and your client and aim toward accomplishing an end goal. Below we discuss several considerations for creating an effective client meeting.

When and Why to Hold a Meeting

One of the first considerations is to determine whether you need to hold a client meeting or if your objective can be accomplished via email or a phone call. In student-run agencies, some account managers tend to call client meetings without thinking through why they want to hold a meeting and what it will accomplish. Remember, you don't want to waste the client's time (or yours). If you want the client to answer a simple question—like if they have photographs available to include in a new website—you don't need to hold a meeting to get that information.

At the other end of the spectrum are account managers who never hold client meetings. This, too, can be ineffective, and worse, could hamper your programming. For example, if you are designing a new website for a client, you'll definitely want to meet with them at the beginning of the project to find out what they want, and again when you provide design options for the website. And, as in the above example, if the client wants to use existing photographs, as well as taking new ones, the creative team might need to meet with them to discuss the complete photo list and get direction for new photos.

So, your first questions should be: Do we need to hold a client meeting? And, Why do we need to hold a client meeting? The answer to the second question will determine the answer to the first. You should schedule a client meeting if

- You need to gather extensive information from the client before moving forward with a plan or program.
- You need the client's buy-in on a new proposal or program.
- You are presenting creative or other visuals to a client where you need to explain how and why you developed the creative and get the clients input and buy-in.
- You have completed a critical planning phase of a client plan and need to show the client your plan and/or creative for that phase.
- You are conducting research for a client and need to present the results.
- A situation arises that involves a challenge that needs to be presented and discussed.
- You have a list of questions for the client that requires discussion and can save time by getting the client's response in person.
- You have completed the execution of a campaign and need to present your final results.

Whenever there is creative involved in a client program, you will want to have a client meeting. There is a big difference between "sending" something to a client and "presenting" it to a client. Proposals, plans, research results, and creative designs require presentation. You want to explain to the client why you took the route you did, what you found along the way, and why you think your plans will be effective. This cannot be done via email. However, if you have already presented options for a website design or other creative and have simply made requested revisions to that design, this can often be done via a shared creative platform or a tool such as DropBox.

Setting Up the Meeting

Once you have determined that a meeting needs to take place, you can schedule the meeting. Before you contact the client, first determine who needs to be in the meeting and what their schedules are. For example, if you are presenting creative, you'll want to have the creative director and the designers/copywriters in the room to present their work.

Determine three dates/times that work for each of the agency members who need to attend the meeting. Then, ask your clients if they are available any of those dates/times. If you simply ask the client, "When can you meet?" you'll inevitably go back and forth between the client and your agency members for each date the client suggests. By narrowing the field to three potential dates/times, you'll avoid this.

It's also important to communicate with the client, in general, the purpose of the meeting so the client can determine who should attend from the client side (later you will send them a more specific agenda). For example, in the client website scenario, if a portion of the website needs to include a sales tool, you'll want members from the client's sales team in the room. Ask the client if they have any issues or topics they'd like to add to the agenda. Instead of having two meetings, you can combine several topics into one. Make sure you estimate how much time it will take to cover every item on the agenda. This will determine whether you hold a 1-hour meeting, or if you need more time.

Also consider where the meeting should take place. If you need to tour client facilities or talk separately to several individuals in the client organization, it might be better to hold the meeting at the client's offices. However, if there are five members from your agency, all of which have classes at different times and locations, it might be easier for the client to come to you. In addition, if you need to show graphics or videos in the presentation and the client doesn't have the capacity for those, it might be easier to hold the meeting at your location. You should suggest where you'd like to hold the meeting and then let the client make the final determination.

Once you have decided on a location, reserve any space you'll need and tour the room to make sure it has the right seating, audio/visual capabilities, and so forth. It's also helpful to rehearse in that space to get the feel for the room.

Preparing for the Meeting

All of the topics and points discussed in the other sections of this chapter apply. Write your story, consider your appeals, prepare your content and materials, and make sure all technical issues have been considered. Again, consider which elements will illustrate the content you want to present and give yourself enough time to have boards or other materials printed and delivered. Most importantly, rehearse!— individually and with your team.

© Trueffelpix/Shutterstock.com

Holding the Meeting

Before the meeting (usually a day or two before), send the client a formal agenda of what will be discussed. This helps the client prepare any materials or answers to questions on their end before they meet with you, which saves time. Print out enough copies of the agenda for everyone who will attend the meeting so everyone is on the same page. Present the agenda at the beginning of the meeting, and ask if there are any topics to be added. As discussed in the chapter on Professional Identity, base your agenda points on the deliverables for the meeting. So, instead of "Discuss website designs," the agenda point would be: "Choose a website design." This way, the client knows they need to make a decision in the meeting on which website design they want to move forward with.

Also, determine how much time you need for each item on the agenda. The facilitator of the meeting (usually an account manager) should make an effort to keep the meeting on track with your schedule. For example, if the meeting is from 3:30 to 5:00 p.m. and you have four topics to present, give each topic ample time within that allotment. You don't want to spend an hour on the first topic and realize you only have 15 minutes to present your creative.

Pro Tip

Lay a watch face up in front of you during the presentation. You can causally glance at the watch to make sure you are staying within your allotted timeframe.

Allow some time at the beginning of the meeting for greetings and introductions. Remember you are building and maintaining relationships and want to interact with your client on both a personal and professional level. So, rather than getting right down to business, work in time to say hello, ask how the client's doing, hear about their vacation, and so forth. And, allow some time at the end of the meeting for casual discussions and leave-taking. It is during these more informal interactions that we build trusted relationships.

CONCLUSION

Becoming a professional at selling your ideas take preparation and practice. With each presentation you make, keep a diary of everything you learned in the process. What worked well? What didn't work well? What do you want to work on for future presentations?

You'll find everyone has a different style when presenting. There is no one size fits all. However, there are a few basics to remember, as we've discussed throughout this chapter.

In addition to selling your ideas, sell your enthusiasm and passion for working on the client's business. Nine times out of 10, your ideas may be a bit off the mark, but if you can sell your passion, the client will be more than willing to work with you on the rest.

REVIEW AND DISCUSSION QUESTIONS

1. What do the terms ethos, logos, and pathos mean?
2. Think of three things on which you would be considered knowledgeable or an expert.
3. Let's assume your client is a barbecue restaurant. Think of two personal stories or experiences you've had that could relate to the client.
4. You are making a presentation to a client recommending Instagram as a message delivery tool to reach a target audience of marathon runners. What logical arguments could you use to sell this platform?
5. Now that you've read this chapter, condense the content down into three key talking points you would use to give a presentation on how to sell your ideas.
6. Using the three talking points from Question 5, what visuals, props, or boards might you use to bring those talking points to life?
7. What is a Run of Show?
8. Think of a presentation you attended that was unique, compelling, or memorable. What about it caught your attention and kept it? Discuss with your team.
9. Think of a presentation you attended that was awful. What could the speaker have done better?
10. Have one person on your team answer the question: Why should a client select your agency to develop a communications campaign? Then, have another person on the team build on that response using the One-Build Rule.

REFERENCES AND ADDITIONAL READINGS

Biesenbach, R. (2014). *11 Deadly presentation sins*. Chicago, IL: Eastlawn Media.

Bohns, V. (2017, April 11). A face-to-face request is 34 times more successful than an email. *Harvard Business Review*. Retrieved from https://hbr.org/2017/04/a-face-to-face-request-is-34-times-more-successful-than-an-email

eMarketer. (2017, April 17). Young millennials are all about Snapchat. *eMarketer*. Retrieved from https://www.emarketer.com/Article/Young-Millennials-All-About-Snapchat/1015675

Levitan, P. (2014). *The Levitan pitch: Buy this book. Win more pitches*. Portland, OR: Portlandia Press.

Solomon, R. (2016). *The art of client service*. Hoboken, NJ: Wiley.

Steel, J. (2007). *Perfect pitch: The art of selling ideas and winning new business*. Hoboken, NJ: John Wiley & Sons.

Stovall, T. (2014). Amplified growth: 15 steps to launch fast, get to contract, and cash checks using NONE of your own money. In J. Comm (Ed.), *So, what do you do? Discovering the genius next door with one simple question* (pp. 183–189). New York, NY: Morgan James Publishing.

Teetak, J. (2014). *Rule the room: A unique, practical and comprehensive guide to making a successful presentation*. New York, NY: Morgan James Publishing.

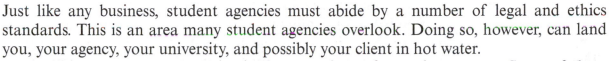

Legal Ease and Ethics Considerations

Just like any business, student agencies must abide by a number of legal and ethics standards. This is an area many student agencies overlook. Doing so, however, can land you, your agency, your university, and possibly your client in hot water.

Legal issues crop up every day in the operations of a student agency. Some of these can be addressed with a basic understanding of media law. Others will be more complex and may require the advice or assistance of an attorney. The key to keeping your agency in good legal standing is to know when and where legal issues intersect with agency processes. If you don't know what to look for ahead of time, chances are you may violate a law you are not even aware of. When it comes to the law, ignorance is not bliss. Lack of awareness is not safe legal ground on which to stand.

Closely related to legal issues are ethics concerns. While laws deal with the way you *must* act according to the laws of any given society, ethics deal with how you *should* act based on the accepted customs and mores of that society. The word "ethics" is derived from two words: the Greek word *ethos*, meaning character, and the Latin word *mores*, meaning customs. Thus, a person or company of good character abides by the ethics of a society.

While law and ethics are closely related, ethics often go beyond what is required by the law. For example, a company could do something that is perfectly legal but which would be seen as unethical in the eyes of its customers. This is often where lawyers and public relations (PR) professionals butt heads. For example, when a negative event occurs, lawyers often recommend that clients say as little as possible to avoid admitting liability where none may exist. The PR professional, however, would be concerned that NOT addressing the issue could affect the company's reputation. Both are doing their jobs, but coming at the issue from different vantage points.

As you walk through your day-to-day work at a student agency, you'll need to be cognizant of the legal and ethics standards of your university, the industry, the client's organization, the society in which you live, and your own values and beliefs. Although this chapter is not meant to be an in-depth reading on these complex issues, it will help you become more aware of some of the issues you should pay attention to. In addition, particularly as the Internet and other new technologies become more prevalent, laws that touch agency or client work change all the time. It is helpful for industry professionals to stay up to date on changing legal standards.

In this chapter, you will learn the following:

- The most common legal issues involved in student agency work.
- Legal terms and definitions related to that work.
- Where to go for legal guidance.
- Issues to consider to make ethical decisions in your work.

LEGAL CONSIDERATIONS

There is a good reason most university communication programs include a course in media law. Even if you are not responsible for dealing directly with legal issues in your professional career, everyone in an organization is responsible for legally and ethically responsible behavior. Perhaps you have already taken a media law course and are aware of the issues and pitfalls. If not, however, you will want to familiarize yourself with the issues that will most likely affect your work. It is highly recommended that student agencies keep a basic media law book in the agency for reference.

Students and advisors must be diligent in considering and addressing legal issues in day-to-day student agency operations. Though the legal issues that intersect with communications agencies can (and do) fill complete libraries, student agencies will likely face issues in three areas: legal issues related to content creation and use, legal issues related to photographing and filming, and legal issues related to programming. Below we address each area, as well as other legal and ethical considerations. Note: *This summation should not be considered as substitution for trained legal counsel. When in doubt seek assistance from professionals.*

Legal Issues Related to Content Creation and Use

Gathering, producing, and distributing content comprise the bulk of what communications agencies do for their clients. Whether you are developing a newsletter, designing a website or ad, filming a video, or producing social media content, there are numerous legal issues to consider.

The first question to ask is: Who owns this content? The term "content" refers not only to text, but also to sound, photographs or images, and videos or film. It is unlawful to use work created by another person or entity without paying for the content or receiving written permission.

When agency members are producing content, they will need to be cognizant of **copyright** laws. A copyright protects original works of authorship including literary, dramatic, musical, and artistic works, such as poetry, novels, movies, songs, computer software, and architecture. The duration of copyright protection depends on several factors. For works created by an individual, protection lasts for the life of the author, plus 70 years. For works created anonymously,

> **Copyright:** Protects original works of authorship including literary, dramatic, musical, and artistic works, such as poetry, novels, movies, songs, computer software, and architecture.

pseudonymously, and for hire, protection lasts 95 years from the date of publication or 120 years from the date of creation, whichever is shorter.

Trademark law will also play a role in student agency operations. According to the United States Patent and Trademark Office (USPTO), a trademark is a word, phrase, symbol, and/or design that identifies and distinguishes the source of the goods of one party from those of others. The significance of this definition is that a trademark protects those who produce it from someone else using it to promote their business or organization.

Similar to a trademark, a **service mark** is a word, phrase, symbol, and/or design that identifies and distinguishes the source of a service rather than goods. Some examples include: brand names, slogans, and logos. The term "trademark" is often used in a general sense to refer to both trademarks and service marks. Both trademarks and service marks may be renewed indefinitely. Why is this important? It is important because those brands have a lot of equity invested in them and represent a substantial value to the companies that own them. Use of the ™ or ® or even © should be considered whenever the names appear in print. There are significant rules that apply to each. Consult the relevant USPTO for specific guidelines or discuss it with your university counsel. The governing statute for trademark registration, infringement, and so on is TMEP §1202.01.

Trademark: Protection for words, phrases, symbols, and/or designs that identify and distinguish the source of the goods of one party from those of others.

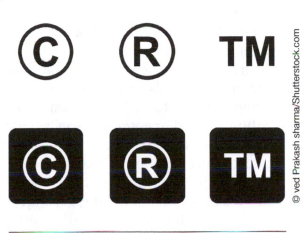

© ved Prakash sharma/Shutterstock.com

Service mark: Similar to a trademark, protects words, phrases, symbols, and/or designs that identify and distinguish the source of a service of one party from those of others.

Agencies often come across copyright, trademark, and service mark issues when creating taglines for clients. You may think that "Fresh from the field to your door" is a perfect tagline, but doing a quick trademark search on https://www.uspto.gov/trademarks-application-process/search-trademark-database is always necessary to determine if someone else is legally using that phrase. Although a quick online search is not as good as hiring a lawyer to do an extensive legal search, it may be the most student agencies can afford. When you do create a unique tagline, it is a good idea to have your client apply for a trademark or service mark to protect the tagline from being used by others.

So, let's put these legal terms into the context of agency work. Let's say, for example, you are writing a blog article about a risotto dish for a restaurant client's website. The first thing you need to consider is the text of the article. As with all academic and professional work, you want to make sure you are not plagiarizing another's work and/or violating copyright law.

Plagiarism is the term used for the stealing of another's work, written or otherwise, and passing it off as one's own. This can include client work and work done by others on behalf of your client. Consider: Your restaurant client has a wonderful review written by an established food critic and you want to include this in your blog. He says, ". . . the risotto was some of the best I have ever had and the service was exemplary." What percentage of that positive review can you use without attribution? The answer is: none. Be sure to attribute who said those wonderful things. If the critique is from another article, you will also need to source the article and, ideally, provide a link to the content if it is online.

Perhaps in your blog article you want to mention some of the brands or products used by the chef in making the risotto dish. Just remember that if you mention a brand or company, you will need to include the proper trademark or service mark for the brand, product or even the brand's tagline.

In addition to using another's work, you will also want to be sure your content is accurate, truthful, and doesn't harm the reputation of another person or entity. **Defamation** is another pitfall that student agencies need to be wary of. Writing or speaking about policy, practices, issues of character, performance, and anything that can be seen as impacting an individual's or an organization's reputation, standing or ability to generate revenue are addressed under defamation laws. The two large categories under defamation are **libel** and **slander**. According to Merriam Webster's online dictionary, harming someone's reputation in speech with falsehoods is known as slander, and doing the same thing in writing is known as libel (which sometimes includes speech as well). So, in your blog post, you might want to stay away from saying the restaurant down the street has cockroaches in its risotto.

Next, you want to include a photo or image with your article to help illustrate your main points. It is a violation of copyright law to simply copy or take a screenshot of a photo or graphic illustration from the Internet. Instead, you will need to shoot your own photo, create your own graphic image, or ask the client if they own photos or images you can use. Alternatively, you can pay for the rights to use a photo from a photo library such as Shutterstock.

Plagiarism: Stealing another's work and passing it off as one's own without attributing the work to the original source.

© Fun Way Illustration/Shutterstock.com

Defamation: Writing or speaking about policy, practices, issues of character, performance, and anything that can be seen as impacting an individual's or an organization's reputation, standing or ability to generate revenue.

Libel: Publishing a false written statement about a person that harms or damages the person's reputation.

Slander: Making a false statement in speech that harms or damages a person's reputation.

Lastly in this scenario, let's say you have the great idea to create a video of the restaurant's chef making the risotto dish. After you have filmed the demonstration, you decide it needs some background music. Universities often purchase the rights to music libraries that students can use for educational purposes in the classroom. Because student agencies are part of the university, many students believe this music can also be used for client work. But this is not the case. Most university music library contracts DO NOT allow the music to be used for commercial purposes. Thus, you will need to purchase the rights to any music used to promote a product, brand, company, cause, or nonprofit entity outside of the university.

If you are diligent in avoiding the violations discussed above but still somehow violate a trademark or copyright issue, the most usual outcome for minor infractions is a **cease and desist** letter. This is a letter drafted by a company attorney informing you of the infraction, asking you to remove the content (cease) and to not use it again (desist). Agencies will usually avoid any punitive issues if they show good faith in abiding by the law.

Cease and desist order: A letter sent by an attorney or company to stop (cease) an illegal activity, such as the use of trademarked content, and to not take up the content or activity again (desist).

Legal Issues Related to Photographing and Filming

Whether you are filming a broadcast spot or PSA, taking photographs for a client's website, or documenting a client event, your work will likely involve the use of people. Laws involved in filming or photographing other people include issues of privacy, permission to use another's likeness (and for what reason), talent contracts, and, as outlined above, questions of who owns the photographs or film. The term **likeness** in legal speak describes the use of a person's name, image (photograph or sketch) and, in some cases, even their voice (see Pember & Calvert, 2011, pp. 248–253).

© Africa Studio/Shutterstock.com

Let's take another real-life student agency example to illustrate how these legal issues would play out. Let's say your client wants to film a commercial for her restaurant. You write a script for a :60 spot that involves an on-camera emcee, shots of the kitchen staff, still shots of menu items taken by another photographer, and shots of people eating in the restaurant.

Likeness: Describes the use of a person's name, image (photograph or sketch) and, in some cases, even their voice. You must get the legal permission of a person before using their likeness.

If the emcee is an actor being paid for emceeing the commercial, you will need to sign a contract outlining the terms of your agreement with that person. This would involve several things. First, it should include the terms of the shoot (how long you will shoot, on what day, etc.), as well as the amount the emcee will be paid for the work. Second, the terms should include how the actor's likeness will be used. For example, will it only be used in the commercial? Or might you also want to use it on the client's website or on a menu or brochure? Unless the specific terms are outlined in your agreement, you could face legal action by the model at a later date if you have used his or her likeness for purposes not agreed to. Lastly, will the actor be paid a one-time fee for services or will they receive **residuals** each time the commercial is played?

Each time you film or photograph people for commercial purposes, you will need to have them sign a **model likeness release**, sometimes called a **talent release** form. This outlines the terms for use of their likeness, and protects you and the client from legal action if you follow the terms of the agreement (see Box 12.1). This includes people who are being paid for their likeness as well as those who are not.

© S_Photo/Shutterstock.com

Residuals: In advertising, residuals are payments to an actor (particularly a Screen Actors Guild actor) each time a commercial is aired. Often, brands will negotiate a buy-out (lump sum payment) instead of paying residuals.

Model likeness release (aka talent release): An agreement that outlines how a person's likeness will be used in communications content.

Box 12.1   Sample Model Likeness Release

Project (Working Title): _____(the "Project")

Person Appearing: _____

Production Date(s): _____

Production Location(s): _____

I authorize _____("Producer"),

Producer's agents, successors, assigns and designees to record my name, likeness, image, voice, sound effects, interview, and performance on photography, film, video, or otherwise (the "Recording"), and to edit such Recording as Producer may desire, and incorporate such Recordings into the Project, any versions of the Project and all related materials thereof, including but not limited to promotion and advertising materials.

It is understood and agreed that Producer shall retain final editorial, artistic, and technical control of the Project and the content of the Project. Producer may use, and authorize others to use, the Project, any portions thereof and the Recording in all markets, manners, formats, and media, whether now known or hereafter developed, throughout the world, in perpetuity. Producer, and Producer's successors and assigns, shall own all rights, title and interest, including the copyright, in and to the Project, including the Recording and related materials, to be used and disposed of, without limitation, as Producer shall in Producer's sole discretion determine.

Signature: _____

Address: _____

City: _____ State: _____ Zip: _____

Telephone: _____

Email: _____

Date: _____

So, for example, when you film customers eating inside the restaurant, do they need to give you permission to use their likeness? The answer is: yes. It is best if you can have each diner sign a release form, as well as any employees of the restaurant. Even though employees are paid for their time at the restaurant, you need their permission to use their likeness for commercial purposes.

At times the crowd being photographed or filmed is too large and transitory (meaning people come and go throughout the shoot) to have every individual sign a release form. In this case, agencies sometimes use a mass release to inform members of the public that filming is taking place. This would entail putting a sign on the door of the restaurant so that all diners can see it as they enter.

When filming in public spaces, issues of **privacy** come into play. If you are not able to obtain a release form from every person being filmed, the legal question becomes whether or not the person being filmed had a reasonable right to privacy. For example, someone dining

> **Privacy:** Describes a person's right to be free from intrusion or observation, and to keep personal information private from other people.

in a restaurant may not have a reasonable right to privacy. However, they WOULD have a reasonable right to privacy if they used the restaurant's restroom. Each situation is unique. Consulting with a legal scholar is prudent when determining what and whom you can and can't photograph in certain settings.

Lastly in this scenario is the issue of using still shots of menu items shot by another photographer. Who owns these photographs? Did the client purchase the right to use them for all commercial purposes? Or does the photographer own the photographs for use other than what they were originally intended? You need to make sure you have permission to use the photos before doing so.

At times in student agency work we hire outside photographers or videographers to shoot client work. In this case, photographers own the initial copyright to the work until the agency purchases it from them. This is called **work-for-hire**. Work-for-hire writers, photographers, or videographers transfer not just publication rights but also actual copyright to the entity purchaser (or employer). In this agreement, the author forfeits all future rights to the material, which can be altered, resold, published under another name, or used in any other fashion the firm desires, without additional compensation to the original author. This protects the firm and prevents the author from modifying the material to sell somewhere else. In fact, under a work-for-hire agreement, the author might actually be guilty of "infringing" on the company's copyright if the new piece is similar enough to the original piece. It is usually best to negotiate work-for-hire compensation prior to producing the actual work.

In addition, when hiring someone to do work for the agency or client, it is recommended that you purchase **all rights**, which include digital, reprints, and so on. *It is also important to note that universities have different arrangements regarding copyrights of faculty work and even student work, so it is best to verify which type of engagements you are operating under before engaging third parties or charging for student work.*

> **Work-for-hire:** A classification of rights, which implies all rights are surrendered once work is provided and contractor is compensated. Recommended for most agency arrangements.

> **All rights:** Rights to reprint work that an author sells. All rights mean essentially that the author is paid once for all work.

Legal Issues Related to Programming

A student agency in North Carolina had a great idea for a national client who sells clothing in the sporting goods industry. In partnership with a children's charity, the agency recommended that the client develop a special sock emblazed with the charity's logo. For each pair of socks sold, a portion of the sales would go to the charity. As you might know, this is called cause-related marketing. The client and the charity both loved the idea and gave it the green light.

The agency was excited. But when the team looked into the legalities of executing the program, they learned the client would need to file paperwork with attorneys general in nearly two dozen states to legally carry out the campaign. What's more, every state's reporting requirements are different. The agency quickly alerted the client, who contacted their attorneys and the paperwork was filed in time for the campaign launch date. But the agency learned a valuable lesson—know the legal requirements for your programming BEFORE presenting ideas to the client.

This is just one example of how legalities can intersect with agency programming. Have you ever read the fine print at the bottom of a contest entry form? Yep. Contests are complicated. Further, each state has different laws for how contests can be executed, what can legally be required for entry and how the prizes are paid or taxed. Professional agencies know this. That is why they hire third parties who are well versed in contest legalities to handle the parameters.

Did you know a brand can't require a Facebook member to "like and share" a post on their Timeline to enter a contest? It's against Facebook's rules. Many advertisers don't know this and launch a contest only to have Facebook ask them to take it down.

© Gustavo Frazao/Shutterstock.com

Although it is beyond the scope of this book to outline all the legalities involved in client programming, the point is this: Always check the fine print. When you have an idea for a program, do a quick online search to determine if there are federal or state laws involved. For example, any program that includes the exchange of goods, services, or money will likely involve some sort of legal reporting. If you are executing a social media campaign, check the promotion and advertising policies of the site where you will launch the program, be it Facebook, Instagram, YouTube, or other sites. Rules differ for every social media site, and often change.

In addition, make sure you are in compliance with Federal Trade Commission (FTC) regulations. The FTC is one of the governing bodies that controls what information can and cannot be published as part of transactions considered as advertising. Under FTC law, claims in advertisements must be truthful, cannot be deceptive or unfair, and must be evidence based. For some specialized products or services, additional rules may apply (Box 12.2). An extremely helpful guide for all things

© Paul Brady Photography/Shutterstock.com

FTC as they pertain to small businesses can be found at: https://www.ftc.gov/tips-advice/business-center/guidance/advertising-faqs-guide-small-business

Box 12.2   FTC Categories for Special Scrutiny

In addition to overall FTC regulations, there are some issues and types of advertising that receive additional FTC scrutiny. When executing programs in these areas, check FTC regulations for additional information. These areas include

Marketing to Children

Use of Professional Endorsements

Environmental Marketing/Green Claims

(Continued)

Health Claims
Made in USA Claims
Online Advertising and Marketing
Telemarketing
Credit and Loans
Debt Instruments and Collection Services
Mortgages and Financial Instruments
Children's Privacy
Consumer Privacy
Use of Credit Reporting Data
Data Security
Tobacco Advertising
. . . and others.

There are also select industries that the FTC pays particular attention to, including alcohol; appliances and energy efficiency; automobiles and related equipment; clothing and textiles—labeling and care instructions; finance; franchises, business opportunities, and investments; funerals; human resources; jewelry; nonprofits; real estate and mortgages; and tobacco. The website https://www.ftc.gov/tips-advice/business-center/legal-resources features more than 2,050 case studies which discuss FTC compliance.

When it comes to agency programming, particularly advertising, many agencies ask their clients to sign **indemnity agreements**. These agreements transfer the risk involved in producing ads or other programming from the agency to the client. Because clients are much more educated about the legal issues pertaining to their business, this puts the onus on the client to thoroughly check work by the agency for any violations. This is particularly helpful when working for industries that are heavily regulated, such as insurance, finance, or health-related industries.

> **Indemnity agreement:** An agreement that transfers legal risk from one party to another. One party agrees to "indemnify," or hold harmless, the other party from any legal loss or damage.

University Legal Standards

In addition to media law issues, student agencies must also be aware of and adhere to legal issues specific to schools and universities. For example, if you are conducting research for a client using human participants, you may be required to go through the university's **Institutional Review Board** (IRB) and abide by the board's ethics guidelines. Universities are also required to adhere to Title IX laws.

> **Institutional review board:** A university board empowered by the Office of Human Research Protections to review and approve any research that involves human subjects. IRBs follow rules and guidelines outlined in the Belmont Report, a report written by the National Commission for the Protection of Human Services of Biomedical and Behavioral Research.

For example, under Title IX, your university may require students to go through training before interacting with children or victims of sexual assault.

Other legal constraints include privacy of data and information under laws including the Health Insurance Portability and Accountability Act (HIPPA), the Family Educational Rights and Privacy Act (FERPA), and others. Thus, if you are interacting with other students, you will need to determine if and how these laws affect your work.

Legal considerations for private universities differ greatly from public universities, and these legal considerations also differ state to state. For example, some public universities do not allow student agencies to enter into legal contracts that involve an exchange of money for services. *Thus, it is imperative that an advisor from the student agency meet with university administrators to discuss any federal or state standards that could intersect with student agency operations.*

Keeping Legal Files

An important component of complying with legal standards and guidelines is keeping good records. It's important to keep a copy of all legal documents—such as talent release forms, client contracts, or work-for-hire contracts—in a secure file. Some laws require that paperwork be kept for a certain number of years. As such, it is best that the agency advisor hold onto the agency's legal documents in a secure location.

In addition, when conducting research, you need to protect the privacy of your participants while maintaining a file of any permissions given by research participants. It is best if this is done through your advisor, who will keep them in a secure, encrypted file, or locked file drawer.

Utilizing Legal Counsel

Although many professional agencies have attorneys on staff or on call, this will not be the case with student-run agencies. However, there are many ways you can connect with legal counsel to answer questions or address specific issues. Below we list four ways to get legal help when needed:

University attorneys: University attorneys will be particularly helpful with issues directly related to the agency itself, or any legal issues that arise between the agency and third parties. For example, if you have a contract dispute with a client, university attorneys will likely step in to help. Since the agency is a legal entity of the university, the university has a stake in solving these types of legal matters. In addition, university attorneys can be helpful when the agency wants to acquire a trademark or copyright for its work, such as securing a trademark for the agency name and logo.

Client attorneys: Many larger clients pay monthly attorney fees or have an attorney on call to resolve legal issues. Client attorneys can be particularly helpful in addressing programming issues, such as filing legal paperwork on behalf of the client for a contest or cause-related campaign. In addition, any time paperwork needs to be signed by a client, such as the client paying for legal rights to photography, a client attorney may be needed to approve the contract.

Law professors: Some universities have law schools or professors who teach law classes on staff. For basic legal questions, law professors can be a good resource for giving students general guidance or point them to resources to do further research. For example, a media law professor can be a valuable resource to answer student questions about copyright law. When embarking on a program, law professors can provide direction when specific issues arise during planning or execution, or can provide students with the basics for setting up a client contract. Although law professors will not officially represent the agency, they can offer general guidance and answer student questions.

Private attorneys: Though student agencies will not likely have the funds to hire their own legal counsel, there may be times when it is beneficial for an agency to hire their own attorney on a limited basis. For example, if you want to make sure you have the proper

legal "kit" to carry out student agency duties, it might be worthwhile to have an attorney draw up sample contracts or model likeness releases. Attorneys just starting out, or alumni who have recently received their J.D., may be willing to provide services for a discounted fee or pro bono. You may also know an attorney who is a family member or trusted friend whom you can consult or get their opinion on whether you need to seek additional legal counsel.

© VP Photo Studio/Shutterstock.com

ETHICS CONSIDERATIONS

There are many ethics challenges students may face in working for a student agency. Some are more generic to business situations whereas others are specific to the communications industry. Understanding ethics considerations are particularly important when you are first entering the business and aren't familiar with common business standards and practices.

In general, the term **ethics** deals with what is considered right and wrong based on the customs of a given society. Although this seems straightforward enough, ethics are not always black and white and can become blurry when facing different situations. What is right and wrong depends on many issues including the culture in which you are working, the values of your agency, the ethics standards of your industry, the considerations of the times,

Ethics: Guidelines or rules that address how a person should act according to the customs and mores of a particular society.

and, most importantly, your own values and moral principles.

Let's take the video news release (VNR) as an example. VNRs are filmed segments that promote a client's product or organization. They are packaged like real news stories and distributed to broadcast stations for use in their newscasts. The VNR has been used in the PR industry for decades as an effective communications tool. However, more recently, the ethics of VNRs have been called into question. As early as 1992, TV Guide deemed the VNR "fake news" and, more recently, broadcasters have developed standards for the use of VNRs including proper disclosure of the VNRs source. The PR industry has had to respond accordingly. This is an example of how standards and practices change over time when ethics issues are called into question (see https://ethicsinpr.wikispaces.com/Video+news+release).

So, how do you ensure you are acting ethically? First and foremost is to develop your own values and moral principles and stick to them. In doing so, recognize that your values and moral principles may differ from others. For example, you may feel it is wrong to work on an alcohol campaign (and cannot legally do so until you are 21 or older), whereas others in the agency may think differently. When asked to do this kind of work, how will you respond? Know what is important to you and how you will conduct yourself when your values and principles are put to the test.

Secondly, know the ethics principles of your agency and university. If your agency doesn't have specific ethics guidelines, ask your advisor to develop them. Most universities have ethics standards to which all students are required to adhere, which include honesty, fairness, and often, principles of diversity, as well as guidelines for conducting research.

Thirdly, know the ethics principles of your industry. The PR and advertising fields have battled unethical reputations since their inception. As a result, industry associations are active in developing and monitoring ethical practices in their industries. For example, the Public Relations Society of America has a Member Code of Ethics that includes general standards of honesty, accuracy, and fairness, as well as specific guidelines relative to disclosure of information, confidentiality, and conflicts of interest. You can read the Code of Ethics here: https://apps.prsa.org/AboutPRSA/Ethics/CodeEnglish/index.html#.WK9ivud2rNQ

Likewise, the American Advertising Federation has similar ethical guidelines, which can be found here: https://www.aaf.org/_PDF/AAF%20Website%20Content/513_Ethics/IAE_Principles_Practices.pdf

Below are a few other guidelines that will help you act ethically in your student agency experiences:

Never misrepresent data/information. We want to make our clients happy and at times may be tempted to "fudge" our numbers to make them look better than they actually are. This might include telling the client you called more reporters than you did, inflating social media numbers, misrepresenting the hours you worked on a project, or saying you had more survey participants than you did. In a nutshell—Don't do it.

Never lie for a client. Many agency professionals have been put in awkward situations when a client asks them to say or do something that is inappropriate. Clients may want to look good for their bosses or try to elevate their product or organization in the market. If a client asks you to lie, misrepresent information, or conduct business in an unethical manner on his or her behalf . . . just don't.

If you see something, say something. If you see a coworker or client conducting unethical practices, you may feel anxious and not know what to do. Rather than keeping that burden to yourself, talk to a trusted adult. Tell your advisor in confidence and rely on them to take the appropriate actions. If you're not sure if something has crossed an ethics line, talk to a parent or another adult you trust. They can walk through the issues with you and offer their experienced advice.

Use the "light of day" rule. It used to be said in the agency business: If you would be embarrassed or condemned for your actions if they appeared on the front page of the newspaper, then you shouldn't do them. Today we might say: If your actions went viral, would you feel okay about them? If not, don't do them. In other words, what we do in the dark may seem fine, but the ethics of our actions become apparent when they hit the light of day.

Be mindful of diversity in your language and actions. Being respectful of others means we sometimes need to put ourselves in others' shoes and see things from their perspective. For example, what may seem like a harmless joke in a social media post or advertising tagline could be truly harmful to someone who has a different identity from our own. When developing content or considering program strategies, be mindful of issues such as race, ethnicity, gender identity, geography, economic status, age, and physical ability, as discussed in Chapter 6.

Guard your conscience. Just as acting unethically can have consequences, at times acting ethically can have consequences too. For example, acting on your values may mean you make a colleague or client angry, or lose an opportunity to work on an account that doesn't sync with

© Rawpixel.com/Shutterstock.com

your values. When making ethical decisions, guard your conscience first, even if there may be consequences in doing so. You can always get another job or account. But, you have to live with your conscience for the rest of your days.

A Word About Sexual Harassment

The U.S. Equal Employment Opportunity Commission (EEOC), the U.S. Supreme Court, and companies around the nation began addressing workplace sexual harassment as early as the 1980's. However, some 40 years later, sexual harassment is still quite pervasive in the workplace. Studies show that 1 in 4 have witnessed sexual harassment, and that 99% of women agree that sexual harassment in the workplace is a problem (Strayer, 2017). Many sexual harassment incidents go unreported. Underlying issues include not understanding what constitutes sexual harassment, the silence of victims and bystanders for fear of disbelief or retaliation, and inaction because employees don't know how to address it.

On rare occasions, student agencies have had to deal with issues of sexual harassment. Sexual harassment can be devastating for victims and is confusing and overwhelming to deal with. Given its prevalence in the workplace, it's important to know how to recognize and address the issue if it arises. Not only is sexual harassment unethical, but also it is unlawful.

Any gender can be both the perpetrators and the victims of sexual harassment. According to the EEOC, sexual harassment can include, "unwelcome sexual advances, requests for sexual favors, and other verbal or physical harassment of a sexual nature" including "offensive remarks about a person's sex" (U.S. EEOC website).

The first, and most obvious, issue to address is: Don't be a sexual harasser. Know what constitutes sexual harassment. Read the EEOC definition as well as your university's policies on appropriate behavior. Then, act accordingly.

If you or someone you know has been the victim of sexual harassment, consult your university's policies on how to report it. Universities can have different processes depending on whether the perpetrator is a client, faculty member, or another student. If you're not sure how to address it, talk to your agency advisor (if trusted), or a counselor at the university. Many universities have health and wellness professionals who specifically deal with gender and sexuality-based harassment and violence.

The American Association of University Women (AAUW) and other organizations also recommend keeping a written log of harassment incidents, including details on what occurred, when and where it occurred, and who witnessed it. These notes are helpful should you need to report an incident and can also help you clarify what happened (American Association of University Women [AAUW], n.d.).

Lastly, if you are sexually harassed, talk about it with someone you trust who can support you. This is not something you should deal with alone. Trusted individuals can include a close friend, parent or family member, faculty member, or even calling a hotline like the National Assault Hotline operated by the Rape, Abuse and Incest National Network (RAINN). Do not second-guess yourself. It is common in sexual harassment and sexual assault cases to begin thinking you didn't experience what you actually DID experience. Know that sexual harassment is not your fault. No one should have to deal with being harassed—period.

CONCLUSION

Each time we embark on a new venture in our lives, we are faced with additional laws and ethics requirements by which we must or should abide. When you entered college, for example, you were required to learn the customs and code of ethics of your university. As you enter the business world, there will be more standards to learn and more situations in which you are required to apply them.

Although learning about these considerations in a classroom is helpful, student agencies give you a chance to apply them in real-life situations. Every situation will be different and will not always be cut and dried. Thus, you'll need to ask yourself a series of questions about how these issues might apply to your current program or situation. As you go through your day-to-day student agency activities, other legal and ethics issues will crop up that were not covered in this chapter. It would be a good idea to document these as they arise so your agency develops standard practices for addressing issues specific to your particular student agency.

REVIEW AND DISCUSSION QUESTIONS

1. What is the difference between a trademark, a service mark, and a copyright?
2. What is the difference between libel and slander?
3. Imagine your agency is working for a local arts' council. The organization is hosting an artist's opening and asks you to film the event and produce an edited video that can be uploaded to the organization's website. What are the legal issues you will need to consider for this activity?
4. A friend of yours is in a local cover band and does a unique rendition of Ed Sheeran's song "Photograph." After hearing his rendition, you decide this would be the perfect background music for the commercial you're producing for a client. What are the legal issues you will need to consider in order to use your friend's rendition?
5. You are writing a blog post for a client on social media marketing. After doing some online research, you find an agency website that includes a good case study on social media marketing that you'd like to use as an example in the post. Would you be able to use the case study on your client's blog? What would you need to consider before doing so?
6. Review your agency's list of clients and the programs you're working on for these clients? Make a list of the legal issues you'll need to be aware of for each client and program.
7. Your creative team recently developed a new logo for a client and the client loves it. You begin using the logo on all client materials. However, after a few weeks you receive a "cease and desist" letter from an attorney. The attorney says the logo is too similar to

another client brand and asks you to take it down and stop using it. After presenting the letter to the client, the client says they're not worried about it and that you should continue to use the logo you developed. How would you handle this situation?

8. Does your student agency currently have a code of ethics? If not, discuss with your team and develop five things that you would include in a code of ethics for your student agency.

9. You are helping a client to develop a presentation that the sales force will use to present the company to customers. The client gives you customer satisfaction numbers to use in the presentation, but asks you to change the 85% customer satisfaction rating to 95%. How would you handle this situation?

10. What are your own values and moral principles that will guide your work in the student agency and your professional career? Write down three principles that you'd like to adhere to and discuss them with your team.

REFERENCES AND ADDITIONAL READINGS

American Association of University Women (AAUW). (n.d.). *Know your rights: Workplace sexual harassment.* Retrieved from http://www.aauw.org/what-we-do/legal-resources/know-your-rights-at-work/workplace-sexual-harassment/

Berkman Center for Internet and Society, Digital Media Law Project. (2007–2016). *Proving fault: Actual malice and negligence.* Retrieved from http://www.dmlp.org/legal-guide/proving-fault-actual-malice-and-negligence

Federal Trade Commission (FTC). (n.d.[a]). *Advertising and marketing.* Retrieved from https://www.ftc.gov/tips-advice/business-center/advertising-and-marketing

Federal Trade Commission (FTC). (n.d.[b]). *Legal resources.* Retrieved from https://www.ftc.gov/tips-advice/business-center/legal-resources

Gilks, M. (2000). *Rights: What they mean and why they're important.* Retrieved from http://www.writing-world.com/rights/rights.shtml

Larson, A. (2014). *Defamation: Libel and slander.* Retrieved from http://www.expertlaw.com/library/personal_injury/defamation.html

Merriam Webster Incorporated. (2016a). *Defamation.* Retrieved from https://www.merriam-webster.com/dictionary/defamation

Merriam Webster Incorporated. (2016b). *Plagiarism.* Retrieved from https://www.merriam-webster.com/dictionary/plagiarism

Pember, D., & Calvert, C. (2011). *Mass media law* (17th ed.). New York: McGraw-Hill.

Public Relations Society of America (n.d.). *Member code of ethics.* Retrieved from https://apps.prsa.org/AboutPRSA/Ethics/CodeEnglish/index.html#.WK9ivud2rNQ

Snyder, W. (2011). Principles and practices for advertising ethics. *Institute for Advertising Ethics.* Retrieved from https://www.aaf.org/_PDF/AAF%20Website%20Content/513_Ethics/IAE_Principles_Practices.pdf

Strayer, J.F. (2017, December 5). Sexual harassment: A workplace pandemic. *Institute for Public Relations.* Retrieved from http://www.instituteforpr.org/sexual-harassment-workplace-pandemic/

Tangent, L. L. C. (n.d.). *Ethics in public relations: Video news release.* Retrieved from https://ethicsinpr.wikispaces.com/Video+news+release

United States Equal Employment Opportunity Commission (n.d.). *Sexual harassment.* Retrieved from https://www.eeoc.gov/laws/types/sexual_harassment.cfm

United States Patent and Trademark Office (USPTO). (2016). *Trademark, copyright or patent?* Retrieved from https://www.uspto.gov/trademarks-getting-started/trademark-basics/trademark-patent-or-copyright

Wikispaces. (n.d.). *Ethics in public relations: Video news release.* Retrieved from https://ethicsinpr.wikispaces.com/Video+news+release

Wrapping Up the Semester

It's time to end the semester, enjoy a vacation from classes, possibly even graduate, and turn your thoughts to fun and seeing family and old friends or maybe even work at an internship. But wait—not so fast. Before you take your leave, there's a bit more to do at the student agency to make sure you end the semester strongly.

Like sticking the dismount in gymnastics, ending the semester right ensures success for your student-run agency, future students, and your clients for many semesters to come. You have worked hard to build a structure for your agency and developed working processes and procedures to make effective strategic communications for clients. The last thing you want now is to lose all that momentum as the agency shifts to another semester because a quality wrap-up with clients and the agency did not occur. And you definitely do not want the semester's worth of knowledge and materials scattered to the wind forever.

Thinking about the end of the semester actually starts at the beginning of the semester, because finishing the job right will make starting right easier next semester. As noted in Chapter 9, the semester is a very natural time-bound parameter your agency operates within. And at the very least, certain deliverables naturally end for clients, but those clients will hopefully return for more agency services next semester.

While a professional agency's work and relationships are year round, your agency will likely have time off for winter holidays and summer vacations. Your agency also differs from professionals in that there is likely a 100% turnover of student staff every 3 to 4 years. Some student-run agencies have near 100% turnover every semester, especially if it is a class for course credit. So, we're thankful for clients who stay with the agency semester after semester as they provide experiential learning opportunities and help train and onboard new and excited, yet uninitiated students to their business and the agency's past work. In fact, just when clients get a team that is clicking, they likely have some if not complete turnover just 16 weeks later. So, part of your job is making sure that turnover from one semester to the next goes smoothly.

Some may liken wrapping up the semester to finishing a marathon. The feeling of accomplishment in running 26-ish miles is diminished if we can't cross the finish line. Perhaps though, wrapping up the semester is more akin to what happens *after* you cross the finish line. What you do after you cross the finish has a tremendous influence on your future performance and needs to be purposeful and deliberate or you might not be able to race effectively again. Watch professional runners when they finish a race. They walk and perform controlled breathing and a cool down (or seek medical attention if they are injured). And they immediately think about muscle health and stretch or seek a massage and pay special attention to hydration.

In a sense, you and your agency have crossed the finish line when you complete your deliverables on time, on strategy, and on budget. But what you do after you cross the finish line has a significant impact on how successful the client and agency will be next semester and for many semesters to come. Rather than being the runner nursing injuries because of a poor postrace physical therapy regimen, be the student-run agency rested and in shape for the next semester thanks to a quality plan to wrap-up the semester.

In this chapter, we'll explore

- Wrapping up in the professional world
- Wrapping up the account with the client
- Wrapping up the account with the agency
- Final agency evaluations

By concentrating on the actions after crossing the finish line so strongly, you can rest assured that personally and professionally you are poised for future challenges and successes, and your agency can be positioned for a new team next semester to continue the great achievements you shepherded that are needed by the clients who have grown so fond of you and your agency.

© Pete Saloutos/Shutterstock.com

WRAPPING UP IN THE PROFESSIONAL WORLD

When we say, "wrapping up," we are talking about finishing with or on a client account. We are not discussing wrapping up a single or even multiple deliverables, such as finishing the investors' brochure or completing the media coverage report or launching the global summer campaign. We've covered the plans and activities that your agency and professionals use to ensure deliverables completion in Chapter 8, and fully detailed a working brief and action steps as the project is managed in Chapter 9, and then of course we'll discuss how to document all these activities for your personal and professional growth portfolio to launch a successful career in Chapter 15. This "wrapping up the semester" is a whole different plan or set of deliverables in and of itself.

There are generally three scenarios in which an agency professional experiences wrapping up with a client: at the end of a time-bound period such as a fiscal or calendar year; when the agency member transitions to another account or position; and/or when a client account is terminated. For both professionals and student-run agencies, wrapping up is a necessary and vital component of the full range of services offered. The agency business is really the agency–client relationship business, as seen in Chapter 7. Client relationships are the foundation for continued opportunities to make great communications plans. While you might not encounter these scenarios directly in your student-run agency, you very likely will in your professional career and you will possibly address these scenarios if you complete an internship at a professional strategic communications firm. It's important to note these scenarios because they have similarities to why you officially close out an account or wrap-up the end of a semester in your student-run agency. Each of these scenarios is discussed in more detail in the following.

Wrapping Up a Time-bound Period

Time-bound periods include endings such as a **fiscal year**, **calendar year**, the quarter, or even a traditional 13-week sales period. Many accounts have some natural time parameters that require the agency to complete certain deliverables or otherwise have some necessary reporting activities so the client can meet their internal expectations. Sometimes the client must meet these deadlines by law or regulation, such as reporting to the Security and Exchange Commission (SEC), or their corporate bylaws necessitate budget reallocations every fiscal quarter, or the nonprofit organization owes a financial accounting report to their donors at the end of each year.

Fiscal year: A year that does not follow the normal calendar and is common in accounting. This is a year as far as budgeting and billing reconciliation is concerned and made often for tax purposes or payroll needs. The date can be set by the organization, and July 1, is a common start date and June 30, is a common end date of the fiscal year for many colleges and universities for example.

Calendar year: A typical January 1 to December 31, year.

The agency will likely be in a time crunch itself to properly estimate and invoice all outstanding items (discussed in Chapter 4). Not performing necessary wrap-up activities as expressed by the client has a detrimental effect on the client relationship. It can take its toll on the people working day-in and day-out to make great communications programs when time and effort is reallocated to needed reporting, billing, or other activities that sometimes don't seem to directly relate to the agency's primary job of providing value through strategic communications strategies and tactics. Your work in the student-run agency to end the semester right will be excellent training for these real situations, so make sure to pay attention to them (and talk about them in your next interview).

Wrapping Up on Behalf of Yourself

Maybe you are **transitioning internally**, that is, moving on to a new account in the

Transitioning internally: Moving off of an account and on to another one at the same agency.

agency. How you transition, gracefully or not, is often remembered longer and with more intensity then all of the great recommendations and flawless execution of tactics you developed in your time on the account. It is not uncommon, especially at larger professional firms, for you to switch accounts. Your agency is hopefully thinking about your career progress so they might move you around to give you exposure to different supervisors and different types of client businesses. You might be promoted to lead an account or you might be shifted to the newest account at the agency after a new business win.

Or, you might be **transitioning externally**, that is, leaving the agency. It is not at all uncommon to leave your current agency to pursue career growth and sometimes needed personal or professional changes. This is espe-

> **Transitioning externally:** Leaving an account and leaving the current agency/employer.

cially common in your early and formative years. Rarely do you resign and walk out of the office that day. It happens, but usually you offer at least a 2-week notice where you begin to wrap-up your activities and transition or prepare your successor or even supervisor to handle the many responsibilities you have been managing.

Many an employee transitions badly and begins to "slack off" or not take their job as seriously as they did before announcing their forthcoming departure. Or even more common, they resist any new or difficult tasks or challenges in the name of, "I'll be out of here soon." These are career-killing mistakes. Your exit defines your total experience with a company. Leaving with animosity or disappointment from your peers, supervisors, and clients can overshadow the many great things you did and follow you for many years to come. If anything, you are more likely to work longer hours, try harder, say yes more often, and persevere through seemingly mundane or unnecessary requests just to end on a positive note. As painful as it might be, it is worth it.

© fizkes/Shutterstock.com

Wrapping Up the Client on Behalf of the Agency

Agency–client relationships end. Sometimes because your agency decided not continue with the client (rare) or the client has decided to fire/terminate the agency (common). Occasionally there is a mutual and friendly parting of ways between agencies and clients. But more often than not, clients choose to fire or terminate their agency and it is difficult and painful for all parties. This happens more often than you might expect. One consulting group cited by the American Association of Advertising Agencies (4As) says,

In 1984, the average client–agency relationship tenure was 7.2 years. By 1997 (13 years later), that number declined by 25% to 5.3 years. Today (2013) the average client-agency tenure is thought to be less than three years.

(The Bedford Group, 2013)

Imagine that. From the time you enter college or university until the time you graduate, a professional agency is likely to have at least half of their clients leave. When clients leave there is some acrimony. Some feelings are hurt. Some blame is assigned. Some revisionist history occurs. Some feelings of disrespect personally and organizationally are hurled under the breath and sometimes publicly. This can be a very tense time for the agency. After all, jobs and paychecks might be at stake. Nonetheless, everyone must professionally wrap-up the account, provide needed and necessary materials and assets, and not withhold information or materials.

How does this compare to your student agency? Do you have clients that stay for 3+ years? It takes great relationship management and a great student staff transitioning twice a year to make the client's investment in time and energy worthwhile. And how you wrap-up the semester directly influences how long a client might be willing to work with your agency. That's a lot of responsibility. Fortunately, you and your team will likely not shoulder the responsibility nor be aware that a client is planning to leave the agency, as that is usually a discussion with the faculty advisor(s). But it is a possibility. Nonetheless, every student has the responsibility to wrap-up the semester in such a way as to bolster their professional career development, position the agency and future students for opportunities, and ensure clients ongoing success.

WRAPPING UP THE ACCOUNT WITH THE CLIENT

So, now it is time for students to wrap-up the semester with the client. Unless your client is brand new to the agency, they have probably been through this process before. And, chances are unless the agency–client relationship has come to an end, they'll be just as interested in learning how next semester's team will be able to do as well as you have this semester.

Wrapping up well with a client also has a personal advantage for students. It allows you to discuss your career ambitions, seek a client reference, and perhaps even develop a friendship or bond that might not only help open doors professionally, but also develop a lifelong mentor. The authors of this book hear from clients all the time about how they are still in contact with past agency employees many years after graduation.

There are many actions and activities to think about when wrapping up the client, as discussed in the following.

Final Deliverables Completion and Transfer

This might be the most important thing the agency does. This is the fulfillment of the semester plan that works to ensure their client organizations' success outlined in the strategic communications plan comes to fruition. These are the executions of the tactics that help clients accomplish goals and fulfill their organization's mission. It is vital to remember this is not merely "a class." Students don't simply turn in their final executions and deliverables on deadline and hope to do well and see what grade they get. Not at all.

Working with a client is a revision and approval process and does not end until the client is satisfied with the outputs and outcomes. So student-run agencies must plan for client suggested revisions and plan to make sure that the work is 100% complete before we close the agencies doors until next semester (or possibly have a skeleton crew during holidays).

End–of-Semester Report, Presentation, and Assets Delivery

In this final client deliverable, agency members capture the accomplishments of the semester and turn over any materials the client will need for the future. This deliverable sets the stage for next semester.

> **End-of-semester report:** A report issued to a client to close out the semester with all needed materials, billings, communication's results reports, and plans for future activities.

An **end-of-semester report** recounts your work for the semester, outlines the results of that work, and summarizes lessons learned that could be used for future programs or campaigns. And, as discussed in Chapter 11, this report should be *presented* to the client in person rather than simply emailed to them. This is a big part of relationship building. You want to show off all you did for your client during the semester, as well as give the client an opportunity to give you feedback and discuss how the work and relationship can be improved for the future. Sometimes the student-run agency faculty advisor(s) will be in attendance for this part of the meeting and sometimes not. Arguments can be made for both scenarios. Sometimes student learning can be enhanced with the frankness of professional clients speaking freely with the students without faculty involvement.

Typically, an end-of-semester report and presentation includes the following.

Outputs and Outcomes

It outlines the activities; provides the actual files, images, or other concrete materials completed; and presents the overall evaluation and measurement results. More specifically this report usually contains

© AYA images/Shutterstock.com

- Semester goals and objectives recap
- Any research findings or planning decisions recap
- Strategies review and tactics created, executed, and implemented
- Results
- Reflective assessment. What worked, what did not? What could be improved?
- Suggestions for short-term (next semester) and long-term planning.

Finances and Accounting Reconciliation

Any billing or invoicing is provided. This is where agency time on projects or on the account is discussed. Out-of-pocket expenses and agency fees are reviewed. None of this should come as a surprise to the client. You likely have been estimating and communicating these activities throughout the semester in accordance with your scope of work and billing practices noted in Chapters 4 and 5. This actual report, and subsequent meeting, gives the client a chance to review spending and ask questions before simply being presented with a bill.

Set Processes for Ongoing Initiatives

Will there be any social media content during holiday seasons when the agency is not active? Who is responsible during this time? Who can the client call if they have any questions or need any previously produced materials from the agency?

More importantly, the end-of-semester report gives students a chance to help shape the future. You might include a work plan for any necessary fast starts or suggestions for deliverables/needs for next semester. What if your client is planning a big event needing promotions in week 2 of next semester? This is a good place to discuss how the agency will be ready to ramp-up fast.

Assets Delivery

A critical part of finalizing your work with the client is making sure you hand over all assets the client will need in your absence. For example, did the client pay for original photography? Those files need to go to the client in case they want to use them for other materials. Did you produce business cards or letterhead for the client? Make sure they have the original artwork so they can reprint them as stock run low.

Even if you will continue working with the client next semester, make sure they have everything produced this semester. You might be surprised how often clients can't find a file the agency provided and need it before the next semester starts. And (THIS CANNOT BE EMPHASIZED ENOUGH) turn over any passwords and pertinent information for social media or web hosting sites. Many a client has had to start a new Facebook page because they didn't have the password to access the existing one, or had their website go down and didn't know how to contact the web hosting company to have it restored (Box 13.1).

Box 13.1   Benefits of a Proper Wrap-Up With the Client

1. Chance for students to receive personal feedback
2. Chance for agency to receive feedback
3. Chance to strengthen and elongate relationship with the client personally for students
4. Chance to strengthen and elongate relationship with the client for the agency
5. Provide client with all needed materials for ongoing success
6. Provide clients with needed contacts/materials/plans during agency downtimes
7. Build strong foundation for next semester prepping others for quick ramp-ups or opportunities

Client Evaluation Forms

Sometimes professionally it is known as the agency report card. This is where the client assesses the agency's work this semester. Some of this information can (and should) be discussed with the client during presentation of your end-of-semester report. But you may also want to send more formal client evaluation forms to all clients at the end of each semester. This can be done via an online survey tool such as SurveyMonkey, or through a paper form sent in the mail.

Formal client evaluations provide two benefits. First, they give the client time to assess the activities of the semester and gather their thoughts about the overall process before responding. Second, client evaluation forms allow agencies to assess their progress and processes as a whole. For example, if 70% of clients say they felt approval turnarounds were too short, then the agency knows it needs to work on those processes.

You will find an example of a client evaluation in Box 13.2. This assessment of the students and agency work generally consists of two parts:

- *Quality of agency deliverables.* Did the agency's work meet objectives? Can we measure and track the success of campaigns or tactical executions? Did the client more closely reach their organizations goals with the help of the agency? Was the client impressed with the strategic thinking and creative executions of the agency? Did the agency provide value through research and strategic recommendations? Is the agency proactively growing and presenting the possibilities for success that strategic communications can achieve? The client can provide valuable positive and constructive feedback that help the students and agency grow in their abilities to research, recommend, and execute strategic communications plans that resonate with audiences and lead to success.

- *Quality of work processes and relationships.* How smoothly did the agency complete deliverables? Was the agency effective in email, phone calls, and live communications? Was the agency positive, flexible, adaptable? Did the team members seem engaged and represent themselves and the agency professionally? Did the team members seem to grow and engage with opportunities and tackle challenges? How can the agency and individual students improve personally, organizationally, and professionally? The client can offer suggestions that students can apply in future internship roles, classroom work, and professional encounters. And, they can offer the agency suggested ways that the relationship can grow and deepen (Box 13.2).

Box 13.2 Client Evaluation Form

This is a sample form that students and/or faculty advisors might encourage clients to fill out. It could also be used as a guide for conversations to solicit feedback from the client on how the agency might always seek to improve and be of even more value moving into future semesters.

The following information is used by [name of student-run agency] to measure success and to make improvements to increase productivity and satisfaction in the future for clients and students. Please complete the questionnaire as accurately as possible. We thank you for your assistance in this matter.

Client Name:_____

How long have you worked with [name of student-run agncy]:_____

Please write the number that corresponds to how you feel.
1 --------------------2 --------------3 -------------4------------------5
Strongly Disagree   Neutral   Strongly Agree

The help and value [name of student-run agency] provided this semester is what I expected._____

My team has completed all assigned work by the established deadline(s)._____

I feel I have an open channel of communication with my account team. _____

I feel I have an open channel of communication with the agency as a whole and the faculty advisor(s). _____

I feel all members of the team contributed to my business this semester._____

The [name of student-run agency] members have conducted themselves in a professional manner._____

I am happy with the work [name of student-run agency] has performed for me._____

I feel I am assisting in offering students excellent professional, hands-on experiences. _____

I hope to continue with [name of student-run agency] next semester._____

I would recommend [name of student-run agency] to other businesses._____

Additional comments/suggestions/constructive criticism:

WRAPPING UP THE ACCOUNT WITH THE AGENCY

Wrapping up for the client inevitably makes wrapping up for the agency nearly complete. But there's a bit more to do to ensure that your agency is ready next semester to pick up on all of the great success you have generated this semester.

The biggest consideration is that the agency needs to be able to find and use EVERYTHING you did this semester. Yes, everything! That includes old conference reports, status reports, internal brainstorming and working briefs, rough concepts, and ideas and recommendations that never even made it to the client.

Even more important than having access to these materials, it is vital for future agency staffers to understand them. So how you title and file your materials is important. It may not seem like it, but that rough draft of a client competitive report, or reputation analysis, or best practices guide for email marketing might contain information that will help this client, or any of the agency's clients, in the future. And, you will likely be long gone embarking on a wonderful career but you can know that your work, thinking, and documentation lives on for others to benefit from.

Knowing that most student-run agencies will have a 100% turnover in 4 years—or possibly every semester—makes your work to archive materials so imperative. Your agency needs you to carefully organize and file everything to be saved ideally on a hard drive or on a backed up archive server. In the old days, these would likely be various folders or even binders, but technology allows us to go digital. In the old days at professional agencies, it was not uncommon for the junior account executive (AE) to have an active client binder and various binders of previous months or years on their desk so that anyone on the account could access this historical archive when the AE was on vacation, or even just in the bathroom, and an answer was needed immediately. And today, agencies regularly look in their archive of their past work for research and inspiration on current client projects.

© Tashatuvango/Shutterstock.com

So you might choose to file your work:

- *Chronologically.* Perhaps title your files by the name of the semester and then try to organize files as they were created, likely starting with the semester kickoff briefing and scope of work and concluding with end-of-semester report. It is also important to title your files with version numbers and being clear when a project deliverable is "final" and has been sent to the client (see Chapter 9 on Project Management).

- *Subject matter relevance.* Perhaps you title your folders in major headings such as, initial semester planning, conference reports, semester plan, creative concepts, final deliverables, media contact list, possible influencers research, and so on.

Let's recap what you did to wrap-up for the client, and then we can get specific to what else your agency needs. Essentially, what you gather and write for the wrap-up for the client is what is needed for the agency wrap-up, plus a few more details for specificity. For instance

1. The client final deliverables completion and transfer is expanded to the **complete agency archive**. You completed all of the work for the client and provided them with the "final" files. Now, make sure you included all the drafts, versions, and initial concepts that might not have ever even been presented for the agency archive.

   Complete agency archive: Organized archival source of all agency documents and created assets.

   This provides more than just a history of the completed files. Think about all of the other materials that were needed to produce client work such as creative briefs, research reports, and even conference reports that your client likely will never need, but sure does benefit your agency next semester as team members try to understand past conversations and agency recommendations. Nothing frustrates a client more than when the agency tries to present the same ideas that were vetoed in the past, or when making a recommendation and the client says, "we tried that last year and it was not successful."

   Equally frustrating is presenting social media content that is not aligned with or has a dissimilar tone to the content that was successful in previous semesters. One author of this book has seen the agency team suggest social media content that mirrored a colossal and controversial failure just two semesters before. If the client has to ask the future team, "Did you see what we did last semester," then you know you have not done your homework or the previous agency team did not provide you with a complete history/archive.

   In addition to the history and inclusion of all of the deliverables and measurement/tracking reports, you should archive everything. And not just dumped into a folder, but organized including
   - Initial client kickoff briefing/scope of work
   - Strategic plans, semester plans, working briefs, and project management timelines
   - Conference reports/call reports
   - Drafts of all deliverables chronicling the development of them
   - Original research and raw sources that might have been used in campaign planning
   - Passwords. Think about clients' social media pages. And, did you subscribe to a creative stock art site or help register a domain name or create Snap Chat filters?

- Old emails. Yes, even client correspondence (and possible internal correspondence) can be helpful for future teams

Proper archiving is tough. Starting early in the semester and thinking about archiving as you complete all the activities of business is the best advice. If you know that at the end of the semester you will leave behind the archive, it is easier to organize and file as you go, rather than make sense of a bunch of files at the end of the semester. And, usually students are so tired at the end of the semester, and rightly so, proud of their accomplishments in the agency and other school work, that this step seems unnecessarily tedious and mundane. Your faculty advisor and future agency team members, and your client will thank you for completing this needed step.

2. The client end of semester report becomes the **agency end-of-semester-report**. It is the client end-of-semester report (discussed previously) but with some additions. The agency also needs to know

> **Agency end-of-semester-report:** All of the elements for the client end-of-semester report plus specific elements that are written by current agency students to future agency students about lessons learned and tips for success on a particular client account.

- Client communications and agency processes. How does the agency current structure and processes aid or hinder effective strategic communications planning or implementation for this client? What challenges did you face working within the agency to help the client become successful and reach communications' goals? How might you suggest working procedures on this client between agency departments/team members in future semesters?
- Areas that the client should or was hesitant to explore. What do you wish the client would explore? What does their business need that the agency can try to recommend and implement in the future? What opportunities or threats do you imagine the client might face next semester and in the years to come?
- A letter for the next team and/or team leader. Think about all of those little nuances of this client and account you picked up along the way that you would use if you were continuing on the account or things you know will help the next account team. Does the client always seem to respond to emails on Monday but not Tuesday? Did posts about a certain subject tend to get the client more excited or lead to more engagement on social media than others? Does the client hate the color blue? Do they never hyphenate a particular subject or always use an acronym for certain terms? What advice would you give the next team to kickoff right, have a smooth semester, and meet client needs and expectations? (Box 13.3)

Box 13.3   Sample End-of-Semester Letter to the Next Team

Dear Next Semester Account Supervisor,

I couldn't have asked for a more fun and exciting client! There is so much creative freedom and a lot of potential.

Over the past semester, my team and I have tried to develop a consistent brand tone that reflects [client organization] as a young, fun, lighthearted personality across Facebook and Instagram through entertaining visuals. If it isn't already, Pinterest will become your best friend for finding cute, clever visuals to give you ideas. And *Pexels* is a great resource for stock photos for social media.

Social media has been a huge success this semester, and you can definitely continue contributing to that success. Because there are so many events going on at [client], I suggest making a social media calendar to make sure each event has a fair amount of coverage (see binder). My team and I also made social media guidelines in order to ensure consistency, since you will most likely have four different people with four different personalities writing posts.

Presenting the creative briefs to the creative team early is important, so you have materials to utilize on Facebook and Instagram throughout the semester. In addition, try to have a photographer from the creative team out to the [client] and the [public events at the client] at the beginning of the semester as well, so you have high-quality photos to use on social media. [student name], the creative team member who photographed the [marquise client event] this semester, mentioned that it is important to bring props and ask [client] for a place to set up equipment at the [client event], for most food comes in Styrofoam containers and does not make for visually appealing images.

On Facebook, we implemented a "Tip of the Week" with the hashtag #[relevant client hashtag] that we posted each Monday, and added monthly event cover photos that showed what events were coming up. Both received a lot of engagement. I really challenged my team to make the social media posts interesting and entertaining rather than merely stating when and where the next event was because otherwise the posts get repetitive and boring. I encourage you to do the same.

To maintain organization and fluid communication, I sent out a weekly email at the end of the Monday night meetings to my team with each account executive's (AE) task for that week. This included when social media posts were due. Because we were producing so much social media and there are so many events with different times and information at [client], I had the AEs edit each other's social media posts before I looked over it— Wednesdays, posts were due; Fridays, comments and edits to each other's posts were due; and Sundays, responses and changes to those suggestions were due. Having the

(Continued)

(Continued)

AEs edit each other's social media allowed an extra set of eyes to catch the simple mistakes before I looked at it.

[Client] is incredibly flexible in terms of creative projects, but it is often hard to get a response or approval from him. I suggest sending everything in advance to give him excess time and if necessary, send him a quick text when there are pressing deadlines.

As far as next steps, I recommend updating their website (both content and design) and branding their [name of client] concert series— logo, color scheme, graphics, flyers, etc.

Please see documents in the [client] binder for more information.

Good luck with everything! You are going to have so much fun! Please don't hesitate to reach out if you have any questions. My number is (###) ###-### and my email is ....

Best regards,

[Student account supervisor]

3. The client wrap-up meeting is rehearsed at the **agency wrap-up meeting**, where each team presents the work they did for their client. It is a practice run-through usually a few days before the end of semester client meeting so the entire agency can share in your accomplishments and successes. This agency-wide meeting to wrap-up all clients provides many advantages and learning opportunities for everyone involved:

Agency wrap-up meeting: A rehearsal for the client end-of-semester report and presentation where all agency accounts report to the entire agency staff to celebrate the successes of the organization.

- It allows the faculty director to offer input on your report and presentation before you go before the client.
- When the entire agency sees the accomplishments of every client, it helps everyone see the big picture of the value the student agency creates for its clients.
- It motivates those agency staffers who might return in future semesters to aspire to greatness and provides a framework for the type of activities they can engage in to grow their portfolios and generate client success.
- It can give all future strategic communications professionals a bigger context of how any agency, and particularly their student-run agency, delivers numerous communications strategies and tactics for a variety of clients.

Wrapping up for the agency is documenting and making available all of the work you did and provided the client. And, it also gives your personal account and reflection for how the agency and future account team members might best manage and create value for the client. It is difficult to prioritize this as the many, many new experiences of the semester conclude both in and outside of the agency, but it's critical. And it is good preparation for similar scenarios you might face in internships and in your career in strategic communications (Table 13.1).

Table 13.1   Transition Wrapping Up With the Client Into Wrapping Up With the Agency

Client	Agency
1. Final deliverables completion and transfer 2. Client end-of-semester report 3. Client end-of-semester meeting	1. Archive all materials generated this semester 2. Agency end-of-semester report 3. Agency end-of-semester meeting

FINAL EVALUATIONS

Client evaluations were covered earlier in this chapter. But that's not the only evaluation that is important to the agency and its members. As we discussed at the end of Chapter 4, the success of your agency also depends on how smoothly your processes worked to deliver client programs, the learning benefits students gained from their agency experiences, the performance of individual team members; the effectiveness of agency leadership, and, often, whether your academic department or dean is pleased with the agency.

You can measure each of these either formally or informally. The first step is to decide what you want to evaluate, the questions you want to ask, and then determine the best way to gather the information needed. As discussed in Chapter 10 on the "gift of feedback," it is best to gather information on individual performance privately or anonymously, while more general learning that would benefit all agency members can be discussed publicly.

For example, you could gather information on agency processes and protocols at an informal end-of-semester all-staff meeting (call it a party— order pizza), where everyone feels comfortable providing informal feedback. This could be part of your agency wrap-up meeting, or a separate gathering. What did students learn this semester that was valuable to them? What DIDN'T they learn that they wish they would have? Do

© Prostock-studio/Shutterstock.com

students have the autonomy necessary to do the right thing for clients? What processes were effective or ineffective? Do they have suggestions for better processes? What types of clients would they like to see the agency add in the future?

Just like you do for clients, you could also conduct an informal Strengths, Weaknesses, Opportunities, and Threats (SWOT) analysis—what do agency members perceive our strengths to be? Our weaknesses? Our best opportunities for being successful? Or, what did they experience this semester that could threaten our success? Write down student input on an easel pad or white board for all to see, then make sure to archive the information when finished.

Since the student agency is first and foremost a learning opportunity, and often taught as a class, an important part of end-of-semester evaluation is measuring the performance of individual agency members. Not only does this provide valuable information that each student can use to learn and grow, it is also helpful for professors who are required to grade students' work.

To do so, you may want to develop confidential peer evaluations for team members and agency leadership. For example, many organizations use **360-degree feedback** systems in which employees are formally and anonymously evaluated by their supervisors, peers, and those that report to them. In other words, members are evaluated up (members evaluating agency leadership), down (supervisors evaluating their teams), and sideways (peer-to-peer evaluations).

> **360-Degree feedback:** A deliberate and organized system of written, anonymous reviews of people hierarchically above, below, and lateral to the one doing the review.

Questions might address issues such as quality of work, quantity of work, ability to work well in a team, leadership responsiveness, professionalism, writing and presentation skills, and other qualities important to your agency and the work you do. These types of evaluations should be confidential and anonymous so agency members feel free to provide feedback without repercussions. It is also helpful for a supervisor or advisor to meet with team members about their evaluation results and help them develop plans for improvement.

Finally, you may want to formally measure the learning benefits of your student agency. Depending on the learning goals of your agency (discussed in Chapter 2), you can determine if students are gaining valuable problem-solving skills, improving their professional identity, learning how to work within an agency structure, and/or gaining effective organizational and time management skills, among other things. While it is valuable to gather this information qualitatively, it can also help to develop more formal, quantitative measurements that can then be tracked over time as you add or change your agency's learning opportunities. In addition, understanding these types of benefits will be particularly relevant when presenting your agency successes to your department head or dean (like when you need more money).

Regardless of how you gather this information, you'll want to keep records of the agency's progress and include any issues for improvement in the next semester's plans. As we discussed in the introduction of this text, the student agency is always "becoming." Just like you do with your client programs, measuring your agency's performance can help you determine where you are succeeding and where you can institute improvements for the betterment of all.

CONCLUSION

So getting to the finish line is an accomplishment, but what you do after you cross it is essential for personal professional growth and for the success of your agency and the future student staff. Planning for the wrap-up at the beginning of the semester eases the natural time crunch and stress that an academic semester naturally brings.

While difficult, archiving and ending the semester is one of the most important things you can do at the agency to ensure that it continues to survive and thrive. And wrapping up accounts and clients successfully and deliberately provides you with a wealth of work samples and discussion points for your next interview. Being able to leave others equipped with the knowledge and files needed to keep the businesses running smoothly is a highly desirable skill for employers and demonstrates your understanding of the bigger picture of business and client relationship management. If you take it seriously, you will make more meaningful networking contacts with your clients and peers that will benefit your agency and your career immediately and likely for years to come.

REVIEW AND DISCUSSION QUESTIONS

1. Why is important to review the types of "wrapping up" of accounts professionals do? How is that applicable to the "wrapping up" the student-run agency does?
2. What are the reasons for very carefully wrapping up an account in the professional world when you transition externally?
3. How is wrapping up the semester similar to completing deliverables outlined in the semester plan? How is it different?
4. Why is a plan to wrap-up the semester valuable to both the student-run agency and to the individual student?
5. What are the components of the end-of-semester report? What is the purpose for the agency to report these to the client?
6. How does wrapping up for the client directly lead to the needed information for wrapping up for the agency? What "extra" is needed when students wrap-up for the agency that might not be included in the client wrap-up?
7. What is the agency wrap-up meeting? Why is it necessary and how might it be beneficial to students and the agency?
8. Why is it important for students to complete 360-degree evaluations? How does it benefit the student and the agency?
9. Discuss with your team ways you can archive client materials (including naming files, where they are stored, accessed, etc.), and effective ways to wrap-up with your own client.
10. What types of questions would you like to see on a client evaluation form? What types of questions would you like to discuss in an agency wrap-up meeting? What types of questions would you like to see on a 360-degree evaluation form (i.e., how do you want your work to be evaluated?).

REFERENCES AND ADDITIONAL READINGS

American Association of Advertising Agencies. (n.d.). *Average tenure of client agency relationships (pdf)*. Retrieved from http://www.aaaa.org/wp-content/uploads/legacy-pdfs/4As-Ave%20longevity%20of%20account%20relationships.pdf

The Bedford Group. (2013). *Client/agency relationship sustainability*. Retrieved from http://bedfordgroupconsulting.com/marketing-insights/agency-relationship-sustainability/

Part III

Professional Practices

Research Real Talk: Revelations, Realizations, and Radical Simplicity

Adrian Fogel
SVP, Strategy Director
Y&R

SEARCH ENGINES AND SIRI DON'T MAKE YOU A RESEARCHER

The essence of research is acquiring information to learn something new. But in a world where information is more accessible than ever before, more and more people assume wisdom can just be Googled or fetched by Siri. It can't. Just because you can Google or use voice activation on your phone, doesn't mean you're a researcher. Great, so wtf do you do now? Exactly. WTF indeed . . . *W*hat *T*ruth and *F*ocus are you seeking? What answers do you need?

When the word *research* falls out of someone's mouth it's because there is a sense that information is missing to help make the best decision possible. The next few pages ask questions that will provide answers that will elevate thinking and eliminate doubts.

W = All the W questions . . . what, why, who, when, where.
T = Truths you need to solve people problems.
F = Focus and freshness to deliver success.

W = WHAT, WHY, WHO, WHEN, WHERE?

Let's start with the WHAT first. The WHAT is usually defined by your research objective. What do you need to achieve?

What?

- *What's your objective?* You need to ask lots of questions and really dig through the lens of the category, consumer, culture, or company. For example, are you solving for a people problem, focused on messaging, leveraging a cultural truth, understanding white space opportunities for innovation, defining your consumer journey/triggers, understanding what's driving consideration, or defining brand perceptions?
- *What is the role of this research?* Knowing the role of the research and how it fits into the bigger picture is critical. This will continue to help you refine and determine the right objectives as well as influencing the analysis and approach.

Things to possibly consider . . . is it to launch a new innovation, understand the motivation and needs of a target audience, determine a shopper journey, provide long-term strategy recommendations, help expand a portfolio or product offering, develop a new creative campaign, launch a new brand, and so on . . .?

- *What does success look like?* The moment you start any project, it's important to know what success looks like. What answers must be delivered to declare victory? You need to know what will make clients feel like this learning is the anchor for whatever they are doing next. How do they need to receive the information to make sure it's usable? Success could range from identifying new insights for packaging to a new brand positioning to what segment to prioritize to competitive advantage to ways to enhance the shopping experience to determining if a new partnership is the right fit to what social cause to support to creating a new loyalty program.

- *What does failure look like?* There's nothing worse than the feeling of sharing research that is nothing more than a deli-sized $*&% sandwich, especially when it's painfully obvious your team knows exactly what they're eating. To avoid this, don't be afraid to ask tough questions. Know ahead of time what failure would look like so you know how to avoid it.

- *What pictures or images do you need to help bring the learning to life?* As the old saying goes, a picture is worth a 1000 words. Knowing most people have the attention span of a gnat, pictures or images can help fast-track the power of the learning. The more visual you can make the data the more compelling it becomes because you have done more than just simply report what you learned. You did something with it. In a world of curated pictures, snaps and infographics and a million ways to create video, think about ways that you can bring the words to life for clients and use consumers, artifacts, pictures, emoji's—whatever it takes to help convey the key learnings.

Advice
If the objective(s) and what success looks like are fuzzy, then it means you are trying to do too much. The best research has one to three simple and clear objectives (each written with eight words or less).

Why?

- *Why do we need to do this?* Once you have figured out WHAT you're doing, you then need to ask WHY you're doing it. The clearer your objective, the easier it will be to answer this question.

- *Why does this matter?* What needs to be answered and how will the learning ultimately be used? What hunches and hypothesis are you starting with?

Advice
This should be single minded, start with a verb, and ideally not be more than two sentences. Ultimately determine if you are giving your client what they asked for versus what they really need.

- *Why do we need to talk to these consumers?* Are there things that you do and don't already know? What new news are you looking for and why?

  Advice
  Make sure you are clear on what you want to learn. To find something new, you need to do something new. The right people get you the right information.

Who?

- *Who matters most?* Those people that will help you discover and unlock the truth so that you can understand why it will matter.
- *Who else do you want to talk to?* Being clear on who you need to speak with goes beyond just the consumer audience. If you are looking for new news, be open to the people you speak with by connecting with category experts or brand haters. Don't forget inspiration can come from anywhere.
- *Who don't you want to talk to?* Making sure you know who *isn't* important to you is just as important as who is. If sales are stagnant, how are you going to bring in new users?

  Advice
  Be open minded. Talking to competitive loyalists could also help ensure that you have a strategy/approach that will be fresh, inspiring, and distinctive.

Where and When Process Needs

- *Where else can you get information?* Based on what you do know, can social listening help fill in the holes? Why or why not? Are there partners who may have intel that could be useful (media, public relations [PR], digital, customer relationship management [CRM], analytics, innovation, design)? Can library tools and a librarian help?
- *When do you need this? What is your timeline?* To avoid time being your enemy, know your deadline and what are key milestone dates. For example, will this learning be part of a big meeting, influencing a budget decision or helping launch something new? It will help you quickly decide how to approach the research and determine the trade-offs within your time frame.

T = TRUTHS

Let's talk about truth for a moment. Most marketers confuse a truth with an insight. The fact is truths don't have tension in them, insights do. For research to really have meaning and solve a people problem, it should have tension in it. No matter whether your approach is qual or quant or both, great research delivers truths with tension. Truths are helpful because you need to uncover the WHY they're true to reveal the insight.

Truth:
A fact or information that is accepted as true.
Findings:
Findings are derived from observations and investigation.
Insights:
Insights explain the emotional drivers of human behavior. Answer the question "WHY?"

Bill Bernbach said something smart about how a good insight inspires a great creative idea . . .

> *"Nothing is so powerful as an insight into human nature . . . what compulsions drive a man, what instincts dominate his action . . . if you know these things about a man you can touch him at his core being."*

Boom. Drop the mic. Point being, it's all about the why, NOT the what. It's less about revelation and more about realization. Getting a feeling. You'll know you have lightening in a bottle when the human truth can be put into an idea and be creatively expressed. The job of the insight is to reveal information that makes it feel like it could potentially change behavior or reflect an unmet need versus just an objective, measureable fact.

To be clear, an insight IS NOT

- Data . . . you need to mine the data and then analyze it to come up with something that can drive a call to action.
- Observation . . . it's something to consider but lacks the why and motivation behind the behavior . . . to be an insight you need to have the WHY or you have just a data point.
- A customer wish or statement need . . . again, you need to understand the WHY behind the need to get to something . . . I'll shut my broken record off now.
- A creative idea.

An insight IS and WILL

- Connect with consumers emotionally and obviously demonstrate that you get them.
- Solve a real problem because it brings together research findings, trends, unmet consumer needs, people behavior, and wider experiences.
- Reexamine existing conventions and challenge the status quo.
- Inspire action, opportunities, and reduce risk.
- Respond creatively to consumer needs.

Examples of insights with tension are . . .

Snickers//You're not yourself when you're hungry.
Ragu//Even kids who have a long day need some comfort food.

Sealy Mattress//A mattress isn't just a bed, it's a horizontal living space.
Purina//Hidden inside every dog is a great dog.

Before I get off my soapbox, these tips are the difference between making you just a great Google fact finder and a great strategist. A stellar strategist is able to take new truths and uncover the unexpressed tensions.

F = FOCUS AND FRESHNESS

Though you are delivering words and data you are ultimately delivering a "feelings palooza" infused with focus and freshness. So much of what you do is rooted in feeling and gut. Research is one of those moments when you shine or get shamed. The power of this feeling comes from the hope of delivering something smart and new that creates possibility. If you are delivering learning that has focus and freshness the team will feel enlightened, energized, and eager because they have something awesome right at their fingertips.

Focus & Freshness Filters

Epic research reporting . . .
- Presents a tension versus just stating common knowledge
- Shares the good, the bad, and the ugly of what you learned
- Provides the WHY's and HOW's, not just the WHAT's
- Translates learning into action (reframing category conventions, white space, etc.)
- Is able to stand alone without needing someone to present it

RESEARCH REAL TALK

You've figured out your objective, why you are doing this research and with whom. Now you need to figure out HOW you are going to do this. Otherwise known as the qualitative (qual) versus quantitative (quant) conundrum. Quantitative research involves counting and numbers—how many and how much. Qualitative research relates more to finding out why people think or feel the way they do. You also need to determine if the client can afford to conduct primary research (aka new research), or if analyzing existing research will achieve your objective (secondary research).

This is where the struggle is real and asking "so, what?" will make the difference in delivering a useless data dump or a goldmine full of truths. The hard question you need to ask is

Are you trying to

explore & discover = qual
define & validate = quant

There are a few terms you need to know to make sure your purpose does not get compromised. These terms are basics like knowing the alphabet.

Approach	Definition	Example
Primary research: (a.k.a. new research)	Surveys, face-to-face interviews, questionnaires, focus groups, retail store, or competitor observations.	**McDonald's**—Conducting a survey to understand how mom's feel about the quality of McDonald's food. **Cars.com**—Creating a questionnaire to improve their website navigation.
Secondary research: (a.k.a. desk research)	Existing client studies on products, brands, or customers, syndicated research like Mintel, Forrester Reports, survey data, sales data, annual reports, or customer service reports.	**Bel Brands**—Leveraging Trend Hunter Report to help identify food culture trends. **Virgin Atlantic**—Using a Forrester Travel Study to understand the attitudes of travelers after 9/11.
Qualitative research: (data comes from words/pictures/ experiences)	Ethnography, focus groups, phenomenology, grounded theory, case study.	**Mini Cooper**—Interviewing people in the back of a Mini-Cooper when it launched. **Ikea**—Interviewing people who were in the process of renovating to understand their relationship with furniture.
Quantitative research: (data comes from numbers)	Segmentation studies, brand and advertising tracking, attitude and usage studies, shopper journeys, positioning, copy or messaging testing, conjoint analysis, and discrete choice modeling.	**Kelloggs**—Conducting a segmentation study to understand the different attitudes toward healthy eating. **Hilton**—Speaking with business and leisure travelers to understand their shopping process and what drives choice.

When it comes to advertising or marketing needs, typically the most common primary research approaches are conducting surveys, testing a creative idea/concept, or conducting research in a focus group setting. Below reflects things I learned the hard way and wish someone had told me before I took on a research project.

Surveys

A particular set of questions is asked to a large sample of people to help provide some validation and direction for the future. Typically, respondents are invited via email to answer a questionnaire with yes/no or multiple choice questions where respondents rate their feelings or share their opinions.

Do	Don't
• Less is more, keep questions short • Ask questions that will instantly impact the business or answer something • A test drive of your survey to make sure your logic is there and everything is working • Make sure to be specific to get what you need • Write questions clearly and simply like you're talking to your grandmother • Break big ideas into multiple questions • Provide simple responses like yes/no, checkbox or multiple choice, dropdown, ranking	• Make your survey length beyond 10–15 minutes • Ask questions that are "nice to haves" • Try to reinvent the wheel, lots of platforms are out there with easy programming and great reporting tools • Write nonspecific questions or offer a response that doesn't get an answer • Write it like a thesis or use industry jargon • Ask more than one question at a time (i.e., what's the cheapest and fastest . . .) • Let your options get too out of control, remember what you need to learn

Idea Testing

You may get asked to test creative work to help get some sense of what is appealing and ways to make the work better. Typically, TV, print or digital work is tested (usually in focus groups or interviews) to get a sense if the message is clear, if people remember which brand it's for and if there is a clear call to action.

Do	Don't
• Be clear that what they are seeing is work in progress, not final; look for opinions to help sharpen messages • Keep questions focused on understanding the what and why • Make sure to understand what they like, what makes it memorable, what makes it breakthrough, why it's relevant to them • Test two to four ideas • Use random letters to code the concepts (i.e., MM, J, etc.)	• Let consumers get hung up on the details/art direction • Let one-person hijack the conversation • Test too many ideas (>5), it gets confusing and hard; avoid blending ideas • Just test one idea . . . to learn you must juxtapose it against something (old work, competitor) • Use 1 or A for coding work, avoid words if possible

Focus Groups

As you try to explore and discover, it may be ideal to bring a few groups of people together at a specialized facility with a one-way mirror for group interviews. The efficiency of this is to gain insight into the way a specific group of people think and to understand what is and isn't important to them.

Do	Don't
• Consider smaller groups of three to four people to get more depth • Make sure your discussion guide truly allows for discussion, manage the time in your prep design • Try to make everyone feel included and comfortable and reassure there are no wrong or right answers • Make sure to understand why someone is providing a response • Prescreen people before they come in the room to make sure they are articulate and in the right state of mind • Record or have a note taker to help capture thoughts • Use an audio recording or have a creative read a script • Make people turn off cellphones when they are in a group • Consider "homework" to help make the most of the conversation	• Allow more than eight people in a group • Use your discussion guide as a script • Let people not participate or give short one word answers • Be afraid to not let people in the group if you have concerns • Do a group by yourself, you always need a wingman • Read a creative script, your delivery can create a bias or distraction • Let them take a phone call or text during the group • Use prework just for an ice breaker, it should have purpose to the learning

RESEARCHER RULE OF THUMB

The point of doing research is to identify the good, the bad, and the ugly. Your data goldmine will depend on how great your gold diggers are. No matter whether it's you or someone else conducting the research, the right skillset, right approach, right technology, reporting style, right temperament, ability to connect with the audience, right match for client culture—all are important ingredients to making the research successful.

When writing up the research report, remember to include INSIGHTS, as well as findings and truths. Ask yourself, do I have concise:

Implications that clearly explain and reframe the way everyone approaches the business?
Recommendations that can immediately be activated and make them feel like they are making informed choices?

Hopefully after reading this you now have raised your research IQ and have the tools to become the researcher you were born to be. So go out there and say "W-T-F" because the more often *you* say it, the less often the people relying on your research will.

Unleashing Your Creativity: A Primer on How to Push Past the Obvious and Create More Engaging Work

Shamika Brown Barbosa
Writer, Entrepreneur, Globetrotter

INTRODUCTION

Welcome to the creative department! While many argue it to be the most interesting department in the building, it is more challenging than it appears to be on TV or in film. While it is a lot of fun, it isn't "easy." Creativity can be very subjective. What's funny to you may not be funny to your boss. So, it takes a special kind of person to work here and thrive. Whether you are an Art Director or Copywriter, you must be resilient, thick-skinned and most importantly, imaginative.

Throughout the creative development process, you will come in contact with key players in other departments. This collaboration is a hallmark of the industry and how well these departments work together can directly impact the effectiveness of your work.

CREATIVE DEVELOPMENT PROCESS

There are seven major phases within the creative development process.

Phase 1: The Briefing

The first step in the process actually begins outside of the creative department. Before any creative work can start, the account team and strategic planners work together to take a deep dive into the client's business problems. Specifically, they analyze the consumer, the product, and the competition to identify the "sweet spot" in which the campaign can succeed within the marketplace.

Once identified, these findings are distilled into a creative brief or strategy and presented to the teams working on the assignment. The briefing is an opportune time to ask questions and gain clarity from those who know the client and its business issues best. Here are some questions to keep in mind when reviewing the brief:

The target: Do you understand your audience, as it is defined? The brief should paint a full picture of the ideal consumer.

The message: Every brief has a key message that the creative work must convey. This one sentence serves as a creative springboard or jumping off point for the teams. As such, does that key message get your creative juices flowing?

The problem: As outlined, does the message you're being asked to convey solve the business problem? Make sure the two connect because the effectiveness of your work will be directly linked to how well it solves the problem.

The competition: Were the category competitors referenced in the briefing? If not, ask about them and do your own research to see what you're really up against in the marketplace.

The tone: Taking a cue from the brand personality, what should be the tone of your work? Your job is to push the creativity of the work and stay on strategy. So, make sure you understand the guardrails when it comes to how far the client is willing to go.

The deliverables: What are you responsible for executing and by when? Is your Creative Director expecting thumbnails (loose sketches) or comps (finished ads) at your first review? These answers impact your creative development and time management. So, know what's mandatory before you leave the briefing.

Phase 2: Creative Development

Once the briefing is complete, it's time to get to work. In creative departments, most teams are comprised of an Art Director and a Copywriter. During this phase of the process, you will spend hours upon hours with your partner as you hash out ideas. You'll want to start with a "big idea" or concept. Many creatives often want to jump into "execution" or make ads right away. But you must think it through first to arrive at the most effective advertising. We call this "peeling back the onion" or digging through layers of thinking to get to an interesting or innovative place. Here are some key words to keep in mind:

Concept: The main idea that is present throughout your campaign.

Execution: How the concept is expressed and what the consumer will see.

Campaign: Three executions or more that feature the same concept.

Message: How your concept is being delivered to consumers through visuals and copy.

Visual: The image in print or a series of scenes in video that consumers see in the execution.

Copy: The written or spoken communication that accompanies the visuals in the execution.

Headline: The main idea of your execution that helps grab the consumer's attention.

Body copy: Longer form text that further explains the concept and sells the product.

Tagline: The short phrase that summarizes the concept of the campaign for consumers.

Dialogue: The copy that is spoken by characters in commercials or video content.

Voiceover: An announcer in a commercial that usually presents the product's selling points.

Throughout this section, let's use Wilson Basketballs as our client. The strategy is to convince parents to spend more time with their kids by playing basketball. You will need to create a print campaign and a 30-second television commercial.

After a few minutes of discussing it with your partner, you decide that a dad and a child playing hoops in their driveway is a great idea and the headline will be: Play basketball together.

As a piece of communication, it's fine. But it probably wouldn't sell many basketballs because it's not a fully developed concept. You jumped into execution. First, you must step back and think about what it means for a dad to play with his child. What feelings does that image conjure up? What meaning can you associate with it? Also, what else can you say about the image to add to the story, rather than just repeating what we already see?

As you think about your own experiences growing up, you may remember time spent with your parents or family members and realize that kids actually gain a lot from these simple moments. So how do you go beyond the obvious? It's simple: You push your thinking.

Tension: Your ad should feature a headline and visual that work off of each other. Together, they create the perfect piece of communication: one draws you in and the other adds to the conversation. Much like puzzle pieces, they should fit together.

Dramatization: Grab the consumer's attention—either visually or through the headline. Show the product being used in a new way or tell consumers something surprising. Draw them in and reward them for stopping to read or watch.

Simplicity: You can only effectively communicate one thing at time. Attempting more than that is the equivalent of talking with a mouth full of marbles. Limit your ideas to one per execution and if you have more ideas, create more executions. That's the beauty of having a big concept worthy of becoming a campaign.

Going back to the Wilson Basketball example, you can keep the father/son moment in the driveway as your visual, but you should revise the headline so it says more about that moment. For example, the new headline could be: You can teach him a lot on a basketball court.

Now, the headline piques the curiosity of the reader or viewer and begins to create an opportunity to have a meaningful conversation. Are we still talking about basketball or something bigger? Also, you could change the pronoun to "she" and take the conversation in a different direction about the importance of girls playing sports.

Other visuals in the print campaign or the commercial could include a mom playing one-on-one with her son. Or a close-up of a basketball being carried under an arm as a parent and child leave a basketball court at sunset. All of the headlines should add to the story about the moments shown. For the television commercial, the voiceover could work in the same way.

Your tagline would sum up the campaign idea. For example, near the Wilson logo, it could read: Where family time meets game time. As a result, the concept of the campaign would invite consumers to create their own memories with their kids—which is more than the original headline stated.

In effect, it's the same concept, but a much deeper message with greater persuasion in the marketplace. The more you do this, the easier it will become. But it will take a while to strengthen your creative muscles. Here are some things to avoid along the way:

See/say: If you're showing a father and child on a basketball court, don't restate the obvious. Add to the story. Provide context and make it mean something to me as a consumer.

The obvious: Write down the first few things that come to mind and then throw them all away! Seriously. The goal is to come up with an original idea that no one has ever thought of before. It will take more time than you think and you will have to dig deep.

Inconsistency: As you are building out your campaign, your executions don't have to be "cookie cutter" or look and sound alike. But, you do need to make sure that they all live under the same concept and strategy. If not, then you may be creating executions for a different campaign.

Puns: It's really difficult to create a successful play on words. Sometimes, even the good ones are bad. Choose clarity over cleverness and let your image do more of the entertaining. After all, the headline and visual should work together.

As you concept, the roles of Art Director and Copywriter may become less defined. Art Directors might come up with headlines and taglines, just as Copywriters might come up with design solutions. It's important to remember that a great idea can come from anywhere. Here are some tips on how to begin ideation:

Brainstorming

First, review your brief and then, start tossing out ideas. Be sure to keep a record of each one and try not to censor yourself early on in the process. Even outlandish thinking is fair game and innovation is key. If this is the first time you're working with your partner, it will take some time to get comfortable sharing your thoughts. But don't take too long. Eventually, you'll have to dive in because you're on a deadline! Here are some thought-starters:

- What are your target's likes and dislikes?
- Where and how do they spend their free time?
- What role does the product play in their lives?
- What role COULD the product play in their lives?
- Is there a visual setting that might appeal to them?
- Does humor fit or should the work be solemn?
- Which subject matter fits best with the feeling you're trying to convey?
- Has this idea been done before?

Breakaways

After your initial brainstorm session, it can be helpful to go off on your own to further develop mutually agreed upon areas. Spend a few hours alone, thinking it through and diving deeper into execution. For example, if a script is required, give the storyline some preliminary thought. If you're working in print, start pulling some visual references. Then come back together and compare notes. You'll be surprised at how you both started in the same place, yet ended up somewhere completely different. If time permits, do this two to three times. Each time, the work will become stronger and more focused.

Editing

When you two come back together, separate the good ideas from the bad by measuring them against the objectives of the brief. Also, try not to become too vested in your ideas because hundreds of ads die every day. Inevitably, some ideas will begin to stand out as being both creative and strategic. As you whittle down the work, try not to keep count of whose ideas are still alive. You are part of a team challenged with coming up with the best creative solutions. The quality of your ideas will matter more than who has the most!

Getting unstuck

If you ever find yourselves sitting in silence and/or staring blankly at each other, you may have hit a wall. If so, try these techniques to break through the creative block.

- *Free association:* Quickly say the first thing that comes to mind. Create a list of 10 to 12 items and review it. Sometimes, you can find a serendipitous connection to your target, their interests or the product. And at the very least, you would have had a fun, mental break.
- *Get out:* Changing your environment can also free up your mind. If you can leave the building, head to a park or a coffee shop. Go for a ride on the subway or go to dinner with a friend. Taking your mind off of "solving it" may actually open your mind up to new solutions. Oftentimes, your brain will keep trying to solve the problem, whether you're sitting at your desk or not. Just remember to write those fleeting thoughts down, because you won't remember them later!

Once you and your partner have agreed upon a few areas, it's time to "flesh them out," or develop them a bit further. This is where the real thinking begins. The goal of advertising is to persuade consumers into action: buying the product you're selling. The easiest way to do this is to make an emotional connection with the consumer through your visuals, copy, and tagline. A visual is any image used in your piece of communication. It can be a still image in print or series of scenes in video. The key is to choose those that resonate with your audience, either depicting them or the lifestyle that they can achieve with the product.

Phase 3: Internal Presentation, Level I

After you and your partner have worked for a few days, you will need to check-in with your Creative Director. These check-ins are critical because when the two of you are toiling away in isolation, the work may seem prolific to you both. But during these reviews, your CD will look at the work from a slightly different, more objective vantage point.

Be sure to schedule a check-in 3 to 5 days after your initial briefing. At this early stage, the ideas will not need to be complete and you should be prepared to show a variety of directions (generally four to six areas). Sometimes, it's enough to present an insight accompanied by a written description of the idea. A seasoned CD will be able to tell whether the idea is worth "fleshing out" and pursuing further.

Depending on the timeline, there will be at least two check-ins. Prepare yourself for some bloodshed. Remember, these are just ideas and it's your job to come up with lots of them. The untimely deaths of your ideas aren't reflections of your talent. You must believe that you can "go back to the well" and return in the next round with even better ideas.

Phase 4: Execution

After the internal reviews, your CD will approve some of your ideas and give you the green light to move into execution. This involves getting your ideas "client ready." Depending on your deliverables, you may be responsible for creating mood boards, key frames, storyboards, comps, and/or body copy. This is also where the official roles of Art Director and Copywriter begin. They include

Art Director Responsibilities
- Creative look and feel
- Selection of visuals
- Photography style
- Placement of creative elements

Copywriter Responsibilities
- Headline and tagline options
- Body copy
- Scripts
- Treatments
- Manifestos

Important terms you'll likely encounter in creative concepting are

Mood boards: These visual treatments give clients an overview of the look and feel of your idea. A mood board typically showcases 8 to 10 images. It also conveys the visual language to the client, as well as the photography style.

Key frames: These are most often used to represent the main ideas of commercials and video content. They feature the script or treatment and one key visual that highlights the main idea or a pivotal moment within the script.

Storyboards: Designed to tell a full story in eight frames or less, storyboards are often used for 15- and 30-second commercials. But when absolutely necessary, they can spill over onto a second page. Corresponding copy and stage directions (as they will be experienced by the viewer) are listed underneath each frame.

Comps: When working within a variety of media (magazine, out of home, digital, social, or experiential) a well-designed example of the consumer-facing execution can help sell the idea. It includes precise placement of everything present in the finished work: the headline, visual, copy, tagline, and logo.

Body copy: When it comes to writing body copy, only use as many words as necessary. Consumers rarely read copy, but clients love it. So, make it succinct. Depending on the subject matter, five to six sentences should be enough. The first sentence should connect in some way to the headline or visual. The middle sentences should sell the product benefit to the consumer and include product support points. The last sentence should connect back to the headline or first sentence of body copy to tie it all together.

Phase 5: Internal Presentation, Level II

Before the client sees your work, the account team and strategic planners must weigh in. After all, they are the most familiar with the client and the business needs. If your CD has kept their concerns in mind during your internal reviews, the revisions required should be minimal. But that isn't always the case. Sometimes, this internal review can lead to major revisions if members of the larger team feel that the work is off strategy.

All parties will eventually come to an agreement on which work makes its way into the meeting and which campaign will be the recommended direction. Typically, two to three campaigns are presented in a client meeting. The order in which the work will be presented is also discussed. Consider showing your recommended work first, your weakest second, and your second strongest third.

Phase 6: Presentation Prep

Congratulations! Now that everyone has agreed on the work, it's time to get it ready for presentation and "prep the deck." This task usually defaults to the Art Director or Designer on the team, with senior team members contributing to the content. The deck will include the market research, creative brief, and all of the deliverables. In many agencies, junior creatives have the opportunity to present their work to the client. Here are some things to remember:

Practice, practice, practice: Review your work and know it inside and out. You should know it well enough to walk through it and only look at it occasionally.

Get into it: When possible, act out your work. Visualizing your ideas for the client helps sell them. You've worked countless hours to get it to this point. If it requires a voice or emotion, go there and leave it all on the presentation floor.

Present democratically: Sell your idea to every client in the room. Connect with them via eye contact. Your vulnerability will make it easier for the client to buy into the characters and storylines you've created.

Phase 7: Client Revisions

During or shortly after the presentation, the client will provide consolidated feedback to the team. At that time, some work will move forward and some work will die. The creative teams will be debriefed and if you're among the lucky ones, your revised work will make it into the next round.

CONCLUSION

Congratulations on your perseverance and hard work! The journey continues until a campaign is chosen for production and could include copy testing, focus groups, or the client simply choosing the winner. Either way, you're now well on your way to understanding how the creative process works. As your career progresses, you'll become more efficient at brainstorming and identifying the "big idea." Until then, keep pushing your thinking and don't forget to have fun along the way.

Media Relations: Best Practices for Working With Journalists

Mary-Elisabeth Grigg
Senior Vice President
DiGennaro Communications

INTRODUCTION

Media relations can be a powerful tool for influencing, engaging, and educating the media. It is the term for activities that involve liaising directly with reporters covering a specific beat. Often, the main goal of a media relations professional is to generate positive coverage by working with reporters. By working with the media, you're in essence generating critical, third-party endorsement for your client's organization, product, or service. Communicating and working with a journalist gives your organization valuable and needed credibility that other forms of communications (say, advertising) cannot match. It's also free.

If media relations is part of your job description, you'll find that you need to engage with the press in various circumstances: launching a product, introducing them to one of your executives or even in a crisis situation.

And if you're talking to the media it's important to keep in mind the environment reporters are working under. Today's newsrooms look very different than, say, the newsrooms of years past. Reporters are under intense pressure to turn around multiple stories throughout the day. Not only are they writing for the print publication, they're also producing stories for the publication's website, blog, and other platforms. For example, writers for the *New York Times* are writing for the print issue, nytimes.com, as well as separate newsletters that go out via email.

They're harried and face intense deadlines. At the same time, they're often worried about a story breaking on Twitter, which has become an incredibly powerful platform for the media. Sometimes, it's more important to break a story on Twitter than it is to get an article out. It's often about being first and less about getting the facts right.

At the end of the day, being effective at media relations will depend on the strength of your relationships with the journalists covering your organization.

These are interesting times, for sure. But in order to be effective at media relations, it's important to keep these changes in mind and to fully appreciate the pressures reporters face. It's also critical that you understand the narrative of the company or organization you represent. As their chief spokesperson and media relations expert, you'll be called upon to articulate their vision. You'll need to represent your organization and know how to tell a story in a clear way.

THE IMPORTANCE OF BUILDING RELATIONSHIPS WITH MEDIA

Effective media relations start with establishing strong and trusting relationships with reporters covering your specific industry. A relationship built on trust will go a long way, not only in helping generate coverage of your organization, but also in some situations positively influencing potential negative coverage. Journalists are more likely to respond to media relations contacts they're familiar with and trust than those they have no prior relationship with.

But building a relationship does not happen quickly and often takes time and patience. You need to demonstrate that you understand their area of coverage and expertise and, more importantly, to show that you would be an incredibly valuable resource to them. Here are a few tips on how you can build better relationships with journalists before pitching them.

Read Everything

This might seem simple but I often remind teams of the need to read everything a particular journalist is covering. Journalists will counsel you to do the same. There is nothing more frustrating to a reporter than being pitched a story that has nothing to do with their beat. Jason Abbruzzese, a business reporter at Mashable, says, "The PR people who have taken the time to get know me, my beat, what I'm interested in and the types of sources I'm looking for always have my ear" (Wing, 2014). Not reading a reporter's work shows that you haven't done your research or taken the time to get to know them. Instead of relying on databases, such as Cision, which can often be outdated, take the time to read a reporter's coverage, follow the conversations they're having on social media platforms, such as Twitter or LinkedIn, and follow blogs and other platforms they're using to post stories.

All of this research will help you craft a relevant pitch that a reporter will find interesting because you've taken the time to research their area of expertise.

Meet Face-to-Face

While email is an important tool for engaging and communicating with journalists, you can't solely rely on this medium. While most public relations (PR) practitioners are understandably sensitive about a journalist's schedule and tight deadlines, some of the best relationships develop and grow through in-person interactions. Whether you're meeting over breakfast, coffee, or dinner, these events are a good way to get to know each other and develop a trusting relationship.

You might also want to meet with reporters face-to-face at industry conferences. Taking the time to meet in-person offers a depth and context that email and social media channels lack.

Use Social Media Wisely

Social media offers PR professionals accessibility to reporters and the opportunity to engage with them. These platforms, especially Twitter and to a certain degree LinkedIn, are used widely by journalists and it's important for PR professionals to follow journalists directly and, when appropriate, to engage with them via these social channels. Social media allows you the opportunity to stay up-to-date on journalists' interests, stories they're working on, and issues they're close to. It also gives you an opportunity to get to know them on a personal level.

When it comes to engaging with reporters on these channels, keep your engagement with press informal and genuine. You want to go beyond your professional expertise and get to know them on a personal level.

CRAFTING A STORY AND THINKING LIKE A REPORTER

The best PR practitioners think like journalists when pitching stories or crafting a client's image. Approaching a story with the same probing mindset of a reporter will ensure you are asking the right questions and exploring all potential story angles.

At the same time, thinking like a journalist forces you to ask the tough questions and prepare your spokespeople for the types of questions an actual journalist will ask during an interview. Having a "nose for news" will also help you determine whether or not a campaign or upcoming announcement is newsworthy. Before approaching a journalist, it's important that you can clearly articulate the story you're about to pitch and get a reporter on board to write the story. Knowing what makes a good story will help you craft a better story.

Thinking like a reporter is also important in helping craft press materials related to your news announcement. For example, a press release will be better written when you approach it in the same way a journalist writes an article. There should be a clear headline, lead, and quotes that actually convey an important message. Quotes should not just be space fillers but should bring to life, in a meaningful way, the story you're trying to tell.

At the end of the day, as a PR person, your job is to not only convince the reporter that you've got a good story to tell but to also help that reporter sell the story to his editor. By arming reporters with the right data, spokespeople, additional sources, and a compelling angle, you'll be making it easier for reporters to convince their editors to let them move forward with the piece.

UNDERSTANDING THE TOOLS: PRESS RELEASE VERSUS A PITCH

A press release and a pitch are very different tools used by PR professionals. While most people still view a press release as the standard for driving earned media coverage, the reality is that a lot of story ideas aren't worthy of a press release and a pitch can be more powerful in selling your idea to a reporter.

So, what's the difference? And when do we use a press release versus a pitch? A pitch is a suggested story idea that's sent to a journalist via email. You're offering the reporter a new story to cover that's relevant to their particular beat. Pitches tend to be brief and more informal; the more personalized the better. If the journalists like the idea, they'll respond with any follow-up questions and write a story based on your idea.

A press release has a set format and follows a specific style. They're written in journalistic style and typically read like a news story. In fact, it should have enough detail to be published as is. The press release lays out the story for a journalist and includes quotes from key spokespeople. In some cases, it's distributed widely across a wire service to reach multiple journalists. A benefit of a press release is they often help improve your company's Search Engine Optimization (SEO).

Both of these tools are essential to a PR function yet a pitch can often be more effective at getting your idea across quickly without having to draft a detailed press release. On the other hand, press releases are incredibly important when announcing major corporate news, such as quarterly earnings and a significant merger or acquisition.

According to PR software company, Cision, there are six simple rules to follow when it comes to using an email pitch (Dougherty, 2015).

1. The most important rule to remember is that every pitch should be personalized to the reporter you're reaching out to. The angle and idea should be unique and appeal to that particular journalist. You should never use mail merge software or mass email a group of reporters.
2. Show the reporter that you've done your research and understand the beat they cover. Clearly explain how your story idea might be relevant to that beat and why it's a story worth covering.
3. Your subject line is valuable real estate and should clearly state the intent of your pitch. Treat the subject line as if it's the headline of your story.
4. Pitches should be short, straightforward, and demonstrate why the story is important to readers.
5. Offering the reporter an exclusive on the story can be incredibly powerful in locking a story in.
6. Reporters generally don't want to open attachments so refrain from attaching images or other files unless absolutely necessary.

When it comes to press releases, you should write your releases using Associated Press (AP) style. Why? Because that's the style used by the news media. The AP has several recommendations to meet editorial standards (Kennedy, 2013). Some of these relate to the clarity of information in your press release, while others relate to formatting and punctuation.

For clarity, you should make sure the journalist understands what your press release is about in the first sentence or two of your release, and answer the five W's in the first paragraph (who, what, when, where, why). For example, if your client is hosting an event, make that clear in the introduction and then answer who is hosting the event, where and when they are hosting the event, and the purpose of the event (why) in the following sentences. If a journalist doesn't understand the point of your press release early on, or have the pertinent information on the event, they're likely to stop reading.

If you are quoting an executive or spokesperson, use the person's first and last name and title in the first mention, then use the person's last name in subsequent mentions. Capitalize the title if it comes before the name (Chief Executive Officer Sarah Brown), but lowercase the title if it follows the name (Sarah Brown, chief executive officer). AP style also does not use what is known as the Oxford comma (the last comma in a series), uses one space between sentences and spells out numbers one through nine.

These might seem like trivial details to follow but they are important when working with reporters. While very few people know that you can generate earned media coverage without a press release, it's very important that as a PR professional you understand the differences and know when to issue a press release for your announcement or to simply pitch a reporter via a simple email.

Making the Pitch

While most PR professionals rely on email to pitch reporters, sometimes a phone call to a reporter can help in pushing your story along and shape the angle of the piece. Over the phone, you can engage directly with the reporter to create a personal connection and be immediately responsive to their tone and interest level.

However, many reporters will often tell you to stick to email and avoid calling them. As a result, many of us in the PR space will hide behind a screen and avoid an actual conversation. Here's what you need to know when calling reporters to pitch them your story:

- Make sure you have a relationship with the reporter before calling them. You should have met them in person, done your research, and know their beat. If you've met them and established a relationship, you'll be more comfortable picking up the phone to talk them through your news.
- Have a good sense of their print cycle and what their deadlines might be. If Fridays is when they go to print, try to avoid calling on a Thursday night or Friday. Make the call earlier in the week.
- Be prepared to answer questions on your announcement. The reporter might have questions for you and you should be ready to address these and clarify any points they need help with. You don't want to lose their interest as you scramble. Be prepared.

Connecting with a reporter by phone may seem daunting but sometimes it can be the best way to sell in your story and determine whether or not a journalist will want to cover the news.

THE RISE OF SOCIAL MEDIA AS A PR TOOL

Social media has absolutely changed the PR disciplines in many ways. Through platforms such as Facebook, Twitter, Snapchat, and LinkedIn, PR professionals have access to a reporter's content and feeds and are able to engage with them in real time. Thanks to social media, PR professionals are able to connect with audiences by inviting conversation, interaction, and feedback. It also means that the workday doesn't end at the traditional time of 5 p.m. Reporters often break news on Twitter (in a rush to be the "first" to break a story) and if it's a story about your client or company, you'll need to be available to manage the situation, no matter what time or day it is. It's a constant news cycle.

Even with easy access to reporters because of social media, it's not common practice to pitch journalists via these platforms. According to Cision's 2015 Social Journalism Study, only "23% of journalists accept pitches via social media." While they still prefer to receive pitches via email, they view social media as a "valuable platform for communication professionals to engage and establish rapport" (Materise, 2016). According to Cision's 2016 State of the Media Report, "73% of journalists use social media to build relationships" (Materise, 2016).

Tips for Using Social Media

There are a few points you'll want to keep in mind when communicating with reporters on social channels, such as Twitter.

- *Twitter:* Twitter can be a great resource for PR professionals. Following journalists that cover your industry and monitoring for story opportunities can be a great way to jump on potential stories. Pitching on Twitter can be done but there's a right way to do it.
- *Your personal brand matters:* Reporters do look for sources they trust to help them with their stories. If you want to pitch reporters on Twitter, make sure your Twitter feed reflects authenticity and demonstrates how you can be a valuable source to them. Establish yourself as a user of the platform before targeting reporters.
- *Build a rapport:* Once you've established a profile, find the right opportunity to interact with a reporter and develop a rapport with them before pitching them. You might want to point them in the right direction for a story they might be working on and establish trust and how you can be a valuable source.
- *Brevity is key:* Once you've established a rapport and have gotten to know a reporter, you should feel comfortable sending a brief pitch by using the Direct Messaging (DM) function (if it's enabled) or via a tweet, as long as it's concise and to the point.

CONCLUSION

This is an exciting time to work with the media. The media business is evolving and so will our roles as media relations professionals. In this current environment, new tools will continue to enhance and amplify how we communicate with reporters. There are more opportunities than ever to connect with media and engage in meaningful dialogue about your company, product, or industry trends.

While these emerging platforms can be useful, it's important to remember the fundamental and basic elements of PR to be most effective in your role.

REFERENCES AND ADDITIONAL READINGS

Buzzsumo. Retrieved from http://buzzsumo.com/blog/pitch-journalist-tips-techcrunch-ny-times/

Cision USA Inc. (2017). *11 tips for pitching reporters on social media*. Cision.com. Retrieved from http://www.cision.com/us/resources/tip-sheets/11-tips-for-pitching-reporters-on-social-media/

Dougherty, J. (2015). *6 simple rules for email pitches*. Cision.com. Retrieved from http://www.cision.com/us/2015/02/6-simple-rules-for-email-pitches/

Kennedy, M. (2013). *6 AP style rules for press releases*. Ragan.com. Retrieved from https://www.ragan.com/Main/Articles/6_AP_Style_rules_for_press_releases_46803.asp/

Materise, M. (2016). *What's the state of the media in 2016?* Institute for PR.com. Retrieved from: http://www.instituteforpr.org/whats-the-state-of-the-media-in-2016/

Wing, H. (2014). *How to pitch journalists: Expert tips from Techcrunch, NYT and more.*

Social Media Marketing: Content Development Planning, Creating and Curating Content, Building a Fan Base, Social Media Analytics

Michael Stern
Senior Vice President, Global Account Director
Leo Burnett

INTRODUCTION

Social media as a marketing vehicle represents one of the single most disruptive digital transformations of the post-Internet era. Social media has changed the way brands/organizations communicate, introducing an entirely new set of channels to reach customers/consumers. It's expanded the definition of creative to include content. And, it's inspired communities of passionate fans (and detractors) to connect with one another. As a result, a brand's identity no longer solely resides with that brand/organization, let alone with its agency partners. Now, when a brand/organization speaks, consumers/customers can talk back—publicly.

What's more, we know whether someone recommended a brand/organization, what they said about it, where they said it, when they said it, and who else saw it. A recommendation is considered the single most powerful determinant of a purchasing decision (Nielsen, 2015). Today, thanks to social media, we can measurably tie these positive recommendations back to changes in attitudes about a brand/organization. And, track how an engagement on a social media channel influenced that audience to take an action. In many cases, thanks to the rapid evolution of social media, we can even track those behaviors back to sales/conversions.

The benefits of social media marketing are not only reserved for big brands and Fortune 500 companies. Smaller challenger brands, as well as nonprofits and local organizations, are using social media to gain greater efficiency and effectiveness with their marketing dollars—often far more than traditional advertising channels (Elder, 2017). The barriers for marketing on social media channels are very low. So, it's an exciting time for clients and agencies of all shapes and sizes to use them.

That said, social media marketing is still emerging from its infancy. As you consider the role social media plays within a campaign or program, there are some things to keep in mind:

1. *If you can't measure it, you can't manage it:* Though social media is a newer marketing channel, it doesn't mean this popular phase doesn't apply. In fact, quite the opposite. Introducing clients to social media marketing means quantifying the return on investment they should expect compared to more traditional

media channels. The social media industry is well aware of the need to establish its measurement credibility. Facebook, for example, has worked tirelessly to bridge the gap between "vanity metrics," like comments and shares; and business objectives, like brand affinity and purchase intent. These platforms have come under heavy scrutiny, along with the rest of the media industry, for ensuring better tracking and transparency of actual media buys (Rath, 2017). So, when measuring social media marketing, strive to go beyond basic consumer outputs in a newsfeed to instead measure actual marketing outcomes. And, once achieved, consider how those outcomes will compare to other marketing channels within the client's marketing mix.

2. *Social media is not an island:* Social media marketing doesn't happen in a vacuum. Rather, it challenges clients to articulate their brand positioning, taglines, and traditional advertising creative in ways that encourage audiences to engage with and share content. Social media influences creative content, media buys, public relations messaging, digital user experiences, and customer service interactions. In fact, many clients today are striving to create "social-first" marketing. Looking at all communications channels through the lens of social media can make their programs more authentic and relevant to the actual consumer/customer journey. In short, social media programming should parallel path all client discussions and become seamlessly integrated into all marketing activities.

3. *Welcome to perpetual beta:* Just like the weather, if you aren't happy with how a social media channel works, just wait 5 minutes because it will likely change. Ok, maybe not in 5 minutes, but often. Platforms like Facebook, Twitter, and Pinterest are constantly evolving, monetizing, and testing new offerings for brands/organizations. This includes retooling the algorithms that dictate which content appears in which users' newsfeeds as advertising inventories expand. It also effects how they balance the expectations of operating a publicly held, profitable business dependent on advertising revenue versus managing a social environment where people share photos with friends and family as part of their daily lives. And, in recognizing the personal nature of all this online sharing, platforms and the companies who advertise on them are constantly revisiting the ethics standards of engaging consumers/customers within that intimate space. All this to say, staying well informed about the changes occurring on social media platforms is essential to helping clients succeed on them. Fortunately, all of these platforms have blogs for businesses that agencies can follow. So, whether it's a subtle change to the creative specs of an ad unit, or a new technology connecting brands with fans, it's easy to stay up to date.

With this in mind, the following article tackles the dynamic world of social media through four key foundational elements: the conversation, the channels, the content, the community. It ends with a framework for measuring the efficiency and effectiveness of executing these elements. And, it also includes a section on transparency to help your team avoid any unintentional missteps.

THE CONVERSATION

According to Google, a conversation is defined as, "an informal exchange of ideas between two people by spoken word." Other than the words being "spoken," an interaction on social media is no different. Successfully engaging a target audience on social media requires a certain level of informality and a two-way dialogue. For that dialogue to work, the conversation must be relevant to both parties. Simply stated, words matter. So does the tone with which they are delivered. And, the persona that is delivering them.

Understand the Current Conversation

The first step in creating a brand's social media voice is understanding the conversation you're about to join. Most agencies subscribe to paid social listening tools, which comb publicly available online conversations. They have the ability to identify the size of a conversation, key brand/organization attributes driving it, as well as popular hashtags used by the target audience. But, what if you don't have the ability to subscribe to these paid tools? Not to worry, many free listening tools exist. Here are some examples:

- *Hootsuite:* Consider testing with a free trial to manage multiple social networks for a client, and to understand their current content and how communities are performing.
- *Twitter Search:* This advanced search functionality allows teams to do more in-depth searches and build queries on specific questions.
- *Blogtrottr:* Interested in following a specific industry or topic online? Consider setting up a series of feeds via this free tool to keep your clients and teams well informed.
- *Google Trends:* Let's not forget about search. Google Trends is a free tool that can help teams understand what was trending during a particular time of year, and the organic search terms and types of keywords used.

Create a Social Voice for the Brand

With these conversation insights in mind, it's time to take a second look at your client's positioning, company mission, or simply its core values as they relate to recent marketing programs. The client's social media voice comes from aligning actual conversation insights with how the brand/organization talks about itself. And, that voice includes a persona, tone, and words. To help create a social voice, ask yourself the following questions after learning more about the client's business and understanding how consumers talk about it:

- *The persona:* Why does the brand/organization have permission to talk to its target audience online? For example, it's something consumers already talk about, or it's present during a specific season or time of year in their newsfeeds already. And, it delivers value in the form of critical information, or cost savings, or simply entertainment.

- *The tone:* If the brand were a person, what endearing qualities would describe it and how would it manifest itself as an individual? For example, characteristics might include witty, intelligent, trust-worthy, or savvy.
- *The words:* How, ideally, would the target audience truly talk about or recommend the brand/organization in their own social media newsfeeds? For example, they may not use the same "corporate jargon," but they do reference similar claims or benefits.

With the answers to those questions informed by real conversations, a summary can be provided to clients and other internal stakeholders for alignment. That summary can inform everything from creative content copy to community moderation. And, it can help the brand/organization deliver a consistent and compelling voice for anything that appears on the client's social media channels. So, how would you describe YOUR client's social media voice?

CHANNELS

According to Pew Research, approximately "seven-in-ten Americans use social media to connect with one another, engage news content, share information, and entertain themselves" (Pew Research, 2017). This stat shows no sign of declining, with 80% of people logging onto Facebook daily, followed by Instagram, Twitter, Pinterest, and LinkedIn.

As a marketer and agency partner, it's important to understand how these platforms can add value to a client's brand/organization. And, which ones to use when. Below is a quick reference summary of today's most popular social media channels, their strengths and an abridged summary of best practices for using them. Additional best practices and case studies can be found on these platforms directly. For example, Twitter offers Twitter Business as does Pinterest with P business. They also offer insights and training programs, such as Facebook IQ and Facebook Blueprint.

Facebook

With a large community of actively engaged users, Facebook allows us a direct connection as well as broad reach. Best practices include

- *Keep a constant cadence:* Use Facebook Ad options to expand your reach, but supplement with organic posts during campaigns to help keep the page alive and interesting for the audience.
- *Be mindful of your text:* Text-only posts aren't engaging. Too much text is overwhelming and ends up being ignored. Text in images can decrease promotional reach and conflicts with Facebook's 20% Rule for promoted copy, which states that no more than 20% of an image promoted on the platform can include text.
- *Video, video, video:* Facebook favors video above all else. Live, Vertical, 360°. Video is now available in cover photos. GIFs are now available in comments. Audiences have come to expect video as a standard.

Instagram

Instagram has an active community that enjoys creative photo and video content, as well as sharing user generated content (UGC). Best practices for using Instagram include

- *See the big picture:* Instagram's focus is on the visuals; design with a visual-first priority, with assets that are tailored to Instagram's strengths and specifications.
- *Be playful and creative:* Boomerangs, Hyperlapse, and Instagram Stories are all tools available on Instagram that people love to see and use. Engage with the latest trends and have fun with your client's target audience.
- *Hashtag it:* Hashtags let brands/organizations join larger conversations and be searched/found organically. Find and vet relevant hashtags and add them to copy. Place additional hashtags in the comment drawer.

Twitter

An open communication tool, Twitter allows for real-time engagement and direct customer service. Best practices include

- *Solve the problems:* Twitter's real-time feel makes it a perfect customer service tool, allowing for quick, speedy service. Solving concerns in public also shows the world how a brand/organization values its customers, and direct messages are great to keep private info private.
- *Catch the eye:* As with all social platforms, the goal is to be eye-catching and thumb-stopping. Include images, videos, and gifs, and design them for Twitter's unique feed.
- *Be real, and be quick:* The Twittersphere moves pretty quickly. According to Twitter, more than one billion tweets are shared every 3 days. Answering tweets and direct messages as quickly as possible helps a brand/organization catch the moment, show audiences it cares, and avoid any potential detractor issues.

Pinterest

Pinterest allows for collection of products, tips, and images, as well as in-app shopping. Best practices include

- *Pin, pin, pin:* Pin new content often to feed the insatiable hunger, and get creative with images and video to attract attention.
- *Curate boards:* Tell a larger story with a brand/organization's boards to further engage Pinners.
- *Let them shop:* Include Buyable Pins and promote content to get your client's product/service in front of Pinners' eyes.

SnapChat

Exceptionally popular among Millennials and Generation Z, Snapchat is a video and photo-sharing app that uses augmented reality filters and lenses to enhance photos. The Discover section allows for snackable content, with a focus on fun, informative videos. Best practices include

- *Consider the context:* Think of the user's mindset. When, how, and where will they engage—and why? Remember, Snapchat users don't just watch ads—they *play* with them.
- *Keep it simple:* Ten seconds is all a Snap needs. Keep away from clutter. Snapchat's audience is used to fast, easy-to-consume content, and they expect a seamless experience between friend posts and branded content.
- *Design for success:* Design for full-screen, vertical video, as all Snap Ads play in this format. Design for sound on, and get the brand/organization in the first 2 seconds. Remember the popularity of Filters, Lenses, and key phrases in the image, like "Mondays Got Me Like" or "OMG."

YouTube

YouTube is a video-centric platform heavily used by Millennials, as well as an excellent SEO tool. Best practices include

- *Playlists keep them hooked:* Place like-content into Playlists for easy viewing. Tell a story with the Playlist and keep the audiences engaged. They'll remember the brand/organization, and come back for more.
- *Don't sweat the comments:* The comment section on YouTube can be an ugly place, and anonymity options allow detractors to flourish. Monitor comments and reply when necessary, but don't worry if you see spam comments.
- *Don't ignore the power of SEO:* YouTube isn't just a place to watch videos—it's also a place where people come to learn. "How To" searches are popular on the platform, and using search engine optimization tags to get videos into those topic searches can help increase views/subscribers.

CONTENT

With the addition of new social media channels comes the need for more content to satisfy them. When building a social media content plan, it's important to think about it from two perspectives: First, where it comes from? And, second, how it will get used?

Unlike other creative elements of a marketing campaign where all content comes from the brand, social media content can come from influencers, partners, or even real consumers who are talking about and sharing user-generated content via their own channels and handles. All are important and serve different purposes:

- *Brand/organization:* From the client or agency, and designed to establish what that brand/organization stands for. For example, to introduce a new product or service.
- *Influencer/partner:* Developed in conjunction with a key thought leader or a media partner on behalf of the client. For example, an industry expert whose disclosure relationship with the organization would serve as a winning endorsement.
- *User generated:* This comes from fans. Consumer/customers who already know, try, or love the product or service. They actively share it on their channels, which the brand/organization can listen for, and ask for permission to use.

In terms of when all this content gets used, there are some different circumstances and considerations. Below are some examples:

- *Campaign:* Content activations for key sales, sponsorship, media, marketing, or fundraising launches or activations.
- *Evergreen:* An "always on," steady drumbeat of preloaded content designed to sustain engagement or conversations on social channels.
- *Real time:* Anticipated or unexpected trends, seasonal moments, or news-inspired content published at the most opportune time, typically inspired by actual consumer/customer conversations.

By understanding where content for a social media program can come from and how it should be used, the social media team can begin to map out activities into a content calendar, and align them with the larger marketing calendar.

A content calendar maps out the types of content you will place, when, and on which channels. Like a regular calendar, it should include important client activities (products launches, fundraising events, promotional specials), as well as common holidays and even fun dates like World Compliment Day or Take Your Dog to Work Week, as they relate to your client's brand and target audience. You and your creative team can then develop and approve content ahead of time (like videos and graphic memes) rather than scrambling at the last minute. It also helps you pulse evergreen content so there are no big gaps in communication. Be flexible with your calendar to allow for real-time content, as described above, and keep an eye on the media for breaking news. For example, if a big snowstorm shuts down flights across the country, that wouldn't be a good time for an airline to post a 2-for-1 special on Twitter.

You can search online for free content calendar templates. Calendars can be scheduled by the month, the season, or for an entire campaign. You can also load content into platform management systems like Hootsuite so content is posted automatically at the correct day and time. Lastly, content calendars make it easier to track which posts are performing well so you can include more of that content in the future.

COMMUNITY

While there are a number of channels to consider and a variety of solutions for content creation, not to mention a myriad of paid media offerings, social media is still ultimately about having a conversation with your consumers/customers. Community moderation isn't only about reacting to questions and customer service requests; it's about engaging your target audience. However, to do this effectively, it's important to have clear protocols and procedures in place to manage the dialogue. Outlining a community management playbook can help to ensure a consistent and compelling conversation. Some elements of that playbook could include the social media voice, channel roles and rationales, proactive engagement topics/opportunities, brand/organization statements/claims, sample responses, and an escalation protocol.

In terms of escalation protocols, the following definitions serve as a helpful framework for the different types of conversations that might occur:

- *No risk:* Comment is not threatening to the brand; most likely coming from a loyal fan or product user. Community moderator should reply.
- *Low risk:* Comment is neutral in nature; no client input required; can be answered with preapproved responses. Community moderator should reply.
- *Medium risk:* Client notification or input required; legal team informed. Do not reply without alignment with client.
- *High risk:* Client notification required, as well as corporate communications, customer service, and regulatory/legal team. Do not reply.

The last thing to keep in mind is that haters are gonna hate. Social media allows an organization's biggest fans, and also its angriest detractors, to openly (and in some cases anonymously) share their opinions. The range of sentiment and the need for acting upon it varies by individual and situation. Unfortunately, an unhappy consumer/customer regardless of how rational or valid their opinion has equal freedom to voice their point of view. Like Winston Churchill once said, "Never let a good crisis go to waste." In other words, sometimes helping an unsatisfied consumer/customer can pay dividends for a brand/organization. Where it gets complicated is that some of these detractors—often referred to as "trolls"—are here to do one thing: hurt your client's brand or organization for the sole purpose of watching them, and their agencies, squirm. Whether we like it or not, these haters are going to hate, but how the agency handles the situation can earn the respect of both your client and their social media fans. Make sure you have a protocol in place.

MEASURING SOCIAL MEDIA

As social media platforms began to monetize their channels through the sale of advertising, what quickly followed was the need to provide advertisers with ways to measure their performance. Comments, likes, and shares, which were indicative of consumers/customers engaging with or enjoying content were no longer enough. Today, social media channels are able to go beyond those basic outputs to provide desirable marketing outcomes.

That said, there are many to consider. The following framework attempts to organize them into activities, attitudes, and actions. Activities are the metrics that help a brand assess audience engagement, such as liking or sharing a piece of content. Attitudinal and action oriented metrics help brands go deeper. For example, incorporating a Nielson brand effects study to survey actual changes in perception following exposure to a social media campaign. Or, matching social media fan data with actual purchasing data from retailers to understand whether or not someone exposed to a campaign actually bought something.

Activities (Outputs)	Attitudes (Outcomes)	Actions (Outcomes)
• Clicks • Impressions generated • Engagements created • Content shared • Conversations earned • Open rates/database growth	• Aided and unaided awareness • Consideration • Brand preference • Purchase intent • Likelihood to recommend	• Redemptions • Leads • Conversions • Traffic to brand website • Customer service solutions • Sales
Measuring activities	Measuring attitudes	Measuring actions
• Native platforms • Third-party analytics tools • Customized dashboards	• Social data into brand survey work • Larger scale MMM • Custom social surveys • Advanced social listening (pre/post)	• Tracking URLs • Embedded pixels • Social coupon redemptions • Sales impact studies • Paid efficiency measures

These measures should be discussed at the beginning of developing any social media programming, and confirmed with all parties. Then, as programs are developed and executed, it's important to revisit how they are tying back to these activities, attitudes, and actions.

TRANSPARENCY AND DISCLOSURES

Since agencies are often given the responsibility of managing clients' social media channels and engaging consumers/customers on their behalf, it's important that teams exercise complete transparency when delivering a branded marketing message and fully disclose their relationship with the brand/organization or the relationship of someone talking on behalf of that company.

Fortunately, organizations like the Word of Mouth Marketing Association (WOMMA) have developed a full Code of Ethics to help all marketing agencies and the companies they work with comply. They define "transparency" as the practice of ensuring that the audience knows the identity of the speaker and the existence of any "material connection" between the speaker and the brand or company the speaker is talking about, as well as any important limitations or restrictions on an offer. They also developed a WOMMA Social Media Disclosure Guidelines (March 2017) to help navigate the nuances of these active, real-time digital channels.

CONCLUSION

One last thing to remember is that unlike any other marketing channel, many of us are native, daily users of social media. Sure, we all watch television, but few of us also produce the commercials, right? However, anyone using social media today is now a social listener, a channel manager, a content creator, and a community moderator. Like the clients we service, we too have a story to tell. We have a unique voice, a personal brand, and our very own fans.

That said, make no mistake that social media marketing is a discipline. It has industry best practices, creative specs, and guidelines. It also has important disclosures and legalities. And, it is the first and last line of defense between a client and its consumer/customer. The strongest social media programming balances two realities. First, continuing to view a client's social media experience through the lens of a real consumer/customer—you. Second, creating a marketing experience within the guidelines and guardrails of what will deliver real business results. I hope that this article has provided a helpful framework for bringing both perspectives together. Good luck!

REFERENCES AND ADDITIONAL READINGS

Elder, R. (2017, January 3). Digital ad spend continues to climb. *Business Insider*. Retrieved from http://www.businessinsider.com/ad-spend-continues-its-climb-2017-1

Nielsen. (2015, September 28). Recommendations from friends remain the most credible form of advertising among consumers. *The Nielsen Global Survey of Trust in Advertising*. Retrieved from http://www.nielsen.com/us/en/press-room/2015/recommendations-from-friends-remain-most-credible-form-of-advertising.html

Pew Research. (2017). *Social media fact sheet*. Pew Research Center, Internet & Technology. Retrieved from http://www.pewinternet.org/fact-sheet/social-media/

Rath, J. (2017). 90% of advertisers are reviewing their programmatic ad contracts as they look for more transparency. *Business Insider*. Retrieved from http://www.businessinsider.com/90-percent-of-advertisers-are-reviewing-their-programmatic-ad-contracts-transparency-wfa-2017-1

Spending Other People's Money: Media Planning and Placement

Theresa Chang
Senior Partner, Group Director
Mediacom

INTRODUCTION

Welcome to the world of Media Planning and Placement. Twenty-five years ago, media was primarily TV, magazines, newspaper, and radio. Today is an exciting time for our industry as technology is changing the media landscape—every day. TV isn't just a box in the living room, but any screen you have at your fingertips and you can find a "channel" for anything you want to see. We have virtual and augmented reality giving us experiences, drones delivering Amazon packages and pizza, refrigerators telling us when we're out of milk, and we have Alexa. She knows everything. And learns more about us every time we interact with her.

The job of Media Planning and Placement today is to know about people. What do they read, see, and hear? How are they taking in information? When, where, and why? You get the picture. By knowing what motivates people's media choices, the better we can offer a message when they are most open to that specific message. This idea can be summed-up by the old adage—Right Place. Right Time. (and now) Right Message.

GETTING STARTED

The actual media plan is one element of the bigger planning process. The process is summarized in the following five steps:

1. Define and quantify the goal
2. Gather research to gain insights
3. Develop the media plan
    a. Defining the media objective
    b. Selecting media tactics
    c. Establishing a budget
    d. Developing a fair price
    e. Calculating how much a plan costs
4. Track performance and optimize
5. Post final results

Step 1—Define and Quantify the Goal

Talk with your client to *define the business goal*. What needs to happen at the end of the advertising campaign so that he or she will be "happy" and consider the campaign successful? Make sure the *goal is quantified*. Business goals are primarily measured by sales—after all, people are in business to make money. As an example, let's say your client is the owner of 10 local McDonald's franchises. In this case, business goals would generally be defined as one of the following:

- *Retention:* Maintain sales by getting current customers to keep coming.
- *Acquisition:* Increase sales by getting people who previously did NOT eat fast-food burgers to eat them, and eat them at McDonald's.
- *Switch:* Increase sales by getting Burger King customers to go to McDonald's instead.
- *Increase current usage:* Get people who eat lunch at McDonald's to also eat breakfast there.
- *Increase market share:* Get people who go to Burger King, Wendy's, and McDonald's to go to McDonald's more often (and Burger King and Wendy's less).

Why does defining a goal matter? Defining business goals impacts your programming in the following ways:

- *What* you say in the message: If you want to get someone to consider going to McDonald's who had not gone to fast-food restaurants before, you may want your message to talk to them about "fresh and healthy" options.
- *When* you place a message: If you want someone to eat breakfast at McDonald's, you may want to have more messages in the morning.
- *Where* you place a message: If you want to get a Burger King person to switch and go to McDonald's, you may place your message near Burger King locations.

Once you have identified your business goals, you'll then want to quantify the goals. Goals are generally quantified as percent growth versus current year. So, whether the business goal is to grow sales by retention, acquisition, switch, or increase current usage or share, be sure the growth is quantified. Why does quantifying a goal matter?

- *How much you spend:* The more aggressive the goal, the more money will generally be spent.
- *Know you met the goal:* Growing 0.1% and 10.0% are both "growing." Which one is the goal?
- *What you say:* A more aggressive growth goal may need an incentive, such as a coupon.

Step 2—Gather Research to Gain Insights

The best plans are built based on data-driven insights, which come from input and knowledge from a team. Collaboration is key as there is strength in numbers. The job of the Media Planner is to take all the information from the specialists and form a story about how the different pieces work together to deliver the client's business goal.

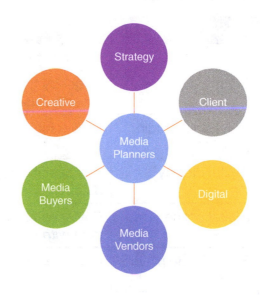

As depicted in this chart, each area contributes information to the media plan in the following ways:

- *Strategy:* Translates data into insights about the consumer that informs who the target is, and how it is best to make an effective connection.
- *Clients:* Provide significant data on their current customers, competitors and category to understand opportunities.
- *Digital:* Provides channels to laser-target consumers via the newest technology.
- *Media vendors:* Connects messaging to people in ever-changing ways—know their offerings.
- *Media buyers:* Specialists in various fields who negotiate the buy – and there's always room to negotiate.
- *Creative:* Media and Creative must work hand-in-hand (if Facebook is part of the plan, make sure the creative team is creating a social post).

Step 3—Develop the Media Plan

Once you have the business goal defined and quantified, and understand the category and competitive landscape to know where the opportunity for growth is, you are ready to put the plan together.

Defining the Media Objective

One of the first steps in developing a media plan is to define your media objective. A media objective is what the plan needs to deliver, which is based on the business goal. If the business goal, for example, is to increase sales by 2% by getting Burger King customers to switch to McDonald's, then the media objective may be: Intercept Burger King consumers throughout the day with an incentive to switch.

General Pros and Cons of Various Media

Media	Pros	Cons
TV	Reaches the masses, quickly	Can be expensive to buy
Print	Target by type of content (Sports, Fashion, Health, etc.)	Lag time to reach full audience potential
(Terrestrial) Radio (AM/FM)	Deliver high frequency of ads	No visual image
Digital display	Buy specific targets based on data	Highly cluttered
Digital online video	Buy specific targets based on data *with video*	Highly cluttered
Full episode players (FEPs)	Broad reach	No targeting
Social	Integrate in everyday conversations	Highly cluttered
Search	Reaches those who are actively seeking information	Competing every day to win top placement, at the lowest cost
Outdoor	Locally targeted	Limited scale
Direct response TV	Low cost	DRTV regulations (800#, website)
Email	Highly targeted	Low response

Mobile is the way to go. When was the last time you left home without your phone? Or were even out of reach for more than a minute? It's probably been a while. Media plans must include and even skew mobile, whether display, online video (OLV), social, or search. And more importantly, creative must be built with mobile first in mind. Meaning, create the ad so it "works" on a 3-inch screen.

Potential Media Tactics

Based on your business goal and media objective, your media plan will include potential media tactics. Back to our example, if the business goal is SWITCH, and the media objective is to intercept Burger King users throughout the day, the media plan needs to be able to target competitive users. Potential tactics, for example:

- Local media, such as *billboards* in close proximity to Burger King locations, would be relevant to meet this business goal and media objective. Reaching people who are near Burger King, and exposing them to McDonald's, perhaps with a special for the month, may entice them to try McDonald's instead.

- *Local radio* should also be considered as radio provides high frequency, and consumers may need to be told multiple times why switching to McDonald's is for them.
- *Mobile ads* (display and/or video)—there are digital media partners who have the technology to target consumers based on location. Mobile in this case would be most beneficial so you can target consumers who are within a two mile radius of a Burger King and McDonald's and serve them a $2 coupon at McDonald's, or a free hamburger offer with any sandwich purchase.
- *Search* should also play a role—especially for people looking for "burgers" near them. Or people who are searching for "Burger King" are served a McDonald's ad with a coupon to incent them to switch

Establishing a Budget

In a perfect world, all companies (and people for that matter) would have a money tree in the backyard that grows $20 bills. In the real world, however, we all need to make choices. Buy an outfit for your new job, or buy a Mother's Day gift? Both important purchases, but fulfilling different goals. Same with your media plan.

The degree to which you can activate multiple tactics will depend on your budget, and you will have to choose which tactics to employ, and how much to spend within each. How do you know how much is the right amount to be successful? There's good news and bad news. Bad news first—there's no magic formula to KNOW what the right amount is. Good news—there's plenty of information for you to come up with a strong recommendation. The key is "KNOW YOUR GOAL." And as you track your progress (next section), you can, and should, adjust your tactics to optimize to what is "working" best. Essentially, your media plan is a "living document," that pivots based on results.

There are three general ways to establish a budget:

1. *Advertising-to-Sales Ratio (A:S ratio)*
   This is a calculation based on the client's projected sales, and most companies have an established ratio. For example, if the client has projected $10 million sales, and the ratio is 1:10 (or 10%), then the advertising budget is $1 million.
2. *Competitive Landscape*
   This approach establishes a budget based on what the competition is spending—historical and recent trends. This can be obtained through services that have to be purchased, such as Kantar. Other sources, although less reliable, are the vendors (sales community) or trade materials (e.g., *Ad Age*).
3. *Zero-Based Budgeting*
   In this case, the client asks "what does it take for the media plan to be successful?" It is up to you to provide the budget. While this is the most tantalizing of the budgeting options, it is also the most pressure packed. Why? Because you need to balance what can the business tolerate (you don't want to spend more than sales can take in) with being aggressive enough to be competitive. If you are asked to

provide a zero-based budget, I suggest you start with calculating the A:S ratio and ask yourself, does this seem realistic?

- Up to 5% is reasonable (generally)
- 6% to 10% is aggressive
- 11% to 20% is very aggressive
- Over 21% is likely not viable

Negotiating a Fair Price for What You Want to Buy

When you open negotiations, vendors will generally start with "rate-card" costs. These are initial offerings. The price you are able to negotiate will be influenced by

- *Market demand:* the more people want, the less willing vendors will be to reduce costs.
- *Volume:* the more you want to buy, the more willing vendors are to do "bulk" deals.
- *History:* the longer you have stayed with the vendor, the more willing vendors will be to reward relationships.

Remember, three important truths when negotiating:

1. *Everyone is in business to make money:* You are working to get the very best deal for your clients, but understand the vendor also has bills to pay, and needs to make money as well.
2. *You get what you pay for:* Everyone wants to pay rock-bottom prices. Be sure you ask what the trade-offs are for the lower costs.
3. *Your negotiating power is commensurate with your willingness to walk away:* If you aren't willing (or able) to walk away from a vendor, be prepared to pay (up to) the asking price.

How to know if you're paying a "fair" price for each tactic? Again, sadly, there's no magic formula. But, the good news is you have plenty of information to guide your negotiations:

- *Compare versus rate card:* If I'm buying large volume, for example, a 6-month radio schedule, I'll start with 50% off rate-card.
- *Ask your colleagues:* Vendors will not share what other clients are paying, but your colleagues will.
- *Look at your results:* This is a more advanced analysis done "postcampaign" and likely involves a third party to do the analysis. There is a type of research study called market mix analysis, which quantifies how much each element of the marketing mix is contributing to overall sales. Essentially, it tells you what is working the hardest at driving volume and profit—your return-on-investment (ROI). From this analysis, you can compare how much you are paying for the media, and what is gained from that expenditure.

You are spending your clients' money. Treat it as if it were your own.

Calculating the Cost of a Media Plan

Each media type is bought on a different "cost per" currency:

- *TV:* Rating point (gross rating points [GRPs])
- *Print:* Page (or fraction of a page)
- *Digital banners:* Viewable impressions
- *Online video:* Completed views
- *Social:* Impressions/post
- *Radio:* Rating point
- *Outdoor billboards:* Showing

What Tactics Should You Buy?

To understand the "optimal" level, or how much you need to buy, you'll again need to look at what is your goal. Let's return to our example from earlier, getting Burger King eaters to switch to McDonald's.

First, let's agree getting someone to switch is not an easy task—after all, they have a favorite place for a reason. So getting someone to *consider* switching will require talking to them a fair number of times—meaning, we would want them to see our ad in multiple places and multiple times—this is called "high frequency."

Second, because they already favor Burger King (in this example), they will need to be convinced why they should try McDonald's. They may be more likely to give it a try if someone they trusted said, "I used to eat Burger King, but now I like McDonald's because . . ."

Third, to even get you to think about trying something different, there likely would have to be something NEW to entice you. And if McDonald's were introducing something NEW—they would want to tell everyone about it—really quickly.
Remember the key Pros and Cons of Media chart? See how they could apply to the above:

- *High frequency:* Radio and OOH
- *Trusted source:* Social
- *News/immediacy:* TV

Step 4—Track Your Progress—Optimize

Tracking your progress during the campaign helps you know what is working and what is not working. Then you can "optimize"—or put more money and resources into what is working to increase your media impact. Again, if we return to the McDonald's example, where I'm looking to grow sales through getting people to switch, let's say I'm finding more people are coming in at lunch, but business has not grown at breakfast. I may "optimize" the media plan to shift to more placements in the late morning (just before lunch) and during lunch hour—seeing that has been where I've seen more growth.

You can also "optimize" creative. Remember in our mobile plan we had two offers—a free hamburger, or a $2 off coupon. If we see more people are coming in with the "Free" coupon, optimize to only have that ad running. Growth should now be boosted as the plan has been optimized for placement (time of day) and message (Free).

Given this example is McDonald's, which serves customers every day, performance should be tracked on a more frequent basis—perhaps daily, or at least weekly.

Step 5—Take a Look Back—Final Results

At the end of the program, it's important to provide clients a performance review. Recap what it is you set out to do. What were the media tactics selected and why? And, of course, what were the results? From you, the media planner, you provide what the media plan delivered. How many competitive consumers did you reach? How many coupons were downloaded (if online)? And the clients will provide if sales increased, and if so, but how much.

CONCLUSION

The learning from this media plan should become part of the "Gather Research to Gain Insight" step for the subsequent year. Every year feeds into the next. Furthermore, with the client's permission, the learning should also become a case study to expand your business relationship, perhaps to surrounding franchise owners.

Key Take-Aways:

1. Define and quantify your goal; otherwise, you won't know if you achieved it or not
2. Media is ever-changing, so be a student of the industry
3. Your team is your greatest asset—be collaborative

A Comprehensive Introduction to Experiential Marketing

Shelby Roehre
Industry Consultant and Production Manager

WHAT IS EXPERIENTIAL MARKETING?

One of the more interesting parts of running your agency can be planning and executing promotional events. One type of event management, experiential marketing (EM), is a growing strategy among many brands. EM creates a unique, face-to-face branded experience, presenting a product or service in a unique and tangible way. Differing from traditional event management, EM creates a deeper emotional response from consumers and produces positive, long-term results for your client.

EM campaigns often involve the creation of a physical structure or footprint. This area is where consumers interact with the brand to create positive experiences. In addition to the physical component, more mainstream marketing strategies and tactics like print and digital support are often included in an EM campaign.

When to Use EM

Applications of EM are often appropriate when brands and/or retailers wish to

- Create/raise awareness of their product or service
- Increase consumer relations
- Generate sales
- Increase positive word of mouth
- Build relationships
- Establish relevance
- Create product or brand desire
- Increase return on marketing investments

Some select brands currently using EM include DICK'S Sporting Goods, Puma, Google, and General Electric.

EM also offers a unique differentiator that can be valuable. Quite simply, the saturation and fragmentation of conventional marketing and media channels have numbed consumers and reduced effectiveness of traditional marketing and advertising. Consumers are becoming immune to typical advertising. EM helps to refocus the consumer on the brand's presence and message. Each campaign is designed specifically to achieve the client's goals in ways that differentiate them from their competitors. An EM opportunity that doesn't force them, but engages with consumers on a personal level, carries more overall impact.

What are some EM opportunities?

Some specific EM applications can include grand openings, e-launches, community partnerships, and interactive advertising campaigns. Some of these types of campaigns include "Sports Matter" by DICK'S Sporting Goods, which utilizes community partnerships and provides charitable sponsorships for youth sports nationwide, and Google's "Building a Better Bay Area," an interactive advertising campaign for Google's corporate philanthropy that raised awareness and positive word of mouth with consumers. Other notable EM campaigns you can review include GE's "Healthymagination," Zappo's "Google Cupcake Ambush," and Adidas' "Jump With Derrick Rose."

HOW TO DEVELOP SUCCESSFUL EM IDEAS AND CAMPAIGNS

To create a successful campaign, one must understand the client's target market and desired goals. To be effective, you must conceptualize a memorable, attention grabbing campaign that addresses the client's wants and desires. You will be creating a unique, tangible experience to engage consumers and create a positive relationship between them and the brand/product. So, you'll want to meet with the client to identify well-defined goals and objectives. Here are a few questions I use with clients:

1. Which customers do you want to target?
2. What is the best method of interacting with these customers?
3. What is the best location and environment?
4. What type of return do you expect from this campaign/event?
5. How will the events integrate into other marketing programs?

Once you have established concrete goals, you are ready to begin the creative process and develop your campaign. After some brainstorming and concept development, you may be ready to establish your campaign strategy. Once this is developed, your next most important tool is your campaign workbook, which includes a running budget, production schedules, approved graphics and creative, your vendors, event renderings, and everything that the process of your campaign needs to be successful.

Constant updating of your workbook and clear communication with all parties involved are key components to running a successful campaign. Communication will be a very intricate part of this process. You should be in constant communication with the creative department for unique and brand encompassing graphics. And, you will need to stay in contact with your clients to create a relationship that allows for open dialogue.

A LOOK INTO A SUCCESSFULLY EXECUTED EM CAMPAIGN

I recently managed a large EM campaign for DICK'S Sporting Goods. This project was for the annual Hood to Coast Race that begins in Mt. Hood, Oregon and ends in Seaside, Oregon. The 199-mile race happens over 3 days and brings in over 40,000 people annually. Teams of 12 runners have to enter a bid to even be considered for a racing spot. Because the race is known worldwide, DICK'S decided to create a community partnership with Hood to Coast and become one of the race's main sponsors. Other race sponsors included Mazda, Nike, Adidas, and GNC.

During the first meeting, the clients provided a semiflexible budget of $200,000 and requested we create three different activations throughout the racecourse that would raise brand awareness, increase customer loyalty, bring an influx of consumers into regional stores, and inevitably, increase sales. In addition to the three large activations, DICK'S also wanted three to four smaller activations at official race stops, and to develop official signage and advertisements throughout the entire 199-mile course.

The Proposal

After determining the client's objectives, we requested a week's time to conceptualize a program deck and finalize our budget. Remember, always give yourself and your agency a reasonable and realistic time frame so you can create a client-worthy deck. The deck represents your agency and your abilities. Done properly with all necessary parts explained in detail, you create the opportunity for budget negotiations. The plan is also important because a program of this caliber with international reach must be done correctly and properly.

Specifically, our proposal included a unique, location-specific event for each activation. At the 20' × 40' footprint at the Mt. Hood race starting point, we provided areas for consumers to get kinesiology tape and race-related promotional items, take photos, and meet the DICK'S Sporting Goods Sasquatch. At the second large activation, we proposed a 100' × 160' "tent city" with over 300 rest tents for race participants. The site would be covered in DICK'S Sporting Good signage and all participants had to do was sign in and provide us their email. Our third large activation was at the race finish line, where we would have multiple activations in a 20' × 20' × 60' footprint size. The finish line activations would provide personal trainers, foam rolling for race recovery, branded promotional items, photo opportunities, and more. For smaller activations along the course, we proposed free kt taping tents, free WIFI tents, water and rehabilitation tents, and promotional item giveaways.

Our proposal went into specific detail about all aspects of the plan and created 3D renderings of the proposed activations. After explaining the parameters of each activation, we included a forecasted return-on-investment (ROI) page and an increased return on social media and advertising page to show the client how we would reach and surpass their goals. By adding all of these important components and defining the scope of work, we objectively budgeted the full event cost.

Depending on your agency, you will either be working on retainer or your company will have a set upcharge percentage that adequately compensates for the agency's time, production, and other expenses incurred thorough managing of the event.

Planning and budgeting are by far the most important part of the initial process. Items to finalize include campaign/event activations, details, timelines, and budgets.

Preparation and Production

For this event specifically, we were given 2 months for preparation, which in industry standards is almost impossible. Events of this magnitude usually demand 3 to 4 months of preparation before the "live" event date. But, our program workbook, client approved deck, relationship with the client, and hard work allowed us to create and run a highly successful event on time and within budget.

During the first month of production, we established relationships with the Hood to Coast committee, scheduled reliable vendors, began the creative process for brand graphics, finalized activation footprints and renderings, secured hotel and travel for parties attending the event, and reserved all needed materials and items needed for our activations. Since the Hood to Coast race is located in Oregon, and our agency is located in Dallas, we also had to establish an economical way of transporting the activation assets we were sending from our warehouse. Items like transport, insurance, loading dock access, secured storage, and other items were also sourced locally. Our budget incorporated these costs and gave us contingency funding for any unforeseen items as well.

The second month of production is when all event assets were shipped in-market and accounted for. We also needed to complete inspections, in-house set-up, packing and shipping, and finalize production of approved graphics, signage, and promotional giveaways. Finally, we set and trained the event staff. For this event, we needed one Production Director, two Field Managers, and 20 Brand Ambassadors. We also contracted eight Brand Ambassador back-ups. Finally, we also paid part of our negotiated contracts to our vendors to secure our market rentals, reserved hotel blocks, acquired rental cars, and other necessary components needed for the event.

An important aspect of planning your EM campaign is quality control. When planning support materials, you should arrange to receive all printed materials 2 to 3 weeks before the "live" event to ensure there are no grammatical errors or issues with your creative presentations. Your creative is a representation of your client and what the majority of consumers will see first. It should stimulate positive word of mouth and market reach; if it doesn't, it could be a public relations (PR) nightmare and humiliate your client.

Similarly, it is important to integrate promotional items within your production so you can successfully increase awareness, achieve positive word of mouth, generate consumer curiosity, and spur demand. These items should be ordered, approved, and ready to be placed on site with plenty of time.

The final week before our events went live was one of the most important weeks of our campaign. About 1 week before the event, all our production and project crews arrived in market to set up activation footprints. At this time, all event assets were accounted for, all structures were built to their renderings, and all footprints were set-up and finalized.

Going Live

Finally after the months of preparations, production, meetings, and planning, our event went live. For 3 days straight the Account Manager and I managed multiple activation locations that were sometimes live simultaneously. In addition to managing the physical activations, we oversaw all necessary vendors for last minute footprint build-outs, and finalized footprint teardowns that were to be done within 12 hours after the event closed. All the while we were checking in with our working field managers and staff to maintain a pristine footprint, sustain customer satisfaction, and receive important metrics for our recaps. We were also available 24/7 for client hospitality and ensured the hotel rooms, meals, and clients were happy and taken care of. Besides the multiple physical activation spots we created and built for this event, we also provided all aspects of hospitality for our clients; we managed their hotel reservations, flights, team buses, meals, snacks, entertainment, and everything they could possibly need before and during the event.

After each day of the "live" event activations, we developed a client recap and incorporated the all-important return metrics. These metrics included social media impressions, photographs taken with branded photo opps, the number of participants kt taped, the number of promotional items given away, the estimated foot traffic at each live activation, and the number of participants who saw our personal trainers and used our foam rollers. The recap also included high quality photos showing the activation sites live and populated with race participants.

These metrics need to be clearly mentioned in short recap summaries to the client with supporting photos of each activation. The recaps should be done after each "live" event day in order to properly record the return and present the results and successes of to your client. Our client used these recaps later to show their success and increase store growth on the West Coast.

At the end of the third and final day, we wrapped up our event. It was clear that DICK'S Sporting Goods had the most brand presence throughout the entire event. Our signage could be seen at every race stop and over 25,000 participants had interacted with one or more of our physical footprints. In addition to surpassing over 1 million impressions through social media channels, we received hundreds of compliments for our activations from race participants. Our clients were extremely verbal about the success of the event and personally thanked us for our work. As a result of our success, we were offered the 2017 Hood to Coast sponsorship contract from DICK'S Sporting Goods.

Each day during the event we worked well over 16 hours and went off of little sleep to ensure our events ran smoothly, that our clients were happy, and that all specified goals were being met. Even with a few unforeseen costs due to damages and additional assets needed, we were still able to come in under budget. To this date, the 2016 Hood to the Coast effort was one of my most exhausting but rewarding events—fun and strenuous but also extremely successful and profitable.

RESULTS AND HOW TO MEASURE SUCCESS

Within EM, things are a little different when it comes to identifying successes and measuring your return. Because EM utilizes physical interaction and innovative ways for brands to communicate with consumers, it achieves visible, measurable results defining a client's ROI. Some of the most commonly used measurements in EM include in-person sign ups, market surveys, and social media metrics.

With the sign-up method, all participants sign a waiver of recognition (for insurance and liability purposes) and then simply sign their name and email address. This method can be done on paper or on a laptop or tablet, allowing multiple sign-ups to happen simultaneously. Collecting a numerical metric of how many people participated/attended your event provides viable contact information for your client.

Another method of measurement for events is market surveys. Many agencies use this method at events and offer some type of incentive if consumers take the survey. When using this method, you are not only recording the number of consumers who participated in your event, this method also allows you to measure your client's current market reach, brand awareness, consumer feelings toward the brand, and provides a dialogue between the consumer and the brand ambassador. Surveys can provide important information to the client regarding future development of marketing campaigns, advertisements, and consumer relations.

One method that many agencies are utilizing is measuring success and returns via social media channels. Social media is a powerful medium of communication that increases brand recognition and visibility, and can significantly increase the reach of your EM campaign. It allows consumers to have open discussions about the campaign, brand, and product, and organically creates more awareness and publicity, thus increasing word of mouth and producing gratis publicity and visibility by consumers simply talking about your campaign.

All campaign measurements should align closely with your client's designated objectives and goals. Because of EM's unique, interactive, face-to-face presentation, you won't be able to provide 100% accurate numbers because you will never operate in perfect markets. There will always be some degree of external factors that are out of our control. However, with constant measurements of consumer perceptions, participation numbers, social media impressions, and brand reach, you are able to successfully show your campaign's ROI and successes.

LESSONS LEARNED

EM is an ever-changing industry, and will constantly be reinvented as consumer demand and technology progress. With each campaign, you will learn lessons about the industry, consumer demands, and how to grow and better perform. Since EM focuses more on qualitative results, you have to reflectively look at your previous campaigns and events and learn from any mistakes/issues that may have taken place.

One thing you will find yourself constantly facing with EM is adversity. In EM, you are the manager of so many different variables, people, projects, and things; all of which you are in charge of maintaining and leading. With this many variables, something is bound to not go as planned. So, you must always be prepared to overcome adversity. This is a lesson that you will learn early on in EM. If you are competent, confident, prepared, and flexible, you will be able to overcome whatever adversity you face.

Another lesson is to always maintain clear channels of communication. When you have a clear line of contact with your client, you are able to notify them of any updates, changes, or issues. This creates a rapport with the client that builds trust and enhances your reputation with your client and within the industry. Communication also plays an important role with your vendors, employees, and all other involved parties. You are the main point of contact for all parties and you hold all the information needed to ensure your campaign goes as planned. You must properly educate them on their objectives, roles, responsibilities, and what your goals are for the campaigns. If everyone is properly informed as to what their role is and the end results are needed, you will create a unified team that is loyal to reaching the desired end results.

CONCLUSION

EM is an invaluable asset to many brands and retailers, allowing them to connect with consumers on an emotional level to create a positive response and outlook. It does this by creating unique experiences that emphasize interpersonal communication and face-to-face marketing. These experiences leave consumers with lasting and memorable impressions about a brand, which then leads to an increase of profitability, loyalty, and awareness.

EM is one of the most rewarding forms of communications that only some will get to experience. You will see your campaign in its manifestation as an actual reality after weeks, months, or even years of creation. You get to witness the creation of your masterpiece in all of its glory. You could have been the sole artist or part of the collective in its creation. Regardless, your campaign will be a live affair for your client and consumer to view and be a part of, and if all is done correctly will stimulate an overall positive and memorable response.

REFERENCE AND ADDITIONAL READING

Crossmark. (2014). Path to Purchase Institute: New report shows importance of experiential and engagement marketing. *Experiential Marketing: Can It Be Localized, Personalized and Scaled Up Affordably, 1*, 2–3.

Video Production: Telling Your Story With Motivation and Passion

Bill Grant
Owner
Cinema Couture

It is a fact of communications life. Video or, more correctly, digital imaging has become a substantial part of our daily media consumption. Increased bandwidth capacities, the rise of streaming entertainment capabilities, and the wild popularity of social media in its many forms have precipitated a paradigm shift in the way we communicate with visual images. In the 21st century, messaging and communications nearly always have to have a visual component to be considered credible.

What are the implications of this for a student-run firm or any other communications consultant? Video production—to include writing, direction, editing, and evaluation—must be tools in your communication consulting toolbox and should be something you can offer your clients. The following are some insights, observations, and suggested best practices for video production.

MAKE IT PERSONAL

The first observation is that video works because it is personal. Video captures symbols, emotions, and experiences, which relay ideas and concepts that people attach to emotionally. Video differs from other forms of communication by personalizing the subject. It doesn't matter what the video is about. When you can see people moving and speaking, or practical applications of ideas demonstrated on screen, it has a way of connecting viewers to a subject like nothing else. It is one thing to hear about animal abuse, for example, but it is an entirely other thing to see the images of results like starved horses, shivering dogs, or bloodied cats. Images have the power to energize with immediate effect. When seen on television or other second screens, powerful emotions are generated, both good and bad. Video has power.

BEFORE YOU START SHOOTING

But let's not get ahead of ourselves. Before you rush to tap into that power, it is best to learn some best practices. Let's start with the process.

Ask the Right Questions

The first part of the process is asking questions, or at least one very important question: What is the goal of the video? What do you want your video to do? For example: if the goal is artistic expression, then what do you want the viewer to think? Do you want to provoke, assuage, inform, challenge? What about emotion? If it's an event or wedding, what do you want the viewer to feel? Joy, excitement, sentiment, love? If it's a marketing video, what do you want the viewer to do? Buy, compare, recommend?

These questions and their answers inform how you should prepare. Is the video going to need a script? Will there be a natural story told throughout the process or will you need to interview key participants? These questions can only be answered through investigating your subject. Most of the time, we can prepare a direction after one conversation. It's all about asking the right questions. Mainly we want to know why. Why are we doing this video? What question are we attempting to answer, and what problem are we trying to solve?

Establish the Narrative

Having established our reason for the video, it is now time to break down the video into two rough categories: words and pictures or, in professional parlance, narrative and b-roll. Best practices dictate you should plan these two components as separate elements of the same recipe. While it is tempting to tell a visual story with all pictures, it is difficult sometimes for the viewer to understand context. How we tell the story is narrative and it often provides perspective and orientation.

In terms of execution, the narrative can be voice over. It can be dialogue between people or it can be interviews with people. The way you set up a narrative then determines the b-roll or supporting footage/images you will shoot. In most cases, you want the supporting footage to match what the narrative is describing.

In general, we tend to shoot b-roll AFTER we capture and understand the narrative so we can be intentional. Note that narrative does not always mean script. A script is one type of narrative, but there are other ways to advance a story/concept using words and pictures including testimonials, actualities, quotations, or on-camera commentary.

Match Equipment/Production With the Narrative

One other distinction before we actually start shooting involves some of the technical aspects of shooting video. We often decide all of our lens, camera, and format choices based on the subject and the tone of what we're working on. For example, if we're telling a dramatic story about drug abuse and recovery, we'll use a shallower depth of field to really isolate the subject. We'll use more dramatic lighting. We'll keep movement motivated and try to present a very intimate look at the subject's journey.

In contrast, if we're telling the story of a school where people are happy to be there and thriving, then our lighting will be brighter with fewer shadows and we'll use a good bit of dramatic movement to emphasize the grandness of it all. It is important to visualize and cater every shot and angle toward the audiences' satisfaction. It is also very helpful to match the actual video production values with the subject material.

For interviews, we typically will shoot a medium shot with the subject looking off camera, and a close up of the same angle. That will give us flexibility in editing. If there are two shots, we can eliminate errors and keep the shots looking smooth.

For B-roll, we generally have one camera shooting close with a zoom lens and one camera shooting wide. That will give us the wide, medium, close combination we need for editing. This is a general rule but we tend to shoot B-roll spontaneously.

As it pertains to equipment choice, in general, you should always use the best equipment you can afford/obtain. In our shop, we use LED panels for lighting. This choice allows for greater color collaboration, a cooler overall set, and the ability to have uniform lighting. In addition, the life of LEDs is much longer than traditional lighting and LEDs are typically less fragile than incandescent or even halide or vapor lights.

In terms of audio, we use a shotgun mic on a boom for most interviews. This way we don't have to hide the mics and can change interview subjects very quickly. It also makes for a more realistic shot. However, for more informal interviews like at an event or wedding, a wireless microphone is optimal for catching all comments and native sounds.

Discussing camera choices, our cameras consist of a variety of makes and models. The different cameras have different roles in the final production. For example, our cinema cameras are versatile with great audio inputs and do very well in lower lighting conditions. However, they are comparatively large and heavy so it is more difficult to use them for capturing movement or moving shots. For that we use some lighter solutions on motorized gimbals, which dampen the jarring but still capture motion.

EDITING: KEEP THE VIEWER'S ATTENTION AND THINK SMALL

Once raw B-roll and narration are prepared, the next step is editing. For this portion of the production, it is all about pacing and control of attention. Remember that

Every 5 seconds or so, the viewer subconsciously rethinks their decision to watch your video.

To that end, you need to understand what drives people's attention. One of the biggest motivators is variety. The edit needs to incorporate differing elements of both the audio and the visual. If you're trying to motivate people, you have to give them a reason to stick around until the end.

Longevity of viewership can be accomplished with music, grand visuals, story, intrigue, or plot. How you do it is up to you but you must achieve it somehow and that's all done in editing. When I edit, I like to think of our production as a song: intro—verse 1—chorus—verse 2—chorus—bridge—chorus—outro. This formatted sequence builds in the variety that is needed to maintain attention.

In addition to compelling narratives and visuals, some productions also depend heavily on graphic elements. We do not use a lot in our videos currently. We feel they can distract from the story and mar authenticity if graphics are not used well. At Cinema Couture, we believe story is everything.

One more characteristic/approach to editing: Think Small. Every edit we do—from 2017 and onward—is designed to be played on a small screen. We know through researching viewer behavior that 60% of our social media content is viewed on a phone. Therefore, if that is where the eyeballs are, that is where we need to be. It is critical that videos play well on mobile and that the mobile experience is painless.

SHOOT WITH PASSION AND AVOID THESE COMMON MISTAKES

A few last words on mistakes . . . Producing video is a combination of art and science. It is an acquired skill and as such beginners will make many mistakes as they are starting out. One of the most important mistakes a beginner makes is shooting without motivation, without passion.

In the best productions, there should be a reason everything is done. Everything from camera movement, to lighting, to sound design should be directly motivated by how it helps to tell the story. One of the biggest beginner mistakes is not having the story motivate the production. To overcome this, ask yourself, what should I do to get people I know excited about this topic? Once you get the answer, move on with deliberate determination to capture that level of passion and enthusiasm as you continue to start your production.

There are a few other simpler mistakes beginners make. One of the most important ones is not varying the framing of shots. It's more comfortable when shooting video of people to stay farther away from them and not invade their space. This creates a situation where it's not as simple to vary the framing. So, be disruptive and dare to intrude upon the space; intimacy provides insight and insight is interesting.

Another common mistake is not backing up audio recording. If you are recording audio at an event or even an interview, there should always be two sources of direct audio (e.g., a shotgun mic and a wireless mic). The primary audio source fails more often than you might guess, so if you have a good backup audio recording, all is not lost.

The last mistake I'll mention in video production is video length. The length of a video is supercritical to its effectiveness. If a video drags at any point, its effectiveness is decreased. Therefore, you have to decide how much story you have, how engaging your video really is, and how to vary the pace to keep it watchable. Even a 30-second TV ad can be too long if it isn't managed properly.

In closing, video production can be a challenging skill to master. But it is an expectation among communicators that any consulting agency offer some exceptional digital media literacy. And, just like any other creative work, it takes time, patience, and motivation to get good at it. But once you succeed, you will be a sought-after commodity, otherwise known as employable.

A Crash Course in Copywriting

Michele Lashley
President, Karacom Creative
Owner, The Smarter Writing Lab

So, lucky you. You're the anointed one who has either volunteered to write copy for your agency's clients OR you've been *volunteered*. Either way, it's a good thing. Why? Because if you can write copy that connects with target audiences in ways that engage them from the very first word, move them to feel good about your client, and inspire them to action (from purchasing to donating to voting)—then you've got a skill that very few others have. And it's also a skill that's in high demand. Ready to start learning about it? Great! Let's go!

SOMETHING TO ALWAYS REMEMBER

Before we get started with the nuts and bolts of copywriting, there's something you need to know:

> The truth isn't the truth until people believe you, and they can't believe you if they don't know what you're saying, and they can't know what you're saying if they don't listen to you, and they won't listen to you if you're not interesting, and you won't be interesting unless you say things imaginatively, originally, freshly. (Bernbach, n.d.)

This was advice given by Bill Bernbach—founder of Doyle Dane Bernbach (DDB) and a leader of the creative revolution that took place in the advertising industry in the 1960s. And, like so much of what he said, this advice applies to the creative industry now more than ever.

If you want to be truly successful as a copywriter, then writing copy that's mediocre or that mimics what everyone else is writing simply isn't an option. There's too much noise, too much competition, and too little attention in today's marketplace. And it's only going to get worse. So, if you want to stand out—and, more important—if you want your *clients* to stand out—you have to be extraordinary. But, first, you have to learn the basics. And that's what this chapter is all about.

WHO IN THE WORLD ARE YOU TALKING TO? THE POWER OF THE BUYER PERSONA

Before you write the first word of copy for your client, you need to understand who it is you're targeting with your message. And here's a hint: IT CAN'T BE EVERYONE! Even if your client *wants* it to be everyone, that's simply not an option.

The bottom line is that not everyone is going to care about what your client is offering. If you're trying to talk to everyone in a way that's meaningful, then you'll end up talking to no one and creating something that's meaningless.

So, what's the answer to writing copy that will help clients reach their goals? **Build a buyer persona first**. According to HubSpot writer Sam Kusinitz, "a buyer persona is a semi-fictional representation of your ideal customer based on market research and real data about your existing customers. When creating your buyer persona(s), consider including customer demographics, behavior patterns, motivations, and goals. The more detailed you are, the better" (Kusinitz, 2014).

Once you have the information you need, you can create a buyer persona that will help you and your client create content that's better focused and much more effective. Why? Because you'll be creating it for that particular person (the persona) instead of nameless, faceless multitudes of strangers.

Here's an example. Let's say your client has come up with a new website that focuses on helping people successfully budget their money. It's called The Most Awesome Budgeting Site EVER, Inc. To access it, users have to pay a monthly subscription charge of $15. Now, a LOT of people are interested in budgeting. However, based on user statistics, your client has found that the majority of subscribers are professional women with young families. Great! So, here's what a buyer persona for The Most Awesome Budgeting Site EVER, Inc. might look like

Sarah (and we'll also provide a photo of "Sarah"—who is a woman who represents our target audience)

Sarah is 38 years old and lives in the suburbs of a major metropolitan area. She's been married for 7 years and has two young children—Amelia who's 2 years old and Jake who's 5.

Sarah is currently an account manager for a local business. Before she and her husband had kids, she was an account executive for an advertising agency. While she earned a significant salary there, she also worked 60- to 80-hour weeks consistently. She earns quite a bit less now—but she wanted to have a job with more regular hours so she could spend more time with her children while they're so young.

Sarah and her husband are getting by financially. But they want to have money to do some extra things for their young family—like taking a week-long vacation during the summer

months. Sarah is looking for ways to make their monthly household income go further and is also trying to figure out better ways to budget so that she and her husband can increase the amount they save each month.

There's a lot of information on the internet about budgeting—but it's overwhelming. Sarah is WAY too busy to sift through all of it. She just needs someone to simplify the budgeting process for her, to answer her questions and to walk her through it step by step.

That's it. Now we have a MUCH better idea about who we'll be writing copy for. We're writing it for Sarah. And, if we focus on that, then we're going to be more likely to write copy that helps our client accomplish their goals.

HEADLINES THAT WORK: HOW TO WRITE HEADLINES THAT GRAB YOUR AUDIENCE'S ATTENTION (AND WON'T LET GO)

The great adman David Ogilvy said, "On the average, five times as many people read the headlines as read the body copy. It follows that unless your headline sells your product, you have wasted 90 percent of your money" (Ogilvy, 1985). That's a pretty strong case for the importance of headlines.

Effective headlines are the key to intriguing people enough to engage with your content—whether that content is a print ad, a blog post, a video, a website, email subject line, or anything else. If you want people to pay attention to what you have to say, you have to grab their attention from the very beginning.

Now, notice that I said "effective headlines"—not "creative headlines"—are what's required. There's a difference. You can come up with a really clever headline, but it might completely miss the boat when it comes to resonating with your target audience. Here's a rule for you: never sacrifice clarity for cleverness.

So, how can you write more *effective* headlines? Here are some tips:

1. *Go back to your buyer persona and answer these three questions:*
   a. What does he or she need (specifically)?
   b. How can my client's product or service answer that need?
   c. Why and how is my client's solution different from competitors?
2. *Write a headline that's specific.* Make the benefit clear. For example, if your client is offering a course on how entrepreneurs can use social media, maybe the headline is something like "Learn How to Build Your Company's Social Media Presence on Pinterest." There's specificity not only regarding building a social media presence for business, but also regarding *which* social media platform. That's very different than a headline that says, "Learn How to Build Your Social Media Presence." Who is this targeting? We don't know.

You can still be creative. For example, "Pin Your Company's Social Media Success on Pinterest." We know that it's for businesses and we know that it focuses on Pinterest.

3. *Consider using numbers.* Think about headlines that grab your attention. Odds are you've been pulled in by articles or blog posts that offer five ways to do this or 10 benefits of that. We love lists. And using numbers in headlines can go a long way in grabbing your audience's attention. For example:

   a. *10 Ways to Improve Your Headlines*
   b. *15 Tricks for Saving Money at the Grocery Store* (Think Sarah, our buyer persona might be drawn to this? Yep.)

4. *Don't underestimate the power of "How To."* From YouTube videos to blog posts to ebooks, people are searching for "how to" information. How do I fix my vacuum cleaner? How do I train my cat to stop scratching the furniture? How do I cook a gourmet meal for under $10? So, it makes sense to use "How To" in headlines when it's appropriate to do so. Some examples are

   a. *How to Get 1000 Email Subscribers in 10 Days*
   b. *How to Find the Best Deals at Your Local Flea Market* (Again—might be a good one for Sarah)

5. *Use AWESOME adjectives.* We've been taught to cut out unnecessary adjectives and adverbs from our writing. But, when writing headlines, you can use them again because this is promotional writing. Effectiveness is key, though. For example:

   a. *A Super Simple Guide to Helping Your Child Learn to Read Before Preschool.* We could have just said "A Guide to Helping Your Child Learn to Read Before Preschool"—but that might imply that it would be a lot of work. By using "super simple" to describe the guide, busy parents' ears are going to perk up because now it sounds like something they might actually have time to do.
   b. *The Money-Making Secrets of Best-Selling Authors.* This is better than just "The Secrets of Best-Selling Authors" because it clarifies what kinds of secrets are going to be provided and it taps into the interest of writers who are looking for ways to use their craft to create a living.

6. *Make a promise (if it's one your client can keep).* When you can make a promise in a headline that clearly addresses a pain point for your audience, this can be a very effective way to grab attention. Here are a couple of examples:

   a. *3 Simple Ways to Monetize Your Blog and Increase Your Revenue 10x in 2018.*
   b. *How to Start a Freelance Copywriting Business That Will Give You the Freedom You're Dreaming of*

   The important thing with promise-making headlines is to be specific about the benefit AND to be ethical in what's being promised.

7. *Address your audience's fears.* People look for solutions to things they're afraid of. So, consider addressing your audience's fears in your headline. But, if you do, the body copy that follows—whether it's a blog post, an article, an ad or anything else—must offer a solution. You don't just want to stir up people's fears and leave them hanging. Here are a couple of fear-based headlines:

   a. *Start Your Own Business and Stop Dreading Mondays*
   b. *The 10 Horrifying Problems Caused by Identity Theft (and what you can do about them)*

8. *Ask a question (as long as the answer isn't "yes" or "no").* You might be surprised how many people will look at a headline that asks a question that resonates with them. For example, for our budgeting site, what if a blog post was titled (headlined): How Will You Pay for Your Child's College Education? My guess is that it would get a LOT of eyeballs on it. By asking the right question in your headline, you can really grab the attention of your target audience.

Writing the right headline can be one of the hardest things you do as a copywriter. If you're assigned a project that needs a headline, write LOTS of options. Not just three or four—but 50 or more. That's how you'll get to the one that will be most effective for your client.

BENEFITS VERSUS FEATURES: SHOW CUSTOMERS HOW YOUR CLIENT'S OFFERING WILL IMPROVE THEIR LIVES

Here's something you need to know as a copywriter: no one cares about you, or your client, or how wonderfully you write. Sorry. But that's the sad truth. And the sooner you hear it and accept it, the better off you'll be. All your audience wants to know is this: ***"What's in it for ME?"*** If you can answer that question clearly and effectively, then you've got a future in copywriting. To help you do that, here are a few things to keep in mind:

1. *People don't buy solely based on cost.* It doesn't matter if the offering is the cheapest on the market or the most expensive, what customers look for is *value*. How much value does the product or service offer? One crucial thing some businesses miss out on—particularly those that sell more expensive offerings—is communicating value in a way that resonates with their audience. For example, a car might be more expensive than other similar cars in its class—but, in the long run, it won't require nearly as many repairs. There's value in that—but it has to be made clear.

2. *Understand the difference between features and benefits.* Too often, businesses focus on communicating about the features instead of how those features will benefit the customer. People don't buy grass seed because it's in an easy-to-open bag. They buy it because it'll give them a beautiful, green yard they can be proud of. Let's go back to our website—The Most Awesome Budgeting Site EVER, Inc.—and our buyer persona—Sarah. Here's the way features versus benefits (or value) might look for that business:

FEATURES	VALUE TO SARAH
Offers proven tips for saving money	Extra money at the end of the month for her family
Provides the most coupons of any site	Everything she needs in one place so that she doesn't have to spend hours scouring the Internet for information
Has easy-to-follow, step-by-step instructions for budgeting	Eliminates the overwhelm and makes budgeting something Sarah can easily implement so that she and her family can achieve their financial goals

SUBHEADS AND BULLETS: HOW TO PUT YOUR COPY IN THE SPOTLIGHT

While it's not true for everyone, a lot of people just don't like to read. At least when it comes to things other than a really good novel. So, that represents a HUGE challenge to you as a copywriter.

Think about how copy looks on a printed page or on a screen. If it's a great big gray blob—it's going to be ignored. Fortunately for you, though, there are a couple of simple solutions to this problem.

1. *Don't write so much.* Do you *really* need to use so much text to communicate your message? If not, trim it down.
2. *Use subheads and bullets.* Regardless of how much copy you have, using subheads and bullets to break it up can make your copy MUCH easier to read. Today, people are more likely to read copy that's scannable rather than copy that requires them to spend a lot of time reading every single word. Subheads and bullets can help with that. Just don't OVERUSE them. Also, it's okay to be somewhat clever with subheads so that they are intriguing, but—as with headlines—clarity comes first.

BE CONVERSATIONAL: WRITE LIKE YOUR AUDIENCE TALKS

People will read copy when it's written in a way that "sounds" familiar to them, that's easy for them to understand, and that feels good. For example, think about the things you *like* to read and *choose* to read versus things you *have to* read or *struggle* to read. How do you feel about each? Which are you more likely to read from start to finish? And which ones are you more likely to talk about with your friends? If you're reading something that uses the language you and your friends use and that talks about things of interest to you in a way that engages you, odds are you're likely to enjoy it. And maybe even share it. That's our goal as copywriters: to write copy that our audience relates to, trusts, engages with, and maybe even shares with their peers.

Writing conversationally can be a BIG switch from how you're used to writing. It's NOT like writing a research paper. And it often breaks certain rules. (e.g., it's okay to start a sentence with "and" like the sentence before this one.) The key is to know your audience and know how they talk. You don't want to use vernacular of millennials if you're writing to an audience of retirees. So, before you write anything, learn how your audience talks and then reflect that in your writing.

In general, here are things you now have permission to do:

- *Start sentences with "and" and "but."* Because that's how we talk. And that's okay.
- *Use contractions.* Again, that's how we talk. It's familiar to us.
- *End sentences with prepositions.* Only if you want to.
- *Have sentences with only one word.* Really? Yep.
- *Have paragraphs with only one sentence.* Sometimes that's all you need.

But, using poor grammar is something you DON'T have permission to do.

Here are a few helpful hints when it comes to writing conversationally:

- *Write to one person—not 1,000*. Remember our buyer persona—Sarah? Write to her (or whoever your buyer persona is).
- *Use words your audience uses.*
- *Don't be afraid to use shorter sentences.*
- *Don't ramble. Get to the point of what you're saying.*
- *Be clear about what you're trying to communicate.*
- *Read what you've written aloud to yourself.*

Writing conversationally takes practice. But, you'll be surprised how much better and how much more effective your copy will be when you write that way.

CALLS TO ACTION: DEVELOPING A CALL TO ACTION THAT ACTUALLY LEADS TO ACTION

Remember that you're not just writing copy for a creative exercise. You're writing it to get people to ACT—calling, asking, buying, donating, voting. But, you can't just leave it to the audience to figure out what you want them to do. You have to clearly TELL THEM. And that's called a call to action. Everything you write should have one.

Forms of Calls to Action

A call to action can take a variety of forms. Some include

- A phone number to call
- A website URL
- A hashtag
- A button on a website (LEARN MORE, GET STARTED, LISTEN NOW)

Be very directive in telling your audience what you want them to do. They won't take time to guess.

"Click Here" Isn't Enough

When you're writing the call to action, you'll often be writing copy for buttons or hyperlinks on a website. And just saying, "click here" isn't enough. You have to provide some type of incentive to get people to click. For example, maybe the call to action

- Removes risk of trying out a product or service
- Demonstrates the benefit very clearly
- Creates a sense of urgency
- Promotes exclusivity

There are a variety of reasons people click on a call to action and understanding what drives your audience to act is crucial.

Some Effective Call to Action Words and Phrases

Finding the right call to action requires understanding your specific audience. But here are a few words and phrases commonly used:

- Guarantee (e.g., a 30-day guarantee that removes risk)
- Change (tap into something your audience wants to change)
- Improve (e.g., improve your sales)
- Results (e.g., by downloading this ebook, you'll get _____ result)
- Try it for free (removes financial risks)
- Limited supply (people don't want to be left out)
- Exclusive (tap into the idea of exclusivity)
- Closing in X days or hours (promotes urgency)

Know What Your Goal Is

You need to know what the goal is for the call to action. What do you want people to do and why? These goals could be anything, but some common ones are

- Creating new business leads
- Connecting with current customers
- Contacting the business
- Signing up for a newsletter or some other type of ongoing communication that allows your client to stay in touch with their audience

THAT'S A WRAP!

So, now you have some of the basics of effective copywriting. But, just reading about them won't make you a great copywriter. Only practice—a LOT of practice—will move you toward that goal. Also, study the work of those who are already great. Check out the award-winning work from the One Show and the Clios, as well as other organizations. Read the trade publications, like *Advertising Age*. Become a student of the industry. Fall in love with the creative process.

As a copywriter, you have the honor and responsibility of telling the stories of your clients in ways that will help them attract their ideal customers. If you can do that—and do it well—then you'll have one of the most valued and marketable skills of the 21st century. So, spend the time it takes to become great. We'll all look forward to seeing your work.

REFERENCES AND ADDITIONAL READINGS

Bernbach, B. (n.d.). *Bill Bernbach quotes.* Doyle Dane Bernbach. Retrieved from http://www.ddb. com/bernbach.html

Kusinitz, S. (2014, March 8). The definition of a buyer persona. *HubSpot.* Retrieved from https://blog.hubspot.com/marketing/buyer-persona-definition-under-100-sr#sm. 00000t09dbqllke86xzh91jld7gug

Ogilvy, D. (1985). *Ogilvy on advertising.* New York, NY: Vintage Books (a division of Random House).

Creating the Essence of a Brand Through Design

Jay Picard
Founder
Think Say Feel

INTRODUCTION

Welcome to the world of brand. For a lot of people a brand equates to one thing, the logo. But a brand is much more than that. The true definition of brand: the perceptions of a product or company people hold based on the sum of all brand interactions. These interactions include the name, the logo and visual language, marketing and advertising, public relations, events, employee behavior, products and innovation, the sales process, corporate values, just to name a few. But the most important and powerful brand interaction isn't created by the brand itself but by consumers—the active sharing of their perceptions and point of view. Think about how consumers shared their anger with the Gap when the retailer attempted a logo redesign in October 2010. The redesign broke the emotional connection consumers had with the brand and they let the brand know it.

So how does a brand create and shape that perception? It starts with strategic positioning. This is the core of what the brand stands for at the highest emotional level vis-à-vis the competition—its ultimate promise to the world. Is the Coca-Cola brand really promising the best soda? No. Coca-Cola promises joy and happiness. In turn, the design of a brand is intended to illuminate that brand promise in order to foster that emotional connection. When done successfully, this emotional connection generates and maintains those positive perceptions of a brand. If the brand veers off track, consumers will step in.

How do clients design or redesign a brand that builds emotional resonance with consumers? Clients can do this themselves but they often hire brand design agencies to lead them through the process. These agencies do this well as they are experts in branding and design, and also provide an important outside lens for clients. If you think about it, more often than not clients are too close to the day-to-day running of the business to see what the brand could be. Simply put, clients oftentimes need help seeing the forest through the trees.

THE PROCESS

Broadly, there are four phases involved in the process of creating a brand but more important than the process is true collaboration with the client. Collaboration allows for two key components for successful brand development: (1) it allows clients to take ownership of ideas early on, which builds client-side brand champions from the start and (2) clients provide the agency with a needed reality check. Can the company really live up to the proposed brand promise?

Phase I: Discovery

This is about getting smart. Learning as much as the agency team can about the company, the competition, the target audience, and even inspirational examples from outside the client's category. This phase includes interviews, audits, and reviewing significant amount of data provided by the client.

Discovery often starts by obtaining the client perspective via stakeholder interviews. This normally happens during the first few weeks of the project and offers a rapid-fire way to quickly learn the client's perspective. It also includes many people from across the client organization in the process. Often this takes the shape as one-on-one interviews and/or small group conversations across the business (think from CEO to receptionist).

Agency designers and strategists team up for these interviews. It is important to have the two key disciplines that will be leading the creation of the brand (design and strategy) hear perceptions directly from clients. There is tremendous power in "being there" versus just reading the report. The goal of stakeholder interviews is to understand strengths and weaknesses of the business. Likes and dislikes with the current brand assets. What's the vision for the future? Who's the enemy? What are the sacred cows that need to remain? What are the biggest fears? After doing this, it's amazing to see the common themes that bubble up from across the company.

Simultaneously, the team will start to pull together competitive and existing client brand audits. The competitive audit is a simple but powerful exercise that allows you to see how the category speaks, both visually and verbally. It literally begins by putting up competitive material on a wall. For each competitor pin up all things the consumer sees, the website, collateral, logos, visual language, advertising, signage, and so on. Before you know it, you can see the entire category right in front of you and clearly see the language or rules of the client's category.

The next step in the audit is to find the commonalities or as some I've worked with call them, category conventions. It's easy. Step back and look at the wall as whole. What do you see that's similar? Is there a lot of one color, say blue? Are there a ton of pictures of babies? You get the picture. As you look at the wall, take some Post-it notes and jot these observations down, then place that Post-it on the wall to mark that observation. Next, get close to the wall and read all the copy across every competitor. Do you see the same words? What's the tonality like? Are the same claims being made? Use the Post-its again to mark similar language across the competitive set.

While you're doing this, another important discovery will emerge—which competitor(s) break category conventions. They'll clearly stand out as they look and speak differently from others in their category. Study these rule breakers closely. How are they getting away with breaking the rules? Do you see other competitors beginning to break the same rule? Can your client's brand break the same rules? After you identify category conventions and which of them some competitors break, have the team answer this question as you enter the strategy and design phases: What conventions must we adhere to and which ones can we break? This is an amazing exercise to do with clients as they frequently don't look at their competitors in this way. They look at their competitors differently—market share, same store sales, year over year growth, and so on.

Auditing the existing client brand's assets is simple. Review all marketing and communications tools the company uses now and has used in the past. Look at ad campaigns, the website, collateral, the logo and visual systems, and so on. This allows you to assess what's working and what's not working. When rebranding, it helps you understand where brand equity may exist. This might manifest itself as a distinctive color that the brand is known for. Think about T-Mobile and their use of magenta; they can't leave that behind. Maybe a mascot or a visual icon like the Energizer Bunny. It could be a tagline that continues to sum up the brand promise. Nike's "just do it."

Another important aspect of the discovery process is to understand the target audience for your client's brand. Yes, the client most likely provides the agency quite a bit of research on their consumers. This research might outline audience segments, illustrate the bulls-eye target, measure consumer perceptions of competitors, purchase behavior or advertising copy test studies, and so on.

All of these are invaluable inputs, but honestly nothing can beat observing and talking to those consumers in person. Observing and talking with them adds a level of humanity, dimensionality, and understanding that research reports can't. After all, these are people we're creating a brand for. Most importantly, this allows you to understand the emotional mindset (value set) and the emotions around the category (often called pain or pleasure points). The proper term for this is qualitative market research.

Clients can spend a lot of money on qualitative research but it can be done with little to no investment for smaller clients. If your client creates a consumer good, go to the grocery store and watch people and even ask them a few questions. It's amazing what you can learn when you do this at a few stores.

Phase II: Strategic Foundation

> *The essence of positioning is sacrifice. Be willing to give up something in order to establish that unique position.*
>
> Ries and Trout (2001, p. 208)

Now that the rapid-fire learning process of the discovery phase is complete, it's time to start creating the brand positioning. This is where you take all of that information and strip away everything but the most important pieces. This is the beginning of differentiation. Whether developing a new brand or rebranding, you're creating the strategic foundation that will inform everything the brand says and does going forward, including the visual design. This process is led by the strategy team, but designers play a valuable role as well.

Brand positioning illuminates the one thing, and only the one thing that will allow a brand to "*differentiate from competitors, resonate with customers, energize and inspire employees and partners and precipitate a gush of ideas for marketing programs*" (Aaker, 2014 p. 26).

But wait, it's not that simple. The notion of a brand standing for "one thing" is really important here and quite challenging. Lots of brands try to be everything for everyone but this results in a brand standing for nothing—for no one. In our fast-paced, message-cluttered world, a single-minded brand positioning allows differentiation to happen through focus.

People don't buy WHAT you do; they buy WHY you do it. And what you do simply proves what you believe.

Simon Sinek (2009 p. 45)

Another important aspect of creating a powerful brand positioning is for it to resonate emotionally. In the introduction, we discussed how brands succeed when they connect with people emotionally. This is the crux of Sinek's point of view—lead with the "why" and prove with the "what." Many brands attempt to differentiate by focusing rational attributes of the products they create—the what. The ones that rise above the rest lead with the emotional reason why they create those products. Mini "Driving should be fun" or Apple "Think Different."

Let's start with what we're creating in this phase, the brand framework. Many agencies and clients that I've worked with use the "brand pyramid" to frame up their brand positioning. I used the one below many times while I worked at Hornall Anderson. I recommend you use this one as it's simple. Feel free to search for other examples, but from my experience, the more content you add to it, the more you run the risk of confusing clients. This framework is made up of six distinct elements:

1. *The target mindset:* The "brand target audience" this rises above demographic descriptors to a set of rational and emotional beliefs.
2. *Brand differentiators:* Three to five things the brand creates or does. This is the "what." Some of these may very well be the same as the competitive set and that's ok.
3. *Functional benefits:* Three or four things the brand gives to customers.
4. *Emotional benefits:* One to three needs the brand fulfills.
5. *Brand promise:* The highest level emotional takeaway a person leaves with after any experience with the brand. This is the "why."
6. *Brand personality:* Literally around five personality traits. This is how the brand acts. When creating these, imagine if the client brand turned into a person and walked into the room. Describe that person.

Here's an example from a client I worked on. This company flew people to amazing destinations around the world via private jets while taking care of every minute detail—for $75,000 a seat.

Target mindset—*for those that:* Comfortable adventurers. Intellectual. Curious. Demand comfort and security.
Differentiators—*the brand creates:* All-inclusive, worry-free travel itineraries to global bucket list destinations that bring you into the culture. Unparalleled service. Knowledgeable, personable, expert staff.

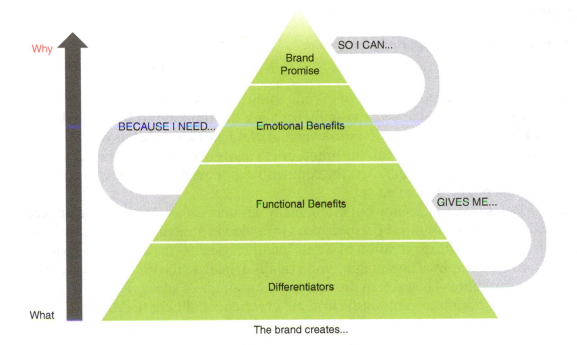

The brand creates...

Functional benefits—*gives me:* Access to rare and intimate views of global destinations in pampered comfort.

Emotional benefit—*because I need:* Transformational experiences.

Brand promise—*so I can:* Discover more . . .

Brand personality—*How the brand acts and behaves:* Adventurous. Dedicated. Meticulous. Resourceful. Attentive.

Start by putting together a brand target mindset. This is who you're creating the brand for and different from a media target. This is who the brand needs to resonate with. Some clients like to create personas and lengthy narratives but these can become confusing so erring on the side of simplicity is best. Distill all the information you gathered about the consumer into a set of emotional and rational beliefs these people hold dear. A set of five to seven characteristics of each works great. Think right brain and left brain. Literally sketch a face and write the characteristics (left and right brain) on either side of it. Now debate and align on the top differentiators and work through the benefits. As you progress, options for the promise and personality will come to light. Keep a list of these going until you can read the pyramid and it all makes sense.

When presenting positioning to the client, give them a few options. Usually present three "pyramids." These should be distinct from one another and focus on different emotional promises. Each promise should be true to the brand but during the presentation have the important discussion with the client about which one could the brand truly deliver on. Be sure to have an agency point of view (POV) on which has more power to differentiate the brand.

Phase III: Design

Design is the silent ambassador of your brand.

Paul Rand (Rand, n.d.)

With the brand strategically focused on that "one thing,"—that promise to the world—designers now take on the challenge of visually bringing the thinking to life. The design phase begins with guidance given to designers via a briefing and a simple, succinctly written, one sheet brand brief. Often visual, the brand brief clearly articulates the brand promise, emotional benefits, the target mindset, the competitive opportunity, key visual equities the new design must retain, and so on.

Different agencies work differently but often, many designers work on the same project to tackle the challenge from multiple perspectives. Grounded in strategy along with strong intuition, designers begin the exploration of a new identity system—the logo, color palate, look and feel, and typography. They imagine and visually articulate the brand promise into many different possibilities. They sketch dozens, likely hundreds of ideas. Their process is creative and iterative taking inspiration from their experiences, different categories, and any useful analogies.

As the process continues, the design director focuses the design team's thinking. Ideas are questioned and focused while other ideas are cut. After this whittling, the broader team meets for a critique or a "crit." At a crit, the ideas are put up on a wall where each designer presents his or her idea to the full team followed by a group discussion. This is a conversation about the possibility these bourgeoning designs have at differentiating the brand. Do the sketches begin to illuminate the brand promise? Designers leave the crit with territories to focus on and additional ideas of how to expand their thinking.

Now designers begin to flesh out their ideas exploring color and typography. Color is of the upmost importance when redesigning a brand. Color is used to evoke emotion, bring to life personality, and provide a key recognition trigger. People shop by using color. I remember hearing a person describe how they bought tortilla chips, "I buy the blue Tostitos for parties." Designers explore how much color versus white space as well as secondary colors used in the palate. A palate of colors allows the final design system to help delineate different product variations. Think about Tostitos again. Color delineates the different flavors and forms across portfolio.

Typography is a core foundational element of and brand identity and conveys emotion personality and character. Designers must select fonts that convey the essence of the brand but also be legible across multiple applications. The identity system will live from business cards to the web to billboards to annual reports, and so on.

Here are a few commonly used font types:

- *Handwritten fonts* come across as welcoming and casual.
- *Italic or script fonts* often a show of high end or sophistication.
- *Sans serif fonts* are clean and modern and express newness.
- *Serif fonts* can convey tradition, seriousness, and professionalism.

At this point, designers have gone from preliminary idea via a sketch to a fleshed-out concept using a new identity idea inclusive of logo, color, and font. They now pressure test this by applying it across some media examples. A brand identity does not live in isolation but out in the real world so the designer needs to show how it lives on the website, on packaging, in advertising, and so on. Another test is how the identity works across multiple product lines.

Now, the team holds another crit (i.e. critique meeting) where the design director will select a manageable number of concepts to share with the client. The concepts selected should be different from one another. As a general rule of thumb, choose three to four to present. Here's a common way to show the difference:

1. Close to what exists today (Safe)
2. Stretching further afield but recognizable
3. Completely new
4. Radical departure

The first design presentation to the client represents a tremendous amount of work and the presentation itself must be thoroughly thought through. The work can't sell itself so the team works together to tell the story of how the new identity options will deliver on the brand promise and differentiate from the competition. Rationalize all to the brand strategy and have a recommendation with a clear point of view why that design concept would work. The presentation should include the problem to solve, the target mind-set, the brand's strategic direction, design inspiration by concept, as well as the new identity concepts.

Congratulations. You've sold a new redesign concept to the client. What's next? Creating guidelines for the new identity system by creating the brand style guide. This is hugely important as it allows for brand consistency across all applications. Consistency is one of the most important rules of branding. The style guide explains in detail how to use the logo, color, typography imagery, and so on. It also gives examples of how not to use it and examples of how to use it in application.

Phase IV: Brand Expression

Activating the new brand. This is about expressing the brand across all applications: website redesign, advertising, new packaging, corporate environments, uniforms, business cards, stationary, and so on. Few clients have the financial resource to do a wholesale change so prioritize. Maybe start with business cards, a web "refresh," and a vinyl temporary sign to place over their existing headquarters sign. The rest will happen over time as budgets are allocated. Instruct the client to use the brand guidelines to ensure brand consistency as they rollout their new identity across all applications. The brand guidelines become the brand bible for creating anything the brand does.

CONCLUSION

The process of creating a brand is part art, part science, challenging, and fun. The reward comes when you know you helped a client create something that not only helps to sell their product, but truly resonates with people emotionally. You helped navigate the client through unfamiliar territory to arrive at a better place for their brand. Be sure to push your ideas both strategically and creatively. Have fun and I look forward to learning of your successes.

REFERENCES AND ADDITIONAL READINGS

Aaker, D. A. (2014). *Aaker on branding: 20 principles that drive success*. New York, NY: Morgan James Publishing.

Rand, P. (n.d.). *Quotes on Design*. Retrieved from https://quotesondesign.com/paul-rand-6/

Ries, A., & Trout, J. (2001). *Positioning*. New York, NY: McGraw Hill.

Sinek, S. (2009). *Start with why: How great leaders inspire everyone to take action*. New York, NY: Portfolio/Penguin Group.

Designing a Solid Website

Blake DuBose
President
DuBose Web Group
www.duboseweb.com

GETTING STARTED

So, your agency is being asked to help a client develop a website. Many questions will be flowing through your mind. Universally, you want a website that reads well, navigates easily, is customer-friendly, colorful, visually appealing, and understandable. Your first step in this process is to ask some questions.

Qualifying Questions

How should the site appear? What feelings/emotions do I wish the site to evoke? Should it be hip, informal, fun, casual, prestigious, formal, or professional?

What is the site's purpose? What do I want the site to do? What are my goals? Do I want to boost awareness about the organization and services? Do I wish to inform or support existing customers, or am I more interested in attracting new prospects? Have I provided information about the company so that it motivates customers to contact me? Do I want to describe and sell products online with credit card capability (promote e-commerce)? Am I wanting to sustain market share or am I out to capture new share instead?

In addition to those purpose questions, you may also want to describe the desired visitor experience. What do I want them to do? Buy a product? Engage a service provider? Support a cause or effort? Think good thoughts about your company/organization and tell others? Participate in an interactive activity? Contribute to the content of the site by sharing their own experiences? Something else?

These questions are important and contribute to your initial design efforts. At DuBose Web, we use the analogy of a beautiful red sports car. Anyone can build a beautiful red car, but most forget (or don't know how) to put a powerful engine in it, and continuously put fuel in the car by evaluating and improving the user experience.

Understanding the Audiences

In addition to defining the client's perspective, you must also understand the audiences'. The best, most effective websites come from teams that work to gain a deep insight into the targets' motivations. That process starts with basic questions like: Who exactly are you trying to attract? How do they think? What strategic tactics will: (1) attract them, (2) convert them to a lead, and (3) close them as a customer?

Once you have this nailed down, the next step is to build conversion paths—guiding the persona through a user-friendly journey, which in the end results in a qualified lead. For this you must stress efficiency, value, solutions, and an easy call to action (CTA).

What Is the Main Domain (or Website Address)?

Related to these efforts, other questions you are probably asking include: What should my domain name be? How do I position my website to be memorable? How do I make it attractive and easy to find? One easy way to do this is choosing a unique, short, easy-to-remember website address. It should relate to the services you provide. Ideally, potential consumers should see your web address and know what your organization does and easily remember it.

If you can, include one of your main services in your domain as this is a very small factor in search engine ranking algorithm. For example, having "web" in the domain, i.e. "duboseweb.com" could slightly help if someone is seeking web-related companies in a search engine.

Research for Insights and Motivation

While all of these questions and more should be asked before you start designing your website, there is also a need to visualize what you are trying to accomplish. One of the best ways to do this, and perhaps foster some creativity, is to proceed with some secondary start-up research.

Size Up the Competition

Start-up research is useful for grounding your efforts in reality. It is relatively easy to imagine what a site could do, but it is instructive to see what other sites are actually doing. A first step is conducting an analysis of competitors' websites. Competitors are great teachers, learn from them and always stay one step ahead.

And while we encourage seeking inspiration through others' websites, color schemes, and layouts, be sure to honor their work, copyrights, and trademarks. Document sites you like to give your designer some ideas, but it is also important to notice that the design world is constantly evolving. So, when possible, connect yourself with industry-leading web sources to stay up to date on industry trends, insights, and different perspectives.

BLUEPRINTING YOUR SITE

Now that you have the client's goals defined, the audiences' perspectives established, the domain name selected, and are sufficiently inspired, it is time to sit down and start planning. Just like a contractor won't start building without a blueprint, you should not start building your site without a map. A map tells you where you are going, how you will get there and how to get back. Following are some observations for planning out your site.

Map It Out (Provide Structure)

Think of the website as a house. Every house needs blueprints so you know what's going to go where. Creating a site map (or content tree) will establish the major, secondary, and tertiary pages you need. During this stage, think about links, visuals, and content. Make sure you know what each page will do and why it is there. Think about how many clicks it may take for a customer to navigate your site (hint it is no more than three).

One other thing to remember when mapping, websites have evolved from text-heavy encyclopedias to less content and more action-oriented graphic experiences. Consequently, as you design, it is important to illustrate and inform (show and tell) the customer that you understand their issues, you can help solve their problems, and then offer an easy way for them to contact you.

KEEPING THE CUSTOMER AROUND (CREATING "STICKINESS")

As you are mapping, in addition to providing basic information and engagement, you should also seek to ensure your site is interactive, attractive, and memorable. Inspire your customer to stick around. Following are some suggested ways to do this:

Video

A great way to engage user interest and impart a lot of information in an easy setting is video. With the evolvement of smartphones, the ease of viewing videos represents an effective way for people and organizations to connect with their audiences.

Couponing and Loyalty Tools

Another way to engender engagement is through couponing and loyalty tools. Rewarding a customer for visiting your site and/or opting in for your content is a great way keep a customer coming back. Just be sure the offerings are relevant and valuable. Unwanted SPAM or self-serving coupons can have the opposite effect and generate resentment. So, be careful selecting these tactics.

Games and Interactivity

Some sites are designed to provide information. Other sites are designed to serve as commerce platforms and still others are promulgated as a form of retailtainment. Depending upon your brand, your budget, and your target audience, certain promotional games can also be seen as a way to maintain engagement and provide value to your target customers.

User-Provided Content

Finally, there is the challenge and excitement of user provided content where your customers can interact with you and the rest of your customer base via your website. Reviews, stories, testimonials, and other "real-life" experiences can be shared on sites as a way to provide solid "word of mouth" endorsements of your product or service. However, be wary of this tool as it can become a two-edged sword and open the door to some negative comments or unwanted information. Should you decide to go down the road of user-provided content, be sure to have someone assigned to monitor the message boards, blog sites, and so on and respond quickly, with tact, to negative messaging.

GENERAL DO'S AND DON'TS OF WEBSITE DESIGN

Getting Your Website Content Copy Right

When designing website content, write text that reflects your business and website goals. The objective is to give visitors enough information (without too many details) so they will contact your company, or you may provide additional links that allow them to purchase your products online.

The content you write should reflect the pages and outline you identified. It should also be written on a high school level so that it is understandable to a wide audience. We strongly suggest using a technical writer or other expert to proof, edit, and refine the content before it goes to the web designer. It should be nearly perfect when the web coding begins.

Other Basic Keys to Credible Copy

In addition to being grammatically as perfect as possible, remember that perception and first impressions are critical in making a good website. So be sure the text on your site projects an aura of credibility. Font types, headings, and text organization can impact readability and retain (or deter) visitors to your site. Be consistent with headers, subheads, body content, and layout. Use a color pallet that is complementary to your brand. Break up copy blocks with subheads.

Search Engine Optimization (SEO)

Something else to highly weigh is SEO: your users are typing keywords into Google seeking your services. Understanding their behaviors and search terms will allow you to create website copy that's centered around these search terms. Text is critical, and if the text users are searching for isn't on your website, then your users have a decreased chance of finding you.

Similarly, one of the keys to performing highly on search engines is to constantly provide new, relevant content to your website. Remember, content is king, and if you fill your website with current, helpful, and valuable information that aligns with your customer's needs, you will attract visitors and delight your customers.

Navigation

As mentioned earlier, organize the site with short navigation (get where you need to go within three clicks). Structure your pages so a viewer can get most anywhere in your site in three clicks or less via tabs and/or embedded links within the copy. Also, design pages using an f-type pattern where the reader reads from left to right and from the top to the bottom.

Calls to Action

Many websites provide a bunch of great content accompanied by a lot of engaging graphics. However, without a CTA, the user is left hanging and doesn't make a decision on what to do next. Remember, your goal is conversion. How do you convert them from a website user to a customer? Throughout your website, you should always be providing CTAs which can be buttons, web forms, phone numbers, and other engaging opportunities for the user to take action.

Build It for Universal Use

Finally, a good website is responsive to mobile media like smartphones, tablets, and other mobile devices. Be sure your designs look good and operate properly on all devices. This is called a responsive web design and it is the approach that suggests design and development should respond to the user's behavior and environment based on screen size, platform, and orientation. Responsive design makes your web pages functional on all devices using CSS and HTML to resize, hide, shrink, enlarge, or move the content to make it look good on any screen.

Related to this concept is browser appearance. While there has been a lot of progress here, not all browsers are created equal: during the design process, examine your site using different Internet browsers. You can then see how your potential customers would see the site based on which browser they are using. Your website should display correctly in all browsers.

Graphics and Photography—Less Is More

The simplified, purposeful, and strategic way you present each page of your website can make or break the experience. A good designer should offer the unique ability to simplify things like navigational bars, create consistent color schemes, insert appropriate, diverse graphics, and identify design inconsistencies. Be sure to use their abilities in these capacities when designing your website.

Always use engaging graphics and photography that are relevant to the material being presented. To obtain graphics and photography, you have multiple options: (1) you can purchase stock photography from online sources that have endless amounts of professional photos, (2) you can personalize the website experience by hiring or taking your own photography, and (3) you can borrow or reuse photography from other websites as long as you have the original artist's permission in writing and provide references.

HOW TO GET WEB TRAFFIC

Now that you have a new website, you'd like to increase your website traffic. Established inbound marketing and a solid content strategy are major players in the success of your website. You want to have a focus on getting found by customers and you do this by constantly sharing relevant, helpful, and valuable content. Do this through blogs, case studies, checklists, e-books, and other content pieces filled with keywords and phrases your customers are typing into Google.

Once you have this content on your site, target distribution channels where your audiences are such as social media and email. Maintain a constant goal of driving visitors to your website and converting them to a customer through a CTA.

Hosting Your Website

As your site is being built, you also have to think about finding server space. Similar to your computer files, the website files and graphics need a place to live so they can be displayed live on the Internet. Because of the advances in technology, "cloud servers" are relatively inexpensive, secure, and the best route to go when hosting your website.

Whether hosted internally or via a third party, be sure to acquire server space that is sufficiently large and fast so it does not impact your operations. Allow extra storage space and bandwidth to allow expansion with future web applications, databases, graphics, and other files.

You should also exercise the option to have company email for you and other employees that includes your website's name in the email addresses (e.g., info@duboseweb.com).

Having personalized, company-related email addresses demonstrates to your customers that your business is a professional, firmly established company and reminds them you are legitimate every time they type in your email address.

Website Analytics—Evaluation Is Better Online

Another huge benefit to moving a client online is the ability to obtain nearly real-time statistics on your website traffic and your visitors' interests. Once your site is operational, analyze your visitors and how they interact with your website. To effectively monitor your website, it is essential to track customer visits, assess which pages are most effective, and understand how customers are finding your website. There is much to learn about how your customers are navigating your site in addition to simply tracking website hits. Some areas you need to consider in your statistics:

- *Worldwide map:* Which cities, states, or countries are your visitors originating from?
- *Visitors:* Are they new or returning? Which pages are they visiting? How much time are they spending on your site? On which web page(s) on your site are these vistors exiting?
- *Browser capabilities:* What browsers, operating systems, do your users' computers have? What features do you need to design in to ensure all of these browsers are operating at peak efficiency for these access points?
- *Traffic sources:* What percentage of traffic reaches your site by typing in the specific web address? Which websites do customers use to find yours? Which search engines are you being found on? What keywords and phrases are being searched that result in visitors locating your site?
- *Content:* What content, subjects, and titles drive visitors to your website? Where do they start and finish on your website? You want your site designed so they not only visit your homepage, but also go deeper to the other pages of your website.

GETTING BY WITH A LITTLE HELP FROM YOUR FRIENDS

When it comes to web design, maybe your students can do it themselves, maybe they need some help. If you decide you need help, here are some suggestions for engaging a web design company.

- Inquire with friends, colleagues, business owners, and nonprofit staff about who they have worked with in the past.
- Contact web designers listed at the bottom of appealing websites.
- Solicit proposals from several web businesses to find the best fit for your needs.
- Before making a final selection, check with your local business bureau to see if there have been complaints filed against the business.

And, as in any field, web companies' philosophies, ethics, work quality, knowledge, experience, financial security, pricing, and customer service vary significantly so be open to a variety of options.

WRAPPING IT UP

To summarize, designing eye-catching websites that work is an art and a science. It takes significant time and effort to refine your website into the powerhouse you need it to be. You can have the best products and services in the world, but if you don't market them the right way—well, you know the rest of the story.

REFERENCES AND ADDITIONAL READINGS

Woods, S. (2013, May 24). How to optimize images for you website or blog. *Shortie Designs*. Retrieved from https://shortiedesigns.com/2013/05/how-to-optimise-images-for-your-website-or-blog/

Woods, S. (2014, April 3). 10 top principles of effective web design. *Shortie Designs*. Retrieved from https://shortiedesigns.com/2014/03/10-top-principles-effective-web-design/

Woods, S. (2016, June 17). Content marketing 101. *Shortie Designs*. Retrieved from https://shortiedesigns.com/2016/06/yourcontentmarketingplan/

Part IV

Leaving a Legacy

Promoting Your Student-Run Agency

Although professional communications agencies rightly focus time and resources applying their trade to benefit clients, many neglect those same skills when it comes to their own business. Ironically, the same communications agencies that work so diligently to execute creative, brand-building strategies for their clients are sometimes unable or unwilling to focus those same important efforts on self-promotions. Lack of time, resources, and a clearly defined identity are just some of the reasons why this happens. Whatever the reason, an agency's inability to strategically focus on its own company's communications plan at best hinders growth and at worst, jeopardizes an agency's very existence.

Make no mistake; an agency's success depends on its ability to make clients successful. If it can't, it shouldn't be in business. Does that mean your student-run agency can simply let great client work speak for itself? Or, do you need to purposefully and intentionally build a strong foundation for future growth and student learning opportunities by

© iQoncept/Shutterstock.com

strategically promoting your agency's value to clients, university **stakeholders**, and students?

The short answer is: agency reputations are built, not born. Yet, when working with limited resources, you may still wonder—why focus on building and communicating the agency's brand when it diverts energy away from the most important function of making clients successful? Without successful clients, all the time and effort in self-promotion becomes irrelevant. The productive agency has to make time for both; after all, failing to communicate your brand is the very thing we caution clients about on a daily basis. Moreover, an agency's failure to effectively communicate its own brand may cause clients to question whether an agency could successfully do this important task for any other client.

Most professional agencies solve this conundrum by dedicating a creative team to develop a **brand identity** and communicate that identity through time-tested tactics such as "taglines," "vision statements," or "philosophies." Reviewing successful agency websites, you will learn their history, often told as "our story," and will likely learn about their accomplishments through their "pressroom" or "awards" or "case studies." Other agencies push their brand identity and self-promotion plans further. Some agency leaders have written books espousing their philosophy, including David Ogilvy and Kevin Roberts of Saatchi & Saatchi. Other agency staffers make it a point to speak regularly at industry conferences and trade organizations, or pen op-eds in the trade press, such as *PR Week, Mediapost,* or *Advertising Age.* Still others create original content to describe their processes, prowess, and personalities, such as the John St. agency in Toronto with their notable ExFEARiential and Jane St. videos. Some have even gotten naked, like Viceroy Creative from New York. While you may not ever streak down Madison Avenue, if your student-run agency seeks to replicate the real world environment of advertising, public relations (PR), or marketing communications, then a self-promotion plan is necessary. It's critical not only for your agency to grow and acquire new clients, but also to meet the ultimate goals of offering professional experiences and engaged learning to prepare students for careers.

This chapter examines the importance of and process for creating a communication plan to ensure your student agency grows not just in size, but in student learning opportunities, outplacements for internships and careers, and reputation for excellence. This plan ultimately helps the student agency to generate success for its clients of all types and allows students to have an active role in helping drive businesses and contributing to their campuses and communities. It will address the actions you should consider to build

Stakeholder: A key audience and/or constituent deserving special attention to validate their initial and/or ongoing support of an organization. Can include any key audience member that holds significant influence in the past, present, or future of an organization such as investors, founders, influencers, strategic partners, and so on.

Brand identity: The way an organization or brand wants to be perceived by the public. Brand identities are developed through visual components such as logos, taglines, fonts and colors, and through an organization's values and the ways it expresses those values.

a strong brand that is worthy of attracting clients, garnering support from your college or university, and delivering on the promise to help launch participants' careers. In this chapter you will discover the following:

- The importance and role of an agency self-promotion communication plan
- Considerations when developing the self-promotion communication planning process
- Elements of brand identity and how they can be captured in the self-promotions plan
- Actions of the agency and outcomes to be communicated in a self-promotion communication plan
- Ways to structure communications with audiences for self-promotions
- Executing the self-promotion communication plan through message delivery platforms

WHY ENGAGE IN SELF-PROMOTION?

The successful student agency starts with a deliberate effort, grounded in strategy and executed flawlessly, to attract quality clients—but it doesn't stop there. Rather, quality clients provide the agency with the opportunity to accomplish all of its other goals such as providing a space for experiential learning or generating revenue. A **self-promotion plan** is a strategic and deliberate effort to communicate your brand identity, personality, and uniqueness to those who need to hear. Creating and executing this plan also provides even more opportunities for students to learn and apply their knowledge and skills. Finally, this plan will generate the needed support from various audiences to ensure that the agency succeeds for many years to come. Why do you need one?

> **Self-promotion plan:** A deliberate, strategic blueprint focused on personal or organizational communications objectives, strategies, and tactics to accomplish goals.

Self-promotion energizes your stakeholders

At your school, someone or several people decided that a student agency is a worthwhile endeavor. Who are these people? Why did—and do—these people support your agency?

- Does the agency bring revenue to the school?
- Does the agency demonstrate your school's commitment to experiential learning and evolving business practices and technologies?
- Does the agency help students succeed in internships and post college careers?
- Does your school offer class/course credit and see the agency as a required or elective part of your education?
- Does your school dedicate faculty and staff to help the agency become successful?

Although student learning is paramount, stakeholders look holistically at how the agency aligns with departmental and university-wide strategic goals. If great clients and great work are happening, but stakeholders do not know or understand the agency's success, then the success is irrelevant.

In short, your agency's self-promotion plan communicates to stakeholders that their investment is worth it. It proves that students are receiving a better education, thanks to the agency experience. It demonstrates professionals are impressed with and hiring agency staff for internships and jobs, and clients are enthused about the high-quality education your college or university is providing. Your student-run agency and its staff signal to the world that the university is on the cutting edge of contemporary business practices and preparing students for careers. Stakeholders need your self-promotions content as evidence that the agency is a worthwhile use of school resources.

Self-promotion is self-defense

Support for the agency can change. Abilities and passion of the agency staff can fluctuate. Enthusiasm and engagement with and from clients can wax and wane. Faculty advisors leave or change roles, deans get promoted, and students graduate. Brand identity and agency culture can be the constant. Are any of the founders of Coca-Cola or the Ford Motor Company still working there today? A strong brand, well communicated, can weather challenges and continue to provide value to stakeholders, clients, and student staff over time. Deliberate, strategic, and consistent self-promotions build a legacy of student learning, client success, and student post college accomplishment for the long term.

Self-promotion is offense

The business of communications changes. Technology and ever-shifting consumer values and preferences push professionals to adapt to new ways of communicating. Just think of all the industry changes in the past few decades—from print to TV advertising; from creating stagnant websites to engaging in Snapchat campaigns; from writing press releases to producing branded videos. Professional agencies had to adapt to these changes and more. Today, technology is moving at an increasingly rapid rate. Through branding and self-promotion, you can secure your agency's place in this emerging communications business. You can carve out a reputation as one that executes and creates in new environments. More than just a theoretical classroom experience, your student agency can engage in practical application of the cutting edge knowledge future employers fervently seek.

Self-promotion attracts clients

Long-term relationships are somewhat rare in the agency business. Clients leave and agencies must create a steady pipeline of potential clients to replace lost business. This concept is regularly addressed in the professional agency world through "new business" efforts—the lifeblood of an agency (see Chapter 3). In addition to simply replacing business, new clients can diversify your agency's portfolio with different business sectors, media efforts, or fresh, innovative work.

However, you don't want to wait until a client leaves to build your pipeline. Self-promotion plans create awareness with potential clients long before you make an agency pitch. A strategic and creative self-promotion plan attracts new clients looking to leverage the abilities and unique perspective of your student agency's budding communications professionals.

Self-promotion attracts talent

A student-run agency is constantly battling for the hearts and minds of fellow creative and strategic talent. Just like clients want to work with a vibrant and innovative agency that delivers on the promise of success, so do current and future employees of the student agency. In school, what student isn't pressed for time? How many clubs or organizations are available and attractive to potential agency staffers? How many students must consider if the agency experience is possible with financial and academic pressures on their time and energy? Self-promoting the culture of personal and career satisfaction can further engage current staffers to perform at their best, and attract new talent who might otherwise not consider joining the agency.

As you can see, self-promotion is about much more than attracting clients. The professional world needs to know about the agency. They need to see how students are applying classroom learning. They need to see how the agency is working in traditional and emerging platforms. They need to see how student-run agency staffers are already doing the job they will do in their careers. Faculty and staff also need to know this to steer talented staff to the agency. University stakeholders need to know this to continue their support with shrinking resources within a culture of accountability. All of this is within your reach, if you have a good self-promotion plan (Box 14.1).

Box 14.1 Five Reasons for Self-Promotion

1. Energize your stakeholders
2. Build a legacy for the long haul
3. Adapt to changing environments
4. Attract new clients
5. Recruit quality talent

HOW TO ENGAGE IN SELF-PROMOTION

In his insightful book, *Paid Attention: Innovative Advertising for a Digital World*, industry consultant Faris Yakob (2015) has a simple formula for generating attention: *Do Things, Tell People.* In other words, the authentic actions you undertake as an agency drive the content you create and share with stakeholders.

Conceptually this should be easy. *Do* activities that create environments of learning and professional experiences, establish thought leadership, and thus generate success for clients and staff. And, have fun! Then, *share* it with others. Notice it is not merely "telling." Sharing implies a mutual reward and the activities the agency completes are more worthy of sharing with the world rather than telling people. Share the activities, greatness, uniqueness, and passion of the student-run agency and all of the talented people who serve in it. First we will examine what to do. Then we can turn our attention to how to communicate those stories to the many publics/audiences of the student agency (Box 14.2).

© EtiAmmos/Shutterstock.com

Box 14.2   Two Crucial Steps for Successful Self-Promotions

STEP 1: *Do*. Take Action Worthy of Communication
STEP 2: *Share*. Plan and Execute Communications of Those Actions

STEP 1: DO. TAKE ACTION WORTHY OF COMMUNICATION

If you believe the agency does not or cannot offer clients success through your strategic and creative efforts, you can stop reading now. You might even consider whether a student agency is viable at all. You know that's not true. You have a group of dedicated, passionate, skillful, and creative innovators applying their classroom learning to real world situations. Good. Now you can engage in self-promotion.

The absolute most important action for immediate and long-term well-being of the agency is doing the work to make clients successful. This is the bedrock for student success in internship and jobs, and the evidence to stakeholders that the agency is providing valuable educational and professional experience, attracting new and innovative clients, and engaging future staffers to do their best work. See Chapters 4 and 7 on how to plan and manage client relationships for success. Once this is solid, you can begin to plan the agency's self-promotion efforts. In other words, actions that are worthy of communicating.

Do Your Brand Audit

The **Brand Audit** is necessary background research needed to understand the present situation and plan for the future. This is usually your first step with any client as you begin to address how the student-run agency will make them successful (see Chapter 8 on how to create a strategic plan). Just like with clients, do your research and ask the hard questions, then write down the **SWOT** and **Situation Analysis**.

> **Brand audit:** Systematic research, review, and analysis of brand identity including elements such as messaging strategies, customer-base demographics and perceptions, competitors, use of and presence on media, logos, taglines/theme-lines, color palates, and so on.

> **SWOT:** Strengths, weaknesses, opportunities, and threats. A model in the communications planning process to develop objectives and strategies to lead to success.

> **Situation analysis:** A description of the current landscape or environment in which an organization exists as it begins to develop plans for near and long-term success.

- *Mission and values.* Why do you exist? How is the world better because you exist? Why is the world incomplete without you?
- *Purpose.* What do you do, literally and figuratively? What can/do you do well? How do you do it? What value do you provide? What are the challenges to successfully fulfilling your mission?
- *Uniqueness.* What makes you special? What's your Brand Identity Statement, Rational Support points/Reasons-to-Believe (RTBs), Emotional Support points/RTBs, personality/tone, Key Insights?
- *Brand assets.* Logo? Website? Established social media channels? Color palette? Tagline/Theme-line? Brand advocates/evangelists like successful alumni or client testimonials?
- *Reputation.* Are people aware of your existence? Are they knowledgeable about your purpose and abilities? Do they believe you are an agency that offers value to staff, the school, and/or clients?
- *Audiences/publics/target.* Who are your primary, secondary, tertiary audiences? Who are your outliers? Demographics, psychographics, perceptions, behavior, usage, loyalty/sentiment?
- *Define communications objectives*-(often per audience/public segment). Raise awareness, educate, reach new audience(s), increase frequency of messages, instill desire/drive an action, redefine identity/offerings/value, combat perception, solidify position, raise consideration?

Capture and Document Client Success

In professional agencies, these are often called **case studies**—stories that outline client successes, including strategies, tactics, and results. Maybe you think in terms of success achieved per semester. Or, you can think in terms of what was accomplished on a single project or campaign. Most importantly, think not just of "what the agency did," but also what the outcome of the effort yielded. *Example:* "We conducted 3 focus groups and fielded a survey with 25 respondents,"

> **Case studies:** Organized narrative and/or visual study created to display the process, output, and success of an agency effort often to reflect a particular theme to demonstrate the agency's capability(ies).

packs more of a punch when we add, "that revealed new insights about the convenience of the client's brand versus the competition, and lead to a two-pronged social media initiative among lapsed customers." Remember numbers and visuals communicate powerfully. Discuss the outcome numerically and show what you did visually (maybe a graph or infographic). Think about how your success can be classified:

- Did your agency show success in a particular business segment (restaurant, non-profit, retail, etc.)?
- Did your agency contribute to business return-on-investment (ROI) success (e.g., increased Instagram reach by 225 new follows for a 63% increase in a 2-month period; average ticket sales increased by 7% during the campaign; 32% click-through rate among those visiting the site)?
- Did your agency show success with a particular type of consumer/public segment (e.g., reached millennials with a unique appeal to their preferences for online content)?
- Did your agency show success with a certain type of media or communications tactic (Facebook campaign, event activation, social media influencer or traditional media relations campaign, crowdsource poll, qualitative research, etc.)?
- Did your agency show success with a creative solution or production capability (branded content video, digital banner ad, speaker points for client media appearance, logo design)?

Establish/Build Credibility and Trust

Saying, "trust us, we're genuine" rings pretty hollow. Saying, "check out our webpage and learn more about us" provides access to tangible proof. So, now you just need to have the proof that people can trust you to deliver on the brand promise of success. How do you do that?

Enter and win awards: First, think of awards related to your client work. Think of local American Advertising Federation (AAF) Ad America awards, and local Public Relations Society of America (PRSA) and American Marketing Association (AMA) awards for your agency's client work. Look nationally as well for places to showcase your client successes such as the University & College Design Association (UCDA) competition. Industry trade publications such as *PR News* and *Mediapost* also offer many award and recognition programs. Also, look to business sector–specific awards, for instance nonprofit, environmental, restaurant, or healthcare communications awards. Additionally, look for platform-specific awards such as social media awards, radio advertising awards, event marketing, or website design awards. Don't forget campus awards. Are there awards for clubs/organizations? Campus citizenship awards? Are there local community awards? Are there small business awards through the chamber of commerce or local news outlets for recognizing community partners? Finally, the agency could consider specific student project awards such as the AAF National Student Advertising Competition (NSAC), PRSSA Bateman Competition, One Club's One Show, The PR Council's Take Flight Competition, Marketing Edge's Project ECHO, or even nonprofit campaign competitions such as Project Yellow Light. The only limit on these opportunities is determined by whether the agency can afford to take time and resources from client work to engage in a project-based competition. If you have the bandwidth, it may be worthwhile, and it certainly can help students build strong portfolios.

Join and attend professional association events: Many professional clubs and organizations offer student discounts and many even allow complimentary access to events for students

in the area. Begin to show the local industry the professionalism and aptitude of the agency staff and leadership through networking and professional development events. From AAF to PRSA to AIGA to AMA, there is an organization for almost any interest in professional communications. Those photos of agency staffers engaging with professionals also make nice posts on social media.

© Matej Kastelic/Shutterstock.com

Activate the agency for worthwhile causes in your community: You have a group of passionate and thoughtful people. How can the agency be a good citizen to build the community? How can the agency serve the university or surrounding area? Can you help an elementary school's tutoring program? Can you take part as an organization in a food drive, blood drive, or a walking team in the next 5K? Can you clean a city park or help to alleviate homelessness in your community? If the student-run agency starts to volunteer, you might be surprised how quickly you are asked to provide communications solutions for community nonprofits. What a great use of your unique talents and abilities!

Open your doors: If you have a physical space, have an open house before the next hiring season. Invite other groups or classes to any events or meetings you have. Hold an orientation "mixer" for first-year students or new majors in your program. Invite faculty/staff for a coffee hour. Invite campus media and local media to tour and perhaps do a spotlight on your organization. Don't forget professionals. Many leaders and junior professionals want to speak to the agency. Believe it or not, coming back to a campus and sharing their perspective and experience is fun for them.

Partner with others: Coordinate with your campus PRSSA, Ad Club or other relevant clubs to cohost guest speakers, screen films, or just have a fun social. Partner with a local agency to be their "millennial soundboard" or offer your services to help with their clients. In turn, they can help the agency solve problems, give advice on best practices, and be great mentors. You can coordinate tours and special educational or networking sessions with area professionals and businesses. Offer to speak about the agency in classes in the major, especially during key hiring/enrollment periods. Consider **strategic partnerships** on campus that might officially or unofficially and directly or indirectly provide mutual benefit. Perhaps coordinating with entrepreneurship education and clubs might provide clients. Or, cinema and production or theater arts students might provide direction, editing, or acting. Or maybe an accounting student interested in law school might be a perfect staff member handling billing, contracts or talent and intellectual property negotiations. In short, make your student-run agency a student-fun agency.

> **Strategic partnerships:** Relationships that provide mutual benefit and pool resources to share, communicate, or otherwise engage with each other to expand opportunities for success.

Engage your alumni: Look at how your university engages alumni in publications, online, and on social media. Think about how organizations such as the AAF Most Promising Multicultural Student Award (MPMS) promote and leverage their alumni base to support students and recent graduates. Consider how the benefit of the student agency experience can extend beyond graduation. A job board? Alumni networking events? An alumni-student mentoring program? Many would argue that a career start or career boost is often attributed to networking and "who you know."

Establish and Communicate Thought Leadership

Every industry has what are known as thought leaders. These are respected people (or organizations) whose informed opinions address the challenges and trends driving the industry forward.

Professional agencies regularly engage in **thought leadership.** Many issue reports in confidence to their clients in the form of "white papers," "POVs," or now even "red papers." FutureBrand, for instance, issues its brand index yearly to provide marketers with respect and sentiment ratings on the "most beloved" brands. Others, like Shift Communications, have attracted large followings, and probably a few clients, thanks to their informative blogs. Some even write recurring guest columns like Marc Brownstein in *Advertising Age.* If you search for an advertising or PR agency, you'll likely find they communicate their aptitudes, opinions, recommendations, and predictions on their website, social media platforms, and blogs.

> **Thought leadership:** Expressing, sharing, and demonstrating expert and informed opinion on matters, trends, and opportunities pertaining to the business one is engaged with.

Student-run agencies also have engaged in this thought leadership initiatives to further brand their organizations. In particular, college students provide unique insights into one of the most sought after target audiences for marketers—Millennials. Two student agencies have tapped into this potential; The University of Florida's The Agency through it's MAVY respondent panel; and Elon University's Live Oak Communications through its Project ECHO, a partnership with global content marketer PACE Communications. These services and successes are, not surprisingly, communicated on the agencies' websites, blogs, and other media vehicles.

© Rawpixel.com/Shutterstock.com

Your student-run agency is now "in the business," so create and share news and perspectives about it with your audiences. You can create and share (curate) important points of view about the changing nature of the communications business. You can offer a stance or position on industry news and activities. You can invite guests to speak with your agency or create a panel to discuss issues facing the profession that might be particularly relevant to students, such as hiring practices, diversity and inclusion efforts, or emerging media planning practices. Stay abreast of industry trends and brainstorm ways to add value to the conversation.

Display Your Professionalism

While other activities in this section promote your work, partnerships and ideas, to display your professionalism you'll want to focus on the agency itself and the people who work there. Consider business-dress staff headshots and an agency group shot. Perhaps you need a brand essence video to communicate to prospective clients or future agency staffers. Consider employee spotlights of staffers who have won scholarships or awards, received industry or university recognition, landed internships with respected employers or participated in philanthropic or other activities. By showing the quality of your people and their accomplishments, you'll increase the professional positioning of your agency.

Display Your Passion and Culture

Have a good time! Do students want all buttoned-up work? Do clients want inhuman communicators singularly focused only on the business of communications? Let's hope not. From informal team bonding over pizza, to bowling, to movie nights, to forming a running club, show how much fun you're having, and how relationships can extend outside of "the agency." People work happier and harder when they are having fun. After all, your coworkers are still students; they just might become some of your best friends and most definitely your professional network base for years to come. Who wouldn't want to associate with a group that not only works hard, but plays hard as well? Consider a staff contest such as an agency March Madness bracket, a taco-eating contest, or end of semester award/superlatives. A video displaying your culture can be very impactful to attract new talent (i.e., staff) to the agency. Those involved in Greek rush know this tactic well (Box 14.3).

Box 14.3   Do Actions Worthy of Communicating

Do Your Brand Audit
Capture and Document Client Success
Establish/Build Credibility and Trust
Establish and Communicate Thought Leadership
Display Your Professionalism
Display Your Passion and Culture

STEP 2: SHARE, PLAN, AND EXECUTE COMMUNICATIONS OF THOSE ACTIONS

When planning how to communicate your actions, once again, think and act in very much in the same manner as planning and executing for a client. The student-run agency should think in terms of crafting the message(s) and delivering the message.

Much of the work has already been done in crafting the message. Mission and values have been identified. Publics/Target audiences have been researched and evaluated in terms of demographics, psychographics, perceptions, and behaviors. By identifying the public/target segments, you should already have a good idea of what motivates stakeholders to support the agency; what industry professionals should hear and see to be encouraged to interview and hire the student-run agency staff; what skills are offered to clients; and what current and future student employees want from this school-to-profession experience. With a strong and consistent brand identity, and the ability to lean on the agency strengths and success for proof of your claims, you can now focus on how best to deliver this message.

Content Marketing: Create and Curate

Content marketing dominates the discussion in the worlds of advertising and PR today. Content Marketing, as defined by the Content Marketing Institute (Pullizi, 2012),

is the marketing and business process for creating and distributing relevant and valuable content to attract, acquire, and engage a clearly defined and understood target audience—with the objective of driving profitable customer action.

Content marketing: Developing audience-centered communication tactics by providing relevant informative, useful and/or entertaining messages designed to engage audiences and encourage communication loops and sharing for the benefit of the communicator.

And,

> a content marketing strategy can leverage all story channels (print, online, in-person, mobile, social, etc.), be employed at any and all stages of the buying process, from attention-oriented strategies to retention and loyalty strategies, and include multiple buying groups.

Said another less formal way by the Content Marketing Institute,

> Content Marketing is owning, as opposed to renting, media. It's a marketing process to attract and retain customers by consistently creating and curating content in order to change or enhance a consumer behavior.

At its core, content marketing evolves the traditional definition of advertising,

From: Paying the media to run your ad,

To: Using the media delivery channels you control (such as your website or social media pages) to distribute your content.

Content marketing also evolves PR definitions and practices,

From: Brands trying to pitch and control media coverage

To: Brands controlling and disseminating messages directly, rather than through a journalist or news outlet.

Created content: You are creating content through your actions at the agency every day. Look at all the great successes and innovative approaches you're recommending and executing for your clients. Look at all your efforts to build trust and credibility on-campus, with stakeholders, and in your community. Look at the actions you've taken to be a thought leader and to display the professional, yet fun and rewarding, culture your student-run agency embodies. You already have the content; now you just need to modify it for specific platforms, such as a social media post, a newsletter article, an email, a video, and so on.

> **Created content:** Developing/executing original content, such as blog posts, videos, infographics, and so on to achieve the communicator's objectives.

Curated content: Similar to curating the best artwork for display in museums, in the communications world the term *curate* means to gather the best content for display on your many media platforms. In addition to creating your own content, you can curate existing articles, industry news, whitepapers, and even

> **Curated content:** Sharing/distributing existing content through owned media platforms that engage audiences, and directly or indirectly support the goals of the communicator.

speeches and expert opinions to share and comment on to your fan base and your followers. Now you just need to deliver it in ways and times and places that educate, inform, entertain, and otherwise provide utility and value to your audiences.

The Media Plan (How to Deliver the Message)

> ### Box 14.4   The Media Mantra
>
> The Right Message
> The Right People
> The Right Place
> The Right Time
> The Right Cost
> The Right Response

In classic media planning, we think in terms of:

> The *Right Message* to the *Right People* in the *Right Place*, at the *Right Time*, at the *Right Cost*, for the *Right Response*.

This has often been called The Media Mantra and is commonly referenced in several iterations in numerous textbooks (see Dickinson, 2008), articles, and conference rooms across the globe. Consider each of these elements as you plan your student-run agency self-promotions:

Audience (internal vs external) + needed message + desired outcome: Who are we trying to reach? Do we wish to reach a broad audience with a general message, or communicate a specific message with a smaller audience for maximum impact? What is the outcome? Improve positive sentiment, attend a guest speaker, share a post, contact the agency to become a client, increase our agency fee?

Timing: What are your key communication periods per public/target audience? Do you want to communicate with future staffers around enrollment or class registration times? Do you need to reach prospective clients in the summer before the semester begins? Do you need faculty/staff/advisors to recommend your agency to new majors before their second year of school? Do you want to communicate with industry talent/human resource professionals around internship and graduation season? Do stakeholders at your school need evidence before board of advisor or budget meetings?

Frequency: Very simply, this means "how much and how often?" Regularly, right before an event? Monthly, to keep current clients excited about the academic and professional success of the student agency team? Daily, for alumni to keep us top of mind when they have a quick job opening and can recruit? For example, Taco Bell probably needs to communicate regularly to many people to stay top of mind among many competitors when a quick decision of where to grab lunch occurs, but Porsche might only need to excite a few people once in their lifetime to buy (when and if they can).

Message mix: Often called the *creative rotation* in the advertising business, the message mix is commonly thought of as a percentage of the types of messages per public/target audience. What percentage of your communications activity ought to focus on news and information, versus entertainment, versus utility/personal development? Of course, this can vary by audience segment, time of year, desired outcome, or any of the other media planning factors previously discussed.

Delivering Your Message

One efficient way many professionals view message distribution is through the **PESO (Paid, Earned, Shared, Owned) media** model. Media decisions are best understood and then executed when we examine them as PEOS (Paid, Earned, Owned, and Shared). That

> **PESO media:** a way to characterize the types of message distribution platforms available and determine most effective communication tactics for each: Paid, Earned, Shared, Owned.

acronym, PEOS is just not as memorable as PESO. But, by addressing a content delivery strategy in the PEOS order, we can see how they might complement each other in a logical and interdependent way. Yet in reality, this interdependence means that PESO is memorable, but really it is not linear and you could address or execute any of these four platforms in any way at any time. PESO, PEOS, ESPO, SOPE, and so on.

In addition, the four parts of the media model are overlapping. For example, on Facebook you control the posted content on your page (owned), interact with and seek engagement with audiences (shared), can place an ad targeted to a specific audience (paid) and garner a mention of your brand on another member's page (earned). To understand the four elements of the model, we'll look at them separately through PEOS.

Paid Media

Paying the media to run your message is often at the very core of any definition of advertising. And today, as emerging platforms and technologies present new opportunities for brands to communicate with their audiences, paid media is most commonly thought of as "traditional advertising."

On the surface, it seems like there may be little to no need to pay for media, considering the student agency's limited marketing footprint, very clearly defined niche audiences, and little need to "sell" a mass-produced commodity. But, if you broaden the thinking and definition of paid media for your agency, you may identify some areas where paying to disseminate your agency message and brand identity could be advantageous. Maybe a small advertisement in the school newspaper or a commercial on university TV (or even just their online extensions) might make sense during hiring season. This is especially true if you're looking to attract new staffers or want to celebrate a huge agency or client success. Maybe a program guide ad in your local community theater *Playbill* or sponsorship of a philanthropic event might help cement your reputation as a community partner. Perhaps an advertisement in the awards annual for your local professional AAF Advertising Club or PRSA chapter could garner higher awareness and positive sentiment among professionals for your student-run agency.

Postcards, flyers, campus LED screens, and posters may be needed, especially if you are engaged in thought leadership by bringing in guest speakers, partnering with other school organizations for educational or social programs, or opening your doors for staff recruitment events. Finally, a newsletter—digital and/or printed—can serve as an historical, yearbook-like summary of all of the agency's activities and successes over the past semester or year. And of course, all these materials build student portfolios and can be entered into award shows to build even more credibility and trust when communicated in your self-promotion plan.

Earned Media

Earned Media is most commonly thought of as a tactic in the arsenal of traditional (marketing) PR. Generally, it involves encouraging journalists or news outlets to cover your events, shoot broadcast segments, or include mentions of your brand in their news stories. In other words, you "earn" a mention in a media outlet by "pitching" story ideas to traditional media gatekeepers. Ideally this coverage would communicate your key messages and strategically align with your communications objectives.

But in today's viral world, Earned Media is more than that. It also involves influencer marketing, creating strategic partnerships, developing affinity for, and hopefully stimulating discussion of your agency among those who have a public following. Maybe a campus leader talks about the agency to their friends and colleagues, or maybe the agency professional you invited to your last event gives you a shout out on their LinkedIn blog. Really, anytime staff, alumni, faculty, business professionals, and so on speak of your agency on their social media pages or in meetings—or even the old fashioned word-of-mouth conversation—you just earned exposure or publicity through Earned Media.

Owned Media

This area allows you to distribute messages without paying to use that medium because you own it. You have the ability to publish, display, or air the messages you want on your own channels or networks.

When investigating Owned Media platforms, first think of physical space. Do you have a space like an office or a dedicated classroom, or even just a door or a faculty advisor's office? Is your logo prominently displayed there? Would a poster showcase your agency mission, aptitude, and brand personality? Are you maximizing all available space? Are you displaying your name and logo wherever/whenever you can (within reason and in good taste)? Are you using your color palette consistently? Are you trying to incorporate your agency tagline/theme-line/mission/purpose? Consider agency swag—t-shirts, stickers, water bottles, umbrellas, and coffee mugs all make great branding tools for your staff and also thoughtful gifts to stakeholders and professionals who support your agency.

Next, think of the forms and templates your agency utilizes every day. Do you have consistent and strategically branded items such as client presentation layouts, new business brochures and folders, conference reports, agency POVs, and email templates when communicating to clients, professionals, influencers, and stakeholders?

Once you've considered your physical space and materials, move on to your digital platforms:

- Are the agency's LinkedIn and Google+ pages accurate and updated? Do they align with your brand identity in terms of color palette, logo, tagline, theme line, mission? If you don't have pages on these sites, consider establishing them. In addition to Twitter, these are the two sites used most often by professionals.
- Do you have a blog? It's a great way for students to express their knowledge and passion for the communications business. It demonstrates to stakeholders how the agency experience enhances classroom learning. It shows thought leadership and **agency capabilities** to current and prospect clients. It also excites talent/HR decision makers to hire agency staffers for internships and full-time jobs by showing students' passion and experience in *doing* communications, not just *studying* it.

> **Agency capabilities:** A description of the literal and figurative uniqueness or abilities of the agency to perform types of work or accomplish specific kinds of goals for clients.

- Do you have a YouTube channel? Video is a powerful communication tactic, and with the skills students learn alongside technological advancements, all of us can conceive, shoot and edit quality branding (professional) and entertainment (culture) videos.
- Is the agency listed as part of your school's website? Again, is it accurate and updated, fully maximizing every word choice to strategically communicate the agency's uniqueness and value?
- How do you perform in key word search? If a searcher Googles the agency name (or reasonably close) your correct URL should show up in the results relatively easily, and route digital traffic correctly to your page. Also, review the text that appears below your link on the search results page. You want to make sure it identifies your brand accurately and succinctly.
- Is your owned agency website accurate, updated, and user friendly? This might possibly be the most important initiative a student agency can tackle. Why? If social

media provides the opportunity to quickly communicate about your agency with your followers, your website is your permanent signage for seekers. Social media is fast—it scrolls and changes. Your website provides the permanence whereby you can communicate the agency's missions/values, client success, agency success, student success, and awards/recognition/accolades now and for years to come. The menu on your page should clearly lead viewers to at least the following:

What we do
Clients
Case Studies
Newsroom, awards, press
Agency blog
Contact Us

- Do you have an email database? Just as important, is it searchable and segmented? Email allows you to communicate your actions more directly to a variety of audiences. For example, you may want to alert prospective clients of new capabilities or expertise within the agency. Or, communicate with industry recruiters about how successful your staff was during their internships this summer. Or, with first-year students who came to an open house last semester to apply for this spring's staff positions. Or, with alumni to visit and speak at your homecoming open house. Or, boast to your dean and faculty at graduation about the jobs agency seniors have secured. Email is a great way to do this.

Shared Media

On one level, Shared Media is easy to understand because it is closely related to social media. It includes platforms like Facebook, Twitter, Snapchat, Instagram, Vine, and numerous other options that will no doubt emerge and disappear before this book is published. In a sense, Shared Media is an owned media platform but also a shared space since followers comment and express emotions and sentiments toward your brand and specific posted content. On another level, Shared Media is more than social media. It empowers and equips the public to make and share content for your brand.

Parry Headrick of Matter Communications notes, "[Shared Media] is trickiest to explain and can take on many forms, but essentially, consumers are working in concert with a brand to create and share/promote the brand's content" (Headrick, 2013). At its core you encourage people to share your created and curated content; they share your posts, forward your emails, comment on, and engage with your social media activity. At a deeper level, you, the brand, give them something worth engaging in. Perhaps this could be a social media poll to solicit answers to a question like, "I joined (name of student-run agency) because . . ." Perhaps one staffer who posts on the agency blog will be selected to attend a writing workshop at a local agency for a day of personal mentoring. Perhaps it could be a contest for staffers to create "the Vine video that defines a day in the life of (name of student-run agency)."

So as you are determining what tactics to use in promoting your agency, be sure to look at all of the options available to you. By adopting the PESO formula, you are ensured that you are building a comprehensive, overlapping media structure that amplifies media opportunities and ensures maximum effectiveness is achieved (Box 14.5).

Box 14.5   PESO Media

P = Paid media (advertising—banner ads, campus newspaper, paid search/AdWords, flyers/posters)
E = Earned media (shares/likes/re-tweets, mentions, articles)
S = Shared media (engaged communications feedback/loops, contests, user created or generated)
O = Owned (website, social media accounts, brochures, newsletters, blogs, office signage/bulletin boards, agency templates)

CONCLUSION

Self-promotion is the art of creating and telling the agency's story. Your story of creative students solving communication problems with great work; your story of the agency as a space for personal and professional growth; your story of the agency equipping and preparing students for career success; and, your story of the fun and friendships made when students embark on this adventure.

By first concentrating on what to do and then strategically planning what to say and how to deliver the message, the story writes itself. Your self-promotion plan is the insurance that the message reaches the right people in the right way at the right time for the desired results. Agency credibility, quality clients and learning experiences, university stakeholder support, and student career success all stem from the self-promotion plan. When you let the world hear and respond to your story, you'll provide a strong foundation that will support your agency now and in the future.

REVIEW AND DISCUSSION QUESTIONS

1. What is the biggest determinant of an agency being deemed a success?
2. Why do students choose to invest passionate energy in a student-run agency? What can a student-run agency do to energize current and future staff members?
3. Why do professional agencies create a self-promotion plan? How are they similar or different to why student-run agencies may create a self-promotion plan?
4. Who are student agency stakeholders? Why are they important or not?
5. How does a student agency start a self-promotion plan from a "Do" and "Share" perspective?
6. How might a student agency "capture" client success? How might they classify or communicate different types of success?

7. What kinds of award competitions might a student agency consider entering?
8. What kinds of strategic partnerships might a student agency consider? Why might they be helpful to a student agency?
9. What media/message delivery tactics seem most relevant or necessary for a student agency?
10. How might a student agency use its owned media such as its website in a self-promotion plan?

REFERENCES AND ADDITIONAL READINGS

Dickinson, D.L. (2008). Media strategy & planning workbook. Chicago, IL: Racom Communications

Headrick, P. (2013). What's the difference between paid, owned and earned media? *PR Whiteboard*, matter Communications blog. Retrieved from https://www.matternow.com/news-views/prwhiteboard/whats-the-difference-between-paid-owned-and-earned-media/

Ogilvy, D. (1985). *Ogilvy on advertising* (First Vintage Books Edition). New York, NY: Random House Inc.

Nudd, T. (2013, November 7). Stolen babies and home abductions: This agency's prankvertising is absolute hell on earth: John St. spoofs hot new trend. *AdWeek*. Retrieved from http://www.adweek.com/adfreak/stolen-babies-and-home-abductions-agencys-prankvertising-absolute-hell-earth-153666

Nudd, T. (2015a, March 9). Why these agency execs went through hell to get naked in these ads (SFW): A rebranding that's more than skin deep. *AdWeek*. Retrieved from http://www.adweek.com/adfreak/why-these-agency-execs-went-through-hell-get-naked-these-ads-sfw-163318

Nudd, T. (2015b, November 5). John St.'s latest merciless satire just destroys the Dove style of marketing to women: "If she's crying, she's buying." *AdWeek*. Retrieved from http://www.adweek.com/adfreak/john-sts-latest-merciless-satire-just-destroys-dove-style-marketing-women-167947

Pullizi, J. (2012, June 6). Six useful content marketing definitions. *Content Marketing Institute*. Retrieved from http://contentmarketinginstitute.com/2012/06/content-marketing-definition/

Roberts, K. (2005). *Lovemarks: The future beyond brands* (Rev. ed.). New York, NY: powerHouse Books.

Yakob, F. (2015). *Paid attention: Innovative advertising for a digital world, series: Cambridge marketing handbooks*. London, UK: Kogan Page Limited.

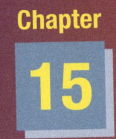
THE CHALLENGE

You have invested 3 to 4 years of your life and a lot of treasure in training for a career outside of college. You have worked your internship(s), had a great time in the student agency—did some great work for some great clients—and now it is time to think about taking flight on your own.

In this chapter, you will discover how to advance your work so it speaks for you, promotes you by building a brand, and invites the world to stand up and take notice of the incredible talent you are. Sometimes this can be a short distance and sometimes it can be a very long road. Hopefully, your time at the student-run agency has shortened your individual journey.

At this juncture, you have done a great job for your clients and your work has been captured, archived and maybe even recognized by professionals in your area. Perhaps, it is now time to consider a larger stage. One challenge to advancing your work is finding appropriate venues to display your brilliance.

In advertising and public relations there are multiple areas where work can be recognized including:

1. *Awards programs.* Almost every professional agency involved in communications has some form of award or recognition. Chapter 1 has more detail about the various categories where you can enter your work. The opportunity and the responsibility are yours, but entering your work can provide a strong springboard that could catapult you into a job. Enter your work, enter it often, and enter it into as many opportunities you can afford. In most cases, there are entry fees associated with the contests. Perhaps your student-run agency can help offset your entry fees. Should you win, be sure to place it on your resume, feature it on your blog, your social media, and your personal brand website.

2. *Service to the community.* Another area where work can be recognized is in pro bono service to the community. Although this effort may involve you creating new work and building new relationships, service on a board or boards, applying your skills to pro bono opportunities and/or volunteering are all good ways to move your work forward and will establish your reputation as an energetic, talented communicator. If your volunteer work results in some finished pieces, all the better.

3. *Teach something.* There is an old saying that if you want to really learn something, teach it to someone else. Take opportunities to share your knowledge, insight, and experience with others by teaching them. The benefits to them are they receive knowledge and profit from your experience. The benefits to you include a greater understanding of the subject matter, a resume bullet, the satisfaction of passing on knowledge and, hopefully, a little bit of cash as well. The world needs good teachers. As a trained communicator, you already have some advantages over others. Leverage those advantages as an opportunity to hone your presentation skills and gain some more experience.

4. *Build an integrated communications brand—about you.* You have done it for other clients, now it is time to do it for yourself. As a way to advance your work, consider building a brand presence. In an article published 20 years ago, author Tom Peters suggested that you are your own brand and that you should behave accordingly (Peters, 1997). And while it does seem somewhat cliché in today's times to speak about branding yourself, other authors and respected publications persist in validating the idea that a branding approach is a great way to promote your work.

A quick search on Amazon and the references at the end of this chapter reveal several books that discuss how to build a personal brand. Each makes different distinctions of how a brand should appear and what you should do to create your own brand. Key points from many authors however circle around points like

- *Truth in advertising*—Make sure you can support what you are promoting.
- *Own the brand*—Understand that it is a commitment to brand oneself and you need to be sure that you are comfortable with who you say you are.
- *Differentiate, don't imitate*—Make sure you are sufficiently different from the others you are competing with.
- *Make your brand relevant*—If you want to work in healthcare communications for example, build a brand around those things that healthcare communicators should care about.
- *Adopt an integrated approach*—Your resume should say the same things that your blog says, show at least some of the same work that your portfolio offers, etc.

THE METHOD

Building Your Own Brand—First Steps

In addition to the tactical communication points listed previously, there are also some strategic steps and tips for starting on your branding process.

Step 1: Discover Your "Secret Identity"

As discussed earlier in this chapter, there are steps to promote your work and, by default, your brand as well. And while there are many tips out there on how to tactically execute a branding campaign (LinkedIn pages, Facebook pages, Blogs, Individual Web Sites, etc.), when it comes to self-promotion, sometimes the first step is to identify which self you want to promote.

Who are you anyway? In the very popular *Guardians of the Galaxy* movie series, in *Volume 2* the main character, Peter Quill, discovers his true origin, a hybrid man-god ("little g") with super powers. He has an inkling of his abilities, (he refers to himself as *Starlord*), yet he is still underestimated by many around him.

But as the story progresses, with some help from his celestial father, Peter Quill discovers his true nature and starts to become known as someone who can get things done, a leader, a friend and a person who can be relied upon. Moreover, he stumbles upon the scope and breadth of his inner strength when his character is tested and his true self is revealed.

In a lot of ways, as you are just starting out, you may need some help in identifying your "secret identity" and "super powers" like Quill. You may not know, or believe, how good you are. As you are just beginning your journey, take the time to seek out mentors, trusted friends, and others to help you discover your strengths. These individuals can help you clarify your future career decisions and encourage your success.

In addition to mentors and trusted friends, there are also tests you can take to help you identify your strengths and weaknesses. One of the most established ones is the Birkman Career Assessment™. The test can be accessed via professional testing agencies and there are also books you can purchase which contain information, passwords, and so forth to take the test yourself.

As you perform these evaluations, don't be surprised if, along with the roses, there aren't a few thorns you have to suffer. Growth is a process—sometimes painful—and professional growth is no different. Welcome the input; accept the good and the bad. Incorporate the suggested changes and keep on striving.

In addition to your mentors' inputs, and any career assessments you may take, don't forget to ask the most important person for some insights as well. Be sure to interview yourself with some probing questions before setting out on your new journey of discovery.

In this chapter are some, (but by no means all), questions you should be asking yourself as you formulate a strategy for transitioning from student to professional and start to think about building your brand. Realize there is no right or wrong answers to these questions

Box 15.1   Self-evaluation Questions

1. In the professional realm, who am I? Am I a leader or do I do better as a support person for a bigger project?
2. In terms of communication functions, what do I really like to do? Am I more of a thinker or am I a planner? Am I more of a director or am I a tactician?
3. In terms of organization, am I a detail-oriented person or am I more of a big picture person?

(Continued)

(Continued)

4. When discussing working as a team and as you look back over assignments you have done and client work you have accomplished, were you happier in a team environment or as an independent operator? Why?/Why not?
5. When thinking of the vast scope of communication platforms and tools available to you, which ones appealed to you the most? Writing press materials? Designing web sites? Blogging? Practicing Social Media? Event planning? Others?
6. In terms of self-fulfillment, where do you see yourself? For example, do you see yourself working for a not-for-profit, or a corporation, or maybe a government entity? Or perhaps you really like the agency environment or maybe you would like to go into business for yourself?
7. Looking pragmatically, what other concerns do you have? Are you limited by geography? Do you have a need to stay or relocate to specific areas of the country?
8. Are you planning a life change (marriage, children, etc.)?
9. How about financial obligations? Loans? Investments?
10. Finally, do you have any existing relationships you can leverage in terms of a job interview or an actual position?

All of these questions and their associated answers are important and should contribute to your personal brand identity. By reflecting on the answers to these questions and others you may ask, you will be able to better focus your efforts to attaining your ultimate goal—gainful, self-fulfilling employment.

Those answers should also help you select what work to promote and what strong points you should focus upon when determining where to apply. For example, if you wanted a job in health communication, the work you did for that hospital client should be the stronger resume item than the sorority council you served. Once you make some of those preliminary decisions, it is time for the next section of your work promotion, developing your brand materials.

MATERIALS

Step 2. Bring Your Identity to Life

Once you've discovered your secret identity, you want to bring that brand to life through materials that show off your work both professionally and creatively.

The Resume

It is sometimes called a curriculum vitae (CV), more often called a resume and it is the key to getting invited to an interview. A RESUME DOES NOT GET YOU THE JOB, THE INTERVIEW DOES.

Similarly, in resumes, talk about your results/successes, not just your job description. Use facts and statistics from your agency successes to illustrate that you know how to quantify your results. Here are a few examples:

1. *Client's first in-store point of purchase campaign generated client reported increase in store traffic by 200 new visitors a month and fostered an estimated 4% increase in monthly sales.*
2. *Social media activity of 15 Facebook posts per month yielded an average 24% reach over the previous year.*
3. *Media list and outreach yielded two feature articles and inclusion in eight new social media mentions by media properties and identified influencers.*

It can also be important to contextualize your experience for the reader and ultimately the interviewer(s). The student agency experience you had may be unfamiliar to their realm of experience, so couch your terminology in language that is understandable to those who work in business. Some things that readily transfer include the following:

Direct client experience. In your student agency role, you may have been responsible for agency deliverables and client happiness and communications success. Speak to those topics. In particular, it is always attractive to future employers if you can demonstrate a stewardship for resources and time while maintaining excellence in your final products.

Managing multiple projects on varying timelines. Multitasking was a fact of life long before it was a term, (particularly in the fast-paced world of communications). Describe how your agency experience provided multiple challenges to time, resources, and people. Talk particularly about how you handled those tensions and how you balanced them.

Liaison between client wants/needs and agency specialists. Particularly if you were an Account Executive, working between clients and your staff carried a very specific set of management challenges. Success in this arena is often difficult and those who can do this well get paid well. Speak to how you performed here and talk about lessons learned.

Path of promotion from contributor to team leader. There is a saying, "Success breeds success" and another that says, "Nothing predicts future success like past success."

In American culture in particular, businesses like to hire people who have already been successful

If you enjoyed any level of added leadership or responsibility while serving in the student agency, discuss this and the processes/procedures you had to learn and/or implement as your role grew. A subset of this opportunity would be to describe your leadership gifts and how you used your managerial positions to motivate and steer a variety of skilled, enthusiastic team members as well as inspiring those less dedicated or focused.

Finally, tailor your resume for each new job opportunity you target, as discussed in "THE HUNT" section below. You want your resume to speak directly to the opportunity that's available. Read the job description thoroughly and drop in key words or phrases—like "self-starter," "ability to relocate," or "team player."

Other Bona Fide Documentation

In addition to your resume, you want to show potential employers samples of your work. First, ensure you have a strong digital presence—LinkedIn, Facebook, Mediabistro, a YouTube channel, and/or a blog. Employers will often "search" for you online. You want to make sure you have a digital brand presence, and that your social media pages are professional.

Second, develop an online portfolio. Appendix A of this text provides a checklist for creating digital online portfolios featuring your work. Incorporate these suggestions into your material. If you did not work directly in graphics/photography/video, but more on the client or agency management side, it still may be advantageous for you to graphically depict some of your highlights like new business development, client renewals, budgets, clients, results, and so forth. Other examples you can share besides finished work or infographics for management success include: fine examples of emails, status reports, conference reports, and bigger deliverables like a strategic plan/campaign or a summary of research report.

THE HUNT

Step 3: Targeting

So, you asked yourself some questions. You processed inputs from your friends and mentors. You developed your brand and brought it to life through your online presence and materials. The input you received and answers you formulated will help you target what jobs/positions you want to chase. **Targeting** is an important phase in the job hunt process. By target, we mean systematically analyze the opportunities, decide which ones you want to seek out and then make a plan to pursue those opportunities.

Target/targeting: The effort of researching and preparing professional communications for the eventual purpose of employment.

In trout fishing, for example, fly casters will target a pool or riffle in the river where they know there are fish. Keeping the objective in sight, they mesh their eyes and body movements to present the perfect fly for their quarry to devour. If they are successful, having shown deliberate effort with nuanced subtlety, and armed with the knowledge of the river, the native species of trout and the proper lure patterns, their efforts are rewarded with a lovely dinner, a great experience, or both.

In this same way, you need to target that firm or organization or other opportunity you want to work for with a deliberate set of steps. Keep your eye on the objective. Arm yourself with the knowledge you need to get your employer interested. Let your experience guide you to the opportunity. Move quickly but with serenity. Know that very seldom will an employer leave an opportunity open for long. So be prepared to cast your best fly when the time is right. However, if you do miss on that one, the good news is, there will be other job openings.

The other part of targeting for that right job is the very important concept of gathering intelligence. A term usually reserved for war fighting, and corporate espionage, **intelligence** is the assembly of facts that help guide decisions and enhance the chances of strategic and tactical success in a job hunt and elsewhere.

Intelligence: Intelligence is information obtained about a company or organization to assist someone in tailoring their work experience, resume, and other communications to secure employment.

When you are targeting a potential employer, you are finding out everything you can about them via secondary and maybe even some primary research. Targeting information/intelligence you want to gather might include questions like those in Box 15.2.

Box 15.2 Twenty Intelligence Questions

1. What is the target organization's primary mission?
2. What clients do they have?
3. What products do they sell?
4. What other services do they provide?
5. How large is their organization?
6. Where are their locations?
7. What is the corporate culture?
8. Who are the key players?
9. Who are their competitors?
10. Where are they in their corporate life cycle?
    a. Start-up
    b. Growth
    c. Maturity
    d. Decline
    e. Reinvention
11. What customers do they serve?
12. How much market share do they have?
13. What are the firm's core competencies?
14. What is their brand?
15. What do they do well?
16. What do they do poorly?
17. What is their presence in the marketplace?
18. What do they say about themselves?
19. What do others say about them?
20. What are their strengths, weaknesses, opportunities, and threats?

Once you have established your targeting intelligence profile, the next questions you should ask are how do you fit into their needs? You'll find a list of helpful questions in Box 15.3.

> ## Box 15.3 Self-Assessment Questions for Targeted Companies/ Organizations
>
> 1. Do you have a set of skills that they are lacking?
> 2. Do you have proven experience that could match up with their core competencies?
> 3. How enthusiastic are you about working for this organization?
>   a. Why? Or why not?
> 4. Do you have any insights into their needs from
>   a. Friends who work there?
>   b. Mentors?
>   c. Others?
> 5. Can you suggest improvements or other benefits they would profit from if they hired you?
> 6. What is uniquely different about your skill set that makes you a good match for this organization?
> 7. In assessing their needs/issues you see, if you were their consultant what would you advise them to do?
> 8. Are you a user of their products or services?
>   a. If so, what was your experience?
>   b. How could it be improved?
>   c. If not, why not?
> 9. Are there any ethical, moral, or other reasons why you would not want to work for them?
> 10. Are there other considerations that may stop you from taking a position with this organization?
> 11. Do you know who to contact about applying for a position?
> 12. Do you have any specific references or contacts that could help lobby for a position with this organization?
> 13. Are there opportunities to get your face and experience in front of management through pro bono work or informational interviews?

THE OPPORTUNITY

Step 4: The Mission

So now that you know who you want to target, and what you want to do to target, it is time to formulate a mission. This is a set of guidelines and tactics that will ensure you make contact with your target in the most positive way for you. A good mission outcome involves getting an interview, showing your work, gaining knowledge, and securing the job. There are several tasks to accomplish this mission. They include

1. *Network.* No doubt you have heard this from hundreds of people but making a network of people who know you and know your work can be extremely valuable.
2. *Get endorsements.* Word-of-mouth recommendations are some of the best endorsements you can offer. Seek these out.
3. *Monitor the target companies'/organizations' web sites, social media, and so forth.* Look for openings. Pay attention to issues and communications these targets are posting.

4. *Ask for an* **informational interview**. Sometimes a sit down with an executive from the company or the organization you are targeting can be extremely useful. Most managers are eager to spend time with people who are interested in their work. An informational interview provides the opportunity to find out about an organization without the added pressure of an interview.

Informational interview: An interview with a professional who discusses with the interviewee their experience, their organization, and so forth. Informational interviews are useful for gathering intelligence from both the interviewer and the interviewee. Occasionally, an informational interview can be a prelude to a job offer.

© Myvisuals/Shutterstock.com

THE INTERVIEW

Step 5: Interview Final Preparations

It's time. You have successfully identified an opportunity and you have received an invitation to interview. You may or may not have gone through preliminary screening interviews. But most jobs are ultimately filled following the in-person interview. Here are some tips to prepare for the big day.

The first step is to maximize your agency experience in the interview. During the interview process, it is important to

© George Rudy/Shutterstock.com)

take every advantage of opportunities to profile how you are an effective communicator. Your experience in the student-run agency is a great segue into proven experience. For example, don't just show your interviewer your final product but also use it as a springboard to discuss how you got there—what was the challenge, strategy, and so forth?

Develop a list of relevant, "gold plated" references you can use. Be sure to communicate with them before your interview. While you are assembling this list, don't forget letters of recommendation from (a) clients, (b) peer supervisors, (c) peer subordinates, and (d) faculty agency leaders.

Proof your work. Do not have a single error on any of your materials. Be sure all your digital material loads properly. While you are at it here, make sure that you are not revealing any CONFIDENTIAL client information in your portfolio or resume bullets. Most interviewers can spot confidential information and if they see you are reckless with someone else's secrets, they may have reason to pause about sharing theirs with you as well.

Ensure your resume is updated and relevant—one last time. Make your bullets quantifiable in terms of measured results. While you are reviewing your resume, take some time to cull your portfolio. Make sure your examples are relevant if possible. Take the time to develop a narrative and a demonstration of the flow leading up to the final work. The more you can articulate the challenges and triumphs of your finished works, the more the employer is going to see relevance for your work and understand that you would be an asset to their firm because you "get it."

Other ways you can prepare for the interview include the following:

- Practice questions and answers. Write some hypothetical questions and rehearse answers. Speak of how your experience is relevant to their issues.
- Know what you want in terms of compensation, benefits, and responsibilities. Know when you can start. Have all of your details worked out in your mind prior to going to the interview.
- Have at least five intelligent questions to ask your interviewers. Make sure the questions incorporate key observations you have obtained from your research/intelligence.
- Be ready to ask for the job. You will almost always be told to wait, but asking for the job displays your interest and motivation.
- Know where you are going. Know how you are going to get there. Plan to be 15 minutes early. Make a "dry run" if possible.

Finally, there is nothing like proven expertise for selling yourself. Consider quotes in this chapter from students who had a positive student agency experience. Inserting talking points like these from your own experiences in the student-run agency can be a powerful incentive for employers to invite you to an interview (Box 15.4).

Box 15.4   Student Agency Graduate Quotes

"There's a major difference between understanding PR and doing PR. I first learned the "doing" at Live Oak Communications and that experience set me apart to land my first job at Ketchum, and ultimately, led to my current role at Netflix.

Getting hired at a major PR firm or brand immediately out of college can be more competitive than getting into college in the first place. Every student or recent graduate vying for these roles understands PR, probably has a strong GPA and an internship or two (or three) under their belts. What set me apart while interviewing was my experience pitching and earning new business, building client relationships, managing teams and understanding budgets. These are core values that cannot be learned in a classroom and often times aren't afforded to interns. It's the catch-22 of opportunity vs. experience.

Student-run agencies, like Live Oak Communications, break this cycle and elevate young PR professionals that are more prepared for the real world."

Sean Flynn
Global Consumer PR Manager, Netflix
Year graduated: 2009

"The Carolina Agency gives students the ability to be a part of a real creative agency which does real work for real clients. It teaches them about work ethic in the real world, outside of the university, and the importance of deadlines and teamwork. Each student is able to use his or her unique abilities to contribute to an award-winning team and make a difference in the lives, and businesses, of the clients. This is a special opportunity for students to grow creatively and professionally and find a direction for their career path."

Meg Parker
Account Manager, Flock and Rally Public Relations
Year graduated: 2016

"Live Oak is most definitely one of the biggest assets on my resume. Many people do not get opportunities to do things like present in front of clients, manage account timelines, pitch media and facilitate client contact until their first jobs. But students at Live Oak are given these opportunities every day. Every time I went to interview for an internship, employers were beyond impressed with the experience I gained through Live Oak."

Grace Ahlering
Assistance Account Executive, Ketchum Public Relations
Year graduated 2016

THE FIRST YEAR

Congratulations, you have won the job!

You have overcome the competition, done great targeting, networked into an opportunity and made yourself so attractive to your employer in terms of professional experience, knowledge of the field and the company that they have invited you onto their team.

Hopefully you have been assigned to the team you want to work for, are servicing clients you are

© g-stockstudio/Shutterstock.com

interested in and experiencing the type of professional freedom that you dreamed of back when you were excelling at the student agency. Now what? Following are a few tips for success in your new position:

Stay positive. You will encounter challenges in your job. Some you will triumph over, and some may send you home doubting your capabilities and career choice. Understand that client service is difficult, fraught with challenges, but filled with opportunities. One of the strongest ways you can ensure success in the long term is to do your best to maintain a positive attitude regardless of the challenges. Find your center and find reliefs for the stresses related to work. Consistent negativity and pessimism can be very toxic to a team environment and works to the disadvantages of group cohesion.

Be part of the solution, not the problem. While we are discussing positivity, it is inevitable that there will be tensions and frustrations. Some can be handled at your level, others may require moderation or attention by those above you in the hierarchy. When these struggles happen, one key phrase to remember is: "be part of the solution, not part of the problem." This means that if you choose to air grievances or frustrations to management, it is strongly recommended that you find and recommend a solution to the problem along with your discussions of the impact of the problem.

For example, maybe your team is missing deadlines because there is a roadblock in graphics. You need to let your supervisors know about the problem because missed deadlines affect everyone. But before you single out one team member or one department, it might be very beneficial to review the process and see if there is anything your department can do to relieve the pressure and performance constriction. Maybe propose a shorter approval chain or take steps to maximize assets in your department to ensure graphics is given sufficient time prior to the deadline to complete the work you need done.

Stay busy contributing. Another way to say this is to "Bloom Where You Are Planted." As you move into your new role, find ways to keep yourself occupied in advancing the future of your firm. Without "stepping on toes" find ways to improve and contribute to the overall strength of the unit. Is there some training you can provide? Are there some suggestions you can offer to improve performance? Are there some duties you can take on that can help take some pressures off the group?

Whatever it is, be sure you discuss it thoroughly before proposing a change, but don't be shy to contribute if your idea will benefit.

© Full_chok/Shutterstock.com

Be a team player. Although individual agendas are common in any organization, one of the best personal goals you can aspire to is making yourself indispensable to the team and to view their success as your success. Adopting the mantra that "none of us is as smart as all of us" and "two heads are better than one," be sure you are reviewing your contributions, collegiality and collaborative abilities as you assess your progress during your inaugural year as a professional communicator.

© Rawpixel.com/Shutterstock.com

CONCLUSION

In summary, as you head out into the professional world, realize your potential. You have worked extremely hard to cultivate experience and results for your clients. Use this experience to your advantage. Make sure you can speak influentially and intelligently about your work. Keep your integrated portfolio current and relevant for the jobs you are seeking. Take the time to quantify your results and translate your achievements into language that your future employer(s) can understand. Furthermore, use your research skills to target opportunities for future employment and when the opportunity presents, don't be afraid to ask for the job.

Finally, understand that the job hunt is a competitive process that requires patience, timing and often, some help. Build and use your references and network to get the interview. It is also helpful to maintain a positive attitude as you navigate the job hunt process and as you adjust to your first professional position.

Once onboard, be sure to maintain a helpful, positive attitude as you grow professionally into your role as a new professional communicator.

REVIEW AND DISCUSSION QUESTIONS

1. What should you do about your portfolio when getting ready for an interview?
2. When considering using references what is an important step you should take before using them for a specific job interview?
3. What is the name of the career assessment test that the text recommends?
4. Describe the process of targeting.
5. When would you want to arrange for an informational interview?
6. Describe why it is important to get inputs from others when constructing your resume.
7. What is the value of networking as it pertains to job hunting?
8. When considering your student-run agency experiences why is it important to add quantifiable values to your results?
9. What are some things you should be prepared for as you go into an interview?
10. Why is it important to "ask for the job?"

REFERENCES AND ADDITIONAL READINGS

About the Birkman Method. (2017). Posted on www.birkman.com. Retrieved from https://birkman.com/assessment-solutions/the-birkman-method/

Clark, D. (2011). Reinventing your personal brand. *Harvard Business Review*. Retrieved from https://hbr.org/2011/03/reinventing-your-personal-brand

Hyder, S. (2014, August 18). 7 things you can do to build an awesome personal brand. *Forbes*. Retrieved from https://www.forbes.com/sites/shamahyder/2014/08/18/7-things-you-can-do-to-build-an-awesome-personal-brand/#22c1548f3c3a

Kayser, M. (2017). *Personal branding secrets for beginners: A short and simple guide to getting started with your personal brand.* Hilton, NY: Blue Ink Publishing.

Kobara, J., & Smith, M. (2017). Job networking tips. How to find the right job by building relationships. *HelpGuide.org*. Retrieved from https://www.helpguide.org/articles/relationships-communication/job-networking-tips.htm

Long, J. (n.d.). 8 tips for building your personal brand in 2017. *Entrepreneur*. Retrieved from https://www.entrepreneur.com/article/287399

Munson, F., Stern, J., & Wills, J. (2016). *Getting the right job: A personal guide to developing your career.* Southlake, TX: Fountainhead Press.

Patel, N., & Argus, A. (n.d.). The complete guide to building your personal brand. *Quicksprout.com*. Retrieved from https://www.quicksprout.com/the-complete-guide-to-building-your-personal-brand/

Peters, T. (1997, August 31). The brand called you. *Fast Company*. Retrieved from https://www.fastcompany.com/28905/brand-called-you

Rhoten, R. (2017). *CareerKred four simple steps to build your digital brand and boost credibility in your career.* New York, NY: Hybrid Global Publishing.

Sweetwood, M. (2017, March 27). 8 reasons a powerful personal brand will make you successful. *Entrepreneur*. Retrieved from https://www.entrepreneur.com/article/289278

VanNas, H. (2014). *Interview like a boss.* New York, NY: Simon & Schuster.

APPENDIX A THE DIGITAL PORTFOLIO eBROCHURE CHECKLIST

It is a fact of life, we live in a digital age. The days of the paper resume and the paper portfolio are numbered in many ways. Just think about your own experiences, how many times have you actually stopped to print something in the last few years? You and/or your friends may not even OWN a printer.

What does that mean for you in your interview process? It means that you need to be digital-savvy and know how to put together a solid digital portfolio—something that can be posted to the cloud, emailed to your future employer and/or displayed during your job interview.

Depending upon your level of experience in this field, this task can be a labor of love or a daunting chore. Whichever it is, use this opportunity to flex your digital muscles or learn what you know you need to know anyway. Don't shy away from the challenge.

You can easily design a web site that features your work. Or you can embark on creating a blog. Or you can do both. Following is a link to a brochure with the information you need as well as tips on how to design your own ePortfolio.

https://www.elon.edu/u/academics/ommunications/wp-content/uploads/sites/23/2017/08/E-Portfolio-Fall-2017-Update.pdf

Notice in this e-brochure there are several emphases:

1. Be sure to include appropriate content that reflects your experience—not all of the content needs to be finished ads or press releases. There are many functions in a student agency and if you excelled in any area(s) of them, be sure to highlight them here. Analytics, for example, may not be as interesting as a :30 television commercial but good data are critical to the long-term health of any communications firm and if you can do it, make sure you tell someone about it.
2. Be sure to provide context to all of your portfolio items.
3. Be careful when creating a site map. Make sure the map works before actually designing the site.
4. Choose a compelling domain name that can be associated with you and what you want to do. Alisha's ads.com might be a good domain for someone named Alisha who is seeking to work in advertising.
5. If you designed it in a certain medium, be sure to include the electronic version of it. For example, if you created a beautiful brochure, then include a final PDF. Or, if you did some television work, make sure your **sizzle reel** highlights both your time behind and in front of the camera.
6. Make the site simple, easy to navigate and multi-platform/multibrowser capable.
7. Have fun with it. This is your brand, make people want to buy it.

Sizzle reel: A video that makes your work "sizzle" by highlighting client work, campaign results, awards, and other successes.

CPSIA information can be obtained
at www.ICGtesting.com
Printed in the USA
LVHW061617160721
692812LV00001B/1

9 781524 919672